THE PAINTINGS OF
Lucas van Leyden

THE PAINTINGS OF
Lucas van Leyden

A New Appraisal, with Catalogue Raisonné

ELISE LAWTON SMITH

University of Missouri Press / Columbia and London

Copyright © 1992 by
The Curators of the University of Missouri
University of Missouri Press, Columbia, Missouri 65201
Printed and bound in the United States of America
All rights reserved
5 4 3 2 1   96 95 94 93 92

Library of Congress Cataloging-in-Publication Data

Smith, Elise Lawton.
  The paintings of Lucas van Leyden : a new appraisal, with catalogue raisonné / Elise Lawton Smith.
    p.   cm.
  Includes bibliographical references and index.
  ISBN 0-8262-0824-X
  1. Lucas, van Leyden, 1484-1533—Criticism and interpretation. 2. Lucas, van Leyden, 1484-1533—Catalogues raisonnés. I. Lucas, van Leyden, 1494-1533. II. Title.
ND653.L85S63   1992
759.9492—dc20   92-18250
                                                                    CIP

∞™ This paper meets the requirements of the
American National Standard for Permanence of Paper
for Printed Library Materials, Z39.48, 1984.

Designer: Kristie Lee
Typesetter: Connell-Zeko Type & Graphics
Printer and binder: Thomson-Shore, Inc.
Typefaces: Garamond #3 and Uncial

To the memory of my mother, Elise Lawton Isleib,
and my father, Robert O. Lawton.

CONTENTS

Preface / ix

Acknowledgments / xv

PART I. Career and Artistic Development

Chapter 1. A Biographical Account / 3

Chapter 2. Stylistic Development of the Paintings / 15

Chapter 3. Iconographic Concerns / 45

Conclusion / 79

PART II. Catalogue Raisonné

Old Testament Paintings / 89

New Testament Paintings / 110

Saints / 145

Portraits / 151

History Painting / 160

Allegorical Genre Paintings / 162

Erroneous Attributions / 181

Illustrations / 203

Appendix: Lucas van Leyden's Appearance / 269

Notes / 273

Bibliography / 343

Index / 379

PREFACE

Lucas van Leyden (1494?–1533) was a remarkably versatile artist skilled in a variety of techniques. During his relatively short lifetime he produced more than two hundred engravings, woodcuts, and etchings, which formed the basis of his early fame and his continued popularity. Although he has been known primarily as a graphic artist, his paintings reveal the talents of an accomplished colorist and draftsman, and his innovative compositions (ranging from the small half-length narratives of his youth to the carefully constructed, multifigured representations of his later years) were influential for following generations. His works were usually executed in oil on panel, but he also experimented with other media. One large-scale canvas in tempera is extant (Cat. 7, Fig. 24), and other works in this inherently fragile technique are mentioned in Carel van Mander's *Het Schilder-Boeck* of 1604, in which van Mander also describes Lucas's skill at painting on glass (see Cat. C4).[1]

The range of Lucas's abilities as a painter has never been fully appreciated. Until recently his oeuvre was inflated with inferior works, including numerous painted copies after his prints that were often mistaken for originals.[2] Due to the wide dissemination of his engravings, he was for several hundred years the best-known sixteenth-century Netherlandish artist in southern Europe. As a result, many paintings related only by the most superficial similarities in appearance were attributed to him in early inventories. By the second quarter of the nineteenth century, a reaction against this indiscriminate treatment had set in. Georg Rathgeber noted in 1844 that Lucas's name had become a catch-all for otherwise unidentifiable works. Out of a group of about one hundred works that he considered falsely attributed to Lucas he was able to identify ten as genuine. By 1868 Alfred Michiels concluded that he had never seen a painting that could with certainty be identified as by Lucas. Other scholars of the period included cautionary notes among their attributions. G. F. Waagen, for example, commented that true paintings by Lucas were as rare as the false were plentiful.[3]

Late in the century a more critical broadening of Lucas's oeuvre appeared in the writings of Franz Dülberg and Wilhelm Bode. In 1899 Dülberg published two detailed articles about Lucas: one an examination of the biographical information that bears on his artistic personality, and the other a lengthy study of the *Last Judgment* in Leiden (Cat. 20, Figs. 17–19). These were followed by an analysis (first printed in 1909) of all of the paintings then accepted as genuine. Dülberg cited eleven of the seventeen paintings still considered originals, but he also included another fifteen or so, now discredited, which continued to complicate consideration of the artist's stylistic development for later writers.

In the next three decades, four important studies of Lucas's paintings appeared: a 1913 monograph by N. Beets; a 1923 book by Ludwig Baldass; the tenth volume (published in 1934) of Max J. Friedländer's monumental *Altniederländische Malerei;* and a lengthy section in G. J. Hoogewerff's *De Noord-Nederlandsche Schilderkunst,* from 1939. Although the corpus of works varied from study to study, a core of incorrectly attributed panels persisted. Most of these, like the *Sermon* in Amsterdam, the *Temptation of St. Anthony* in Brussels, and the *Portrait of a Man* in the Thyssen Collection, are now thought to have been painted by Lucas's contemporaries in Leiden. Because the erroneous corpus was composed of paintings by several artists, the development of what was believed to be Lucas's style was characterized as experimental, erratic, inconsistent, even capricious.[4] The culmination of this era of scholarship—which produced analyses that were occasionally enlightening but more often perplexing—was Friedländer's *Lucas van Leyden,* written before 1950 but first published (posthumously) in 1963. In reviewing Lucas's oeuvre, he concluded that there was no uniformity or logic to the artist's development, and that there were scarcely two paintings that showed any convincing technical similarity to one another.[5]

In the last twenty-five years further research on the works of Aertgen van Leyden and the three sons of Cornelis Engebrechtsz., as well as on Lucas himself, has brought some order to our thinking about the Leiden school, although much still remains to be clarified. In a 1960 article on Aertgen, Joos Bruyn reattributed to him the three paintings mentioned above and cleared the ground for a reconsideration of Lucas's oeuvre. A dissertation by Walter S. Gibson on

Cornelis Engebrechtsz. contained a detailed study of that artist's workshop, further refining our picture of the early artistic circles in Leiden. A 1974 dissertation by Peter Parshall, which investigated certain iconographic problems in Lucas's oeuvre, included chapters on gaming and betrothal scenes and on the *Dance around the Golden Calf* in Amsterdam (Cat. 11, Fig. 32). More recently, exhibitions of Lucas's paintings and drawings in Leiden (1978) and of his prints in Amsterdam (1978) and Washington (1983) prompted a variety of articles, catalogues, and reviews. Rik Vos's *Lucas van Leyden,* published in conjunction with the Leiden exhibition, raised provocative questions related to iconographic and stylistic aspects of Lucas's oeuvre. A lengthy article by J. P. Filedt Kok on the paint technique and underdrawing style of fifteen paintings attributed to the artist further reduced Lucas's corpus and redefined his chronological development on scientific grounds.

Despite this upsurge of interest, no comprehensive review of Lucas's paintings has yet appeared. This study is a first step toward that end. I begin in Part I with a survey of biographical data, focusing on Lucas's disputed birthdate, his artistic training, and his travels to the southern Netherlands. An analysis of his stylistic development follows, with special attention given to the influence of Albrecht Dürer, Marcantonio Raimondi, and Jan Gossaert. Finally, Lucas's paintings are examined with reference to recurring thematic motifs.

The catalogue raisonné of Part II provides more detailed considerations of the dating, provenance, condition, and subject of each work. The catalogue is divided into sections based on subject matter, and the works within each section are organized chronologically. The seventeen paintings accepted here as originals are interspersed with a few works known through descriptions in Van Mander's *Het Schilder-Boeck,* as well as with now-lost paintings known only through sixteenth- and seventeenth-century copies. These are included with the extant originals in order to provide a comprehensive survey of Lucas's concerns as a painter, but the copies are distinguished from the originals by the letter *C* placed before the catalogue number. The final section in the catalogue deals with a number of paintings no longer accepted as originals. Many paintings once attributed to Lucas have been convincingly removed from his oeuvre by earlier scholars, and only those works that were still questionable or that had not been treated in sufficient depth in terms of their relationship to Lucas are analyzed here.

The inclusion in this monograph of numerous sixteenth- and seventeenth-century copies after lost works by Lucas effectively doubles the number of compositions in his oeuvre, providing us with a richer understanding of his accomplishments as a painter. It is important at the outset to clarify my reasons for identifying these, first, as *copies*—rather than pastiches or later variants—and second, as copies after lost *paintings* rather than prints. The first distinction is problematic: one can only try to weed out compositions whose motifs seem incompatible with Lucas's stylistic or iconographic concerns during the period in question. It is certainly possible that works like the *Betrothal* in the Morris Collection (Cat. C45), for example, or the *Card Players* in Budapest (Cat. C39) may be pastiches, with the idea of the fool drawn from Lucas's woodcut *Tavern Scene* and then added for moralizing emphasis to a basic composition by Lucas. I deal with these in Chapter 3 as copies, however, since the moralizing overtones do not in fact seem at all foreign to Lucas's interests in the 1520s. The second distinction is easier to make: of the late sixteenth- and seventeenth-century copies after lost compositions by Lucas discussed in this book, most seem to be more directly related to the style of his paintings than to that of his prints. Lucas took up different challenges in various media at different times in his career. Copies with multifigured, full-length compositions, datable to the late period on the basis of other stylistic criteria, are easily identified as modeled after lost paintings because they are quite different from the more restricted compositions of his prints and drawings from the 1520s (for example, Cats. C9, C10, C18, C24, and C33). Only two of the copies are less easily characterized: *Fall of Man* (Cat. C5) and *Virgin and Child in the Clouds* (Cat. C17) show marked similarities to prints of the period and might be after lost engravings or drawings rather than paintings. I decided to include them here in the Catalogue Raisonné since both copies are by Jan de Bisschop, whose other drawings after Lucas are all clearly after lost paintings.

While the examination of Lucas's works in the catalogue is divided thematically, the illustrations of the paintings are arranged chronologically, with the extant originals and copies of those works (Figs. 1–39) followed by copies after now-lost originals (Figs. 40–64). I hope that any frustration caused by the use of two sets of numbers to refer to the catalogue entry and the illustrations will be more than offset by the benefits of illustrating all of Lucas's works in chronological order. Following the paintings by Lucas are illustrations of a number of comparative works (Figs. 65–80).

The reader should note that in the captions all measurements are given in centimeters, with height preceding width. References in the text to engravings use the numbers of Adam Bartsch from *Le Peintre Graveur*, identified as B.

* * *

As a contributor to the development of allegorical genre, as an innovator in religious iconography, and as an experimenter with half-length as well as multifigured compositions, Lucas should be considered one of the most noteworthy northern European artists of the early sixteenth century. His importance as a painter has usually taken second place to his achievements as a printmaker, but his painted oeuvre, presented here in a more complete form than in previous publications, can now be studied with greater understanding and appreciation for its significance.

ACKNOWLEDGMENTS

This volume is a revised and amplified version of a dissertation completed in 1981 at the University of North Carolina, Chapel Hill; without the support of numerous individuals and institutions it would never have been completed. I would like to express my deep appreciation, first, for the following fellowships: a Fulbright-Hays Grant for work in the Netherlands during the academic year 1978–1979; a Samuel H. Kress fellowship and travel grant for 1979–1980; and a Chester Dale Fellowship for 1980–1981. During this period I was able to see all of the original paintings by Lucas, most of the copies, and many of the works whose attribution to the artist I reject.

I am grateful for the assistance given me by personnel in a number of museums, libraries, and photograph archives, in particular the Rijksbureau voor Kunsthistorische Documentatie in The Hague; the Kunsthistorisch Instituut, Gemeente Universiteit, Amsterdam; the library in the Rijksprentenkabinet, Amsterdam; the Frick Art Reference Library, New York; and the Center for Advanced Study at the National Gallery of Art, Washington.

I would also like to acknowledge several colleagues. In Amsterdam, Joos Bruyn of the Gemeente Universiteit kindly agreed to be my academic sponsor during 1978–1979, and Jan Piet Filedt Kok of the Rijksprentenkabinet gave unstintingly of his time and knowledge. Maarten Wurfbain, director of the Stedelijk Museum "De Lakenhal" in Leiden, welcomed me as a fellow Lucas enthusiast. Jeremy Bangs, at the Gemeente Archief, tirelessly answered many questions about archival documents and cultural matters related to artistic life in early sixteenth-century Leiden. Larry Silver, of Northwestern University, offered useful guidance in the early stages of my research.

The members of my doctoral committee were supportive of my ideas and patient with my mistakes, devoting much time and energy to reading early drafts of the dissertation. Jaroslav Folda was particularly helpful with iconographic matters, and Innis Shoemaker with Lucas's relationship to Marcantonio Raimondi. Walter Gibson provided invaluable assistance with his knowledge of the early Leiden school and the iconographic tradition of card and chess scenes and has continued to provide advice and encouragement. To J. Richard Judson, who challenged me through my years at the University of North Carolina, I offer my respect, admiration, and gratitude.

I would like to thank Kathy Cohen for her close reading of much of this manuscript, and Jane Carroll for her friendship over the years, so important for my enjoyment of the academic roller coaster. Finally, the love and humor of my husband, Steve, were steady bulwarks against the tides of scholarly confusion.

PART I

Career and Artistic Development

CHAPTER 1

A Biographical Account

Biographical information about Lucas van Leyden is relatively limited and at times difficult to interpret. The single most extensive source is *Het Schilder-Boeck,* a collection of artists' biographies written by Carel van Mander and published in Haarlem in 1604. According to Van Mander, Lucas was born in Leiden in late May or early June 1494 and was taught first by his father, Huygh Jacobsz., also a painter. Van Mander reported that Lucas moved to the studio of Cornelis Engebrechtsz. after the death of his father. He learned engraving from a man who made armor and also studied with a goldsmith. Later Lucas married a noblewoman of the Van Boschuysen family. Van Mander described Lucas as rather short and slight of build and mentioned a self-portrait in which the artist wore a large feathered hat and carried a skull (B.174, no longer identified as a self-portrait). He was visited by Albrecht Dürer, a meeting that Van Mander erroneously placed in Leiden. At the age of thirty-three, around 1527, Lucas went south to Zeeland, where he was joined by Jan Gossaert, and together they toured Flanders and Brabant. After this trip Lucas's health seriously deteriorated, and he died six years later in 1533 at the age of thirty-nine, believing he had been poisoned during his travels. He was survived by his widow and by one child, an illegitimate daughter. Two grandsons later became painters as well.[1]

In addition to this biographical sketch, Van Mander described four paintings still extant: the *Virgin and Child with Mary Magdalene and a Donor* and the *Annunciation,* two halves of a diptych, both in Munich (Cats. 14–15, Figs. 12–13); the *Last Judgment* in Leiden (Cat. 20, Figs. 17–23); the *Dance around the*

Golden Calf in Amsterdam (Cat. 11, Figs. 32-34); and *Christ Healing the Blind Man* in Leningrad (Cat. 25, Figs. 35, 37-39). A number of paintings mentioned by Van Mander are presumed missing or cannot be securely identified. These include a few portraits (one of which is described as a nearly life-size head; see Cat. 31), a *Madonna* (see Cats. C22, 23), a glass painting of the *Triumphal Entry of David into Jerusalem* (Cat. C4), and several pictures in tempera on canvas representing *St. Hubert* (Cat. 27), *Rebecca and Eliezer at the Well* (Cat. 8), and the *History of Joseph* (Cat. 2). Many of Lucas's prints are also described, although these compose only a small portion of his graphic oeuvre.

There are minor inaccuracies in Van Mander's descriptions of Lucas's works, and scholars have questioned the reliability of his biographical account. Many of his statements have been proved erroneous, including those concerning the death of Lucas's father, the locale of Lucas's meeting with Dürer, and the identification of his self-portrait. The most controversial aspect of Van Mander's biography remains his identification of 1494 as the year of the artist's birth. Upon review of the evidence, however, I see no reason to doubt his account on this point. Despite its errors, the section on Lucas in *Het Schilder-Boeck* should still be considered the best and most complete early source for information on Lucas's career.

The Artist's Birth

Since no contemporary documents exist concerning Lucas's birth, the earliest source is the account in *Het Schilder-Boeck*. Of the many early Netherlandish and German artists treated in this compendium, only one other not still living in 1604 is given so precise a birth date. Van Mander was usually forthright about admitting facts not known to him, and in this case he specifically mentioned the "nearly incredible" stories about this child prodigy, "told by those who still know." It has been suggested that he received his information on this point from a grandson of the artist, Lucas Dammesz. de Hoey, who died in Utrecht in 1604. Despite the family connection, the evidence would still be hearsay, for Lucas Dammesz. was just nine days old when his grandfather died.[2]

If the birth date of 1494 is accurate, Lucas's first dated work, an engraving from 1508 of *Mohammed and the Monk Sergius* (B.126), would have been made at the remarkably youthful age of fourteen. Several paintings can be placed in this period, including *The Chess Players* in Berlin (Cat. 34, Fig. 1) and *The Fortuneteller* in Paris (Cat. 35, Fig. 2), and a number of prints can be assigned an even earlier date on stylistic grounds (B.17, 24, 28, 42, and 108, among others). Although such precocity may seem unlikely, Van Mander consistently portrayed the artist as a prodigy. He reported, for example, that a painting of *St. Hubert* made for the Lord of Lochorst was finished when Lucas was only twelve (see Cat. 27). Repeated references to Lucas's early virtuosity in *Het Schilder-Boeck* give the impression that his reputation was well known. Van Mander wrote, "I know of none who was the equal of the gifted Lucas van Leyden . . . , who seemed to be born with brush and burin in hand and with a natural talent for painting and drawing." He described the *Ecce Homo* engraving of 1510 (B.71) as "a work of art which fills one with amazement that such a young boy possessed such abundant spirit and intelligence," and added, "I wanted to describe these prints in order to demonstrate, and to keep in mind with amazement, what perfectly ripe fruits could drop from such a green sprout."[3]

Such statements are unconvincing as evidence of a specific birth date, however, being so general that they might be applied to any supposed prodigy. Van Mander's birth date for Lucas has often been questioned, and a number of scholars have attempted to set it back by five or six years, suggesting that Van Mander was confused about the timing and number of trips taken by the artist. We know that Lucas met Dürer in Antwerp in 1521, and Van Mander reported that Lucas made a trip through Flanders at the age of thirty-three. Van Mander also reported that Lucas had met Dürer in Leiden, rather than Antwerp, leading to speculation that he had somehow conflated his accounts of Lucas's two journeys. Thus, it has been argued that Lucas might have been thirty-three in 1521, pushing the birth date back to 1488.[4] Obviously an important element in the controversy over the artist's birth date is Van Mander's report of that trip to the southern Netherlands:

> When Lucas was about thirty-three years old he had the urge to visit the painters of Zeeland, Flanders and Brabant, so he set out on his journey and traveled like a man of means, I believe with a ship he outfitted himself, with everything in sufficient supply. Arriving in Middelburg, he took pleasure in studying the works of the industrious and artistic Jan de Mabuse [Jan Gossaert], who was living there at the time and had executed various works there. Lucas entertained Mabuse and other painters with a banquet that cost sixty guilders, and he did the same elsewhere, namely in Ghent, Mechelen and Antwerp, each time treating the painters for sixty guilders; he was accompanied everywhere by the above-mentioned Jan de Mabuse.[5]

If we accept the birth date of May/June 1494 in *Het Schilder-Boeck,* this trip would have occurred in 1527–1528. Gossaert was in Middelburg at the time, and there is no evidence of any commissions or personal business that would have prevented his leaving Zeeland for a while. Lucas would presumably have just completed the monumental triptych of the *Last Judgment* (Cat. 20, Figs. 17–23) and the canvas of *Moses after Striking the Rock* (Cat. 7, Figs. 24–25); at some point after his projected return he began the *Dance around the Golden Calf* (Cat. 11, Figs. 32–34), a work that, along with several others from 1528–1530, clearly shows the influence of Gossaert's style.

Some of those who favor the 1488–1489 birth date have tried to date the journey 1521–1522, but in fact Gossaert was nowhere near Middelburg during this period. From 1517 to 1523 he was in the service of Philip of Burgundy at Wijk bij Duurstede, southeast of Utrecht. Although Dürer was sufficiently interested in Gossaert to describe his triptych in the abbey at Middelburg in a diary entry of December 8, 1520, he makes no mention of meeting with the Fleming. It seems unlikely that he would not have encountered him in Antwerp if indeed Gossaert had been Lucas's companion there in 1521.[6]

Another theory proposes a birth date of 1489 based on the premise that Lucas had reached the age of majority by 1514. In that year he was paid an annuity that most scholars believe to have been conditional upon the recipient's status as an adult. Some uncertainty still exists, however, about what the age of majority was at this time in Leiden, and it has recently been suggested that Lucas could have received the annuity even as a minor.[7] Other arguments for changing the birth date given in *Het Schilder-Boeck* have been proposed, but none is entirely convincing.[8]

Life in Leiden and the Family Circle

Lucas Hugensz. van Leyden was the son of Huygh Jacobsz., described by Van Mander as "an outstanding painter in his time."[9] Lucas's mother was long thought to be Beatrys, daughter of Dirck Florisz., but in 1959 information was published establishing that Beatrys was Huygh's second wife and Lucas's stepmother. A document dated December 23, 1500, records Huygh's guarantee of the maternal inheritance due to the five minor children of his first wife, Marie Heynricxdr. The children are listed as Lucas, Katrijn, Marie, Griet, and Barber.[10]

The next documentary source for Lucas concerns the annuity payment described above, to "mr [meester] Lucas Huge Jacopsz." In the same year, on March 6, Lucas became a member of the Oude Schutters (Old Archers), one of the archers' guilds formed to defend the city. Cornelis Engebrechtsz. was a member of the same guild in that year, while Lucas's father was in the Voetboogschutters (Crossbow Archers). On May 23, 1515, Lucas joined the Voetboogschutters, and he appears again in their membership roll on May 7, 1519.[11]

Lucas's only child, Marijtgen, was born out of wedlock. Her mother is unknown, as is the date of her birth. Van Mander mentions that Marijtgen had married and given birth by 1533, which suggests that she was born between 1510 and 1515.[12] This is consistent with the later birth date for Lucas of 1494 given by Van Mander.

Lucas was married to Elysabeth van Boschuysen after June 11, 1526, when a document shows that she was still married to her first husband, and probably before 1528, by which time the artist had moved out of his father's home and established his own household. The Van Boschuysens were well known and wealthy members of the nobility—in 1480, three of the four burgomasters of Leiden were members of the family, and Elysabeth's father, Jacob, and brother Jan were both influential in government circles. Van Mander remarked that after his marriage Lucas lost "to his regret a lot of time with parties and good cheer, as is the habit of the wealthy and noble." This passage refers to the last five to seven years of the artist's life, during which time his health was failing: "it is a fact that he was in bed for much of his time until his death six years later."[13] Lucas overcame this combination of high living and ill health to produce a number of important paintings during the years 1527–1531, but no works in any medium can be assigned to the last two years of his life.

Van Mander's date of 1533 for Lucas's death has been confirmed by Jeremy D. Bangs. The burial is listed in an account book of St. Peter's in Leiden, and municipal documents also record a dispute that erupted during the summer of 1534 over the settlement of Lucas's will.[14] In 1538, after the death of his widow, Lucas's siblings brought an additional (and unsuccessful) suit against Marijtgen and her husband, demanding half of the estate, or three hundred Carolus guilders.[15] This suit gives us some insight into the financial status of the artist.

At the time of his death Lucas must have been one of Leiden's more prosperous citizens. His prosperity is corroborated by Van Mander's description of his southern tour, when Lucas hosted banquets for other artists costing sixty guilders apiece. His prints were apparently a more lucrative source of income than his paintings. Van Mander observed that large prints, such as the *Dance of Mary Magdalene* (B.123), earned him one gold guilder, or 1.40 Flemish pounds, each. To put this in perspective, this sum was slightly more than the earnings of a carpenter or bricklayer for six days work in Leiden in 1520 and was considerably more than the amounts paid for Dürer's prints during his trip to the Netherlands in 1521. In contrast to his financial success as a printmaker, Lucas appears to have earned relatively little from his paintings. He received two pounds, five stuivers in 1523 for a *Flight into Egypt* (see Cat. C21), and only thirty-five Flemish pounds for the large triptych of the *Last Judgment*.[16]

Travels

In addition to his tour of the southern Netherlands at the age of thirty-three, Lucas apparently made only one other trip, to Antwerp in 1521. Conflicting accounts of the artist's travels outside Holland are given by Van Mander and Giorgio Vasari. In the second edition of his *Vite* (1568) Vasari mentioned Lucas "with many others, who were all in Italy to study and draw after the antique." Van Mander specifically refuted this, saying Vasari was "mistaken" and "poorly informed" and "thought all the famous painters of our Netherlands had to have learned the art in Italy." Attempts have been made to renew the idea of a trip by Lucas to Italy, although his style shows little Italian influence other than what would have been known to him through engravings.[17] Van Mander's sources would also surely have informed him of such an important event in Lucas's life.

Vasari's account of Lucas's trip to Antwerp in 1521 is more reliable, since it is corroborated by Dürer's diary. Vasari tells us that Dürer, "having traveled to Flanders, found another rival, who had already begun to make many fine engravings in order to compete with him: and this was Lucas d'Olanda." Van Mander, on the other hand, as we have already noted, described a visit by Dürer to Leiden, apparently an incorrect account of the German artist's stay in Antwerp: "They studied each other's prints with the greatest admiration, Dürer finally coming to Holland, and while visiting Lucas in Leyden, each of them drew on a tablet a portrait of the other from life, and they enjoyed themselves in each other's company in friendship." Dürer's trip to the Netherlands in 1521 is reported in detail in his diary, from which it is known that the meeting between the two artists took place in Antwerp rather than in Lucas's hometown. Sometime between June 8 and 29, 1521, Dürer wrote: "I was invited to be the guest of master Lucas, who engraves in copper; he is a short, slight man and native of Leyden in Holland, who was in Antwerp . . . I made a portrait of master Lucas van Leyden in silverpoint." The portrait has been identified as the drawing now in Lille (Fig. 70). There is no extant companion portrait of Dürer by Lucas, and Van Mander might have been in error on this point. That the artists exchanged prints during this meeting or shortly thereafter is known through another entry in Dürer's diary: "I have traded 8 guilders' worth of my prints for Lucas's complete graphic oeuvre."[18]

Friedländer has suggested that Lucas was in Antwerp in 1520, but there is no confirmation of this earlier date.[19] Whether he traveled to other cities in the southern Netherlands in addition to Antwerp is not ascertainable, but the influence of Flemish art is clearly visible in a number of his works from 1521 to 1522. Some scholars have identified Lucas as "Lucas de Hollandere, scildere" (Lucas the Hollander, painter) in the list of masters received in 1522 into Antwerp's St. Lucas Guild of Painters. We know, however, that Lucas returned to Leiden soon after his meeting with Dürer, since he stood bail for his stepbrother Dirck Huyghensz. on June 28, 1521, and it is unlikely that Lucas would have made a second trip to Antwerp by the date of the guild entry. One explanation, first suggested by Beets in 1935, is that this "Lucas de Hollandere" referred to Cornelis Engebrechtsz.'s youngest son, Lucas Cornelisz. de Kock.[20]

Teachers

Van Mander mentioned that "Lucas, a born master, studied first under his father, and then under Cornelis Engelbrechtsz." He went on to describe Lucas's extraordinary diligence and long hours of apprentice work, consistent with the nature of artistic precocity. In the biography of Cornelis he added, "It is believed that the following Lucas Hugensen van Leyden lost his father early, and studied with [Cornelis]." In this case, Van Mander's source was incorrect, since Huygh outlived his son by several years. Lucas's father was indeed a painter, as we know from several references in guild membership lists and from a receipt issued for payment of an annuity.[21]

Huygh Jacobsz.

Although his date of birth is unknown, by 1469 Huygh was assistant to Brother Tymanus, the foremost painter of the Hieronymusdal monastery on the outskirts of Leiden. Other documentary evidence suggests that from 1480 to 1485 he lived in Koudekerk, a small village to the east, returning to Leiden in 1485. Bangs has shown that between 1488 and 1496 Huygh painted an altarpiece for the chapel of the Fullers' Guild in St. Peter's, Leiden. He was described in the commission as "Master Huge Jacopsz. of Koudekerck, living in Gouda," although he had returned to Leiden by 1494 when he registered in the guild of Longbow Archers. The diary of Arnoldus Buchelius, written between 1590 and 1605, describes him as "Hugo from Leiden, Gouda, or Ghent."[22]

A number of paintings by Huygh are known from early records, although none of these is extant.[23] Various attempts have been made to reconstruct his oeuvre. Several groups of works have been attributed to him on the basis of their stylistic relationship to fifteenth-century Ghent or Gouda schools and to the paintings and prints of Lucas. The most plausible arguments have been made for his authorship of the works assigned to the Master of the Turin Crucifixion and to the Master of the St. John Panels.

The triptych in the Galleria Sabauda, Turin, for which the first master is named, is composed of a central *Crucifixion* flanked by an *Ecce Homo* and *Christ Crowned with Thorns* on the wings (Fig. 65). It was at one point attributed to Lucas himself, as was the case with a small panel of the *Crucifixion* by the same artist, now in Frankfurt. The figures of Christ in both show the influence of compositions associated with late fifteenth-century Ghent, particularly those by Hugo van der Goes.[24] Parallels with the early works of Lucas have been enumerated by Gibson, who concurs with Dülberg and Hoogewerff in identifying the painter as Lucas's father and first teacher. Gibson finds evidence of a close stylistic relationship with Lucas when comparing the head of the bearded figure just to the right of the cross in the Turin panel with that of Potiphar in Lucas's *Potiphar's Wife Accusing Joseph* in Rotterdam (Cat. 1, Fig. 4). This evidence is not convincing, however; although the facial types and positions of the heads are indeed quite close, this type of averted head with sidelong glancing eyes was commonly used for the figure of the bearded centurion in Crucifixion scenes. Gibson has also pointed out the similar poses of the man in the right foreground of the *Christ Crowned with Thorns* wing in Turin and a figure in Lucas's engraving of the same subject from the 1509 *Round Passion* series (B.62). Once again, the figures are comparable, but contorted, exaggerated figures seen from the rear are used frequently for soldiers in representations of the Passion.[25] It does not necessarily follow, therefore, that Lucas must have seen and been influenced by this particular triptych.

The Master of the St. John Panels is named for three paintings of similar size, perhaps part of one large altarpiece, each representing a scene from the life of John the Baptist: the *Birth of John the Baptist* and the *Flight of Elizabeth,* both in the Museum Boymans–van Beuningen, Rotterdam, and *John the Baptist Preaching, with Christ and His Disciples* in the Johnson Collection, Philadelphia (Figs. 66–67).[26] They have often been assigned to Huygh's supposed period of activity in Gouda, primarily because of their similarities to the woodcut illustrations in the *Chevalier délibéré,* a poem by Olivier de la Marche published in Gouda around 1486.[27] There are a number of affinities among these works: the facial types with strong cheekbones, the short-fingered hands, the drapery folds, the use of the lost profile, the bare, rolling hills, and the high horizon of the landscape. Whether the woodcuts are by the artist of the St. John panels is difficult to determine, given the different media, but the similarities do point to the artist's association with the Gouda school.

Comparison of the three St. John panels with a series of cartoons now in the Rijksprentenkabinet, Amsterdam, reveals a further connection with Gouda. The cartoon series is composed of twelve chalk drawings, nine of which are by the same artist. Of these, eight depict the sacraments of Baptism, Confirmation, Communion, and Ordination, and the ninth represents *A Young Man with an Angel*. They are almost certainly the drawings associated in 1714 with the glass paintings in the windows of St. John's in Gouda. The eighteenth-century author remarked that the drapery was so naturalistic that Lucas van Leyden might have drawn it, and the drawings have been attributed to Lucas by many scholars since. It is more likely, as K. G. Boon has suggested, that the nine drawings were made in Huygh's workshop around 1508, with the help of Lucas and perhaps Pieter Cornelisz. Kunst. Boon based this attribution on stylistic parallels between the cartoons and the St. John panels. Both are characterized by simple, somewhat awkward representations of figures and drapery, compact clusters of men and women, and the repeated use of a figure seen from the back as a *repoussoir*.[28]

Other comparisons can be drawn between the works of Lucas and those of the Master of the St. John Panels. The short figures in the St. John panels, with their large, square faces, prominent cheekbones, and fine, carefully drawn hair, are close to types in Lucas's *Chess Players* (Cat. 34, Fig. 1) and early engravings such as *David Playing the Harp before Saul* (B.27). Small, rounded hands, stubby fingers, and projecting thumbs are also typical of these works. So is the compositional grouping of figures in stiff, awkward clusters, with heads overlapping so that background faces are only partially visible. As J. Q. Van Regteren Altena has pointed out, the prominence given to landscape in the *Flight of Elizabeth* (Fig. 66) and *John the Baptist Preaching* (Fig. 67) might have sparked Lucas's early interest as a printmaker in landscapes. The distinctive mountains used so frequently in Lucas's engravings from 1505–1508 are unrelated to the St. John panels, but the bare, rolling hills in these paintings, with trees arranged to lead the eye into the background, might well have influenced Lucas's representation of low hillocks in the middle ground of his *Holy Family* engravings from this period (B.38–39).[29] The foliage of the trees in the *Flight of Elizabeth*, curved in gentle arcs to cover the trunks, has a close parallel in Lucas's *David and Abigail* (B.24) and *Raising of Lazarus* (B.42).

Van Regteren Altena has also described certain features common to the St.

John panels and a small triptych of the *Adoration of the Magi* in the Barnes Collection. He attributes this triptych to Lucas, as did many early scholars, but the painting is now generally excluded from his oeuvre (see Cat. A7). It is certainly closely related to the early sixteenth-century Leiden school, however, particularly to the art of Lucas. The resemblance to the St. John panels of this *Adoration*—and of two other works clearly by the same artist, the *Last Supper* in Aachen and the *Feeding of the Five Thousand* in Koblenz—strengthens the identification of the St. John Master as Huygh Jacobsz. Van Regteren Altena has noted, for example, that the head of the man third from the left in the Philadelphia panel is seen in the same position on the left wing of the *Adoration.* This man also appears as the servant in the right foreground of the *Last Supper.*[30] The importance of background landscape, the high horizon, the simple, rolling hillocks, and the foliage on the trees in these three small triptychs may also point to a connection with the school of Huygh Jacobsz.

Given their associations with the early Leiden and Gouda schools mentioned above, these three St. John panels may well have been painted by Huygh Jacobsz. If so, Lucas could have learned a range of skills from his father around 1505–1508. He certainly must have acquired at least the basic techniques of painting and drawing from Huygh, although Jan Piet Filedt Kok has observed that Lucas's lively manner of underdrawing and application of pigment have little in common with the more painstaking style of his father.[31] Lucas's precocity may account for the dissimilarities between his works and those of the St. John Master. By the time he learned to paint (which was, apparently, after he became proficient as an engraver), his prodigious talents would have quickly surpassed the rather pedestrian abilities of his father.

It seems to have been during this period that Lucas became familiar with certain compositional motifs that he repeated throughout his career. Particular mention should be made of a figure placed in the foreground as a *repoussoir* or transitional device between the real and the imagined world—a device inherited apparently from his father, whom I identify as the Master of the St. John Panels. Lucas also must have been impressed at an early age by the compositional arrangement of figures in a tight cluster, animated by the positioning of the heads. He frequently employed this formal device, even in paintings as late as *Christ Healing the Blind Man* from 1531, now in Leningrad (Cat. 25, Figs. 35, 37–39). Both Lucas and Huygh in the St. John panels used landscape as a vital unifying factor in their compositions, already evident in the earliest of Lucas's engravings. The paintings in Rotterdam and Philadelphia (as well as the woodcuts from the *Chevalier délibéré,* which I tentatively associate with the same artist) exhibit an interest in landscape that can be seen as a precursor to Lucas's own.

Cornelis Engebrechtsz.

According to *Het Schilder-Boeck,* Lucas's second teacher was Cornelis Engebrechtsz. Van Mander's report that Lucas moved to a new studio as the result of Huygh Jacobsz.'s early death has been proved incorrect. The date of Lucas's admission to the workshop of Cornelis is still unknown and has been surprisingly difficult to determine. Lucas's work shows little influence of his second teacher, and for this reason it is particularly unfortunate that Cornelis's *Adoration of the Magi* is now lost. This large watercolor painting, said to have hung in the city hall of Leiden in the early seventeenth century, seems to have been an important stylistic link between the two artists. Van Mander said of it, "A beautiful manner of [depicting] poses and drapery is visible, from which one can easily see that Lucas learned or practiced from his [Cornelis's] things."[32] Gibson has suggested parallels between the works of the two artists, especially in Lucas's prints and paintings from 1508–1509. But his theory that Lucas entered Cornelis's studio as early as 1508 is based on the incorrect dating of several engravings. I consider it more likely that Lucas's association with the workshop began in 1509. There are compositional affinities, for example, between Cornelis's small *Christ Carrying the Cross* in Leiden—which probably dates from the 1490s—and the same scene in Lucas's engraved *Round Passion* series of 1509 (B.64). In particular, the figures of Christ in these two works seem related. Also Lucas's background figure who supports the crossbar with one arm, raising the other to strike Christ, is essentially a mirror image of the man depicted by Cornelis. Of course, Lucas might well have seen this early painting by Cornelis in a context unrelated to his supposed sojourn in the older artist's studio. In fact, Bangs suggests that Lucas was never Cornelis's pupil.[33]

Lucas's figure types are generally quite different from those in Cornelis's works, but the deep, rich colors in his paintings may well have been inspired by an association with Cornelis. Most noteworthy is the use of bright red tones as a unifying device in many of Lucas's works. Filedt Kok has also noted similarities in both artists' techniques and styles of paint application. He suggests that Lucas (already proficient in the graphic media) probably learned more of the painter's art in Cornelis's studio than in that of his first teacher. But the energy, detail, and variety of Lucas's underdrawing style—evident even in his earliest paintings—has nothing in common with that of the St. John panels and is only slightly more similar to that found in Cornelis's works.[34] If he did study with both of these men, Lucas took from them only the most basic of skills. His experimentation with the possibilities of various media must have sprung from his innate artistic drive and curiosity.

Gibson has posited the absence of Cornelis's influence on Lucas's work as a reason for dating Lucas's birth in 1489 rather than 1494.[35] Thus, Lucas would have been admitted to the studio of his second teacher at age twenty, serving more in the capacity of assistant than of pupil. In defense of Van Mander's account, Lucas at age fifteen would also have been relatively independent of a new master's style, especially given his precocity and his earlier study with another artist.

CHAPTER 2

Stylistic Development of the Paintings

It has been unusually difficult for scholars to establish a chronology for Lucas's paintings. In large part this difficulty has been due to the inflation of his oeuvre with works by other artists, but even with the recent and rigorous investigation of his panels certain problems remain. Only two extant paintings by Lucas are dated: the *Virgin and Child with Mary Magdalene and a Donor* in Munich (Cat. 14, Fig. 12), from 1522, and *Moses after Striking the Rock* in Boston (Cat. 7, Figs. 24–25), from 1527. Only two others can be securely dated without appeal to stylistic evidence: *Christ Healing the Blind Man* in Leningrad (Cat. 25, Figs. 35, 37–39), originally with the year 1531 on an exterior panel that was either lost or destroyed during later alterations, and the *Last Judgment* triptych in Leiden (Cat. 20, Figs. 17–19), which can be placed in 1526–1527 based on an archival reference to its commission. My approximate dates for the paintings in the catalogue raisonné and my analysis of Lucas's stylistic development are based to a large extent on comparison with the artist's sizable graphic oeuvre. More than half of his engravings are dated, ranging from 1508 to 1530, which provides a useful framework for arranging the paintings.[1]

In studying Lucas's paintings, we must take into account the numerous copies after works no longer extant, remembering that they transmit the original image only through the filter of the copyist's artistic training and abilities. Dating of these works is a hazardous undertaking; the style and technique of the lost original are often difficult to detect, and composition, figure types, and setting are subject to alteration by the copyist. The drawings of Jan de

Bisschop, a lawyer and amateur artist from The Hague active from around 1655 until his death in 1671, form the largest body of copies after Lucas's paintings. De Bisschop reproduced seven or eight panels by Lucas as well as works by a number of other sixteenth- and seventeenth-century artists. According to one early source, De Bisschop wanted to simulate the styles of other painters, and as a result he was able to create remarkably exact imitations of the originals.[2] His works after Lucas can be considered relatively faithful reproductions, allowing for the unavoidable distortions present in any copy.

Circa 1506–1512: The Half-Length Narratives

The paintings of the youthful Lucas are remarkably free of the influence of the two teachers mentioned by Van Mander: Huygh Jacobsz. and Cornelis Engebrechtsz. Although Huygh's distinctive treatment of landscape as seen in the St. John panels appears to have had a powerful influence on Lucas's youthful engravings, and might well have inspired his lifelong interest in landscape, the two earliest extant paintings by Lucas show a complete disregard for and even denial of the setting. These two panels, the *Chess Players* in Berlin (Cat. 34, Fig. 1) and *The Fortuneteller* in Paris (Cat. 35, Fig. 2), were painted around 1508. But one earlier work, now lost, because of its subject may have depended on the St. John panels more than the two allegorical genre scenes. Van Mander mentions a canvas in tempera, the *History of St. Hubert* (Cat. 27), made when Lucas was twelve years old (or in 1506–1507, calculating from the 1494 birth date cited in *Het Schilder-Boeck*). No further description is given by Van Mander, but it seems likely that landscape played an important narrative function in the painting, since the most frequently represented episode of St. Hubert's life was his conversion while out hunting.[3]

In 1930 Friedländer described what he saw as a paradox in Lucas's style: although his engravings were crafted with the vision of a natural painter, his early paintings exhibited the constraint characteristic of an engraver.[4] This paradox was due to Lucas's investigation of distinct problems in the two media. In the early engravings he concentrated on conveying a sense of expansive space inhabited by three-dimensional forms, and in order to achieve this spatial extension he experimented with various methods of lighting, with the foreshortening of limbs, heads, and even entire bodies, and with the representation of deep landscape settings. Both Vasari and Van Mander praised Lucas's portrayal of atmospheric recession in these prints, and the Dutch writer singled out the "level, continuous ground of his landscapes."[5] The high point of his early graphic development is found in the engraving *Mohammed and the Monk*

Sergius (B.126), dated 1508. Here, spatial concerns meet with a secondary interest in physiognomic types and emotional content.

The early paintings, which are narrative rather than devotional in character, reveal Lucas's emphasis on psychological mood with minimal attention to an architectural or landscape background. The settings of the *Chess Players* and *The Fortuneteller* are played down in favor of emphatic gestures and carefully articulated facial types. Even in these early and rather clumsy works, the somber tones and thick application of pigment convey an appropriate mood of tension, and highlighted faces and hands, the primary vehicles of expression, project dramatically. The squat, thickset figures are densely clustered in an airless space, but the clarity of the composition in these small, overcrowded panels imposes an order on the confusion. The principal characters in the foreground are balanced against the background frieze of heads. Lively gestures, which animate the dense structure, reinforce the basic lines of the composition. The use of background figures as filler is not characteristic of the early engravings, although a similar closely set, overlapping crowd appears in *David Playing the Harp before Saul* of circa 1508 (B.27).[6] As in the two early paintings, the crowd in this engraving forms a backdrop for the dramatic interaction of the protagonists.

It has been suggested that the background figures in Dürer's woodcut of the *Martyrdom of St. John the Evangelist* (1498) influenced Lucas's *Chess Players*.[7] A more direct link with the German print can be seen in Lucas's *David Playing the Harp before Saul*, with striking similarities in the placement and arrangement of figures behind the balustrade as well as physiognomic affinities between the emperor Domitian and Saul. It may be that Lucas experimented in the print with the compositional and narrative possibilities of Dürer's dense crowd of onlookers before using the motif so effectively in his two early panels. Lucas's compact, half-length painted compositions seem to have been the result of his innovative, experimental variations on an indirect graphic source. He might also have drawn inspiration from the religious narratives in half length that became so popular in the early sixteenth century, a type he himself was to depict only a few years later in *Potiphar's Wife Accusing Joseph,* now in Rotterdam (Cat. 1, Fig. 4). There is a similarity, for example, between *The Fortuneteller* and Petrus Christus's *St. Eloy* of 1449 in the position of the main figures and their location behind a foreground table. Lucas might have been exposed to this Bruges composition through his father, Huygh Jacobsz., whose sojourn in Ghent (near Bruges) was mentioned by several sixteenth-century sources. Dürer's *Christ among the Doctors* in the Thyssen-Bornemisza Collection in Lugano is much closer to the intense mood, the emphasis on gestures, and the crowded, overlapping figures of Lucas's panels. But Dürer's work was painted in Venice in 1506 and could not have been known to Lucas unless through some now-lost intermediary.[8]

Several authors have suggested the influence of Massys and Bosch on the early paintings of Lucas, but his half-length compositions closely crowded with figures predate the most likely comparisons. The chronology of Bosch's paintings is difficult to determine, and it is possible that some of his small Passion panels, or copies after them, may have been seen by Lucas prior to 1508. Although all three artists were apparently fascinated by physiognomic types, the figures depicted by Lucas were as a rule less grotesque and caricatured.[9]

Both *Potiphar's Wife Accusing Joseph* and *Susanna before the Judge* (Cat. 3, Fig. 6) may be dated several years after the *Chess Players* (circa 1510–1511 and circa 1512, respectively), based on an analysis of compositions, figure types, and styles of underdrawing. The backgrounds of these works are more open, with a view leading into a distant landscape at the left. The setting has now become a more integral part of the scene, providing a structural backdrop for the action and, in the case of the architectural decorations in *Susanna*, adding allegorical meaning to the biblical story. The figures themselves, taller and thinner than those in the *Chess Players,* have more space in which to turn and gesture. Compared with the rather muddy browns, dull golds, dark blue-greens, and intense reds dominating the two earlier panels, the lighter, more golden tones of *Potiphar's Wife* add to the atmospheric ambience. The use of color shows a greater sophistication and dramatic flair, as in the pale blue and reddish violet dress of Potiphar's wife. The thin layers of paint are applied with more flowing strokes, as opposed to the relatively viscous handling in the earlier works. The brushwork of the *Chess Players,* for example, is quite labored, curiously at variance with the bold and varied strokes of the underdrawing. This difference indicates that while the young Lucas was an able draftsman, he was still hindered at that stage by his awkward handling of paint. The *History of St. Hubert* is the only known earlier painting by Lucas, and its medium of tempera on canvas would not have fully prepared the young artist for the challenge of working in oil. By 1510–1512, however, Lucas's paint technique was marked by greater ease and assurance, and it began to approach the vitality of his detailed early underdrawing style.[10]

It has been suggested that *Potiphar's Wife* and *Susanna* were pendants, but the dimensions of the two panels are different and the works appear to be separated in time by at least a year or two.[11] They are thematically related, however, both portraying biblical stories in which a virtuous young person is falsely accused of wrongdoing, and compositional affinities between the two works suggest that Lucas was experimenting with the same fundamental problems of figural grouping and interaction. In both paintings a scene of confrontation involving a man and a woman is centrally located, and around these protagonists are clustered subsidiary participants and spectators. The figures in *Potiphar's Wife* are more closely pressed between the picture plane and the background wall, and the composition lacks the relief of the low balustrade and the two males in the foreground of *Susanna*.

The energy and dynamism of the paintings derive not from the still somewhat stiff poses and expressionless faces but from the cluster of gestures at the heart of the semicircular compositions. In *Potiphar's Wife Accusing Joseph*, Lucas continued the experiment begun in the *Chess Players*—to locate meaning in gesture. He chose the moment of the denunciation of Joseph by Potiphar's wife rather than the more popular scene of her attempted seduction of the youth. His 1512 engraved series of *The History of Joseph* (B.19–23) includes both episodes, and its greater expansiveness, narratively as well as compositionally, points to an earlier date for the more constricted representation in paint. In the engraving of the accusation of Potiphar's wife (B.21) the poses are also freer and looser, and the gestures play a less central symbolic role as they are diffused throughout the composition. The density of the figural grouping in the panel enhances the power of Potiphar's reaction to the news, expressed in the recoil of his body, his head twisting away and his eyes slit. His *contrapposto* form is the axis around which the other figures are posed in stiff verticals. The emotional force of the scene is encapsulated in the violent movement of Potiphar's upraised right arm. This gesture is also at the heart of the spatial arrangement, conveying the reflexive horror and astonishment of the injured husband in the face of the accusation.

Circa 1513–1520: The Development of Landscape

Lucas's growing interest in landscape after 1513 is found in the *Card Players* in the Thyssen-Bornemisza Collection in Lugano (Cat. 37, Fig. 7), a variant of the early chess and fortune-telling scenes. This small panel (in rather poor condition, with overpainting in evidence throughout) can be securely placed in the period 1513–1515. It reveals an increased sophistication in Lucas's compositional skills since the painting of *Susanna before the Judge*. Although the individual figures are still rather awkwardly posed, there is now a much greater sense of three-dimensional extension. This new spaciousness is largely due to the dramatic simplification of the scene, here limited to the three participants in the game. There is now more room for the figures to move, and the interstices between each have not been filled with a crowd of "extras" as in the earlier paintings. Although the table in the foreground forms a barrier between the real and the imagined worlds, and the two men at each side are cramped by the frame, the landscape that runs the breadth of the composition was a new step for the young painter. By setting the game in the open air he expanded the earlier, more limited vista of *Susanna,* combining his early interest as an engraver in landscape and his emphasis as a painter on human interaction. He focused attention on the card game by creating a grid of verticals and horizontals with the trees and fence, comparable to the background framework he had already experimented with in engravings such as *Two Couples in a Wood* (B.146, 1509) and *The Milkmaid* (B.158, 1510). This structuring of the background, serving to order the major compositional elements, is a variant of the enframing architecture in *Potiphar's Wife* and *Susanna,* but here it also provides the scene with a greater sense of light and air.

The *Triumphal Entry of David into Jerusalem* (Cat. C4), a work known only through copies (Figs. 41–42), integrates the figures and their landscape setting less successfully. The lost original is a work of the early period and should be dated circa 1510–1515. There are variations in the format and the number of figures among the different versions, but the composition in each is timid and cluttered, lacking the bold simplicity of design and naturalistic landscape setting of the *Card Players* in Lugano. The women who welcome David at the gates of Jerusalem form a single compositional unit, with full-length and rather elongated figures as crowded together as those in the earlier *Chess Players.* The foreground scene is arranged as if on a stage, and the setting—a plateau dropping precipitously to a distant landscape—had apparently been reduced to a formula by this time, since Lucas used it in many engravings from this period.[12] Despite these problems, the work provides interesting evidence for another stage in the development of Lucas's merging of graphic and pictorial concerns. If, as Van Mander stated in 1604, the original was painted on glass, perhaps the very nature of the medium provided the stimulus and opportunity for experimentation.[13] As an intermediate between printmaking and painting, glass painting may have prompted Lucas to represent, on the small scale of an engraving, a group of full-length figures in a landscape setting comparable to so many of his prints from this period.

Greater maturity and assurance are evident in the *Card Players* in the collection of the Earl of Pembroke, Wilton House (Cat. 38, Fig. 9). Dating from 1515–1517, this painting can be seen as the culmination of Lucas's early half-length narratives. Although similar to the youthful works, it achieves a more careful balance through the juxtaposition of complex forms and varied tones. As in the earlier paintings, the figures are still tightly framed at the sides and seem pressed between the picture plane and the background wall, but there is a greater sense of spatial freedom. The figures, more naturalistically and gracefully proportioned, have ample room in which to turn and gesture. The number of spectators is held to a minimum, and those that are included are important to the composition. In addition, the man and woman at the foreground left and right now begin to invade the space between the table and the picture plane, adding to the sense of depth. These *repoussoir* figures seen from the back are in this way both more emphatically placed and more compositionally useful than those in the *Chess Players* and *Susanna before the Judge*.

Although the small window gives a more restricted view than in the paintings from 1512–1515, the simplicity of the landscape relieves the action of the main scene in a novel way. Attention is drawn to this distant view in several subtle ways. The two main lines of the composition (which run through the heads of the female players at the left and the male players at the right) lead directly out the window. The principal figure, both iconographically and spatially, is the elderly man placing his bet on the table. He is slightly off-center to the right, and the placement of the window to the left of the central axis is a counter to his weight. This asymmetry enlivens what had been a static balance in the Lugano *Card Players*. The vitality of the painting is increased further by the circle of figures around the table, with the outstretched arms of the players forming the spokes of a wheel. As in so many of Lucas's paintings, gestures are at the heart of the composition. Even the angles of the tilted hats lead the eye down to the hand of the elderly man.

The use of different shades of red further unifies the composition. The orange robes worn by the men at the left and right accent the lateral edges, and the circular motion of the composition as a whole is strengthened and stabilized by the repetition of brilliant scarlet details at key points. The hat of the man at the lower right is countered in tone as well as in angle by that of the man advising the young woman. The coloristic equilibrium is more complex than that of the slightly earlier *Card Players* in Lugano, in which the simple pyramidal arrangement of the figures is underscored by shades of scarlet in a V pattern.

Lucas's *St. Andrew* in Karlsruhe, originally part of a triptych from around 1512–1517 but now cut down on three sides (Cat. 28, Fig. 8), is painted with similarly bright color combinations. The rich red of the saint's robe was used earlier in Potiphar's costume, and in both the Lugano and the Wilton House *Card Players* this color also appears in conjunction with the same cool bluegreen of the background of *St. Andrew*. The colors of Andrew's cloak, one half a light pinkish tan and the other dark brown, are repeated in the cloak of the man in the background of the *Card Players* in Wilton House. In these works, as well as in *Potiphar's Wife*, Lucas was experimenting with the potential of color as an expressive tool—a unifying and articulating element—although these early efforts are less sophisticated than the remarkably complex tonal balance achieved in late paintings such as the *Dance around the Golden Calf* (Cat. 11, Figs. 32–34).

The *St. Andrew* panel is thickly painted, with broad strokes of white highlighting the saint's face and hands and a rapidly brushed background—a far cry from the thin, flowing paint style of *Potiphar's Wife* and the *Card Players* in Wilton House. Filedt Kok dates *St. Andrew* around 1518, citing its direct brushwork reminiscent of Lucas's late paintings, particularly *Dance around the Golden Calf*.[14] The hasty manner in which the paint is applied should perhaps be seen, though, as more akin to the style of the very early *Fortuneteller*. The summary, almost careless brushwork tends to flatten the forms at times, and in this respect Lucas was far from achieving the plasticity of the broadly painted figures in *Dance*.

The broad, thick application of the paint in the *St. Andrew* panel may perhaps be due to its original purpose and location on the inside right wing of a triptych. *St. George* (Cat. C29), now lost and known only through a drawing by Jan de Bisschop (Fig. 43), may have been its counterpart on the left. The similarity of *St. Andrew* to Lucas's *Annunciation* in Munich (Cat. 15, Fig. 13) helps to explain the unusual technique. Both were once subordinate members of a larger work, and both were executed with the same sketchy brushwork. The central panel of the *St. Andrew–St. George* triptych is now lost, but its paint was probably more flowing and finely drawn than that on the wings—similar to the interior of the Munich *Virgin and Child* (Fig. 12) and to paintings closer in time such as the *Card Players* in Lugano and Wilton House. Lucas would have been deliberately juxtaposing the relative roughness of the peripheral panels with the delicacy and detail of the major scene, emphasizing the importance of the latter. This hypothesis would help to explain the vast differences between the paint technique of this panel, which for other reasons seems to date from 1512–1517, and those of other works from the 1510s. He used different techniques in other polyptychs from the 1520s, as in the *Virgin and Child* and *Annunciation* diptych in Munich and the *Last Judgment* triptych in Leiden, but in these works the distinction is between the exterior and interior representations. A change in style between the central panel and the interior wings, as suggested here for *St. Andrew*, might well have seemed jarring. But if a continuous scene was not represented, there already would have been a certain visual break between the saints and the image in the center: Jan Provost's triptych in the Mauritshuis, for example, includes a half-length Virgin and Child on the center panel and full-length saints on the wings.[15] If this was the case, Lucas might have wanted to emphasize the break rather than to smooth the transitions.

Both St. Andrew and St. George are shown standing in landscape settings (Figs. 8 and 43), which would have been much more extensive in the original triptych, of course, since the figures were probably full length. Lucas's interest in landscape, evident in his earliest prints, developed gradually in his paintings of 1510–1520. The landscape plays a dominant role for iconographic reasons in the *Fall of Man* (Cat. C5), known only from a drawing by Jan de Bisschop (Fig. 44) that probably copies a lost painting of 1517–1520. Adam and Eve are set in a carefully observed and detailed Garden of Eden and are completely overpowered by the huge tree to their right. The subject requires a natural setting, of course, but the scope and grandeur of the landscape are more reminiscent of the artist's engravings from this period than of his other paintings.[16] Most of the early panels had an architectural setting, and if a landscape view was included, it was always subordinate to the action of the main scene. The unusual prominence of landscape in this work seems to be an offshoot of Lucas's graphic development. The *Fall of Man* was his favorite theme as a printmaker, repeated more than any other subject.[17] Although Lucas rarely painted a subject he had already treated in another medium, it is not surprising that his continuing fascination with the Fall would have led him to explore this theme in a painting. His growing interest in the incorporation of landscape elements in his paintings from this period seems in some ways dependent on the more fully developed topography in his early prints, as we have seen, and the breadth and scope of the large-scale landscapes in his late paintings are more directly linked to the early engravings than to these still rather limited environments in the panels.

Circa 1521–1525: The Influence of Antwerp

Lucas's trip to Antwerp in the summer of 1521 had a marked effect on his work in the following years. Antwerp had replaced Bruges by that time as the commercial heart of the Netherlands and was one of the leading ports in northern Europe. It was a burgeoning center of international trade and had attracted painters and printmakers as well as merchants from many parts of Europe. The artistic life of the city was active and varied, supporting prominent painters such as Quinten Massys, Joos van Cleve, and Joachim Patinir. In 1520–1521 Albrecht Dürer was in Antwerp, and his presence in the city may have been the primary reason for Lucas's trip. Lucas had long been an admirer of Dürer's woodcuts and engravings and had borrowed poses and compositional motifs from them for some of his own early prints.[18]

It was not until their meeting in Antwerp, however, that Dürer's figures and compositions came to have an influence on Lucas's paintings, although his renewed acquaintance with Dürer's art was at first more readily apparent in his prints and drawings. The *Small Passion* of 1521 (B.43–56) was closely based on Dürer's engraved *Passion* series of 1507–1512 (B.4–18), and an engraving of *St. Jerome* (B.114), as well as a drawing in Oxford, was inspired by Dürer's painting of the same subject in Lisbon.[19] Lucas's six portrait drawings from 1521, three of which are signed and dated, also show the effects of this meeting of the two artists. During his travels in the Netherlands, Dürer drew numerous portraits, usually bust length and in three-quarter poses. Lucas borrowed the pose for his own studies in black chalk, but he achieved greater solidity and stability through the use of a horizontal format rather than Dürer's vertical. This difference is evident, for example, in a comparison of Lucas's *Portrait of a Man* drawing in Leiden and Dürer's portraits of young men in Berlin and Paris.[20]

In the painted *Portrait of a Man Aged 38* in the National Gallery in London (Cat. 31, Fig. 10), Lucas reverted to the more traditional portrait composition typical of fifteenth- and early sixteenth-century Netherlandish art. The bust-length figure is tightly enclosed in a vertical rectangle, as in many of Dürer's portrait drawings, but the space is even further restricted by the cramped placement of the hands. The composition and the extremely fine detailing of the flesh areas are ultimately derived from Netherlandish rather than German sources. It is interesting to note that Dürer's painted portraits of 1520–1521 reveal that he too temporarily came under the influence of this Netherlandish style, returning to a format he had used in his youth. It is not clear whether Lucas's portrait should be seen as a direct descendant of this early Netherlandish tradition, which was continued in Antwerp by Joos van Cleve and Quinten Massys, or whether it came through the indirect channel of Dürer's resuscitation of the style.[21] Certainly Dürer seems to have been an important influence on the resurgence of Lucas's interest in portraiture during the early 1520s, just as the boldness and clarity of his drawing style had an impact on Lucas's draftsmanship.

For two years following his return to Leiden in 1521, Lucas devoted himself almost exclusively to paintings of the Virgin and Child, apparently as a result of his contact with artists such as Joos van Cleve and Massys and his renewed interest in Dürer's prints (although Dürer himself by this point seems to have largely turned against such Catholic imagery). The art market in Antwerp produced large numbers of devotional images of the Virgin and Child for export to southern Europe. Dürer's many prints of the subject, especially those from 1518 to 1520, clearly inspired several engravings by Lucas, including his *Virgin and Child on a Crescent Moon* (B.82) and *Virgin and Child with Angels*

(B.84), both from 1523. Lucas's composition of the *Virgin and Child in the Clouds* (Cat. C17, 1522–1523), known only through a drawing by Jan de Bisschop (Fig. 46), is reminiscent of Dürer's engraving of the *Madonna Nursing*, from 1519 (B.36), especially in the position of the two main figures and the movement of their hands. Other variants of this composition by Dürer may also have been used as source material by Lucas: the woodcut B.99, for example, has a similar representation at the center top of God the Father and the dove of the Holy Ghost to complete the Trinity. The motif of the Virgin and Child encircled by cherubs is roughly comparable to Dürer's woodcut of 1518, the *Virgin Crowned by Two Angels* (B.101), and the view of the earth spread beneath the celestial scene could have been inspired by any one of a number of prints by Dürer, including his engraving of *Nemesis* (B.77) or several woodcuts from his series of the *Apocalypse* (for example, B.68, 71).

Lucas's painting of the *Virgin and Child with Angels* in Berlin, circa 1521 (Cat. 12, Fig. 11), may reflect the popularity among artists in the southern Netherlands of the theme of the Virgin and Child enthroned and accompanied by musical angels. Versions of this subject have been attributed to Massys, the Master of the Morrison Triptych, and the Master of Frankfurt.[22] The central panel of an altarpiece by Jan Gossaert, now in Palermo, is closest to Lucas's painting in the appearance of the cherubs. Although the extremely elaborate Gothic setting in Gossaert's work is very different from Lucas's architecture, many similarities exist in the way the plump, curly haired little angels cluster around the Virgin and Child. In both panels several angels sing from an open book of music, others play musical instruments as their bodies seem to extend into the spectator's space, and another hands a flower to the Christ Child. This altarpiece was probably in Bruges when Lucas was in Antwerp. Although there is no evidence that Lucas made a trip to Bruges, he could have seen one of the copies after Gossaert's altarpiece by Adriaen Isenbrandt.[23]

Lucas's *Virgin and Child with Angels* is also reminiscent of Dürer's work, most notably in the inclusion of musical angels. Dürer's interest in the compositions of Gentile Bellini (whose paintings of the *Sacra Conversazione* almost invariably include at least one musical angel in the foreground) is evident, for example, in his *Feast of the Rose Garlands* (1506), in which an angel playing the lute is placed at the feet of the Virgin. Dürer elaborated on this theme in various drawings and prints, such as woodcuts of 1511 (B.97) and 1518 (B.101) in which the cherubs are similar in type to the ones in Lucas's paintings. By the time he traveled to the Netherlands, Dürer was at work on an unfinished altarpiece of the *Sacra Conversazione,* and he included in his preparatory sketches Bellini's figure of the musical angel seated in the foreground before the Virgin.[24]

The strict symmetry of the architecture in *Virgin and Child with Angels* provides a geometrical framework for the central placement of the Virgin and lute-playing angel in the foreground. Despite this apparent order, the elements of the background architecture fail to describe a comprehensible space, and any indication of measurable depth is negated by the thin body of the Virgin sandwiched between the balustrade and the tapestry. Although a sense of bulk is suggested by the great width of her torso, which is enveloped in a voluminous red cloak and acts as the pyramidal center of the composition, the sharp contours and awkward foreshortening of her body counteract any appearance of depth. The distorted perspective and deep shadows of the balustrade or table in the foreground add to the confusion, making it impossible to determine either the ground plan of this interior or the various levels of the floor. It is not clear, for example, where the youths at the side are standing or how the ledge or steps in the foreground relate to the balustrade in front of the Virgin. The angel's head at the bottom of the frame serves to dissolve the boundaries of the scene, but at the same time it adds to the ambiguity of the spatial arrangement. The pose of the cherub in the foreground with his back to the spectator acts as a transitional device between the onlooker and the Virgin and Child. The glance, the curve of the body, and the outstretched arm lead the eye inward toward the thematic center of the composition. This use of a *repoussoir* occurs frequently in Lucas's engravings (see B.14, 40, 61, 136). The motif of a child seen from the back, in the foreground gesturing inward, is also found in the *Crucifixion* in Basel by Cornelis Engebrechtsz., circa 1515, and Gibson considers that this motif in Cornelis's work was borrowed from engravings by Lucas (such as B.61 and 71).[25]

The *Virgin and Child with Joseph, Anne, and Two Male Saints* (Cat. C13), known from a later drawing now in the Louvre (Fig. 45) and from a later engraving, is a more successful composition, probably made by Lucas shortly after his return to Leiden. The arrangement of the full-length figures is similar to Massys's *Holy Kindred* altarpiece in Brussels, dated 1509. Like the Flemish artist, Lucas grouped the saints symmetrically in an open portico and included figures behind a low balustrade to add a sense of depth. Although the *Holy Kindred* was commissioned for St. Peter's in Louvain, it is possible that Lucas saw a copy or drawing of it during his stay in Antwerp.

The *Virgin and Child with Mary Magdalene and a Donor* in Munich (Cat. 14, Fig. 12) was originally a diptych dated 1522, although it has suffered considerable alterations. Diptychs like this one featuring a seated Virgin and Child facing a donor and saint in three-quarter length were uncommon, the only example known to me in northern art being Jean Fouquet's *Melun Diptych,* circa 1450. Full-length, single-panel formats were much more frequently used; examples include Hans Memling's *Virgin and Child with Donor and St. Anthony* in

Ottawa and Jan Provost's *Virgin Enthroned* in The Hague. Another popular format was that of the small devotional diptych with the Virgin and Child on the left wing and the praying donor on the right. In these, however, the limited size prohibited the inclusion of a saint as intercessor. A number of examples by Rogier van der Weyden are known, and Memling's *Nieuwenhove Diptych* in Bruges is a later version.[26] Lucas's work should probably be considered an enlarged and elaborated form of these diptychs rather than an indirect descendant of Fouquet's work.

The sense of space in this painting is especially striking when compared to the *Virgin and Child with Angels* in Berlin (Fig. 11). The plasticity and foreshortening of the figures are more accomplished, and the placement of the figures and the throne at an angle to the picture plane eliminates the harsh frontal composition of the Berlin panel. The spaciousness is enhanced by the absence of a balustrade in the foreground, allowing the figures to move more freely, and also by the inclusion of a broad landscape in the distance. The landscape is fluidly painted, creating an expansive, atmospheric backdrop that is more fully developed than in the panels from the 1510s. As so often in Lucas's work, his prints from the same period reveal different priorities and interests. Certainly landscape is used as a significant compositional element in the *Dance of the Magdalene* of 1519 (B.122), with a luxurious spread comparable to and supportive of the foreground narrative (and with a craggy mountain like that in the Munich *Virgin and Child,* referring to the Magdalene's hermitage in St. Baume).[27] But his engravings from 1520–1522 show a more restricted, intimate space. Closest in mood and composition, and in the combination of volumetric form with spacious surround, is his engraving of the *Virgin and Child with Angels* from 1523 (B.84). It seems, in fact, to be a reworking in a unified scene of the ideas Lucas had been experimenting with the year before in the diptych, in particular the use of a background rectilinear grid to enhance the main figural action (balustrade, fence, horizon, pier, and mountain in the diptych; trees, post, and rocky ledge in the engraving).

The *Annunciation* (Cat. 15, Fig. 13), originally on the reverse of the diptych, derives from the traditional format used in the Netherlands and Germany in the fifteenth century. Gabriel flies in from the upper left, landing with both legs bent, and finds the Virgin kneeling at the prie-dieu in her bedroom. These components were popularized by Rogier van der Weyden in his *Annunciation* in the Louvre, and Lucas might have known any one of a number of variants of this painting. That this compositional type was known in Antwerp in the early 1520s is evident from a panel by Joos van Cleve in New York, painted around 1525.[28] Dürer's prints were also readily available to Lucas at this time, of course. Several woodcut *Annunciations* by Dürer (B.19, 83) are roughly similar to Lucas's composition, and one detail in particular may indicate a specific link. In the print from Dürer's *Life of the Virgin* (B.83) the curtains are swept aside by Gabriel's entrance in such a way that Lucas could have reinterpreted the drapery as part of the Archangel's robe.

Lucas's *Christ as Man of Sorrows and Virgin of Sorrows* (Cat. C16) is now lost but was reproduced in numerous sixteenth- and seventeenth-century copies. A date of 1522 on the etched copy attributed to Simon Frisius (Fig. 47) can be confirmed by comparison of the figure types with other paintings and engravings by Lucas from the early 1520s, especially the Munich diptych and the *Small Passion* series (B.43–56, 1521). The subject matter and format reinforce a date closely following Lucas's trip to Antwerp, since this type of devotional diptych was especially popular in the southern Netherlands in the late fifteenth and early sixteenth centuries. Examples were produced in quantity in the studios of Dirk and Albert Bouts as well as the workshops of Memling and Massys.[29]

The works from 1521–1523 reveal the profound influence of southern Netherlandish art on Lucas's thematic and compositional concerns. His interest in allegorical and biblical narratives, which dominated the first decade of his career, underwent a dramatic, though temporary, change as a result of his association with artists in Antwerp. During this period he was almost exclusively concerned with the production of devotional images, ranging from the closely framed, bust-length *Christ as Man of Sorrows and Virgin of Sorrows* to the full-length, expansive setting of the *Virgin and Child in the Clouds* (Cat. C17, Fig. 46). Lucas's figures were gradually becoming more robust, as can be clearly seen in the full, rounded faces and broad shoulders of the females. The proportions of the figures were still clumsy at times, however, and foreshortening remained a problem. The pyramidal solidity of the Virgin in Berlin (Fig. 11) is offset by the unconvincing three-dimensionality of her torso, and in a similar way the monumentality of the Virgin in Munich (Fig. 12) is diminished by her very slender forearm. By 1523 Lucas had become more consistent in the depiction of fully rounded forms, as in the *Virgin and Child in the Clouds* and the engraving of the *Virgin and Child with Angels* (B.84).

The corporeality of individual figures increased in several allegorical scenes from 1522–1525, all known only from copies: *A Family Surprised by Death* (Cat. C40, Fig. 49), the *Allegory of Transience* (Cat. C41, Figs. 50–51), the *Temptation of a Young Man* (Cat. C42, Fig. 52), and the *Card Players* (Cat. C39, Fig. 53). Although the solidity of the figures in these works could be the result of the copyists' efforts rather than Lucas's, it is more likely a reflection of Lucas's own interests since the greater amplitude of form as well as other aspects of figure type and costume are close to his engravings from 1523–1525.

The crones in several of these paintings, for example, are comparable to similarly grotesque old women in *The Musicians* (B.155, 1524) and *Virgil Suspended in a Basket* (B.136, 1525), and the young women and children are found again in the engraving of Virgil and works such as *The Dentist* (B.157) and the *Virgin and Child with Angels* (B.84), both from 1523. In some ways, though, he was returning in these works to thematic and compositional concerns that predated his trip to Antwerp, especially in his renewed interest in allegorical content and in the arrangement of figures around a foreground table.

Circa 1526–1531: The Late Works

As he matured, Lucas apparently turned increasingly to the medium of paint to experiment with large, complex, multifigured compositions. Sixteen paintings from this period are known, some only from copies, and more than half of these are monumental biblical scenes with full-length figures, with less attention paid to allegorical genre and to small devotional images. As in Lucas's earliest period, his prints are concerned with strikingly different problems from his paintings. None of the engravings from 1527–1531 includes more than three figures, the emphasis being on the graphic representation of plastic, three-dimensional forms seen at close range. Settings in the late prints are more generalized, even in the case of landscapes, and their primary function is to form a relatively abstracted backdrop for the action of the figures (see B.3, 5, 10). But there is common ground between the two media, especially in the influence of Marcantonio Raimondi and Jan Gossaert on some of the figure poses and on Lucas's increasingly monumental forms.

Unlike his contemporaries Gossaert and Jan van Scorel, Lucas never traveled to Italy. His knowledge of Italian models must have come exclusively from prints, drawings, and paintings available in the Netherlands. The engravings of Marcantonio Raimondi, a Bolognese printmaker who moved to Rome around 1509 and became closely associated with the workshop of Raphael, were vital to the development of Lucas's late style. The two artists were linked even earlier, however, since Marcantonio had been influenced in his early period by the prints of both Lucas and Dürer. In a number of copies after figural compositions by Raphael and other artists, Marcantonio had borrowed landscape backgrounds from northern artists. In his print of *Lucretia* from circa 1512–1513 (B.192, Fig. 71), for example, which is probably after a design by Raphael, the landscape is partially drawn from Lucas's *Susanna and the Elders* (B.33).

The earliest evidence of Marcantonio's influence is seen in Lucas's engraving of *Lucretia*, circa 1514–1515 (B.134, Fig. 72).[30] Its relationship to Marcantonio's *Venus and Cupid*, circa 1512 (B.311, Fig. 73), provides useful insights into the first stage of Lucas's interest in Italian models. *Venus and Cupid*, modeled after Raphael, was one of the most influential engravings in northern Europe. In addition to being the primary inspiration for Lucas's *Lucretia*, it was also the model for Gossaert's painting of *Venus and Cupid* in Brussels and Van Scorel's *Lucretia* on the reverse of a portrait in Berlin.[31] Like Van Scorel, Lucas changed the figure from a graceful Venus into a suicidal Lucretia. There are a number of other variations between the prints by Marcantonio and Lucas, including slight changes in the pose of arms and legs and in the treatment of hair, but in general, and most significant for his later works, the new monumentality of Lucas's figure was clearly dependent on the Italian prototype. Compared to Lucas's earlier nudes, such as his *Mary Magdalene*, circa 1506 (B.123), Lucretia shows a greater sense of weight and corporeal solidity as well as more naturalistic proportions. This amplitude is a result of the broadened silhouette of the figure and of the actual burin technique borrowed from Marcantonio. The hatching of the inner modeling is more regular and deeply incised than that in Lucas's early engravings, and the crosshatching of the shadowed areas is beginning to approximate Marcantonio's systematic, gridlike application of lines. The full impact of Marcantonio's engraving style becomes apparent in Lucas's late prints.[32]

Despite these influences, Lucas's Lucretia is still decidedly northern in appearance, identifiable as such by her facial type and by the irregularities in the surface of her flesh. Marcantonio simplifies and idealizes, which is characteristic of the Italian approach, whereas Lucas emphasizes the descriptive details of an individual. The projection of northern characteristics onto an Italian model is an important aspect of Lucas's later paintings, beginning with the *Last Judgment* in Leiden of 1526–1527 (Cat. 20, Figs. 17–23).

Art historians throughout the nineteenth century sharply criticized this monumental triptych, especially because of its pale tonality. One early scholar likened it to an unfinished study of nudes. The figure poses were often described as clumsy or mannered, and the anatomy was considered poorly executed. The composition itself was seen as fragmented and empty.[33] Lucas did indeed omit the traditional scene of the weighing of souls by the Archangel Michael and dramatically underplayed the role of the Virgin and John the Baptist as intercessors. These elements, so significant in fifteenth-century versions such as Rogier van der Weyden's Beaune polyptych, were generally minimized by the sixteenth century, as in Bernard Van Orley's triptych in Antwerp and Joos van Cleve's panel in New York, both painted in the early 1520s. But Lucas went further, and the result of his greatly simplified representation is an original interpretation of the theme, with the remarkable sense of spaciousness reinforced by the light, golden coloring, the masterful representation of atmospheric perspective, and the diminution of many distracting iconographic details typical of earlier *Last Judgment* scenes. The contrast with an altarpiece by Hans Memling, dating from the 1470s and now in Danzig, reveals the innovations of Lucas's triptych. Memling concentrated on the sacred protagonists, and the swarming profusion of resurrected figures almost equals the complexity of Gothic fretwork. In Lucas's *Last Judgment*, on the other hand, the visual emphasis is on the relatively small array of nudes in the foreground.[34]

The orderly, symmetrical upper zone of the central panel is composed of tiers of angels, apostles, and saints flanking the centralized images of God the Father, Christ, and the dove of the Holy Ghost. Despite the brilliant golden light above the head of Christ and the unusually dark coloring of the apostles' dress, this upper area remains subordinate because of its placement back from the picture plane. Contrary to tradition, Lucas also downplayed the views of Heaven and Hell on the wings. Nothing competes with the representation of the resurrected nudes ranging across the foreground of all three panels. The prominent void in the center of the composition provides access to the stark, sweeping landscape in the distance, also dotted with nudes.

The fluid application of thin layers of paint on the interior barely conceals the underdrawing in brush, wash, and chalk, but the paint technique and underdrawing of the exterior are less careful and detailed: the black chalk underdrawing of Peter and Paul is sketchy, and the paint layers, except on their costumes, are simpler and more hastily applied (Fig. 23). The rich, saturated tones in the foreground of the exterior panels also contrast sharply with the pastel and golden hues of the interior. As in the Munich diptych (Figs. 12–13), this distinction in technique was probably intended to emphasize the difference between the open and closed states of the triptych.[35]

On the exterior, Peter and Paul, heralds of the Last Coming as well as patron saints of St. Peter's in Leiden, are posed in the foreground of a landscape that reflects the influence of Joachim Patinir, whose work Lucas would surely have seen in Antwerp. The relatively high horizon, the tonal gradations from brown and green to blue, and the craggy mountains and wide expanse of water have much in common with paintings by Patinir such as the *Baptism of Christ* in Vienna and *St. Christopher* in the Escorial. The loose brushstrokes and blurred contours in the background of the triptych bear little resemblance, however, to Patinir's more linear, detailed landscapes. The great sea unites the two panels and provides the locus for scenes from the lives of the two saints.

The nudes in the *Last Judgment* (Figs. 17–19, 21) rely on a number of figural models, predominantly Italian, although in the late nineteenth and early twentieth centuries a series of writers specifically mentioned the lack of Italian influence on this triptych. They often added that many of the forms were inspired by Dürer, and some later scholars pointed out the influence of Gossaert, although his style is in fact much less conspicuous here than in several later prints and paintings. Prior to the 1978 exhibitions in Leiden and Amsterdam, Marcantonio was rarely mentioned as a source for the figures of the *Last Judgment,* and even now the extent of his influence on these nudes has not been fully elaborated.[36] The man fleeing from a devil at the far right of the central panel (see Fig. 17), for example, can be compared to several figures in Marcantonio's *Massacre of the Innocents* of 1512–1513 (B.18, Fig. 74)—most closely to the woman to the left of center, particularly in her rounded shoulder, head turned in profile, and exposed lower body. Lucas was apparently impressed by the pose of a figure fleeing in terror, associating it with the theme of the *Last Judgment.* When he was struck by a particular pose or group of poses he often continued to experiment with them in later works. The figure of the man just mentioned, for instance, together with the woman at his right whose upper body is obscured by the frame, are quite similar to Adam and Eve in his engraving of the *Expulsion* (B.4), dated 1529.

The upper body of the prominently featured woman in the Hell wing of the *Last Judgment* is comparable in pose to that of the man discussed above, although her head is less fully turned over her shoulder (Fig. 19). This parallel is not as close in the underdrawing, where the woman's head was originally looking forward (Fig. 20). Its position was altered at the earliest stage of painting, apparently to reinforce the link between the separate panels of the triptych. The interruption posed by the frame is ameliorated by the woman's glance toward the center and by the duplication of images, echoed in the figures further in the background. Other figures scattered throughout the *Last Judgment* also seem to have been drawn, with varying degrees of exactitude, from the *Massacre.*

Several times in this triptych Lucas used a variation on the pose of the seated man looking out at the spectator in Marcantonio's *Judgment of Paris* of circa 1517 (B.245, Fig. 75), for example in the man seated in the center foreground. The curve of his back and the placement of his elbow on his knee, with his head supported on one hand, are clearly derived from the figure in the *Judgment of Paris.* As noted by several scholars, the ultimate source for Marcantonio's pose must have been the *Belvedere Torso,* now in the Vatican.[37] Lucas never went to Italy, and was probably unaware of this Roman marble unearthed in the fifteenth century, but with Marcantonio as intermediary and with his own keen observation of nature he was able to capture the spirit of the ancient sculpture. The curved back reappears in a man at the left of the central panel, who except for his glance toward the viewer seems unconnected with Marcantonio's figure. Inspired by Italian forms, Lucas revealed his creative powers by avoiding unimaginative, line-for-line duplication.

In the background of the *Last Judgment* is a group composed of three standing figures and several kneeling and seated ones. The careful balance and symmetry of the group are striking, most obviously in the rather artificial doubling of poses of the two standing figures at the left. The woman clearly derives from Marcantonio's *Orpheus and Eurydice* of circa 1509 (B.295, Fig. 76): Eurydice's arms, legs, and head are remarkably similar to those of Lucas's figure, and the enveloping hair of the woman in the *Last Judgment* echoes the curve of the drapery around Marcantonio's nude. The pose can be traced back to its ultimate source in the Greek *Venus pudica* sculptures. Examples include the *Capitoline Aphrodite* and the *Venus de Medici,* both known only in Roman copies. Thus Lucas was once more, if perhaps unwittingly, borrowing from the antique as seen through the eyes of Raphael and his engraver Marcantonio. The man in the middle of this trio was originally drawn with his head upturned and both hands raised to his chest (Fig. 22). As originally planned, he would have been a simple copy of the woman at the right, but Lucas changed the position of the head and arms by roughly sketching in chalk over the original brush contours. By doing so he created an almost perfect mirror image of the woman based on Marcantonio's Eurydice. A pose of modesty, like this one, was not unusual in fifteenth- and early sixteenth-century northern representations of the *Last Judgment,* serving, perhaps, as a reminder of man's fallen state.[38] Although the details mentioned above point to Marcantonio rather than any particular northern work as the primary source for this figure, Lucas was surely aware of the symbolic appropriateness of the pose and its recurrence in traditional Netherlandish representations of the Judgment. He must, then, have been attracted as much by Eurydice's apposite modesty as by her graceful stance.

Lucas's ability to produce distinctive variations on a prototype is characteristic of his late style, often making it difficult to determine a specific model for any given "Italianate" figure. Even the poses borrowed fairly clearly from Marcantonio sometimes appear in more than one print by the Italian, so that Lucas's free transposition of what could be considered stock poses in Marcantonio's engravings significantly increases the number of possible sources for any given figure. The pose of the woman in hell (Fig. 19), for example, is a subtle variation on the figure in the foreground of the *Massacre* (Fig. 74), augmented slightly with figures from other prints by Marcantonio. Most notably, the head of the damned woman in the *Last Judgment* is turned in three-quarter rather than profile view and in this way is similar to Lucas's *Lucretia* (B.134,

Fig. 72), discussed in relation to Marcantonio's *Venus* (B.311, Fig. 73), or to his earlier *Venus* engraved circa 1505 (B.312). Wurfbain has suggested Raphael's *Galatea,* engraved circa 1513–1517 by Marcantonio or his school, as a possible source for this same figure.[39] Lucas could have had such nudes in mind as he adjusted the tilt of the head and the torsion of the upper body, although the graceful, easy movements of Venus or Galatea have here been given another meaning. If Lucas used his Italian sources so freely, with so many variations, why should we even attempt to identify them? Primarily because they underscore Lucas's increasing interest in Italian art, both as a painter and as a printmaker, and reveal the importance of Raphael in the development of his late style—whether Raphael's figure types as filtered through Marcantonio, evident most clearly in Lucas's *Last Judgment,* or Raphael's compositions as transmitted in the Vatican cartoons, evident in several of Lucas's later paintings.[40]

Certain figures in the *Last Judgment* also seem related to works by Michelangelo for which no engravings are known. A close look at the seated man just to the right of the three standing figures discussed above (see Fig. 17) reveals a remarkable resemblance to several of Michelangelo's *Ignudi* on the ceiling of the Sistine Chapel. The nudes above the Cumaean and Libyan Sibyls are in comparably contorted poses, with their heads turned sharply toward the near shoulder. It is possible, of course, that Lucas arrived at this figure by adapting for a seated position the male at the far right of his panel, taken from Marcantonio's *Massacre* (Fig. 74). On the exterior of the triptych (Fig. 23), the apostles Peter and Paul exhibit a powerful and highly concentrated energy of expression. This energy, combined with their unusual monumentality of form, immediately suggests a link with developments in early sixteenth-century Italian painting. Perhaps the most striking comparison is with Michelangelo's *Prophets* on the Sistine ceiling. The similarity between the massive forms and *contrapposto* poses of Lucas's Peter and Michelangelo's Isaiah is clear, although not suggestive of a direct copy. Only tentative parallels can be drawn, but consideration of such possibilities helps reveal the undercurrent of Italianism evident in many of Lucas's figures.

By the late 1520s Lucas turned more frequently for inspiration to Italian prints than to Dürer—for poses and larger compositional motifs as well as for the development of his burin technique. Nonetheless, figures reminiscent of Dürer continued to appear in the later works. The woman in the left foreground of the central panel of the *Last Judgment* (Fig. 21), for example, echoes the profile of Dürer's *Nemesis* of 1502 (B.77), although her head and orientation to the left more closely match his woodcut of the *Fall of Man* from 1511 (B.17).

The group at the left foreground of the central panel, composed of an angel leading several of the blessed to heaven, derives from traditional northern fifteenth- and early sixteenth-century sources. Perhaps the closest parallels can be drawn between the angel with the nude female in profile and similar figures in a *Last Judgment* originally painted on the vault of the choir of St. Laurens, Alkmaar.[41] The man in the pinwheel pose in Lucas's painting seems to be a composite of several figures in the earlier *Last Judgment*. His striding legs appear in some of the nudes clustered around the angel in Alkmaar, and the twist of his torso and head is found in another of the figures. Certain minor elements of the Heaven and Hell panels of these two works are also comparable, but most striking is the woman stretched full length in the foreground of the central panel. Although the poses vary, the prominent positions of both figures and the similar way in which the demons pull them to Hell suggest that Lucas had studied this *Last Judgment*.

Throughout the triptych Lucas experimented with the doubling of images, either individual figures or whole groups, as with the man and woman fleeing from demons at the right and the mirrored figures in the middle distance. Also noteworthy is the succession of seated figures in the central panel that leads the eye back into depth (see Fig. 17). From the man at the far left who looks out at the viewer, our gaze follows the direction of his pointing finger to a figure with a similar curved back in the center of the composition. The more frontal torso and profile head of the man to his right are echoed slightly further back in the figure gesturing toward heaven. Finally, the woman seated beside the gesturing figure is paralleled by a man directly above her in the background. To unify the composition by means of repeated poses, Lucas designed the group in the left panel (Fig. 18) as a variant of the three standing figures at the left of the central panel (see Fig. 21). The woman with the profile body has clearly been changed into a man at the left, but their poses and the turn of their heads are roughly similar. Both groups are completed by additional figures, a member of the opposite sex and an angel guide, whose heads are clustered together and turned back in much the same way. The doubling of images here and on the right side of the triptych helps to unite the three panels, minimizing the disruption of the frame.

Following the completion of the *Last Judgment*, Lucas painted a series of smaller panels devoted to images of the Virgin and Child and to allegorical genre scenes. Most of these seem to have been made after his second trip to the southern Netherlands, which according to Van Mander took place when Lucas was thirty-three years old. He met Gossaert in Middelburg, and they then traveled together through Zeeland, Flanders, and Brabant. As noted earlier, scholars have attempted to conflate this trip with Lucas's journey to Antwerp in 1521 by pushing his birth date back to 1488-1489, but the obvious influence of Gossaert's style on several late paintings by Lucas argues against this. If Lucas was born in May or June 1494, then the trip with Gossaert would have taken place in 1527-1528, and in fact Lucas's *Virgin and Child* paintings from around 1528 are closely related to paintings of the same subject by Gossaert.

The most noteworthy of these paintings is Lucas's *Virgin and Child* in Oslo (Cat. 23, Fig. 29). Although he could have seen similar works by Dirk Bouts and Joos van Cleve in 1521, it was probably through the agency of Gossaert that Lucas absorbed the early Netherlandish compositional tradition. The half-length format in which large, bulky figures are closely confined by an architectural background and foreground balustrade or table was frequently employed by Gossaert in the 1520s and copied by his followers. The bare breast and use of symbolic fruit are also common in Gossaert's representations of the Madonna, the closest parallel to the Oslo panel being Gossaert's *Virgin and Child* in the Prado.[42] The facial type of Gossaert's Virgin is strikingly similar to the one in Lucas's painting, as is her partially exposed pyramidal body, which acts as a foil for the vertical pose of Christ. In both paintings the standing Christ Child looks up at his mother, reaching out to her with his left hand and holding a large apple in his right. Although the spatial relationship between the two figures has changed, along with a number of subsidiary details, the similarities make it likely that Lucas either saw the Prado painting in Gossaert's workshop or saw drawings after it or a similar composition.

Gossaert's influence is also readily apparent in another composition of the *Virgin and Child* from around 1528 (Cat. C22), now known from copies in Norfolk (Fig. 58) and Amsterdam. The reclining Christ Child and cradling arm of the Virgin are found in a number of Gossaert's paintings from the 1520s, most notably a probable shop work in the Metropolitan Museum.[43] The copies after Lucas's *Rest on the Flight into Egypt* from 1527 (Cat. C21, Fig. 57) show the impact of Gossaert's style in the *contrapposto* pose of the curly haired Jesus and the increased plasticity of the forms.

Lucas's massive, fleshy figures from this period, with their rounded faces and wide, dimpled hands, inhabit a realm of greater spaciousness than is found in most of Gossaert's paintings. This feeling of space is achieved less by the actual setting of the scene than by the quiet, restrained poses. In Gossaert's Virgin and Child representations the figures erupt from their frames, and the panels seem unable to contain them. The energetic embrace of the mother, the playful wriggling of the Child, and the animated folds of the drapery are markedly different from the rather stolid figures in Lucas's late devotional paintings. The pyramidal solidity of Lucas's Virgin in the Oslo panel is relieved only by the slight tilt of her head and the detailing of her costume, but the swirling drapery is still very mild in comparison to the exuberant clothing favored by Gossaert. Unlike the cheek-to-cheek poses in many of Gossaert's compositions, a certain formality and coolness are achieved by Lucas's separation of the two figures. Although Lucas's Virgin and Child scenes are in many ways dependent on Gossaert's mannered, energetic paintings, he has given them a classical stability more reminiscent of Dürer.[44]

The increasing monumentality of form at this time reveals a gradual development in Lucas's style, beginning with the Munich diptych of 1522. The paintings of Gossaert, as well as the prints of Dürer and especially of Marcantonio, influenced his style in the direction of a greater corporeality of the individual figures. Several allegorical genre scenes from Lucas's late period also reveal this emphatic three-dimensionality. The broad shoulders, rounded face, and fleshy jawline of the woman in the Strasbourg *Betrothal* (Cat. 44, Fig. 26) are reinforced by the heavy folds of her drapery. Lucas's fascination with monumental form continued in the larger, more complex composition of the *Card Players* (Cat. C43), known from a sixteenth-century copy in Washington (Fig. 54). During this decade his portrayal of three-dimensional form was matched by his increasing facility at arranging these figures in a more spacious setting, culminating in the triptychs of *Dance around the Golden Calf* (Cat. 11, Figs. 32–34) and *Christ Healing the Blind Man* (Cat. 25, Figs. 35, 37–39). The composition of the *Card Players* in Washington is similar in a number of respects to that of the *Card Players* in Wilton House (Fig. 9), particularly in the gathering of figures around a circular table and in their gestures, but in the later copy the composition is less tightly framed at top and bottom. The figures are depicted in three-quarter rather than half length, with more room to move, and the apparent depth of the room has also been augmented by the representation of a table in the left background and by a curtain at the right that helps to divide the interior. The still-life objects in the background make the setting more natural and the space more comprehensible, an improvement on the neutral wall that confuses the sense of depth in the Wilton House panel. The figures in Washington have increased in bulk and weight, and even the costumes seem more substantial compared to the relatively thin cloth in the earlier panel. The subtle asymmetry of the first composition is repeated: the table in the Washington copy has been pushed off-center to allow more room for the heroically proportioned woman at the left, who acts as a visual balance for the weight of the furniture. Similarly, the spectator in the left background is offset by a darkened alcove in the wall to the right. As in the earlier *Card Players* at Wilton House, the complexity of the composition is effectively unified and concentrated by the gesturing figures who point inward to the bets on the table.

The framing figures, who add weight and stability to the foreground corners, are repeated in the monumental biblical paintings of the late period. An additional function of these figures is to direct our attention to the thematic and compositional heart of the scene, as do the woman looking directly out at the spectator while pointing toward the center of the *Card Players* in Washington and the similarly located man in the *Last Judgment*. The L-shaped pose of the woman in the left foreground of *Moses after Striking the Rock* in Boston (Cat. 7, Fig. 24) reinforces one corner of the composition, as does the group of figures at the lower right. The limits of the Boston scene are set by this arrangement in the foreground and by the outcropping of rock in the background that follows the contours of the figural groups. The scope is enlarged by the view into depth at the left and, less conspicuously, by the figures in the middle ground who walk out of the composition. This method of dissolving boundaries was used by Lucas as early as 1510 in his engraving of the *Milkmaid* (B.158), where a half-seen cow serves the same function.

The Israelites in *Moses after Striking the Rock* (Figs. 24–25) are carefully grouped in asymmetrical patterns, but the center of the composition, as in the *Last Judgment*, is empty. The poses of the protagonists are marked by strong, static verticals that stand out against the active lines in the rest of the scene. In addition, several subtle diagonals lead the eye from the lower left to Moses and Aaron at the upper right: the leg of the man seen from the rear in the lower right sets up the diagonal echoed in the heads of the two figures seated at the feet of Aaron and in the casual pose of the man with the jug just to the left of center. These three directional lines are further emphasized by the bright scarlet of the tunics and hats worn by the Israelites. The painting is unfortunately in poor condition because of the fragility of tempera on canvas, and the tonal balance may have been weakened by the fading of some of the colors.

Moses after Striking the Rock must have been painted just before Lucas's travels with Gossaert, whose massive forms are not to be found here. Given the subject matter, it is perhaps not surprising that it has no affinities with the style of Marcantonio. Several scholars have noted Dürer's influence, citing the costumes in his engraving of the *Large Cannon* (B.99, 1518) and the landscape and figural grouping in his painting of the *Martyrdom of the Ten Thousand* (1508) in Vienna. There is a remarkable resemblance between Lucas's Moses and the figure of Nicodemus at the far right of Dürer's *Lamentation* (circa 1500) in Munich. The positions of the head, torso, and arms are similar, as are the knee-length costumes and curving folds of the drapery held in one hand. Dürer might have brought with him to the Netherlands a portfolio of drawings with sketches of his important paintings, in order to give Charles V, whom he intended to petition for an extension of his pension, an idea of his work to date. It is known that he carried a great deal of art with him, including many of his own prints, works by other Germans, and even some small paintings.[45]

Unlike *Moses,* Lucas's *Dance around the Golden Calf* in Amsterdam (Cat. 11, Figs. 32–34), circa 1529–1530, clearly reflects Gossaert's stylistic influence. The women, in particular, have much in common with paintings by Gossaert such as the *Vanitas* in Rovigo and the *Virgin and Child* in Madrid, both dating from the 1520s.[46] Lucas's small triptych of the *Dance* is filled with heavy, rounded forms, striking in their powerful plasticity but still skillfully subordinated to the overall design.

The composition is united by a series of interlocking, undulating lines and by the repetition of dominant shades of red throughout the foreground. Numerous subsidiary details, including the poses and gestures of some figures, were used to underscore the principal curves. In the right wing, for example, two women seen from the rear form a *U* that leads the eye up to the elegantly dressed man in the cape and plumed hat who points across the central panel. Several other figures in the right half of the triptych gesture inward, emphasizing the directional flow toward the center. At the left another man in a plumed cap echoes the pose of the gentleman in the red cape. These mirror-image figures at the extreme left and right of the central panel serve to frame the main scene and link it with the wings. At the core of the composition, in the center foreground, is a circle of men and women drinking and exchanging fruit.

Despite the essential differences between these multifigured paintings and the late engravings with their more limited format, the broad compositional rhythms of the *Dance* triptych are quite close to the long, undulating lines in the prints from 1529–1530 (for example, B.1, 16). The relatively tight figure groupings and the compact, angular design of Lucas's engravings from the early 1520s developed into a more spacious extension of forms. The cramped, reclining postures of *St. Jerome* (B.114, 1521) and the woman in the foreground of *Virgil Suspended in a Basket* (B.136, 1525) differ dramatically from the lazy, sinuous curve of Adam's body in the *Creation of Eve* (B.1, 1529) and of the female in the extreme right foreground of *Dance around the Golden Calf.* The amplitude of form in this late painting is complemented by a more spacious atmosphere in which the individual figures move easily and without constriction. A similar stylistic change is readily apparent in the 1524 and 1529 engravings of the *Murder of Abel* (B.13 and 5). The figures in the earlier print are closely confined by the frame, and their bodies move in angular opposition to each other. The 1529 interpretation of the theme is closer to the *Dance,* both in its spacious setting and in the circular lines of the bodies echoed by the drapery and the background smoke. The use of background accessories or landscape elements as a foil for the grouping of the figures is typical of several engravings from 1529–1530 (see B.3, 5, 16) and also can be seen in the intricate composition of the *Dance*. The central axis of the right wing, formed by the woman standing in the middle ground, has a counterpart in the tree trunk supporting the tent in the left panel, and the mountainous landscape of the two wings conforms to the shape of the frame as it leads the eye to the central panel.

The dance of the Israelites around the golden idol is represented in the far distance, and it serves only as a framework for the moralizing message of that circular cluster of figures in the center. The foreground figures in general are carefully painted, with great attention to detail and a lively variety of colors, while the distant figures are broadly and hastily depicted with a severely restricted tonal range.[47] The calf itself is pushed to the left of center in the background, and the tall pedestal on which it is placed does little to highlight it. The foreground scene, spread across all three panels, represents the merrymaking of the Israelites. Although this episode was an important feature of the account in Exodus, it was usually subordinated in artistic representations to the idolatrous dance around the golden calf. This relegation of the principal narrative to the background was not unusual in Lucas's art, however; it can be seen as early as his engravings of *Ecce Homo* (B.71) and the *Baptism of Christ* (B.40), both from 1510.

The emphasis on genre details of eating, drinking, and lovemaking is more generally associated with scenes of the *Feeding of the Five Thousand*. Three works on this theme have been compared to Lucas's triptych. One, formerly in Berlin and lost during World War II, is now attributed to Cornelis Engebrechtsz. and an assistant (Fig. 68). The others—one in Koblenz and the other formerly in the Collection Bührle, Zurich (Fig. 69)—are also associated with the early Leiden school.[48] As in Lucas's *Dance*, the biblical protagonists in these three panels are relegated to the background, and the foreground is filled with figures in contemporary sixteenth-century dress. Groups of women and children are prominent in all these works. The woman seen from the rear in the right foreground of the Zurich panel is similar to the women in the right wing of Lucas's triptych (compare Figs. 34 and 69), although somewhat less gracefully posed. Connections can also be drawn between Lucas's painting and the work in Koblenz. The scene stretches across all three panels of both triptychs, and foreground figures seen from the rear bridge the gap between the spectator and the painted representation. In the right wing of the Koblenz triptych, the seated man turning away with his hand to his mouth is similar to

Lucas's elderly man in the left wing. In the central panels of both works there is an exchange of food between a man and woman, and the bowl set in the foreground center of the Koblenz triptych is reminiscent of the barrel in Lucas's work (although Lucas was much more adept at integrating the object into the surrounding scene). The dating of these panels is uncertain, but in any case the complex, well-knit composition of Lucas's *Dance* should probably be seen as the original on which the Koblenz and Zurich paintings depend. Cornelis Engebrechtsz.'s *Feeding of the Five Thousand* must have been painted before Lucas's work, of course, given Cornelis's death in 1527. Its emphatic diagonal thrust into depth was transformed by Lucas into a composition based on figural zones set parallel to the picture plane. The frieze of figures in the foreground of the *Dance* is essentially self-sufficient and seems to preclude penetration into the distance by virtue of its broad, horizontal layout. The fact that the primary biblical event is set in the background provides an extra dimension, however, iconographically as well as spatially. This compositional format was used occasionally by earlier artists, although Lucas's repeated use of it was unprecedented in the north. Israhel van Meckenem's *Dance of Salome* (B.9) and Dürer's drawing of *Calvary* in the Uffizi are unusual instances of this mode of representation. Jacopo Bellini, whose sketchbooks include many drawings in which the religious theme is relegated to the background, seemed more interested in the perspectival challenges of leading the eye back to the main event.[49] So Lucas's works form an important early stage in the use of compositional inversion that reached a high point in Netherlandish art by midcentury in the works of Pieter Aertsen.

As in the *Last Judgment*, a number of poses in Lucas's *Dance around the Golden Calf* derive from Italian prototypes. The combination of a body seen from the front with the head in profile was frequently used by Lucas in his late works, including the *Last Judgment* and the engraving of *Pallas Athena* (B.139). It also appears several times in the *Dance*, in the women in the middle of the central panel and the right wing (see Figs. 33–34). This unnatural pose afforded an opportunity to exhibit parts of the body in their purest aspects. This was the case in Dürer's 1504 *Adam and Eve* (B.1), which influenced Lucas's late drawing of the same subject in Hamburg. The woman who stands in the center of the right wing of the *Dance* (Fig. 34) shares some features with Dürer's Eve but is closer to types in Italian prints: a woman and child with downturned profile are found, for example, in Marcantonio's late engravings of *Peace* (B.393) and *God Appearing to Noah* (B.3). The position of the legs derives from Marcantonio's *Lucretia* (Fig. 71), a print from which Lucas had drawn his figure of Eve in the *Lamentation over the Body of Abel*, 1529 (B.6). Once again we see Lucas's interest in extracting and isolating details from Italian prints and then combining them to form new variations on a familiar theme.[50] Although specific parallels can be drawn, these are the exception rather than the rule, and his late paintings can in no way be considered groupings of stock Italianate poses. Even in the *Last Judgment* Lucas's figures remain essentially northern in their physical characteristics, especially apparent in facial structure and features. Lucas's selective appropriation of ideas from the south allowed a more complete assimilation of Italian poses into a northern setting.

The composition of the rather broadly painted *Christ Healing the Blind Man* in Leningrad (Cat. 25, Figs. 35, 37–39) exhibits a classical stability and symmetry that is especially noteworthy when compared to the central void of the *Last Judgment* and *Moses after Striking the Rock* or to the inverted composition of *Dance around the Golden Calf.* Although Christ and the blind man appear slightly behind the foreground plane, they are exactly centralized. The healing is further emphasized by the child in the foreground who points in the direction of the miracle. Such children who introduce the main scene are a common compositional device in Lucas's works. The remaining figures in *Christ Healing the Blind Man* form two balanced groups extending into the area at the sides that once formed the wings. Gibson has explored the possibility of the influence of Raphael's tapestry cartoons for the *Acts of the Apostles,* citing compositional devices in *The Death of Ananias* (which could have been available to Lucas in prints by Agostino Veneziano and Ugo da Carpi).[51]

In the original triptych form of the *Healing of the Blind Man,* as in the *Dance around the Golden Calf,* the continuous narrative and landscape helped to dissolve the barriers of the frame. The inclusion in each wing of a figure who gestures toward the miracle in the center also served to bridge the gap. Even while striving for visual unification of the triptych, Lucas carefully preserved the compositional integrity of each panel. The two wings and the central panel were bracketed by figures in the foreground corners who turned to face each other, thus subtly reaffirming the formal divisions.

In its general mood the exterior of the triptych (Fig. 39) contrasts strikingly with the interior. The classicism of the miracle scene gives way to agitated complexity, and the *Shield-Bearers* can be compared to Cornelis Engebrechtsz.'s mannered painting of *Constantine and Helena* in Munich. The extreme attenuation and elegant swaying forms have been blended by Lucas with an Italianism evident in the increased plasticity of the figures and the severity of the architecture. In its impact the *Shield-Bearers* is similar to Gossaert's *Neptune and Amphitrite* in East Berlin, where the bulky figures are placed in a cramped setting, and also to his *St. John the Baptist* and *St. Peter* in Toledo, Ohio, with an overlay of surface agitation. The monumentality of Lucas's figures is increased, indeed exaggerated, by the strong shadows and by their shallow, restrictive niches, which propel the figures forward, creating an ambiguous space. The result is a tension between figure and setting similar to that in Gossaert's *Portrait of a Man with a Rosary* in London. The appearance of steps or depressions in the foreground corners further disrupts the established, classical mode of spatial representation: a weakness is suggested at precisely the points that should provide the most solid support of the composition. Since Lucas was aware throughout his mature period of the need to augment these outer corners, this playful divergence should be seen as a deliberate rebuttal or revision of the classical norm. It appears again in his late engravings, most clearly in *Fides* (B.127) from the *Virtues*. As in the *Shield-Bearers*, the bulky figure of *Fides* is disconcertingly unstable in pose, and the simple, stone architecture is offset by the unexpected and somewhat unsettling variation in the levels of the floor. Lucas's late works defy categorization, despite a recent attempt to describe the engravings from this period as strictly classicizing in form.[52] Italian figural proportions and poses were certainly important in Lucas's late works, but they were combined with (and transformed by) the dramatic energy of late Gothicism and the manipulations and distortions of the classical ideal found in the northern mannerism of Gossaert.

As in the *Last Judgment, Moses after Striking the Rock,* and *Dance around the Golden Calf,* the broadly brushed landscape in the background of *Christ Healing the Blind Man* is carefully arranged to complement the compositional structure of the foreground. Lucas's landscape settings have certain affinities with those of Jan van Scorel, for example his *Baptism of Christ* in Haarlem dating from 1527–1529.[53] Both artists use dark trees and rocks set against a pale blue-green range of mountains, which, in turn, blends with the color of the sky. Both were also known for their cityscapes and thinly painted *staffage*. The question of a relationship between these artists is a difficult one. There is no recorded meeting between them, although both lived in the northern Netherlands and are known to have traveled in that area. The possibility remains, therefore, that they arrived independently at a similar method of composing and painting landscapes. The settings in Lucas's late paintings can be traced within his own oeuvre to early engravings such as the *Conversion of Paul* (B.107), the *Baptism of Christ* (B.40), the *Return of the Prodigal Son* (B.78), *Calvary* (B.74), and the *Dance of Mary Magdalene* (B.122).

Several copies by Jan de Bisschop after lost paintings from this late period expand our knowledge of Lucas's interest in multifigured biblical scenes. Two of the works are particularly close to *Christ Healing the Blind Man*. As in the Leningrad painting, De Bisschop's drawings after Lucas's *Meeting of David and Abigail* (Cat. C10, Fig. 61) and *Christ Healing the Lepers* (Cat. C24, Fig. 63) show centrally placed protagonists flanked on both sides by relatively tight clusters of spectators. The carefully balanced, roughly symmetrical foreground grouping in all three works is set against a broad landscape peopled with *staffage*. A similar, although much more restricted and narrowly focused format, is used for De Bisschop's copy of the *Procession of the Holy Sacrament* (Cat. C33, Fig. 62). His lost copy of the triptych of *Susanna in Her Bath* (Cat. C9, Fig. 60) was also characterized by this sort of compositional restraint, although here the subject called for fewer figures and a greater intimacy in the setting. In the case of *David and Abigail* and *Susanna in Her Bath,* it is instructive to compare these late compositions, classically balanced and ordered, with engravings of the same subjects made earlier in Lucas's career (B.24 and 33, circa 1507–1508): those engravings lack the clarity and straightforwardness of the later works, and the aggressive asymmetry of the design is controlled by the narrative focal point being pushed off-center and into the distant background. The most rigorously symmetrical of Lucas's late designs is the *Judgment of Solomon* (Cat. C6, Fig. 59), in which the pyramidal structure of Solomon and the two grieving mothers is reinforced by the lines of the architectural interior. The severe regularity of the background architecture in this composition lacks the inherent vitality and irregularity of a landscape or the playful surprises of the setting for the *Shield-Bearers* in Leningrad (Fig. 39). It is relieved only by the curvilinear decoration of the canopied throne and by the strong diagonals repeated in the king's hat and the executioner's sword.

Lucas's maturation as a painter is marked by greater facility and freedom of brushwork, a more subtle tonal range and more complex use of colors, and a decreasing reliance on underdrawing as a preliminary stage in the design.[54] He also developed under the influence of Marcantonio and Gossaert the ability to portray powerful three-dimensional forms. His skill in weaving a number of figures into a complex, varied, yet unified whole remains one of his more remarkable achievements. He had experimented much earlier with multifigured narratives in prints such as the *Conversion of Paul* (B.107) and *Ecce Homo* (B.71), but his late paintings are in general more successfully integrated and more compositionally coherent than these rather diffuse early prints. The relatively tight clusters of figures characteristic of Lucas's style throughout his career are more effectively used as building blocks in his late paintings. Although his sense of balance became increasingly refined, his compositions from 1526 to 1531 are never static. The varied poses and gestures, even within the most compact, tightly knit figural units, are much more naturalistic than the stiffer, more awkward movements in his earlier works. Lucas's maturity as a painter is perhaps most evident in his ability to impose order on complexity and to create unity from multiplicity.

CHAPTER 3

Iconographic Concerns

Of the forty to forty-five paintings by Lucas that are known in the original, in later copies, or in descriptions by Carel van Mander, more than half represent biblical subjects, and the largest number of these depict the Virgin and Child. Lucas painted no mythological scenes, and only a few portraits are extant. The remainder of his painted oeuvre can be classified as allegorical genre, and these works consist largely of gaming scenes. In this chapter, the card and chess scenes, as well as the fortune-telling and betrothal paintings, will be discussed in relation to late medieval allegories of love and the popular theme of the Power of Women. The domination of women, specifically by means of seduction, continued as one of Lucas's concerns in certain of his Old Testament paintings. His depiction of gypsy life will be analyzed as a late manifestation of his interest in the human inclination toward intemperance, profligacy, and promiscuity. Finally, his late works will provide a framework for discussing his awareness of the theological debates between orthodox Catholics and the Erasmian, Lutheran, and Sacramentarian reformers.

Chess Players

The theme of prosperous men and women amusing themselves at a table game frequently recurs in Lucas's paintings. Although not appearing in his graphic oeuvre, this subject is found in five paintings, known either in the original or in later copies and ranging in date from around 1508 to 1525

(Figs. 1, 7, 9, 53, 54). Such chess or card games appear at first glance to be simple genre scenes: objective renditions of an early sixteenth-century pastime. This has been the interpretation of many scholars, but several recent studies have shown that Lucas was not entirely free from the late medieval traditions of didactic and moralizing representations of play.[1]

Chess became popular in Europe in the eleventh century and for the next three hundred years was primarily an aristocratic pursuit. During this period it was a favorite amusement of the court, and to a lesser degree of the clergy, despite various legal and religious attempts at prohibition. In 1061 Cardinal Petrus Damiani wrote a letter to Pope Alexander II condemning games such as dice and chess and alluding to his punishment of a Florentine bishop who spent an evening in a public inn playing "the vain game of chess." In the twelfth century, Alexander Neckam devoted a chapter of his *De naturis rerum* to a condemnation of the consuming passion of chess players and the inherent vanity of the game. Chess was condemned by the Council of Paris in 1212 and by royal decree of Louis IX in 1254. Occasionally championed as a game of skill, it was praised in an early German poem as a game in which no money is exchanged and no deceit practiced. While games of chance continued to be banned by municipal ordinance in the fourteenth and fifteenth centuries, chess was sometimes accepted on grounds that it exercised the intellect.[2]

The gradual relaxation of the prohibitions against the game, even among the clergy, probably resulted from its use as a moralizing allegory of the transitory nature of life. The earliest example of such a written morality dates from the thirteenth century. Entitled *Quaedam moralitas de scaccario*, it presents the world as a chessboard, arranged with men of different rank and station. By the end of the game (that is, life) all meet with a common fate. An early sixteenth-century passage from Philipp Melanchthon, in which he imagines God playing chess and cards with real men as his pieces, is similar in intent: the outcome, of course, is that all are thrown into the bag together, including "the Pope with Luther." The most popular of these moralities was a compilation of didactic anecdotes and exempla gathered in the late thirteenth century from various literary sources by the friar Jacobus de Cessolis. As in the works cited above, the chessboard is presented as a mirror of earthly life, with its figures representative of various occupations and social standings. This idea of Death as the ultimate leveler also appears in the *King in Check*, an engraving from the late fifteenth century by the Master BR.[3]

The most widespread use of chess in late medieval art, however, was as an allegory for the game of love. In the poem *Huon de Bordeaux*, written around 1200, a prince disguised as the servant of a traveling minstrel arrives at court and boasts of his prowess at chess. As a test, the king arranges a game between the young man and his daughter, also an expert. The stakes are high, the life of the hero against the virginity of the princess, plus one hundred marks. During the course of the game, the maiden falls in love with her opponent and, losing her concentration as well as her desire to win, also loses the match. The allegory of *Les Eschez Amoureux,* a poem written in the late fourteenth century, features a more abstract competition, one between reason and sensuality, Pallas and Amor.[4] The central event, which transpires in a dream, involves a game of chess between the poet and a young woman. Descriptions of the paradisiacal garden setting and the chessmen and board of precious materials add to the atmosphere of elegance and refinement appropriate to the aristocratic tastes of the readers. The individual chessmen are representative of human characteristics such as Beauty, Regard, Simplicity, and Youth, and their moves parallel the course of the love developing between the protagonists. Unlike the princess in *Huon de Bordeaux,* here the woman wins the game.

In courtly art of the late Middle Ages—in ivories, tapestries, and other media—chess was frequently used as a metaphor for the maneuvering and eventual capitulation inherent to the pursuit of love. Manuscript illuminations of love poems often include a young, elegantly dressed man and woman playing chess. One of the best-known examples is a miniature from the early fourteenth-century Manesse Manuscript, representing Otto IV of Brandenburg and a maiden seated at the board. Ivory boxes and mirror covers were commonly decorated with scenes of recreation, including hunting and game playing. Chess was a recurrent theme, and the scene usually involved a young man and woman at play beneath a tent in a garden. Such images have often been considered illustrations of *Huon de Bordeaux,* but they are probably simply part of the repertoire of courtly pastimes.[5]

This is also true of chess-playing groups on certain tapestries. An example in Basel dating from 1460–1480 shows five couples in modish dress, enjoying themselves in a Garden of Love. They play chess and cards, gather fruit, kiss, and converse (Fig. 77). Similar representations from the later Middle Ages are found in other media, including stained glass, manuscript illumination, and prints. The amorous, aristocratic players in the fifteenth-century grisaille window of Villefranche-sur-Saone are comparable to those on the ivories and tapestries mentioned above. Couples in the miniature of a chess game in the Willehalm Codex of 1334 and in the engraving of a *Garden of Love* by the Master E. S., circa 1460, are also part of this tradition.[6]

Although the eventual victor in these games is not always clear, the parallels with the game of love are strongly suggested. An engraving by the Master of the Berlin Passion, for example, shows the chess players surrounded by an ornate frame in which the foliate decoration is intertwined with hunters and animals. The course of love, symbolized in the game of chess, is here likened to hunting. With few exceptions, these late medieval chess scenes involve a handsome young man and lovely maiden, elegantly dressed. They are typically shown in a Garden of Love with other conversing, caressing couples, and their gestures also frequently emphasize the amorous overtones of the scene. The glances of the participants, sometimes coy, sometimes more direct, suggest a romantic link, and in at least one case the culmination of the game of love is even more clearly drawn. In *Das Guldin Spil,* a treatise published in Augsburg in 1472 by the Dominican monk Johannes Ingold in which the virtues and vices are compared to various games and recreations, one of the woodcuts shows the conclusion of a chess game. The pieces are scattered at one side of the board, and the man and woman look across at one another and join hands.[7]

The setting of these medieval allegories and moralities associated with the game of chess was usually aristocratic. This courtly, idyllic treatment persisted well into the fifteenth century in ivories and tapestries and even in the more generally accessible medium of engraving. During the course of that century, however, chess left the preserves of the nobility and began to be included among the recreations of the middle class. It seems, though, that these burghers were more attracted to games of chance than to the intellectual challenge of chess, since the game appeared infrequently in art and literature of the later fifteenth and sixteenth centuries.[8]

Panel paintings of the subject were extremely rare in this period, and in fact only one is known to predate Lucas's painting. The *Chess Players* attributed to Francesco di Giorgio, painted sometime after 1485 and now in the Metropolitan Museum, is considered by many scholars to be an illustration of *Huon de Bordeaux.* The young man is winning the game, and even as the heroine's female attendants register their distress at her loss, she rests her hand lightly on his arm as a token of love. It has been suggested that this painting originally formed one side of a *cassone,* or wedding chest.[9] If this is the case, Lucas's *Chess Players* in Berlin, from around 1508 (Cat. 34, Fig. 1), would be the earliest known independent panel painting representing the game of chess.

At first glance Lucas's *Chess Players* reveals few points in common with the late medieval allegories of love already described. The idyllic garden or pavilion setting, the elegant dress, and the frivolous air of amorous intrigue that marked the earlier Gothic scenes are gone. The atmosphere is charged with tension, reinforced by the dark, overcrowded room, the active gestures of the figures, and their serious, spotlit faces. The costumes are those of the Leiden middle class, the fur collars projecting a sense of prosperity.[10] Could this simply be a scene of everyday life, as Friedländer suggested, without any moralizing or didactic overtones? The answer is found in the parallels that exist between this painting and the earlier literary and artistic tradition.

For his opponents Lucas chose a young man and woman, thereby reiterating the allegorical notion of a contest between the sexes. Artists of the medieval chess allegories favored the climactic moment, the culmination of the game, in which one of the players gestures with an upraised hand to indicate surprise, chagrin, or defeat. It is usually the woman who is identified in this way as the loser, symbolizing her capitulation in the game of love. Occasionally, however, the woman triumphs, suggesting that the man has succumbed to her charms or wiles. Such is the case in *Les Eschez Amoureaux* and in the miniature from the Willehalm Codex, in which the man reacts to the move of his opponent with an expressive gesture. The Garden of Love engraving by Master E. S. is more subtle. Here the man smiles in anticipation of victory as he removes a piece from the board, but the woman, far from conceding the game, is ready with a countermove. The owl perched on the fence by her side probably symbolizes the folly of this sport.[11]

In Lucas's painting, the woman has the advantage. Under the guidance of her elderly male adviser, she is in the process of capturing what appears to be an important piece. The game being played is actually not the traditional form of chess, but a variant known as courier. Unfortunately, the difficulty of identifying the specific pieces depicted by Lucas makes it impossible to interpret fully the course of the game. But it is apparent from the man's reaction that he is losing.[12] He half-turns from the board, his eyes uplifted, and his left hand is raised in a variation of the gesture of capitulation so frequent in the medieval allegories. Lucas has transformed the traditional gesture of a raised, open palm into the more subtle and carefully observed movement of the hand scratching the side of the head.

It is clear that the painting represents a contest between the sexes symbolized in the game of chess, and that the woman is the winner. This much at least has its basis in the earlier allegories of love. As noted above, however, the mood of the work is entirely different from the lighthearted, courtly, and rather innocent medieval representations. The moral of the scene seems couched in negative rather than positive terms, and Parshall's suggestion that the painting reflects the current popularity of the Power of Women theme is the most likely interpretation.[13] Various historical, literary, and religious subjects involving the deception or betrayal of a man by a woman were portrayed by graphic artists of this period. The cunning and guile of women, rooted in their sensuality, was emphasized in depictions of Adam and Eve, Samson and Delilah, Jael and Sisera, the Dance of Salome, and the Idolatry of Solomon. These representations were meant to be read as a warning to unwitting men, similar to that implied in this fifteenth- or sixteenth-century Netherlandish proverb: "Since Adam, our first father, / together with David, Samson, Solomon / were deceived by women / then who shall remain undeceived?"[14] By depicting an anonymous young man and woman in contemporary dress, rather than well-known biblical or historical characters, Lucas dramatically contemporized and localized the warning. His interest in the theme is obvious in two later woodcut series of the *Power of Women,* circa 1512 and 1517 (see B.1-2, 5-13, 16), but he could certainly have been aware of such imagery earlier. References in the moralizing literature of the period were frequent, as were representations in the minor and graphic arts. In addition to the standard scenes from the Bible and other early sources, some fifteenth- and sixteenth-century artists drew on the events of everyday life to illustrate the woman's mastery of her mate. Engravings of the *Henpecked Husband* by the Master bg and Israhel van Meckenem show a woman beating a man over the head with her distaff. Representations of the Battle for the Britches were also common, and such works were important, although considerably less subtle, ideological precursors to Lucas's *Chess Players.*[15]

This painting should therefore be read as a competition between the sexes, symbolized by the game of chess. Unlike the medieval allegories of the game of love, however, Lucas's *Chess Players* does not postulate an idyllic, amorous outcome. In these moralities, as well as in many artistic representations, the end result is the same whether the man succumbs to the charms of the woman or the woman surrenders to the man. Borrowing his subject from these courtly chess scenes, Lucas acquired the mood and moral for his painting from the theme of the Power of Women. The painting is far from being a genre study, for its didactic, moralizing message is couched in terms of a warning to mankind against the wiles of women. The chessboard is a mirror of life, as suggested in such works as *Quaedam moralitas de scaccario,* but Lucas has altered the focus of the moral. No longer does the message concern the vanities of life and the inevitability of death; it reveals instead the treacherous temptations that beset men in the contest between the sexes.

Card Players

The majority of Lucas's gaming scenes involve various forms of card playing. Cards allowed for a greater number of participants, from two to four, and a corresponding increase in the crowd of spectators and advisers. Whether Lucas's paintings of card players should be interpreted in the same way as the

Chess Players can only be determined after a survey of the artistic and literary tradition.

Like chess, card playing first became popular in Europe among the aristocracy. There are records from the late fourteenth century of expensive decks of cards, elaborately painted on parchment, purchased by various members of the nobility in northern Europe. The mass production of woodcut decks probably began around the turn of the century, and by the mid-fifteenth century engraved cards were also common. These packs were affordable for the lower classes, and the number of games rapidly increased.[16] It seems that most were games of chance involving gambling, often supplemented by the use of dice, and it was this mercenary aspect of the sport that most concerned civic and religious authorities. Cards were already among the games prohibited in Leiden in 1397, and transgressors were required to pay a fine and absent themselves from the city for two weeks. Frequently, stakes were exorbitantly high, and the reckless betting involved not only large sums of money but also such important items as a knight's armor, a monk's crucifix, and even a man's wife and children. Attempts were made to reduce the stakes; in the 1430s, for example, the Duke of Savoy restricted his subjects to certain games with meat and drink as the prize. The same decree made it illegal to play cards except in the company of women, presumably to inhibit any rough or imprudent behavior, and betting was confined to pins. Municipal ordinances against gambling were widespread in the fifteenth century, but the number of such laws and the frequency with which they were invoked seem to indicate a singular lack of success.[17]

Religious authorities condemned gaming of all types. In the early fifteenth century, St. Bernardino of Siena preached a sermon vilifying cards as an invention of the devil, and in 1452 a sermon by the Franciscan Johannes Capistranus prompted the burning of 3,640 game boards, 40,000 dice, and an even larger number of cards in Nuremberg. A woodcut was made by Hans Leonhard Schäufelein to commemorate the event. Similarly pointed sermons, sometimes accompanied by bonfires as a sign of repentance, took place in various cities in Germany and the Netherlands. One speech condemned the "ruffians and rascals" who play dice and cards when they should be tending their business, and another described gaming as "great nonsense and folly" that destroyed reason and led to shame and disgrace.[18]

A number of manuscript illuminations, tapestries, prints, and even a few large-scale paintings from the fifteenth century attest to the fact that games of cards, like chess, commonly included women. Women were specifically mentioned in a number of municipal ordinances—sometimes given permission to play for small stakes, sometimes prohibited from gambling of any sort. Because of their sex, women gamesters were often doubly condemned or satirized in literature of the fifteenth and sixteenth centuries, and the locus of play in taverns and brothels may have promoted this attitude.[19]

In some artistic representations, the love arising in the midst of gaming is seen as false and foolish, but others give it a more positive, innocent, romantic character. The latter continue the tradition of courtly depictions of the Garden of Love. Several tapestries in Basel, for example, show the card players in a garden with other couples. One from around 1490 shows a young man and woman seated at a table in an elaborate tent. While they play, a servant pours something for them to drink. Banderoles with inscriptions are intertwined in the upper zone, recording the conversation: the young man compliments his opponent for her good play, while she remarks that she has won the game. An engraving by Martin Zasinger, dated 1500, represents a ball given by Duke Albert IV of Bavaria (Fig. 78). A man and woman are seated behind the dancers in a background alcove playing a game. The card that the woman has just presented, a five of hearts, suggests that a game of love is being enacted, and the score chalked on the table indicates that she is winning.[20] The woman also has the upper hand in an engraving from the late fifteenth century by Israhel van Meckenem. She is smiling, while the man is shown with one hand raised in a gesture of shock or defeat. In a mid-fifteenth-century engraving by an anonymous artist from the lower Rhine known as the Master of the Love Gardens, six elegantly dressed couples eat, converse, and play music and cards in what appears to be an idyllic Garden of Love. But the animals in the garden give an added dimension to the scene, apparently symbolizing various characteristics of love: the dog may represent fidelity and the unicorn chastity, while the rabbits, pigs, goat, and ape are all references to lust.[21]

In an engraving by the Master of the Housebook dating from the 1480s an even more satirical view of the game of love is presented (Fig. 79). Although the leisurely dalliance of the participants is emphasized by their elegant dress, the folly of the young woman's game as she sports with three men at once is underscored by the presence of a jester. The amorous overtones are made more explicit by the background couple who ride off into the woods followed by a leaping dog. The game depicted in a woodcut illustration of Meister Ingold's *Das Guldin Spil* conveys a similar meaning. Here the setting is entirely different, a rough interior perhaps indicative of a tavern. The four players are of a lower class than those depicted by the Master of the Housebook. Two men, a youth, and a woman are shown, with piles of money and cards on the table. That the woman is the focus of the moralizing message is apparent not only from the rather sly, sidelong glances of the two men, but also from the condemnation in the text of unchaste women who tempt men to wrongdoing.[22]

An entire chapter of Sebastian Brant's *Das Narrenschiff,* published in Basel in 1494 and printed in the Low Counties in 1500, is devoted to the folly of gambling. The woodcut accompanying the text shows a group of two young women and two men, all wearing foolscaps and playing cards and dice (Fig. 80). A tankard of wine is on the table. The opening lines of the chapter "Von Spielern" read:

> Some foolish idiots I could name,
> They love the cards, the dice, the game,
> Preferring never to exist
> Before from gambling they'd desist,
> And day and night they game and rattle
> With cards and dice, and drink and prattle.

With regard to the inclusion of women, Brant laments:

> And many women are so blind
> That they forget their sex and kind
> And know not that propriety
> Forbids such mixed society.
> They sit together 'mongst the men
> And never feel dishonored when
> They shake the dice and bet and game,
> For all good women great the shame.[23]

Erasmus also admitted game players into his society of fools, describing those who gamble away all their possessions in *The Praise of Folly,* first published in Paris in 1510.[24]

The idea of gaming and gambling as foolish and sinful continued to find expression in artistic representations of the sixteenth century in northern Europe. Bosch included dice and game boards in the *Hell* wing of his *Garden of Earthly Delights,* and Hans Burgkmair's allegory of *Greed* (B.59) represents a corpulent woman holding a goblet in one hand and a deck of cards in the other. The vice of sloth is connected with gaming in several sixteenth-century prints, one example being H. Aldegrever's *Socordia* (Indolence) of 1549. Here the personification holds a game board and a deck of cards. A satirical woodcut by Cornelis Anthonisz. Theunissen, circa 1540, shows a man who has succumbed to a number of vices. The pig-headed figure, dressed in a barrel, holds a tankard and is crowned by a wreath of grape leaves, playing cards, and dice.[25]

The close association among gaming, drinking, and love is apparent in a number of tavern or brothel scenes and representations of the Prodigal Son. One candle-lit *Tavern Scene* attributed to the Brunswick Monogrammist shows five half-length figures grouped around a table playing cards. Tankards of wine are close at hand and the lovemaking has already begun. The view into the bedroom in the background, with a woman in bed and a man drinking, underscores the message. A late fifteenth-century German preparation for confession, the *Spiegel des Sünders* (Mirror of Sinners), asks: "Have you become used to spending your nights in drunkenness, overeating, lovemaking, games, cards, arguing and cursing?" Given the association of these vices, it is not surprising that the theme of the Prodigal Son's reckless life-style before his return home (Luke 15:13) became so popular in the sixteenth century. Konrad Renger's iconographic study emphasizes the didacticism with which these scenes characterize the profligate as a drinker, carouser, and gambler.[26]

This survey of card playing and gambling can be used with advantage in the interpretation of Lucas's paintings. Two original card scenes dating from the 1510s are extant, one in the Collection Thyssen-Bornemisza, Lugano (Cat. 37, Fig. 7), and the other in the collection of the Earl of Pembroke, Wilton House (Cat. 38, Fig. 9). Two other compositions by Lucas, painted in the 1520s and now lost (Cats. C39 and C43), are known through copies in Budapest (Fig. 53) and Washington (Fig. 54). Given the prevailing view of games as allegories of love or illustrations of folly and vice, it is unlikely that these works were intended as pure genre scenes. Like the *Chess Players,* the card scenes fit remarkably well into the allegorizing, moralizing tradition.

Lucas's painting in Lugano (Fig. 7) shows a card game played in an outdoor setting by a young woman and two men, one approximately her age and the other much older. The central placement of the woman immediately suggests that her two comrades are involved in a competition for her favors. In this instance the young man would seem to be ascendant, since his king outranks her jack and the elderly man's eight. The woman's glance at her youthful suitor further indicates the eventual outcome of the game. This painting has much in common with the engraving by the Master of the Housebook, in which a woman dallies at the game of love with several eager young men (Fig. 79).[27] The folly of these two idle, speculative pastimes, game playing and lovemaking, is satirized by the presence of a jester in the engraving.

Lucas's composition may reflect the theme of the Love Triangle, which was a variant of the popular subject of the Ill-Matched Pair. In many of these works the woman allows an elderly man to fondle her breast while she steals money from his purse. At the same time she keeps the interest of a handsome young gentleman by holding his hand. In a woodcut from around 1511–1512, Urs Graf placed his three figures at a table on which we see various games, a deck of cards, fruit, wine, and a lute.[28] Lucas probably intended his work to convey a similar moralizing attitude, although it lacks the memento mori content so clearly expressed in Graf's woodcut inscriptions.

An explicitly satirical commentary on card playing is also provided by the fool who peers from behind a curtain at the young man and woman at play in the Budapest panel (Fig. 53). The youth, closely watched by another man looking over his shoulder, presents an ace of clubs. This may or may not be trumped, depending on the rules of the game, by the ten of clubs that the woman is about to play under her counselor's guidance. As in Zasinger's engraving of the *Ball of Duke Albert IV* (Fig. 78), the suit of hearts in the woman's hand leaves no doubt about her eventual victory in the game of love, if not in the game of cards.[29]

More expanded versions of the same theme are seen in Lucas's paintings in Wilton House and Washington (Figs. 9, 54). In the Wilton House panel two men and two women take part in the game, while others look on or make suggestions. The emphasis is on the complex web of relationships among these figures, and the level of psychological observation is heightened by refinements in tonal and compositional balance. But even in these paintings there seems to be a close tie to obviously moralizing representations of the subject, especially to the warning given to gamblers in Brant's *Das Narrenschiff.* The participation of young women is described and lamented by the German author, as is the kind of betting going on in the Wilton House painting. The elderly man depicted with one hand hidden in his cloak in the right background of this painting provides further commentary on the game. He is emblematic of the vice of sloth, as described in Proverbs 19:24: "A slothful man hideth his hand in his bosom." The practice of showing the lazy or the poor in such a pose was prevalent in northern Europe from the fourteenth century on and is seen, for example, in an engraving of an idle but pretentious peasant with a blank escutcheon by the Master bg.[30] Lucas himself used the gesture in his engraving of *Beggars* (B.143) from circa 1509.

A figure in the same pose appears in the background of the panel in Washington. In the foreground, two men and two women play at a game that has been described as primero, of Spanish origin. Although variants in the rules were common, and depended on the custom in the area, the game shown by Lucas has been identified as one in which the ace of spades is the wild card.[31] This card, which can be assigned any value by the player, is held by the man at the right. He points at his money on the table, apparently in anticipation of victory. His female opponent in the left foreground also points to the coins he has staked, but her meaningful glance at the spectator as she shows her card in the suit of hearts suggests she may be the victor in the game of love.

The well-to-do men and women in these four paintings are all fashionably dressed and at first glance do not appear to be the sort who would gamble away "their wife's clothes," as condemned in Leiden's municipal ordinance of 1528. But the large piles of money on the table in front of each player indicate that they are playing for high stakes. In 1508 gambling of any sort was prohibited within a mile of Leiden, but this seems to have had little real effect on the gaming habits of the populace since "frivolous and lazy fellows," or gamblers, were the subject of another punitive law in 1528. Lucas's paintings would have represented a daring, though apparently fairly widespread, pastime of great local interest. The intended audience for such scenes, suggested by the fashionable dress, was probably the well-to-do middle class of Leiden.[32] The owners of these works would surely have enjoyed the gaming scenes at face value and been titillated by the amorous overtones of the competition between the sexes. They also would not have missed the clear references to the popular theme of the Power of Women, found in at least three of Lucas's card and chess scenes. The warning against the feminine power to beguile and entrap, as well as the beguiling nature of idle, foolish, and wasteful games, would have added spice to an already entertaining subject. Even with Lucas's innovations, especially his perfection of the half-length composition and his acute perception of the nuances of human interaction, his gaming scenes are still within the didactic tradition of late medieval moralizing allegories. Independent of each other, it would seem, Lucas and Quinten Massys were key promoters of this satirical view of venal love and sexual competition that grew out of and soon replaced the earlier courtly allegories of love.

Other Allegorical Genre Scenes

The *Fortuneteller* in the Louvre (Cat. 35, Fig. 2) is a thematic variant of Lucas's paintings of card players. Cards are a central motif in this small panel, but the representation does not involve competition. A young woman is seated at the table in the foreground, looking down at some cards grouped rather haphazardly before her. She has just turned up a four of diamonds, and with the other hand she is either giving a red carnation to or receiving it from the young man beside her. The background is crowded with bystanders, including a fool with his *marotte*. The woman standing at the right holds a shallow bowl of red liquid, presumably wine poured from the tankard on the table. The painting has proved difficult to decipher since it has no known visual precedents, but the consensus among most scholars is that the arrangement of the cards involves some form of fortune-telling.[33]

There are no earlier representations of this method of fortune-telling, and very few references of any sort to it, although palm reading, usually by a gypsy woman, was fairly common. This subject appears as a peripheral detail in several French and Flemish tapestries of the late fifteenth and early sixteenth centuries and in the foreground of Bosch's *Hay Wain* in the Prado, painted in the 1490s. Rolling dice was another popular means of prediction, but the first reference to cards being used for this purpose is found in *Eyn Loszbuch ausz der Karten gemacht* (A Book of Fate Made from Cards), printed in Mainz circa 1505–1510. Unfortunately, neither the suits nor the pattern of laying out cards in the *Loszbuch* corresponds to the scene in Lucas's panel.[34]

Despite the differences, some of these literary and artistic representations of fortune-telling may help us interpret the underlying message of Lucas's painting. In Bosch's triptych the fortune-teller is used as an example of falsehood and avarice. Card games and divination are mentioned together as inventions of the greedy and depraved in *Commentaires urbains,* written by Raffaël Maffi in 1480 and published in Rome in 1506. In a *Losbuch aus der Karten* published in Strasbourg in 1520, cartomancy is described as an idle pastime and readers are warned, "If you believe in this, I say to you that you are hoaxed and also deceived."[35]

Given the prevalent view of divination as an instrument of deceit, combined with the consistent record of Lucas's interest in the Power of Women topos, this painting can be outlined as a warning against the fraudulent predictions of fortune-tellers and more broadly, perhaps, against the unreliability of women in general. The woman at the right holding the cup of wine may exemplify loose living and depravity. The close association among gaming, drinking, and lovemaking was discussed above in relation to Lucas's other card scenes, and early proverbs in many languages also connect wine, women, and gaming (of which fortune-telling might be considered a loose variant): "Würfel, Weiber, Wein," "Femes, dez, et taverne," "Alea, vina, venus."[36] The presence of the jester seems to satirize misplaced belief in the predictions of cartomancers as well as the words of women. With this in mind, one might go a step further and read into this image a caution against marriage. The carnation, or pink, being exchanged between the young man and woman was commonly used as a symbol of betrothal and was found as such in a number of betrothal and marriage portraits. Examples include a miniature from 1481–1482, in which Maximilian of Austria and Mary of Burgundy exchange a ring and carnation, and the *Self-Portrait* of Joos van Cleve in the Thyssen-Bornemisza Collection, where the flower is a reference to his marriage in 1519.[37] The young man in the *Fortuneteller* may be hearing a prediction of his betrothal as he receives the flower and doffs his hat.

Another painting by Lucas, his half-length *Betrothal* in Strasbourg (Cat. 44, Fig. 26), may provide further insight into this view of women as a threat to the "natural" order. A man at the left, seen from the rear in three-quarter view, puts a ring on the left index finger of his betrothed, who in turn rests her other hand on his shoulder. The meaning of the painting seems straightforward, although the composition deviates in certain respects from traditional betrothal and marriage portraits. In the fifteenth and early sixteenth centuries pendant portraits were more common in the north than single-panel representations of a couple, but regardless of the format both figures were almost always shown facing forward.[38] A link between the man and woman was customarily suggested by a very slight inclination of the body or head, and sometimes by the gestures of their hands. Lucas's portrayal of the actual exchange of the ring and of the woman's loving gesture is also unusual.[39] Should this painting be interpreted simply as a compositional variant of the popular betrothal theme, stemming from his lifelong interest in depicting the narrative moment with the greatest dramatic potential, or does he specifically intend a warning about women?

We may find the answer in a second painted version of Lucas's composition, a copy in the collection of M. Q. Morris, London, after a now-lost panel (Cat. C45, Fig. 28). This work is larger than the painting in Strasbourg, with the addition of a fool at the left. From the mouth of his *marotte* curls a long banderole inscribed "Het es haest ghetrowt dat langge rowt" (Who marries in haste must suffer for a long time or, more familiarly, Marry in haste, repent at leisure). Although the fool might have been an insertion of the copyist, it seems more likely that this variation was Lucas's, given his moralizing interests throughout his career and his use of the fool as commentator in various prints. For example, Lucas's early engraving of a *Young Couple Followed by a Fool* (B.147), circa 1508, shows a youth with a torch, traditional symbol of lust, leading a maiden down a dark street. The presence of the jester in this case is surely a warning against yielding to the pleasures of the flesh.[40] In his woodcut *Tavern Scene* (B.20), circa 1517–1519, a jester points to a loving couple in the tavern and invites us, as inscribed in the banderole, to "wait and see how it turns out." And the results of the young man's folly are plainly visible: even as she fondles him, the conniving woman has taken the money from his purse and passed it to two of her accomplices.

In both the Strasbourg and the Morris collection paintings Lucas followed the customary format based on the rules of heraldry in placing the man on the dexter side of the composition, reserved for the husband in his role as master of his wife.[41] He subtly manipulated the mood of the scene, however, by turning the man to face his betrothed. With his back to us and his face seen only in lost profile, he becomes no more than a subsidiary element, dominated by the massive, frontal form of the woman. This compositional subordination, as in many representations of the Fall of Man (including Lucas's woodcuts of circa 1514 and circa 1517 [B.1–2] and his engraving of 1529), becomes even more pointed when supplemented by the fool and his inscription. Lucas's warning against hasty marriage was clearly intended for the man who succumbs without thinking to the seductions of a young woman, only to find his position as master of the household usurped by a domineering wife.

Satirical references to a woman's ability to come out on top, using her cunning and her powers of carnal temptation, are found in various representations of marital discord in the fourteenth through the sixteenth centuries. There was a proliferation of images showing a subversion of the traditional hierarchy, with the male descended from dominance to uxorious subordination by a stereotypically tyrannical wife. Scenes of the Hen-Pecked Husband or the Battle for the Britches can be found as marginalia in fourteenth-century manuscripts, and there are engravings of the subject by Israhel van Meckenem and other fifteenth-century printmakers. In an anonymous engraving printed in Antwerp in the 1550s the conflict between husbands and wives is illustrated by several bickering couples.[42] The woman gets the upper hand in all the vignettes, as the men are shown submitting in various ways to their wives. A banner held by one of the women at the left reads "D'OVERHAND" (The Upper Hand), and one of the verses written on a plaque on the wall states: "Where the woman has the upper hand, and wears the trousers, / There it is that Jan the Man lives according to the dictates of the skirt."

Although no overt reference to this tradition is made in Lucas's painting, the placement of the figures and the fool's warning were probably easily deciphered by his audience. As Erasmus said in his *Praise of Folly*, "What man would be willing to offer his neck to the halter of matrimony if he applied the usual practice of the wise man and first weighed up its disadvantages as a way of life?"[43] Compositional placement was used for a different purpose in Lucas's engraving of *The Musicians,* from 1524 (B.155). There the man is dominant— larger than the woman, placed closer to us, turned more frontally, and with the larger instrument. Van Mander described the print as "a well thought-out and fine representation of an old man and woman, naturalistically tuning their musical instruments to the same pitch; it seems to be taken from the philosopher Plutarch's passage on the laws of marriage, where he writes that in marriage, at home, the man's voice counts for most, just as the thickest strings of the largest instrument often reproduce the loudest tones: for Lucas has the man holding the larger instrument."[44]

A view of marriage more similar to that in the Strasbourg panel is found in another painting of the *Betrothal* in the style of Lucas, perhaps a copy after an early, now-lost original (Cat. C36, Fig. 40). A young man and woman, hands clasped, have apparently just exchanged the betrothal ring or vows, while two elderly men appear as witnesses in the background. A fool in the right foreground admonishes the couple. It is tempting to interpret the placement of the woman's hand, shown uppermost in the clasp, as a reference to her domineering nature, but it may simply have been the best means of prominently displaying her ring.

It may be that the popularity of Lucas's late betrothal composition, now known only in the copy in the Morris collection (Fig. 28), led to the production of the simplified version in Strasbourg (Fig. 26). The man and woman in both are characteristic of the physiognomic types used by Lucas throughout the 1520s and should not be considered portraits of specific people. Although the satirical nature of the version in the Morris collection is clear, the meaning of the Strasbourg painting is less obvious when considered independently. It could well be, as Parshall has suggested, that the Strasbourg *Betrothal* was intended to be an engagement or bridal gift, with the negative view of marriage well submerged.[45] The Strasbourg panel might have served a purpose similar to the painting of the *Young Couple* in Gotha, from the circle of the Housebook Master, circa 1480. The couple in this panel are exchanging a *schnurlin,* or braided tassel, which was sometimes given as an engagement present. Although these protagonists are an idealized pair of lovers, they were personalized by the addition of a coat of arms at the top of the composition. Without the family arms, which were never added in the Strasbourg painting, such a generic couple would of course have been suitable for any purchaser.[46]

The original misogynistic message evident in the Morris Collection composition, although greatly weakened with the omission of the fool and his warning, might still have been apparent to the more discerning viewers through the unusual placement of the figures—a sort of inside joke at the expense of the wife. This is indicated, for example, in a pen drawing by Jan Muller of *A Couple,* dating from around 1620 and now in Constanz.[47] This artist, who also engraved copies after a number of Lucas's prints, was clearly influenced by the earlier composition in posing his two figures. But an important change has been introduced, altering the specific narrative content while retaining the underlying warning against women: while the man offers a ring to the young woman, she surreptitiously reaches for his purse. Muller might well have borrowed this motif from Lucas's woodcut *Tavern Scene* (B.20) or from one of the many late fifteenth- and sixteenth-century representations of Ill-Matched Lovers. Rarely in these is the woman the gullible one (despite one view of the Fall as being due primarily to Eve's credulity). Much more often it is the man, older and flattered by the attentions of his young and beautiful partner, who is shown in the process of being fleeced. Quinten Massys, for example, who was also under the influence of Lucas's *Tavern Scene,* included a fool in his *Ill-Matched Lovers* painting in Washington.[48]

Sometimes after money, sometimes in pursuit of power or sensual gratification, women were commonly portrayed during this period as deceitful connivers in the game of love and as domineering tyrants in the arena of marriage. Whether by stealth or by force, they usually managed to get the upper hand. Lucas's interest in this subject should not necessarily be seen as evidence of a personal dislike for women, of course, but rather as a response to the commercial popularity of the theme. In addition to being highly marketable, the subject provided him with the opportunity to portray interaction between the sexes in a wide variety of dramatic situations—occasionally quite subtle, at other times fairly blatant.

The Power of Women Theme in Several Old Testament Paintings

While the Power of Women topos refers specifically to a rather limited series of biblical, mythological, and historical subjects, we have already seen that Lucas borrowed the idea for a broader range of subjects. Woman's power to manipulate man is the underlying theme of the great majority of his allegorical genre paintings and prints and also appears in some of his religious works. That the woman is always at fault is predicated on Eve's role as temptress in the Fall of Man. She was conceived, according to one early adage, as "an imperfect beast, without faith, without law, without fear, without constancy."[49] Eve was the archetypal woman, and according to many biblical commentators from Tertullian on it was her carnality, so effective a means of temptation, that was the primary inheritance of later women. Woman's sensuality was set in opposition to man's rationality, resulting in an overturning of the "natural" sexual order first established by God in prelapsarian Eden (at least according to the more influential account of the Creation in Genesis 2). References to the seductive power of a woman's body abound in the art and literature of the late fifteenth and sixteenth centuries, most obviously in the Power of Women series that warn males against those dangerous attractions. As mentioned earlier, Lucas produced in the 1510s two woodcut series devoted to this theme, each beginning with the Fall of Man.

In keeping with his continuing preoccupation with love in its various manifestations, it should not be surprising that the subject most frequently represented by Lucas was the Fall of Adam and Eve. There are nine versions dating from around 1506 to 1530: five engravings (B.3, 7–10); two woodcuts (B.1, 2); a drawing in Hamburg; and a lost work, probably a painting, known only through a drawing by Jan de Bisschop (Cat. C5, Fig. 44). In most of these Lucas highlighted the role of Eve as temptress by putting her in a physically dominant position, with Adam below her, or half-hidden behind the tree, or contorted in contrast with her more forthright pose. In the drawing by De Bisschop, Eve sits on Adam's lap with her legs crossed (a common sign of sexual proclivity) and actively guides his hand holding the apple.[50] As in several of Lucas's representations of the Fall, her gesture parallels the movement of the serpent. This equation of Eve with the arch-tempter recurs, for example, in the engravings of 1519, 1529, and circa 1530 (B.8–10) and is an especially important indicator of her sin in the 1529 version, a print in which her role as protagonist is otherwise downplayed. These images reflect the standard patristic interpretation of the events in Genesis: Eve, having succumbed to the lure of the serpent and become thoroughly imbued with the spirit of evil, seduced Adam away from God's will. In Augustine's words, "Then began the flesh to lust against the Spirit, in which strife we are born, deriving from the first transgression a seed of death, and bearing in our members, and in our vitiated nature, the contest or even victory of the flesh." Lucas's representation of the Fall of Man in both of his woodcut series about the Power of Women was highly unusual, although Eve's temptation of Adam was a standard element in the literary treatment of this theme. In his letter *To Nepotian on the Duties of the Clergy,* for example, St. Jerome warned: "You cannot be a man more saintly than David, or more wise than Solomon. Remember always that a woman drove the tiller of Paradise from the garden that had been given him." A similar passage occurs in Dirc Potter's *Der Minnen Loep,* an early fifteenth-century didactic poem composed of historical and literary tales of love. In the section on "foolish love" Potter asks all "good men" to consider "how David and Solomon were deceived, / Samson, Lot, and also Adam, / Who all succumbed to women."[51]

Lucas's earliest extant religious painting, dating between the *Chess Players* in Berlin and the *Card Players* in Lugano, also reflects his early interest in the conflict between the sexes. *Potiphar's Wife Accusing Joseph,* painted around 1510–1511 and now in Rotterdam (Cat. 1, Fig. 4), has as its subject a woman who, like Eve, has long been an emblem of temptation. In Meister Ingold's *Das Guldin Spil* of 1472, Potiphar's wife appeared as an example of promiscuity, and Brant used her as a paradigm of the wicked woman in *Das Narrenschiff.*[52]

Lucas's unusual representation depicts the moment when Potiphar's wife, using Joseph's cloak as evidence, falsely accuses him of rape. It was much more common for painters to show the unsuccessful seduction, with Joseph fleeing from the woman. Popular for its titillating illustration of virtue preserved, this episode was included by Lucas in a series of five engravings of the *History of Joseph,* made a year or two later (see B.20). Lucas's portrayal in the panel of the accusation rather than the seduction was probably due in large part to its greater potential for the exploration of psychological interrelationships. The emphasis here is on Potiphar's reaction to the news of his trusted servant's supposed betrayal, as opposed to the physical action so central to the bedroom scene. In addition, the woman's cold-blooded revenge, resulting in Joseph's imprisonment, is a revelation of her calculating as well as her lustful nature.

The architectural reliefs in the background of *Potiphar's Wife* show allegorical counterparts to the biblical story. The panel behind Potiphar's wife represents Eve, the archetypal seductress.[53] Just to the right of her, at the top of the composition, a nude woman is balanced on a globe. This figure shares characteristics of both Venus and Fortune: the globe, a common attribute of the personification of Fortune, is a reminder of the vicissitudes of fate but can also allude to Venus's power over men's actions and to the inherent instability in her domain, as in Lucas's late engraving of *Mars, Venus, and Cupid* from 1530 (B.137).[54] Further reference to the world of love is found in the third relief, where the nude putto, though wingless, is probably meant to represent Cupid. The emphasis of the painting is therefore on the manipulation of men, both Joseph and Potiphar in this case, by the guiles of a woman's sensual nature. Potiphar's wife is represented as a true daughter of the first temptress, Eve, with her actions under the aegis of a fickle goddess, whether it be Venus or Fortune or some combination of the two.

It is significant that Lucas's next known painting, dating one or two years after *Potiphar's Wife,* depicts the Old Testament story of *Susanna before the Judge* (Cat. 3, Fig. 6). Both works center on the false accusation of a virtuous young person. The presentation of woman as corrupt and treacherous, typified in *Potiphar's Wife* and also found to a certain degree in some of Lucas's gaming and betrothal scenes, is balanced here by his tribute to the purity and innocence of Susanna. She was an exemplar of chastity throughout the Middle Ages, appearing as "a fair and good example," for instance, in a collection of models of virtue written in 1371 by the Chevalier de la Tour Landry for his daughters. In fact, the name *Susanna* means "lily" in Hebrew, a further reason for her use as a symbol of purity. She was lauded as a good wife in Dirc Potter's *Der Minnen Loep* and was recognized for her unusual moral strength in resisting the snares of passion.[55]

In this pair of thematically and compositionally similar Old Testament paintings, Lucas depicted the denouement rather than the more frequently represented episode of the narrative. As Parshall and Gibson have shown, this choice of the moment before or after the climactic moment is also characteristic of Lucas's dramatic sense in his prints, for example his early *Susanna and the Elders* (B.33).[56] These two panels present a warning to both men and women against the enticements and deceptions of the opposite sex. Lucas's early fascination with the conflict between the sexes was certainly influenced by the general popularity of the theme in the early sixteenth century, but his continuing interest in the pitfalls of sexual relations may also have been based on personal experience. His only child, an illegitimate daughter, was the product of an extramarital affair probably conducted sometime in the early 1510s. Nothing more is known about this episode, however, and there is little reason for speculating further about its possible impact on his thematic concerns.

Also indirectly related to the Power of Women topos is Lucas's late triptych in Amsterdam, the *Dance around the Golden Calf* (Cat. 11, Figs. 32–34). The actual idolatrous dance has been relegated to the background, while even further in the distance Moses and his assistant Joshua descend with the tablets of law. The foreground in all three panels has been filled with Israelites who "sat down to eat and drink and then gave themselves up to revelry" (Exod. 32:6; compare 1 Cor. 10:7). Aaron was talked into his sinful construction of the golden calf by "the people," with no attempt in this case to assign guilt more specifically, but there are other episodes in the Old Testament in which women are cited as the primary temptresses; for instance, the story of the Moabite women, used as an example of promiscuity in Meister Ingold's *Das Guldin Spil,* relates how the Israelites were turned against their religion by "intercourse with Moabite women, who invited them to the sacrifices offered to their gods" (Num. 25:1–3).[57] Throughout the Old Testament the sensual nature of woman is seen as an obstacle to man's faith in God, from the story of Adam's disobedience to the account of Solomon's worship of pagan cults. Lucas provided a similar explanation for the *Dance around the Golden Calf,* as explicitly stated in the embracing couple prominently placed in the foreground of the right wing (Fig. 34).

The theme of a dance also supports an exploration of the vices of concupiscence and *luxuria.* Dancing was connected with drunkenness and sexual depravity by the Church Fathers and was still viewed as morally reprehensible in the fifteenth and sixteenth centuries. Brant judged that "dance and sin are one in kind," and Agrippa and Calvin also condemned dancing, while Luther warned only against excessive or immoderate behavior. A number of writers brought up biblical examples of the sinful effects of dancing, including, of course, the Israelites' dance at the base of Mount Sinai, although in one French dance manual of 1588 the reader is reminded that Moses was disturbed not by the dance itself but by the fact that it took place around an idol.[58] Lucas had earlier linked dancing with sinful worldliness in his engraving of *The Dance of the Magdalene,* from 1519 (B.22). There, too, the religious narrative is obscured by a panoramic display of genre details, in which drunkenness, music, dancing, and lovemaking are all included. A jester at the side points at the multiple folly, comparable in pose to the gesturing figures at either side of the central panel in the *Dance* triptych that serve a similar compositional, and perhaps moralizing, function. Characteristic of a number of Lucas's works is the central alignment of significant symbolic elements in *The Dance of the Magdalene:* the linked arms of the lovers at the bottom, the feathered cap of the Magdalene's partner (also referring to unchastity, as in Cornelis Anthonisz.'s woodcut of that vice from 1546), and the drum of the dance. Perhaps this line should be extended to include the small figure of the Magdalene on horseback in the background, since the hunt, like Lucas's card and chess games, may here be a reference to the course of love.[59]

Another significant allegory of human weakness is found in the circular group of figures at the center of the *Dance around the Golden Calf* (Fig. 33). It has been noted that the exchange of fruit between the man and woman in this group is a clear parallel to the Fall of Man.[60] The child in the woman's arms is an unexpected addition, if Lucas did indeed intend this to be reminiscent of the Fall. The updated version of Eve is dressed as a gypsy—appropriately emblematic of immorality, as we will see—so the child might simply be one of the ubiquitous gypsy babes-in-arms. But he also serves as a reference to the transferral of Original Sin from the first couple to their descendants. He eats with one hand, and with that taste of the fruit his libidinous instincts, like those of Adam and Eve, are aroused. With his other hand he holds a suggestively shaped and placed stick that corresponds to the symbolic genitalia on the other side of the circular grouping: the sexual gesture of the man paired with the open flagon that he holds up. Silver has already convincingly shown Lucas's use of visual puns with natural elements like tree trunks and twigs to emphasize the sexual undertones of two early engravings, *Susanna and the Elders* (B.33, circa 1508) and *The Milkmaid* (B.158, 1510), and here in the *Dance* Lucas returns to that metaphorical language.[61] The placement of the woman in a dominant position, looking down on the seated man, also reflects a common compositional motif in scenes of the Fall, alluding to the woman's powers of seduction.[62] The sexual element is further emphasized by the clearly visible breasts and abdomen under the woman's clothing, very unusual in Lucas's art.

The central axis of the panel passes through the hand of the man with the fruit, as well as through the pouring of wine above and a wine cask below. As discussed above in relation to Lucas's card scenes, drinking to excess was commonly associated with other sensual indulgences, particularly sexual gratification. The most obvious parallel in Lucas's own oeuvre is his engraving of *Lot and His Daughters* from 1530 (B.16): the drinking implements are also aligned along a central axis, one of the daughters is placed in a dominant position over her father, and sexual symbolism is included with the rounded flagons and the prominent sword. Clearly here the sin of promiscuity is the explicit result of drunkenness. In the chapter on gluttony and feasting in *Das Narrenschiff*, Brant warned:

> A drunken man neglects his friends
> And knows no prudent moderation,
> And drinking leads to fornication;
> It oft induces grave offense,
> A wise man drinks with common sense.[63]

Brant went on to blame the "wanton" dance of the Israelites around the golden calf on their feasting and their overfull bellies. As Van Mander described this triptych by Lucas, "The festivities give a very true-to-life picture of the people's profligacy and the base lust that shines in their eyes."[64] The painting serves as a warning against intemperance in all its forms: gluttony, drunkenness, sexual promiscuity, and idolatry. The gypsy costumes worn by a number of the Israelites in this triptych may have been intended as a further reference to these vices.

Gypsy Costumes

It has often been observed that Lucas used fifteenth- and sixteenth-century Dutch costumes as a means of contemporizing his representations of Old and New Testament events. He depicted Samson and Delilah, Joseph and Potiphar's wife, Solomon and his harem, even the witnesses of the miracles and Passion of Christ in the garb of Dutch citizens. This undoubtedly helped to dramatize the relevance of the biblical stories for the men and women of his day. An acknowledgment of the subject at hand is evident, however, in his use of nonspecific or antique garb for certain figures. Christ, his apostles, and the saints, for instance, are frequently shown in voluminous cloaks or robes suggestive of the biblical period or of an antique civilization. Lucas also sometimes introduced an exotic Near Eastern touch in the form of elaborate turbans. This orientalizing motif was commonly used in the fifteenth century in an attempt to give an air of authenticity to biblical scenes.

Lucas's fascination with the details of costume was also expressed in his occasional use of gypsy dress in biblical prints and paintings. Bands of itinerant gypsies had been known in western Europe since the 1410s, welcomed initially as pilgrims fleeing the Turks. Soon, however, widespread reports of their unsettled, hand-to-mouth existence based on deception and thievery led to their condemnation and persecution. From the mid-fifteenth century on, numerous anti-gypsy laws were passed, and the literature contains many prejudicial descriptions of the gypsies' appearance and life-style. During the first half of the sixteenth century they were characterized as "underdeveloped, black, ugly, dirty, and thieves," "depending for a living on highway robbery, stealing, deceiving and barter, amusing people with fortune-telling, purporting to tell the future by palmistry and other impostures."[65] Notable for their dark skin and long black hair, they usually wore loose robes or shifts with blankets or cloaks fastened at their shoulders as overgarments. The women and children often went barefoot and wore earrings, and the unusual headdress, or *bern,* of the women was also cited in early descriptions. It was identified in one early gypsy vocabulary as "a wheel wound round with bands." This wide, flattened turban formed of strips of cloth wrapped around a light, wooden frame appears in woodcut illustrations of gypsy costumes in books by Sebastian Münster, François Desprez, and Cesare Vecellio.[66] Gypsies began to appear as artistic subjects in their own right in the late fifteenth and early sixteenth centuries, for example in a series of tapestries from Tournai depicting the daily life of a wandering band. Specific references to their underhanded, fraudulent behavior are made in some of these tapestries, with scenes of fortune-telling and petty thievery. Bosch's *Hay Wain* in the Prado includes a group of gypsies and a fortune-teller, who are almost certainly intended to reinforce the allegory of deceit and avarice.[67]

Lucas's depiction of gypsy costumes is difficult to interpret. The *berns* and cloaks tied at the shoulders (sometimes used to carry a baby, as seen in the woodcuts by Desprez and Vecellio) appear throughout the paintings of *Moses after Striking the Rock* (Cat. 7, Figs. 24–25) and the *Dance around the Golden Calf.* On one level the dress of the Israelites is surely intended as an allusion to their sojourn among the Egyptians, from whom the word *gypsy* derives, since popular belief held that they originated in that land. But a secondary meaning may also have been intended. The loose living of these gypsies was generally acknowledged, and their religion, at first believed to have the support of the Pope, was soon recognized as highly unorthodox. They were condemned in Germany in the late fifteenth century as "traitors to Christian countries," and in the Netherlands they were commonly called "Heidens" (heathens) as well as "Egyptenaars" (Egyptians).[68] This taint of moral and religious turpitude would certainly have been appropriate for a representation of the Dance around the Golden Calf, especially since gypsies were known for music making and dancing. The Israelites in *Moses after Striking the Rock* are also characterized by a lack of faith and an overriding concern for sensual gratification. In both paintings, a moral as well as geographical significance should probably be assigned to the gypsy costumes. The gypsy-like turban worn by Mary Magdalene in Lucas's engraving of the *Descent from the Cross* (B.53, 1521) may also be a moralizing allusion to her past as a courtesan. The Magdalene was generally shown in elaborate attire, however, and the headdress in this case may simply be an attempt to give a certain exoticism to her costume. In contrast, the gypsies among the spectators in *Christ Healing the Blind Man* in Leningrad (Figs. 35, 38) seem to have been included only in order to add local color to the contemporary setting of Christ's travels. A similar explanation should be used for the gypsy woman in the right foreground of *John the Baptist Preaching in the Wilderness* (Fig. 56). In both cases the gypsies simply illustrate, along with the Dutch burghers, the sort of people who might have been encountered on a road or in a large gathering in sixteenth-century Holland.

Reformation or Catholic Ideology in the Late Paintings

Unusual characteristics in some of Lucas's late paintings have led recent scholars to analyze them in light of the challenges to the Catholic faith presented by Martin Luther's revolutionary theses of 1517. News of the events in Wittenberg spread rapidly, and by 1521 the first condemnation of Lutheran thought in the northern Netherlands was issued by Margaret of Austria. In 1523, the Leiden publisher Jan Zevertsz. was summoned to the Court of Holland in The Hague to answer a charge of printing and selling heretical books, and in 1524 he fled the authorities. Erasmus related in a letter of 1525 that "the largest part of the people of Holland, Zeeland, and Flanders know the teachings of Luther."[69] During this period numerous incidents took place in Leiden involving the destruction of papal bulls and the dissemination of heretical and anticlerical poems and pamphlets. In 1526 poems were tacked to the doors of St. Peter's, Leiden, and strewn inside, warning pious men to guard their wives from all monks and stating that no good could be done for God in the church "since he is not in there." The Leiden prison was filled with men and women "infected with the Lutheran sect," but in general the punishments were mild. They usually consisted of some sort of public penitence, such as participating in religious processions or wearing the image of the chalice, although occasionally a sentence of brief imprisonment or banishment was passed.[70]

Lutheran sentiments were clearly known in the Netherlands, but most Dutch heretics during this first decade of the Reformation held beliefs that were at times radically opposed to both the Catholic and the Lutheran faith. Luther's doctrine of consubstantiation, for example, in which the real presence of Christ coexists with the actual bread and wine at the Eucharist, was not acceptable to the Dutch reformers. The Sacramentarians of the 1520s held that the communion wafer was nothing more than bread, only a symbol of Christ's presence. But in other matters the two groups had much in common, particularly in their struggle against the abuses of the church.

What was Lucas's attitude toward these changes? He was certainly aware of anti-Catholic sentiment.[71] His trip to the southern Netherlands in 1521 was made in the same year that four hundred unorthodox books were burned in Antwerp by the papal legate, and his meeting with Dürer in June occurred only a month after that artist lamented, in response to the rumor of Luther's abduction and assassination: "Oh God, if Luther is dead, who shall henceforth so clearly expound to us the Holy Gospels? . . . O all ye pious Christians, help me to weep over this God-illumined man and beg Him to send us another enlightened one."[72] There is no record that the two artists discussed religion, but on his return to Leiden, Lucas could scarcely have missed the controversy centered around the heretical publications of the printer Jan Zevertsz. It has been suggested that the visit to Leiden in 1522 of Francis van der Hulst, head of the Inquisition in the Netherlands, was in response to this increased circulation of anti-Catholic books.[73] Jan Zevertsz. was apparently a former employer of Lucas, having commissioned designs for woodcut illustrations for several books printed in the 1510s. This occurred before the circulation of Lutheran ideas, of course, but it is reasonable to assume that Lucas would have followed with interest the later career of the printer in Leiden. By 1526, when Lucas was working on the *Last Judgment* triptych for St. Peter's (Cat. 20, Figs. 17-23), he must have been aware of the anonymous poems that were posted on the church doors and scattered inside the sanctuary. Bangs suggests that religious disputes in Leiden were kept private and were handled with some secrecy, so without further proof it should not be assumed that Lucas knew of particular Sacramentarian issues.[74] Although it is impossible to determine to what extent the artist was able or willing to follow specific, detailed points in the theological debate, it is evident from the preceding summary of events that Lucas must have been at least in a general sense aware of the religious situation in his hometown.

The relationship, if any, of Lucas's late paintings to the ideas of the Reformation is questionable. The artist's profound interest in devotional images of the Virgin and Child during the period following his return from Antwerp, circa 1521–1523, would seem to indicate that at least in these years his artistic concerns were still consonant with those of the Catholic Church. In the matter of religious imagery, Luther's teachings were certainly more lenient than those of John Calvin, since he even hung a painting of the Virgin in his room. But in his commentary on the *Magnificat,* Mary's words of praise in Luke 1:46–55, Luther criticized "the masters who so depict and portray the blessed Virgin that there is found in her nothing to be despised, but only great and lofty things." He suggested that artists show instead "how the exceeding riches of God joined in her with utter poverty, the divine honor with her low estate, the divine glory with her shame, the divine greatness with her smallness, the divine goodness with her lack of merit, the divine grace with her unworthiness."[75] Even the moderate Erasmus, who wanted to reform the church from within, criticized the Catholic veneration of images: "How many are there who put more trust in the safeguard of the Virgin Mary, or St. Christopher, than Christ himself? They worship the Mother with images, candles, and songs; and offend Christ heinously by their impious living." The influence of Erasmus's position should not be underrated, especially in the Netherlands. Hieronymus Aleander, the papal legate to the Diet of Worms, wrote in a letter of 1520 to Cardinal de Medici that Erasmus's teachings were instrumental in the spread of Lutheran ideas in the Low Countries.[76] Given the above comments by Luther and Erasmus, it would seem that most, if not all, of Lucas's works during the early 1520s were painted for traditional Catholic patrons.

It has been suggested that a reflection of the Reformation controversy is visible in the exterior panels of Lucas's *Last Judgment* triptych, representing Saints Peter and Paul in a landscape (Fig. 23).[77] This work was commissioned in 1526 by one of the leading families of Leiden, closely involved in municipal government and church affairs, and was apparently hung just outside the baptistery of St. Peter's. It is therefore highly unlikely that Reformation sentiments would be expressed in this triptych, and the presence of the tonsured monk burning in hell in the right wing of the interior (Fig. 19) should simply be considered in light of the critical attitude often taken toward the ignorance and immorality of monks throughout the late Middle Ages.[78]

The pairing of Peter and Paul, seated before a broad seascape linking the two exterior panels of the Leiden triptych, is based on several traditions. Perhaps most important was the fact that the church of St. Peter's in Leiden was dedicated to these two saints. Peter and Paul are also said to have spent some time together in the course of their travels (Gal. 1:18–19). In addition, they are closely linked in the Catholic hierarchy of saints because they were believed to have been martyred in Rome on the same day (June 29). As the patron saints of Rome they were frequently shown together with an image of Veronica's veil, which is one of the relics in St. Peter's in Rome. Furthermore, they are often prominently placed in representations of the Last Judgment because of their attributes. Peter's keys, symbolizing salvation through the church, give entry to the gates of Paradise, and Paul's sword, although specifically related to his martyrdom, is often seen as a type of Christ's sword of retribution.[79] So the presence of the two saints on the exterior of Lucas's *Last Judgment* is appropriate, in that they are the patron saints of the church and harbingers of the act of judgment depicted on the interior panels.

A question remains as to whether these two saints should also be interpreted as the figureheads of opposing religious camps. As the spiritual rock on which the church was founded, Peter was commonly identified with the papacy, whereas Paul was associated with the ideas of the reformers. Luther's tenet of justification by faith alone was based on Paul's Epistle to the Romans (1:17), and much of his subsequent writing was heavily influenced by Paul. In the *Leipzig Disputation* of 1519, he denied the primacy of Peter among the apostles. Luther's attitude toward the two apostles was undoubtedly known to Dürer, and in his *Four Apostles,* painted in 1526 and now in Munich, Paul and John the Evangelist occupy the foreground of the two panels while Peter and Mark are relegated to the back.[80] Whether Lucas was also aware of the Lutheran *Primatus Pauli* is unknown.

Parshall and Silver have cited the turbulent sea in the background of these two panels, as well as the contorted poses of the saints with Peter's back turned on his companion, as evidence of Lucas's concern over the strife between Catholicism and Lutheranism.[81] The seascape, though, can best be interpreted on iconographic grounds unrelated to current religious matters. The most probable explanation is that Lucas, in search of a background that would unify the two panels of the exterior, realized that important events in the lives of both men took place on a stormy sea. Behind Paul, Lucas depicted an episode from Acts 27: in transit as a prisoner from Palestine to Rome, Paul's ship was destroyed in a violent storm, and the passengers were forced to swim to the nearby island of Malta. It was there that Paul performed several miracles, in accordance with Christ's prophecies concerning the missionary activities of his disciples (Mark 16:17–18). In the background of the other wing, the ships may be an allusion to Peter's vocation as a fisherman before he became an apostle. More particularly, one detail represents the story of Peter walking across the tempestuous water toward Christ (Matt. 14:28–33).

The *contrapposto* poses of the two figures probably have little to do with spiritual conflict and should be seen instead as a sign of Lucas's interest in the dynamic and monumental forms of Italian art. The relatively unusual poses of the saints, looking in the same direction rather than toward each other, seem to be an indication of the original placement of the triptych on the wall to the right of the baptistery in St. Peter's. In this case, both Peter and Paul would have directed the viewer's attention to the chapel, the locus of human redemption through Christ. The background seascape may also have had an underlying reference to the baptismal font. Even though the glances of the two saints lead the eye away from the center of the composition, the two panels are united by their gesturing hands and by this symbolic background setting. The hand movements of both figures seem to serve more of a compositional than an iconographic purpose, although they may also be interpreted as gestures of invitation to open the triptych. The obvious debate between the two apostles in Lucas's engraving of 1527 (B.106) is not as apparent here. Whether a reference to theological conflict was intended or not, there is no evidence here of any commitment to Reformation views.

Recent scholars have also identified Reformation issues in several of Lucas's late paintings that deal with the period of the Israelites' journey to Canaan, specifically *Moses after Striking the Rock* and the *Dance around the Golden Calf.* Certainly Moses was an important figure in Lutheran writings, described by Luther himself as the "main fountainhead, source, father, and master of all prophets." In reference to the miracle of the rock at Meribah, Luther follows the typological association made by Paul between the miraculous gift to the Israelites of water, that "supernatural drink," and the wine of the Eucharist (1 Cor. 10:3–4).[82] This was a common parallel in early Christian and medieval writings about the Old and New Testaments and was reflected in artistic representations in which the water released by Moses was related to blood spouting from the wounded side of the crucified Christ. An example of this mentioned by Bangs is a triptych in Kassel attributed to Aertgen van Leyden. The three wings represent the *Miracle of the Rock,* the *Crucifixion,* and *Moses and the Brazen Serpent,* also considered an image of man's salvation through Christ (see John 3:14–15).[83]

It is precisely this issue of redemption through faith that forms the core of the theological discourses on the Miracle of the Rock, a message that was dramatically depicted by Lucas. He chose to emphasize not the traditional positive association between the water in the desert and Christ's sacrificial blood, but the negative view of the Israelites' lack of faith in God's redemptive powers. Silver has elaborated on the fact that Lucas's painting depicts the moment after the striking of the rock, in which Moses stares fixedly at his rod in recognition of his sin.[84] In calling forth the water by smiting the rock rather than speaking to it, he doubted the word of God and disobeyed (Num. 20:7–12).

This faithlessness on the part of Moses is central to the message of the scene. The "arrogant and stubborn" nature of the Israelites throughout their journey from Egypt was repeatedly cited in later books of the Old Testament as evidence of the essential worthlessness of humanity and of God's continuing grace and compassion (for example, Deut. 9, Neh. 9:9–31). By concentrating on the aftermath of the miracle, Lucas emphasized the solemn acknowledgment of wrongdoing on the part of the main characters, who are grouped together in the right middle ground (Fig. 25). The Lord's punishment for the lack of faith shown by Moses and Aaron is clearly stated in Num. 20:24 and 27:12–14. Neither lived to see the Israelites led into the Promised Land, and it was Joshua, Moses's assistant (Exod. 24:13), who was chosen by God for this task (Num. 27:15–23). Lucas probably portrayed Joshua at Moses's right, gazing at the rod not, like Moses and Aaron, in recognition of sin but in awareness of his future responsibility. But Lucas's primary focus is on the Israelites who are spread across the foreground of the composition. They are apparently unaware either of the miracle that precipitated the stream of water or of its effect as a symbol of broken faith on their leaders; instead they are concerned only with the immediate gratification of their physical needs.

The depiction of the moment after the miracle is rare in Netherlandish art of the period. A drawing in the British Museum by Jan Swart, or from his circle, shows a similar portrayal of the account in Numbers.[85] Moses is represented in the foreground walking away from the spring with his rod still held upright, followed by Aaron as they exchange glances. Although psychological analysis is uncertain ground for an art historian, the expressions of the protagonists seem to reveal a troubled, almost tormented spirit, supporting the interpretation of the scene as the recognition by Moses of his sin. The left wing of the triptych in Kassel attributed to Aertgen van Leyden, mentioned above, was also clearly influenced by Lucas's painting. Not only did Aertgen, like Lucas, depict the moment after the miracle, but he also based several of his women and children on those painted by Lucas. But Aertgen used these elements from Lucas's composition in a triptych juxtaposing two Old Testament scenes (the Mosaic miracles of the rock and of the brazen serpent) with the central image of the crucifixion. In doing so he altered the message of Lucas's painting by having Moses and Aaron look directly at the rock and spring as the source of salvation, rather than at the rod as the instrument of transgression. Jan Steen's painting now in Philadelphia, painted a century later, appears to represent the same moment as Lucas's *Moses,* without the iconographic changes made by Aertgen. It is also compositionally similar to Lucas's painting. The foreground is filled with groups of Israelites quenching their thirst, while Moses and Aaron are pushed off-center in the middle distance. Steen clearly showed Moses reacting to God's reprimand (Num. 20:1–2), gazing upward with hands outstretched.

As in the *Dance around the Golden Calf,* Lucas or his patrons chose to interpret the subject of pride and faithlessness by focusing on the overriding human desire for sensual satisfaction. Moses's lapse of faith is secondary in this composition to the Israelites' sin of self-gratification. This inversion of the theme is probably the result of Lucas's own interpretation of the commission, given his lifelong interest in the subject of humans held in thrall to their carnal desires. The choice of subject, involving the sin of Moses and the heedlessness of the people rather than the more frequently chosen moment of the miracle itself, suggests that the painting was commissioned as a private affirmation of faith. The certainty of punishment would be a warning for those, like Moses, who doubt and disobey.

The medium of the painting further supports the idea that it was intended not as a public commission but for a large private home. Relatively few Netherlandish paintings in tempera on canvas have survived. This is the result of the fragility of the backing in high-humidity conditions and the practice common in the fifteenth and early sixteenth centuries of hanging canvases directly against the wall in lieu of tapestries as a quick and inexpensive way to decorate large expanses. Van Mander described Lucas as a skillful painter in watercolor as well as in oil, and he mentioned a canvas in this medium depicting the history of St. Hubert, painted when Lucas was twelve (Cat. 27). He further described a canvas in the house of Heer van Sonneveldt or Heer Knotter showing Rebecca at the well (Cat. 8). It has been suggested that in this case Van Mander actually saw the painting of *Moses* and identified its subject incorrectly, but given his close description of the work it is unlikely that he would have overlooked or misread the figure of Moses.[86] In light of the apparent similarities between the paintings of *Moses after Striking the Rock* and *Rebecca and Eliezer at the Well,* it seems possible that the works were originally part of a tapestry-like series hung together in a single large room. The technique of the two was similar, as was the thematic emphasis on water and the compositional format of a group of figures set in a landscape. This hypothesis is further supported by Van Mander's description of another series of now-lost canvases in watercolor by Lucas, representing the history of Joseph and seen by Van Mander in the house of a Delft brewer or malt maker (Cat. 2).[87]

A similar series of large canvases might therefore have been executed by Lucas, with scenes representing some of the many biblical stories in which water plays a major role. The scarcity of water as a natural resource in Palestine explains the biblical preoccupation with its importance. It was frequently used in both the Old and New Testaments as a symbol of the Lord's power, beneficence, or approval, and the devastating effects of a drought were explained as a sign of his displeasure (Jer. 14:1-9). In the story of Rebecca and Abraham's servant, water was a means of guiding the faithful toward God's will (Gen. 24:10-27, especially 7 and 27). As a kind of moral proving ground, water functions in this story much as it does in the story of Moses striking the rock. The belief of the doubting Israelites would surely have been renewed by the miraculous appearance of water, but Moses's lack of faith at a critical moment weakened the effect of the miracle. If a series based on this theme was, in fact, intended by Lucas, a number of other stories in the Old Testament would also have been suitable for inclusion. One appropriate parallel, for example, would have been the miracle of the well in response to the plight of Hagar and Ishmael (Gen. 21:14-20), a subject that Lucas had already explored in engravings of circa 1507 and 1516 (B.17 and 18). The Lord's provision of water for the Israelites at Beer (Num. 21:16-18) or the purification of the water at Mara (Exod. 15:22-26) would have been even closer to the paintings of *Moses* and *Rebecca* in also having a large cast of characters. The miraculous deliverance of the Israelites in their crossing of the Red Sea (Exod. 14:21-31) is described in the New Testament as an act of faith (Heb. 11:29) and is directly related to the striking of the rock as a prefiguration of the baptism through Christ (1 Cor. 10:4; compare Ps. 78:12-16). In the story of Christ and the Samaritan woman at the well, Christ promises to provide "living water" to the faithful (John 4:4-15), closely allying this story to the Old Testament tradition of the Lord as the "fountain of living waters" (Jer. 17:13).

Whether or not Lucas's *Moses* was originally part of such a series, the emphasis on redemption through faith found as an underlying theme in many of the water miracles of the Old and New Testament parallels the central issue in Lucas's painting. As Silver has shown, the representation of the sin of Moses as opposed to the moment of the actual miracle could well have been a reflection of the religious turmoil of the period.[88] But it is exactly this choice of moment that suggests a Catholic rather than a Reformed point of view, reasserting the importance of faith in the face of those who doubt.

The triptych of the *Dance around the Golden Calf* is similar to *Moses after Striking the Rock* in condemning the faithless Israelites. For this reason the event is included in the accounts of the "stubborn" resistance of man to God's will given in the ninth chapters of Deuteronomy and Nehemiah. In the *Dance*, Lucas is also, and indeed primarily, concerned with a moralizing representation based on the immoderate behavior of the Israelites, as discussed earlier. The *Dance* was associated with anti-Sacramentarian sentiments by Maarten Wurfbain, who identified one of the figures as the heretic David Jorisz. His suggestion that the triptych was intended as a warning against such Reformation ideas lacks any corroborating evidence. Filedt Kok and Bangs have argued convincingly that the letters in the underdrawing that Wurfbain read as "D JO^r" are instead a color notation.[89]

Parshall related the triptych to the question of idolatrous images under discussion in Lutheran circles in the 1520s. His analysis of the visual paradox set up by the depiction of an idolatrous subject, the golden calf, in a format traditionally used as an icon, the triptych, led him to the conclusion that the painting probably reflected the Erasmian position against image worship. Silver, however, returned to the idea that the painting was related to the current debate of Sacramentarian issues.[90]

These analyses have failed to recognize the thematic continuity in Lucas's painted oeuvre.[91] When seen in light of his earlier warnings against physical excess and carnal indulgence, his choice of these two subjects focusing on the sensual gratification of the Israelites should come as no surprise. Although it remains possible that both *Moses after Striking the Rock* and the *Dance around the Golden Calf* have an underlying reference to the theological debates of the period, it should be emphasized that this would have been neither their primary message nor their raison d'être. The use of a triptych format for an Old Testament subject such as the *Dance around the Golden Calf* is unusual, but it is characteristic of Lucas's compositional interests during the later period. Like the *Last Judgment* and *Christ Healing the Blind Man,* the *Dance* shows the artist's fascination with the problems of composing a large group of figures against a landscape background, and the challenge posed by the physical divisions of a triptych provided Lucas with the opportunity for an increasingly sophisticated design. Certainly his interests would in any case have been subordinate to the patron's specifications. The use of the traditional altarpiece form for such a biblical narrative implies a relaxation of the original liturgical function of the triptych.[92] The unusual subject of the painting, its small size, and its plain exterior painted in imitation marble have led to a great deal of speculation about its original location. It was probably commissioned for a private chapel, although no definite conclusion can be reached without further information on the commission or patron.[93]

The theme of faith was important to Lucas's late period and may well have been a result of the religious confusion of the period. The central scene of Christ healing the blind beggar in *Christ Healing the Blind Man* is underscored in the background by the episode of the sterile fig tree (Mark 10:51–52 and 11:20–24). This explicit call to faith is paralleled in another late painting of *Christ Healing the Lepers* (Cat. C24), now lost and known through several copies (Fig. 63). Again, the primary message is found in Christ's words, "Your faith has cured you" (Luke 17:19).

After considering the possibility of Lutheran and Sacramentarian ideas in Lucas's late paintings, both Parshall and Silver concluded that the artist remained within the Catholic fold.[94] Certainly his private religious beliefs need not have echoed those of his patrons, but he continued to work for the leading families of Leiden. It is unlikely that Claes Dircxz. van Swieten or his family, for example, who were closely involved in municipal and church affairs, would have commissioned the *Last Judgment* from an artist even remotely associated with Reformation ideas.

Several late works by Lucas shed further light on his religious beliefs. His engraved series of the *Seven Theological and Cardinal Virtues* (B.127–33), dated 1530, has been analyzed in some detail by Silver and Smith.[95] Unusual in their nudity and highly unorthodox in their contorted, exaggerated poses, the Christian Virtues might at first suggest an underlying satirical or negative view. But they are probably intended to be read as serious illustrations of the subject and are not unlike the nude *Virtues* by the German Master IB (B.23–29). The figures share the mannerist spirit of the *Shield-Bearers* formerly on the exterior of *Christ Healing the Blind Man* (Fig. 39), but their inscriptions and attributes are perfectly conventional. The personification of *Faith* (B.127), for example, is shown with the standard cross, chalice, and wafer of the Eucharist.

Finally, Lucas's late painting of the *Procession of the Holy Sacrament* (Cat. C33), now lost and known only through a drawing by Jan de Bisschop (Fig. 62), seems to be a further indication of his traditional views. Religious processions were common in sixteenth-century Holland, their purpose being "to pray humbly to God Almighty that it please his divine clemency to be merciful and full of grace for his people."[96] They were held to pray for political protection, for salvation from plagues and other diseases, and even for good weather. Because of the frequency of such processions, the Leiden burghers became increasingly indifferent to them and attendance seems to have dropped. As a result, an order was issued on April 2, 1513, requiring everyone to follow the Host with appropriate reverence during the processions held on the first Sunday of every month. A common punishment for heretics during the 1520s was the performance of public penance during these processions. None of the figures in Lucas's composition can be identified, but he clearly contrasted the devotion and pious attention of the poor and infirm in the foreground with the indifference of the middle-class burghers at the right. Perhaps the painting was commissioned by the municipality as a reminder to the populace of the need for renewed faith in the Holy Sacrament.[97]

Thus, there is no evidence from Lucas's paintings and prints of the 1520s that he followed Dürer in converting to the Reformed movement. Some of his late paintings have as their central message the need for faith and as such might be considered reflections of the religious turmoil of the period. In general, however, his primary concerns remained with the refinement of his compositional abilities and with the development of the theme that had been uppermost in his mind throughout most of his career, that of humanity's intemperate or profligate nature.

CONCLUSION

Max J. Friedländer described Lucas's career as a painter by noting in frustration, "Everything should be expected except for a consistent and logical development."[1] His confusion was primarily the result of his acceptance of many paintings incorrectly attributed to Lucas. Recently Lucas's oeuvre has been pared down to a more unified corpus, resulting in a more comprehensible painting style. A clarification of Lucas's compositional and iconographic development leads us to a new recognition of his versatility and the experimental nature of his work.

Lucas has often been described as a child prodigy, based on the birth date of 1494 given in Carel van Mander's biography. Certain scholars have attempted to push this birth date back five or six years, but none of the arguments has been convincing. Lucas's earliest paintings exhibit an innovative approach to structure and theme, with little apparent influence from his two teachers. He may have become aware through his father, Huygh Jacobsz., of the value of *repoussoir* motifs as transitional elements and of the impact of tight clusters of figure as compositional blocks, enlivened by pose and gesture. His paint technique and color range, especially the deep rich reds serving as unifying tones, seem at least partly indebted to Cornelis Engebrechtsz. But what is most striking in the young Lucas is his remarkable independence, as well as his surprising ability to confront the challenges posed by different media. As a printmaker, his early works dealt with problems of space—figural illusionism, foreshortening, landscape and architectural surround. But as a painter he chose compositions that were tightly confined, restricted to the half-length format and emphasizing the psychological drama of the event rather than its spatial extension. One element uniting these disparate interests, not only in the early period but throughout his career, was his strong and often unconventional sense of narrative meaning, of what constituted the moment of greatest impact. His Old Testament scenes, for example—from *Potiphar's Wife Accusing Joseph* to the *Dance around the Golden Calf,* from the engraved *Susanna and the Elders* to the woodcut *Power of Women* series—often undermine our expectations. In some cases he focused on an unusual moment before or after the traditional climax; in others he manipulated the composition to highlight different aspects of the story, thereby providing a new and deeper understanding of its meaning.

Lucas's concern for compositional and tonal balance, physiognomic description, and psychological study began with his earliest works and remained with him throughout his relatively brief career. He never went to Italy, unlike such artists as Albrecht Dürer, Jan Gossaert, and Jan van Scorel, but he became aware of the Italian style through the art of these contemporaries and, more directly, through the prints of Marcantonio Raimondi. He also achieved greater assurance and skill through contact with the graphic art of Dürer and Marcantonio, from whom he borrowed poses and compositional motifs as well as a new language of monumental form. In addition, his trip to Antwerp in 1521— when he could have seen works by Quinten Massys, Joos van Cleve, Bernard van Orley, and others—and his travels through Zeeland, Flanders, and Brabant with Gossaert later in the decade proved to be of great significance to his development of massive, weighty figures. All of these artists were influential for his graphic as well as his painting style in the 1520s, but his experiments in these media again took very different forms. During the course of that decade his engravings became increasingly focused as he concentrated on a few monumental nude forms set close to the picture plane, while his late paintings are more panoramic, with many figures extended across a wide landscape. His latest paintings also exhibit a compositional classicism, more stable and balanced than Gossaert's or Van Scorel's, but even while under the influence of Italian structural considerations he retained the northern ability to transform biblical and allegorical themes into real events, emotionally vivid and naturalistically detailed.[2]

His interest in painted landscape settings may have been influenced by works he saw in Antwerp, in particular those by Joachim Patinir, but his style is quite different in effect from Patinir's more tightly painted, meticulously detailed bird's-eye views. There are parallels with Van Scorel's broadly brushed backdrops, as in his *Baptism of Christ* painted around 1528 for the Knights of St. John in Haarlem. The appearance of darker foreground elements set against cool blue-green mountains in the distance, for example, as well as certain staffage elements appear in the work of both artists, but we have no indication that the artists ever met or had the opportunity of studying each other's paintings. They may have arrived independently at a similar representation of landscape, in which case Lucas's late paintings would perhaps be best understood as variations in a different medium of his early engraved environments.

Many of his works throughout his career, in various media, explore the theme of the relationship between the sexes. His early allegorical genre panels, like the allegories of Quinten Massys and Jan van Hemessen in Antwerp, were important transitional works in the movement of Netherlandish art away from its roots in the medieval church. These allegories set him apart, however, from his northern Netherlandish contemporaries such as Jan Mostaert in Haarlem, who concentrated on portraits and devotional panels, Jacob Cornelisz. in Amsterdam, who painted a range of religious works imbued with the northern Mannerist style, and Jan van Scorel, whose ecclesiastical and noble patrons throughout the north largely determined the nature of his production. Lucas had been inspired by the topos of the Power of Women in two woodcut series, and he seems to have taken the idea of woman's dangerous wiles—with its corollary warning against temptations of the flesh in general—and extended it as an underlying theme to other biblical and allegorical genre scenes. Another sign of his narrative experimentation is the inclusion of gypsies among the participants and spectators in biblical scenes, serving as representatives of physical and spiritual depravity to strengthen the metaphorical message. Many of his paintings and prints reveal an underlying interest in the fundamental issues of temptation, sin, and faith, although there is no substantial evidence that he entered into the religious debates of the Reformation, and he seems to have remained a Catholic.

Very little is known about his patrons, but most of those whose names have come down to us from archival documents or from the biography in *Het Schilder-Boeck* were important figures in Leiden and the surrounding area. His early canvas of the *History of St. Hubert* was commissioned by the Lord of Lochorst, according to Van Mander, who also describes the Munich diptych of the *Virgin and Child with Mary Magdalene and a Donor* as being in 1604 in the collection of Frans Hooghstraet in a manor outside the city. It may be possible to identify the donor from this information, since Franchoys van Hoogstraten, who was mayor of Haarlem from 1521 to 1524, lived in the Castle Teijlingen near Leiden.[3] The *Last Judgment* was also painted for the ruling elite. It was commissioned by members of the Van Swieten family in memory of the Leiden timber merchant Claes Dircsz. van Swieten, who had been active in the municipal government. The donors of *Christ Healing the Blind Man* were Jacob Florisz.

van Montfoort and Dirckje Boelensdr. van Lindenburgh. Jacob was a manufacturer of bricks and a member, like Van Swieten before him, of the town council. Both the Van Swieten and Van Montfoort families continued to patronize the arts: Cornelis van Swieten's collection included twenty-two paintings in 1547, and Jacob van Montfoort's family commissioned on the occasion of his death in 1554 a memorial triptych of the *Last Judgment* by Aertgen van Leyden.[4] Otherwise we know nothing about Lucas's patrons.

Most controversial, perhaps, is the small triptych of the *Dance around the Golden Calf,* described by Van Mander as being in a private collection in Amsterdam in 1604. Although the triptych format was normally reserved for altarpieces, the subject here makes it highly unlikely that it was intended for a church altar, providing as it does an unmistakable commentary on idolatry by means of an Old Testament story. Perhaps painted for a private chapel, it may well have been placed in a purely secular setting, as some of Bosch's triptychs apparently were. Much less is known about Lucas's patronage than about that of Jan van Scorel, for example, who received many important commissions from the ecclesiastical hierarchy and from the nobility in Utrecht and elsewhere.[5] Many of Lucas's works, especially his small allegorical genre panels and his various representations of the Virgin and Child, were probably sold without commission from his workshop or on the open market, and the popularity of certain compositions would explain the existence of copies and variants.

In contrast to the widespread influence of his prints, Lucas's impact as a painter was limited during his lifetime to his colleagues in Leiden. The figure style and compositional format of his biblical scenes from the 1520s may have affected works such as Cornelis Engebrechtsz.'s triptych of the *Healing of Naaman* in Vienna and several Leiden School paintings of the *Feeding of the Five Thousand* (Figs. 68–69).[6] But his interest in allegorical genre scenes was apparently unparalleled at this time in Leiden, or for that matter anywhere in the northern Netherlands. The didactic satires of Lucas and Massys seem to have developed independently of each other, those of Massys having more of an impact in the south than Lucas's did in the north. Secular scenes of folly, often set in a tavern or brothel and occasionally featuring the Prodigal Son, were popular in the mid-sixteenth century, but it is impossible to identify specific works dependent on Lucas's panels.[7]

The compositional shift of focus in many of his paintings and prints, in which he pushed the conventional narrative center of interest into the background or off to one side and replaced it with secondary elements (which in turn often assumed metaphorical significance), may have influenced in a general way certain Netherlandish artists active during the middle of the century.

This clever manipulation of the viewer's expectations appears in paintings by the Brunswick Monogrammist, Jan van Hemessen, and Pieter Aertsen, among others.[8] The link to Lucas is tenuous, however, and it must be concluded that his pictures had little real effect on the art of the mid-sixteenth century.

His influence on the style of later artists was largely due to the widespread popularity of his engravings and woodcuts. His prints were well known in the sixteenth century, even in Italy, and he was described by Giorgio Vasari as a rival of Dürer's in the graphic arts.[9] In addition to borrowing from his Italian contemporaries, he provided them in turn with models for figure poses and landscape design.[10] Although his prints were of greatest importance in the spread of his ideas, being easily reproduced and transported, some of his paintings were also significant for Dutch artists of the late sixteenth and seventeenth centuries. Renewed interest in his art is evident from the fact that a number of his now-lost painted compositions are known only from copies of this period. Artists such as Jan Muller, Jan Saenredam, Bartholomaus Dolendo, Simon Frisius, Nicolas de Bruyn, and Jan de Bisschop reproduced works by Lucas.

This appreciation for Lucas's painting style beginning in the late sixteenth century is expressed in the diaries of the lawyer and art lover Arnoldus Buchelius during the period 1583–1639. He praised Lucas's skills in the pictorial arts and judged his works to be of eternal worth, adding that he deserved a place among the great painters of the world.[11] Van Mander's enthusiastic description of Lucas's pictures in *Het Schilder-Boeck* includes several laudatory poems by other writers, and he himself stated: "There are few paintings by him that one can see today, and few that one comes across, but these few are extraordinarily praiseworthy and appealing thanks to their exceptional quality." Van Mander's interest in Lucas's art takes on concrete form in his own *Dance around the Golden Calf,* now in Haarlem, which probably owes its inverted composition and certain details of figure type, pose, and costume to Lucas's triptych of the same subject.[12]

The account in *Het Schilder-Boeck* of the efforts of Emperor Rudolf II of Prague to acquire a painting by Lucas is another testimony to his popularity at the time. Aided by the Amsterdam engraver Jan Muller, among others, Rudolf at first tried to purchase Lucas's *Last Judgment,* which was then in the Leiden Town Hall. Although his offer was supported by Prince Maurits and the States General, the Leiden Council refused to sell the monumental triptych. According to a letter of 1602 by Muller, both Van Mander and his fellow Haarlem artist Hendrick Goltzius were instrumental in keeping the work in Leiden. In 1603 the emperor, a connoisseur and collector of early Netherlandish and German art, again attempted to acquire a painting by Lucas. The object of his efforts, *Christ Healing the Blind Man,* was at that time owned by Goltzius, but Rudolf was thwarted by what his agent considered Goltzius's exorbitant price. In 1604 Rudolf's quest was finally successful, and he acquired Lucas's diptych of the *Virgin and Child with Mary Magdalene and a Donor.*[13]

Goltzius's appreciation of Lucas's work was noted in *Het Schilder-Boeck:* "His expert knowledge of art had led him to love and covet Lucas's works."[14] In addition to *Christ Healing the Blind Man,* Goltzius owned a glass painting by Lucas of the *Triumphal Entry of David into Jerusalem* (Cat. C4), and his collection also included a painting by Lucas's contemporary Aertgen van Leyden. He was influenced by Lucas's engraving technique, and in 1593 he used the earlier artist's *Adoration of the Magi* (B.37) as the model for his own *Epiphany* (B.19). A number of drawings by Goltzius were also made in Lucas's manner. In particular, a sketch in Oxford of a *Shield-Bearer,* dated 1586, is apparently based on one of the figures on the exterior of Lucas's *Christ Healing the Blind Man.*[15]

Lucas's influence on the style of the later sixteenth-century Dutch mannerists can be traced in several other works. The inverted focus of his *Dance around the Golden Calf,* with the primary event hidden behind the spectators, appears in paintings such as Van Mander's of the same subject and Cornelis van Haarlem's *Wedding of Peleus and Thetis,* both in Haarlem, and Abraham Bloemaert's *Sermon of John the Baptist* in Amsterdam.[16] As in Lucas's *Dance,* these paintings emphasize genre details of eating and drinking, women with their lovers, and mothers with their children. Also comparable is the occasional use of gypsy dress, and the reclining poses of foreground figures in these late sixteenth-century works are closely related to Lucas's figures in the *Dance* and *Christ Healing the Blind Man.* Jan Steen was later attracted by the same characteristics, as seen in his *Dance around the Golden Calf* in Raleigh and *Moses after Striking the Rock* in Philadelphia.[17]

The influence of Lucas's art on the Netherlandish Caravaggisti takes another form. These artists were primarily interested in the half-length genre or allegorical genre scenes of Lucas, Massys, and midcentury followers such as Marinus van Reymerswaele and Jan van Hemessen. Caravaggio's representations of cardsharps and fortune-tellers can be traced indirectly to Lucas's gaming scenes, although it is unlikely that he knew them at first hand. While Caravaggio was a major source of inspiration for the Utrecht artists of the early seventeenth century, the gaming, tavern, and brothel scenes of their Dutch predecessors were also important for Hendrick Terbrugghen and Gerrit van Honthorst. For example, Lucas's glass painting of the *Triumphal Entry of David into Jerusalem,* owned by Goltzius, seems to have influenced Terbrugghen's representation of the same subject in Raleigh.[18] Terbrugghen's work is in half length and therefore more concentrated, but his compositional treatment is otherwise remarkably similar to Lucas's, as is the motif of a woman in the foreground with her back turned to the viewer. The bearded head of Goliath, held by a lock of his hair, is probably taken from Lucas's engraving of around 1513 (B.26).

Lucas's prints and a number of his paintings were well known and greatly admired in the late sixteenth and seventeenth centuries, but various artists appear to have been attracted by different aspects of his style. The Haarlem mannerists, and later Jan Steen, modeled some of their works on Lucas's large biblical paintings, while the Utrecht Caravaggisti were drawn to his more compact allegorical genre panels. Lucas's thematic and compositional versatility not only distinguished him from his contemporaries in the Netherlands, therefore, but also proved of some importance for later Dutch artists. The variety apparent in his choice of narrative and devotional themes reveals his interest in relatively unusual aspects of allegorical genre and Old Testament subjects, as well as more traditional biblical themes, and his compositions—ranging from small, crowded, half-length panels to spacious, many-figured representations—exhibit the great diversity and richness of his painted oeuvre.

PART II

Catalogue Raisonné

Old Testament Paintings

Cat. 1. *Potiphar's Wife Accusing Joseph* (Fig. 4)

Museum Boymans–van Beuningen, Rotterdam, inv. no. 2455; panel, 24 x 34.5; circa 1510–1511.

Provenance: Coll. Baumgärtner, Nuremberg, sold 1820;[1] Coll. Count Silva Taroncca; inherited by Count Sternberg, Prague;[2] with P. Cassirer, Berlin, 1922; with Goudstikker, Amsterdam, 1930; Coll. D. G. van Beuningen, Vierhouten, 1930–1958; acquired by the museum in 1958.

Exhibitions: Amsterdam, Goudstikker, 1930, no. 33 (as *Jephthah's Daughter*); Rotterdam, Museum Boymans–van Beuningen, 1930–1931, no. 11 (as *Jephthah's Daughter,* painted directly after the Bremen *Susanna* [Cat. 3]); Rotterdam, Museum Boymans–van Beuningen, 1936, no. 80 (as *Susanna before the Judge*); Rotterdam, Museum Boymans–van Beuningen, 1938, no. 10 (as *Susanna*); Amsterdam, Rijksmuseum, 1939, no. 70a (as *Susanna*); The Hague, Mauritshuis, 1945, no. 63 (as *Joseph and Potiphar's Wife,* ca. 1509); Rotterdam, Museum Boymans–van Beuningen, 1949, no. 16 (ca. 1509); Paris, Petit Palais, 1952, no. 54; Rotterdam, Museum Boymans–van Beuningen, 1955, no. 14 (ca. 1509); Amsterdam, Rijksmuseum, 1958, no. 127 (ca. 1512; similar to Lucas's engraving of *Joseph and Potiphar's Wife,* B.12); Leiden, Stedelijk Museum, 1978, no. 2 (ca. 1512).

Literature: Müller, 1820, p. 20, no. 57 (by Lucas, *Susanna;* see Copy 2); Kahn, 1918, p. 24; Friedländer, 1930, pp. 498–99 (ca. 1509; probably *Susanna,* although certain details suggest *Joseph and Potiphar's Wife*); Dülberg, 1933, p. 7 (*Jephthah's Return Home,* ca. 1512); Beets, 1934, p. 50 (ca. 1510); Gerson, 1936, p. 137; Beets, 1940, pp. 47–51 (*Joseph and Potiphar's Wife;* first to identify background scene as Joseph being led to prison); Hoogewerff,

1936-1947, 3:230-31, 278 (*Jephthah's Daughter,* ca. 1512); Hannema, 1949, p. 30, no. 16 (ca. 1509);[3] Beets, 1954, p. 445; Leymarie, 1956, p. 48; Rotterdam, Museum Boymans-van Beuningen, 1962, p. 77 (ca. 1512); Friedländer, 1963a, p. 51 (ca. 1510); Boon, 1964, col. 351 (ca. 1510); Reznicek-Buriks, 1965, p. 244 (ca. 1512); Ringbom, 1965, p. 192 (an Old Testament prefiguration of the theme of *Christ and the Adulteress;* probably influenced by Venetian half-length paintings); Gibson, 1970b, p. 93 (ca. 1508; head of Potiphar similar to that of a man in the Turin *Crucifixion,* attributed by him to Huygh Jacobsz.); Friedländer, 1967-1976, 10:51, 82 (ca. 1509); Parshall, 1974, pp. 127-28, 130-31 (ca. 1508); Brown, 1978, p. 782 (must date from the earliest years of the second decade); Filedt Kok, 1978, pp. 26-32, 120, 125 (ca. 1512; careful, detailed underdrawing in brush and black paint; paint technique less draftsmanlike, more flowing than the Berlin *Chess Players* [Fig. 1, Cat. 34]); Silver and Smith, 1978, pp. 263-64, 288, n. 56; Vos, 1978a, p. 32 (ca. 1512); Vos, 1978c, p. 500, n. 98 (ca. 1509); Wurfbain, 1978, pp. 205-6; Renger, 1979, p. 58.

Copies: (1) Painting, artist unknown; location unknown; panel, 24.5 x 40, with an extension of the panel at the left.[4] *Prov.:* Coll. Semmel, Berlin; sale Geneva (Galerie Moos), May 23, 1936, no. 90 (as *Susanna before the Judge,* atelier of Lucas). *Lit.:* Friedländer, 1930, p. 499 (as an old copy).

(2) Engraving, artist unknown (Fig. 5); in reverse, with an additional strip behind the figure of Potiphar's wife; published in Müller, 1820, p. 20, no. 57.

This panel represents a scene from the Old Testament account of Joseph in Egypt. Joseph was bought by Potiphar, the captain of Pharaoh's guard and a eunuch, who soon put the young Israelite in charge of his household (Gen. 39:1-6). Joseph became the object of unwanted attentions on the part of his master's wife but refused to succumb to her repeated attempts at seduction (39:7-10). During one such episode, the woman grabbed Joseph's cloak as he fled from her and used it as false evidence in her slanderous accusation of rape (39:11-20). This is the moment depicted by Lucas. Potiphar's wife is shown at the left, holding the cloak and looking across at Joseph, who is situated in the lower right corner. Between them stand five men, including Potiphar, who holds a decorative scepter and reacts with anger and astonishment to the news. Through a window at the left, Joseph is seen being led off to prison in the distant background (39:20). Before the background scene was identified by Beets, there was a good deal of confusion about the painting's iconography; most scholars called it either *Susanna before the Judge* or *Jephthah's Daughter.*[5] Although this work is similar to representations of *Susanna* in certain respects, the reaction of the man in the foreground is not appropriate for the role of a judge, and the cloak held by the woman has no place in the story of Susanna (see Cat. 3). The account of Jephthah and his daughter also has little relationship to the event depicted in this panel, beyond the presence of the young woman confronting an older man (Judges 11).

The extreme youth of the figure at the lower right, presumably Joseph, is problematic. According to Genesis 37:2, he was seventeen years old. Perhaps Lucas intended to emphasize in this way the innocence of the young man and the corruption of his older seductress. The episode of Potiphar's wife accusing Joseph seldom appeared independently, although it was sometimes included as part of a history of Joseph, as in the *Bible moralisée* and Lucas's own engraved series (B.19–23).[6]

The painting has been dated between 1508 and 1512, with recent scholarship divided between these two extremes.[7] It has relatively little in common with Lucas's earliest panels, the *Chess Players* in Berlin (Fig. 1, Cat. 34) and *The Fortuneteller* in Paris (Fig. 2, Cat. 35). The rather viscous application of paint, the dark colors, and the crowded and airless compositions of these works from around 1508 are not in evidence here. The touch is more delicate, the paint is thinner and more smoothly applied, the highlights are dissolved rather than additive, the colors are lighter, and the spaces are more open.[8] The work has many similarities to Lucas's *Susanna before the Judge,* formerly in Bremen (Fig. 6, Cat. 3), especially in the facial types and poses and in the representation of the hands and drapery. The Rotterdam panel appears to date slightly earlier, circa 1510–1511. The relatively tight clustering of figures and the woodenness of the poses distinguish it from an engraving of the same subject, dated 1512 (B.21), and place it closer to Lucas's *Ecce Homo,* from 1510 (B.71). The comparison is particularly convincing in the detail of the spectators grouped at the far left of the 1510 engraving, although the gestures in the painting are slightly freer and more naturalistic.

Cat. 2. *History of Joseph*

Location unknown, presumably lost; tempera on canvas.
Literature: Van Mander, 1604, fols. 213v–214r; Rosenberg, 1877, p. 8; Colvin, 1882, p. 137; Hymans, 1884, p. 146, n. 1; Silver, 1973, p. 407; Vos, 1978c, p. 500, n. 98; Wolfthal, 1989, pp. 17 and cat. 126.

This series of paintings, now lost, is known only through a description in *Het Schilder-Boeck* by Van Mander:

I have also seen in Delft, in the house of a brewer or maltmaker, some watercolor canvases representing the history of Joseph that are very beautiful in invention and draughtsmanship, with some beautiful drapery, especially in [the scene of] the wine-steward and baker lying in prison: but it is unfortunate that time and age have ravaged them, and destroyed them by the moisture of the walls that is a common malady in the Netherlands.[1]

The *History of Joseph* might have consisted of a number of scenes taken from the biblical account of his brothers' treachery and his subsequent enslavement and rise to power in Egypt (Gen. 37, 39–41). Lucas painted a small panel around 1510–1511 of *Potiphar's Wife Accusing Joseph* (Fig. 4, Cat. 1) and slightly later, in 1512, engraved a five-part series (B.19–23). Three of these prints deal with Joseph's explication of dreams (Gen. 40–41), and two treat his encounter with Potiphar's wife (Gen. 39:7–20).[2] Whether the series in tempera represented the same subjects is unknown. Only one episode, that of the wine steward and the baker in prison (Gen. 40; see also B.22), is mentioned specifically by Van Mander.[3]

Van Mander described the use of large paintings in tempera on canvas as substitutes for tapestries, so it is likely that related scenes would be chosen for a decorative series.[4] Although tempera on canvas is less expensive than tapestry as a means of covering wall space, Silver's suggestion that the brewer's choice was dictated by financial considerations is problematic. First, it has been pointed out that the profession of brewing was one of the most lucrative in Holland at this time.[5] Also, the brewer who owned the series in the early seventeenth century could not have been the same man who commissioned it more than seventy years earlier. We have no way of knowing, therefore, whether financial constraints dictated the choice of medium in this case.

Cat. 3. *Susanna before the Judge* (Fig. 6)

Destroyed during World War II; formerly Kunsthalle, Bremen, inv. no. 62-1851; panel, 34 x 46; circa 1512.

Provenance: legacy of H. Klugkist, 1851.

Exhibitions: Rotterdam, Museum Boymans–van Beuningen, 1936, no. 81.

Literature: Hurm, 1892, pp. 48–50, no. 62 (attributed to Lucas's grandson, Joan de Hoey, based on the signature "Hoey" on the drapery at the lower right;[1] most complete description of the colors); Dülberg, 1899b, pp. 157–58 (attributed to Dammes Claesz. de Hoey, Lucas's son-in-law; too close to Lucas's style to be by Joan de Hoey); Bredius, 1901 (by Lucas); Pauli, 1907, p. 24 (by Lucas); Dülberg, 1909, p. 12; Beets, 1913, p. 81 (ca. 1510-1511); Conway, 1921, pp. 472-73; Baldass, 1923, pp. 15-16, 30 (ca. 1512); Winkler, 1924, p. 264; Burger, 1925, p. 155; Dülberg, 1929, p. 168 (ca. 1515-1520); Di Lentaglio, 1929, p. 18; Wescher, 1929, p. 168; Friedländer, 1930, p. 498 (ca. 1509); Dülberg, 1933, p. 7 (ca. 1512); Beets, 1940, pp. 47-51; Hoogewerff, 1936-1947, 3:230-31 (ca. 1512); Benesch, 1945, p. 85 (one of Lucas's earliest paintings, possibly done when he was fifteen); Bremen, Kunsthalle, 1948, p. 54, no. 23 (in the list of paintings lost during the war); Leymarie, 1956, p. 48; Friedländer, 1963a, p. 51 (ca. 1510; cites incorrect measurements); Boon, 1964, col. 351 (ca. 1510); Reznicek-Buriks, 1965, p. 244 (ca. 1510); Ringbom, 1965, p. 192 (probably influenced by Venetian half-length paintings); Friedländer, 1967-1976, 10:51, 82 (ca. 1509); Parshall, 1974, pp. 128-31 (close in date to *Potiphar's Wife Accusing Joseph*, but slightly later); Filedt Kok, 1978, p. 27 (ca. 1512); Vos, 1978a, p. 187 (ca. 1512); Renger, 1979, p. 58.

This small panel represented an episode from the *Historia Susannae*, chapter 13 of the book of Daniel in the Latin Vulgate. Susanna, the beautiful and devout wife of a wealthy Babylonian named Joachim, was the innocent victim of an attempted seduction. Two elders of the community, who were appointed judges, threatened to accuse her of infidelity if she repulsed their advances. Her unequivocal response helps to explain her popularity as an exemplar of chastity and marital fidelity during the Early Christian and medieval periods: "I will not do it. It is better to be at your mercy than to sin against the Lord" (verse 23). The next day the elders bore false witness against her before an assembly at Joachim's house, and she was condemned to death (compare Deut. 22:23-24).[2] Hearing her cry of despair, the Lord inspired the young Daniel to protest, and it is the scene of Daniel's intervention that Lucas represented (verses 45-49).

Lucas's painting showed Susanna about to be led off to execution by the gaily dressed young man seen from the back in the left foreground. Her hands are folded in an attitude of submission and modesty, and she faces her judge with downcast eyes. According to the biblical description, she was not condemned by a single judge but by the entire assembly of people gathered at Joachim's house. Lucas did show a small group of men in the right foreground who look at and gesture toward Susanna and her young defender, but he followed the pictorial rather than the written tradition by clearly designating a single judge. He is distinguished by his position just behind the balustrade and under the architectural decoration, as well as by his scroll and staff, probably intended to be symbols of authority and wisdom.[3] Daniel, whose name in

Hebrew means "God is my Judge," stands at the center of the composition. His lips are slightly parted, and his rhetorical gesture refutes the case against Susanna. A similar symbolic gesture is found in Lucas's *Potiphar's Wife Accusing Joseph* in Rotterdam (Fig. 4, Cat. 1). Here in *Susanna* the composition is more sophisticated, with several secondary figures whose pointed forefingers direct the eye toward Daniel. The man seen from the rear at the far right is a transitional device: like the almost identical young man at the left of the *Chess Players* in Berlin (Fig. 1, Cat. 34), he forms a bridge between the spectator and the painted scene and directs attention to the main action.

Daniel's right index finger touches the thumb of the left hand as the various points of his argument are enumerated. This gesture was frequently used in Italian Renaissance representations of scholastic debate or discussion. In northern art, it appears in one of Gerard David's *Justice* panels of 1498, *Cambyses Arresting the Judge Sisamnes*, while Dürer's *Christ among the Doctors* in Lugano is even closer to Lucas's work.[4] The paintings by Lucas and Dürer share the motif of "speaking hands" as their thematic and compositional focus, and both were executed in half length, although the figures of Lucas's panel were more loosely organized than those of Dürer's highly concentrated painting. It should be noted that Lucas could only have seen Dürer's work, which was painted in Venice in 1506, through the means of some now-lost intermediary. Half-length religious narratives were popular at the time, especially in Venice. One north Italian example, probably painted under the influence of Dürer's work, is Rocco Marconi's *Susanna before the Judge*.[5] It is like Lucas's *Susanna* in the more spacious grouping of half-length figures set before an architectural background, as well as in its highlighted gestures. Whether Lucas was aware of this trend in Italy and its relationship to early sixteenth-century German art is not known, but his early religious paintings seem closer to this tradition than to the half-length representations of the Infancy and Passion of Christ that were prevalent in the north in the fifteenth century. As Ringbom and Parshall have observed, the closest comparisons to the panels of *Potiphar's Wife* and *Susanna* are works from the north Italian tradition.[6] Considering the early date of Lucas's half-length compositions, it is more plausible that they developed independently of Italian works and as a result of his native gift for experimentation.

The panel has generally been dated sometime between 1509 and 1512. A comparison with Lucas's engravings of the period helps to fix a more exact date. His prints of 1509–1510 are executed in a clearly more youthful and inexperienced style than this painting. The architectural perspective of the 1509 *Round Passion* series (B.57–65) is abrupt and confused, the movements of the figures are awkward and unnatural, and the heads and limbs are curiously misshapen. The 1510 *Ecce Homo* engraving (B.71) also demonstrates Lucas's early interest in gesture as a means of unifying and enlivening a composition, but the specific gestures of the *Susanna* panel are closer in style and type to those in the *History of Joseph* (B.19–23), dated 1512. In this engraved series the *computat digitas,* rarely found in Netherlandish art, appears in three of the five prints (B.19, 22, 23). In addition, the format of *Susanna* closely approximates that of the *History of Joseph.* The narrative composition in breadth, with a focal scene in the right foreground balanced by a distant view at the left, is repeated in several of the 1512 engravings (B.19, 21, 23, with a variant in B.20). The architectural background of *Susanna* is also similar to that in the *History of Joseph.* The slim, articulated colonnettes and the Italianate relief sculpture on the pier are closer to *Joseph Interprets Pharaoh's Dreams* (B.23) than to the Gothic decoration in *Christ before Annas* of 1509 (B.59). In light of these comparisons, a date of 1512 for *Susanna before the Judge* seems reasonable.

Cat. C4. *Triumphal Entry of David into Jerusalem* (Figs. 41–42)

Location unknown, presumably lost; glass; circa 1510–1515.
Provenance: owned by Hendrick Goltzius, Haarlem, 1604.
Literature: Van Mander, 1604, fol. 214r (a glass painting representing the Israelite women dancing out to greet David; owned by Hendrick Goltzius);[1] Hymans, 1884, p. 147, n. 5; Floerke, 1906, p. 127, n. 67; Stechow, 1966, p. 36, n. 27; Van de Wall, 1969, p. 451, n. 27; Vos, 1978a, p. 145, n. 64; Vos, 1978c, pp. 503–4, n. 117.
Copies: (1) Painting, artist unknown (Fig. 41); Galleria della Biblioteca Ambrosiana, Milan, inv. no. 54; grisaille on glass, 23 x 17. *Prov.:* perhaps Coll. Hendrick Goltzius, Haarlem, 1604; Coll. Federico Borromeo, Milan, by 1625. *Lit.:* Blok, 1884a, p. 282, n. 1 (identified by Bredius as the original by Lucas); Stiassny, 1888, pp. 390–91; Dülberg, 1903–1908b, p. 25 (after the Saenredam print [Copy 10]); Dülberg, 1909, p. 10; Hirschmann, 1916, p. 41, n. 2; Von Frimmel, 1920–1921, p. 149 (not by Lucas, and not the painting mentioned by Van Mander); Wolter, 1926, p. 228 (after Saenredam's print [Copy 10]; not by Lucas, but probably the painting seen by Van Mander); Tea, 1932, p. 20 (copy after Lucas); Hoogewerff, 1936–1947, 3:314 (by Lucas, owned by Goltzius); Galbiati, 1951, p. 170 (attributed to Lucas); Gibson, 1970a, p. 86 (copy after Lucas); Vos, 1978c, pp. 503–4, n. 117 (not by Lucas; after Saenredam's print [Copy 10]; perhaps the work mentioned by Van Mander); Kloek and Filedt Kok, 1983, p. 20, n. 31 (copy after Saenredam's print [Copy 10]).
(2) Painting, artist unknown; Museo del Prado, inv. no. 2098; panel, 51 x 65.

Prov.: from the Royal Palace, Aranjuez, 1828. *Lit.*: De Madrazo, 1903, p. 237, no. 1416 (copy of Lucas); Von Frimmel, 1920-1921, pp. 149-50 (perhaps the painting owned by Rubens [see Copy 5]); Wolter, 1926, p. 228 (an enlargement by the copyist, after Saenredam's print [Copy 10]); Hoogewerff, 1936-1947, 3:318 (probably owned by Rubens).

(3) Painting, artist unknown; location unknown; panel, 35 x 46. *Prov.*: with S. Hartveld, Antwerp, 1935, no. 983; Coll. Brökmann, Lyon.

(4) Painting, artist unknown; location unknown; panel. *Prov.*: Coll. Emperor Rudolf II or Maximilian I, Prague, 1621 (a bad copy after Lucas).[2] *Lit.*: Zimerman, 1905, p. xxxix, no. 866; Vos, 1978c, p. 504, n. 118; Kloek and Filedt Kok, 1983, p. 20, n. 31 (cut on upper, lower, and left sides; copy after Saenredam's print [Copy 10]).

(5) Painting, artist unknown; location unknown; panel. *Prov.*: Coll. Peter Paul Rubens, Antwerp, sold 1641 (as Lucas).[3] *Lit.*: Rathgeber, 1844, col. 213, no. 702; Michiels, 1847, p. 128, no. 8;[4] Von Frimmel, 1920-1921, pp. 149-50 (perhaps the painting in the Prado [Copy 2], since many of the paintings owned by Rubens went to Spain); Wolter, 1926, pp. 228, 234 (not the painting in the Prado, since surely Rubens would have recognized a poor copy; probably the painting discovered by Wolter [Copy 7]); Hoogewerff, 1936-1947, 3:318 (probably the painting in the Prado); Stechow, 1966, p. 36, n. 27 (possibly the model for the glass painting in Milan [Copy 1]).

(6) Painting, artist unknown; location unknown; panel, 51.1 x 36.5; signed with monogram "L." *Prov.*: Coll. Eduard Arie, Vienna, 1921. *Lit.*: Von Frimmel, 1920-1921, pp. 149-53 (the original by Lucas after which Saenredam made the engraving [Copy 10]); Wolter, 1926, p. 228 (after the Saenredam print); Hoogewerff, 1936-1947, 3:317-18 (not by Lucas; after the Saenredam print).

(7) Painting, artist unknown; location unknown; tempera on canvas, 102 x 74. *Lit.*: Wolter, 1926 (the original by Lucas, ca. 1520-1527; owned by Rubens [see Cat. 5]); Hoogewerff, 1936-1947, 3:315-16 (Wolter's attribution far from convincing); Friedländer, 1963a, p. 71 (may be the original); Stechow, 1966, p. 36, n. 27 (a poor copy, in reverse, of the painting in Milan [Copy 1]).

(8) Painting, artist unknown; location unknown; panel, 29.5 x 34.5 (fragment). *Prov.*: Coll. C. J. Reijerse, The Hague, 1939. *Lit.*: Hoogewerff, 1936-1947, 3:316-17 (perhaps an original by Lucas; originally measured around 62 x 52).

(9) Drawing, artist unknown; Rugby School, Warwickshire (as eighteenth-century copy of the engraving by Saenredam [Copy 10]); red chalk on vellum, 26.8 x 36.7. *Prov.*: Coll. M. H. Bloxam.

(10) Engraving, by Jan Saenredam (Fig. 42); 25 x 19; inscribed at the bot-

tom "I. Saenredam sculp.," "N. de Clerck ex.," and "1600 L"; also with a two-line inscription in Latin relating the events of 1 Sam. 18:6. *Lit.*: Bartsch, 1803–1821, 3:253, no. 109; Rosenberg, 1877, p. 7; Evrard, 1884, p. 643, no. 275, and pp. 740–41, no. 440; Stiassny, 1888, pp. 390–91; Dülberg, 1909, p. 10; Von Frimmel, 1920–1921, pp. 149–53; Wolter, 1926, pp. 228–31; Buchelius, 1928, p. 89; Hoogewerff, 1936–1947, 3:314–15; Hollstein, 1949–1974, 10:242, no. 64; Kloek and Filedt Kok, 1983, p. 16.

(11) Engraving, published by Pieter Fierens, after Copy 10. *Lit.*: Hollstein, 1949–1974, 10:241, no. 32.

(12) Engraving, by P. van Serwouter, after Copy 10. *Lit.*: Hollstein, 1949–1974, 10:242, no. 65.

(13) Engraving, by P. Perret, after Copy 10. *Lit.*: Hollstein, 1949–1974, 10:242, no. 60.

(14) Engraving, by Johan Schmidt, after Copy 10. *Lit.*: Von Frimmel, 1920–1921, p. 151.

(15) Engraving, published by Petrus de Jode, in reverse of Copy 1. *Lit.*: Bartsch, 1803–1821, 3:253, no. 109; Hollstein, 1949–1974, 10:241, no. 32.

(16) Woodcut, by C. von Sichem, after Copy 10. *Lit.*: Hollstein, 1949–1974, 10:242, no. 66.

There are essentially two different variations among these numerous copies, all of which seem to derive from a lost work from Lucas's early period. The first is a vertical composition (Copies 1, 4–16; Figs. 41, 42). In the print by Jan Saenredam (Copy 10, Fig. 42) the figure of David, represented in profile at the right, holds his sword upright with the huge head of Goliath impaled on the end. He faces a group of Israelite women who are grouped before the city gate of Jerusalem singing and playing music in welcome (1 Sam. 18:6–7). According to the biblical account, Saul accompanied David on his entry into Jerusalem, but he is not included in any of these copies. Copies 1, 4–6, 9, 11–14, and 16 are identical, while Nos. 7, 8, and 15 show the scene in reverse.[5]

The second variant presents the narrative in a horizontal format (Copies 2–3). The figure of David and the group of Israelites are reproduced exactly as described above, but separated by a wider expanse. Three women with a small dog cavorting before them have been inserted in the middle background. Copy 2 is the same as the engraving by Saenredam, while Copy 3 reverses the composition. Whether this enlarged composition goes back to Lucas, or was a variation on the original by a later copyist, is impossible to determine. The three additional figures are in the style of Lucas, and the dog is of a type that appears in his *Calvary* (B.74). Why Copy 3 should be in reverse is puzzling, since there are no prints in this enlarged horizontal format.[6]

To judge from photographs, none of these versions of the *Triumph of David* composition can be considered an original by Lucas. Even the glass painting in Milan (Fig. 41), which most closely fits Van Mander's description, is executed in a hard, linear manner that suggests the work of a copyist. It is possible Van Mander saw this copy in Goltzius's collection and mistakenly identified it as a work by, rather than a copy after, the Leiden master. Wolter and Hoogewerff have convincingly argued, based on the use of left and right hands, that the original by Lucas must have had the figure of David at the left of the composition.

The original was dated circa 1520-1527 by Wolter and 1517-1519 by Hoogewerff, but the figure types and composition are more reminiscent of Lucas's early period. The high hillock in the foreground and the steep drop at the right with an abrupt transition into the background are similar to the landscape in the *Return of the Prodigal Son,* circa 1510 (B.78). The proportions of the figures are less elongated and the poses less stiff and angular than in this engraving, however, and the glass painting seems more akin to the prints of 1512-1514. The compact group of women at the left, enlivened by the positioning of the heads, is similar to a group in *Joseph Interprets His Dreams to Jacob,* 1512 (B.19). Extravagant feathered hats and grape-leaf wreaths are common features of Lucas's prints from 1510-1515 (for example, B.30, 37). The decorative slitting of the costumes is seen in his *Pyramus and Thisbe* of 1514 (B.135) and in certain woodcuts of 1513-1514 (for example, B.6, 8). The triumphal return of David was treated in an engraving by Lucas from 1513-1514 (B.26) and in a woodcut for a *Biblia Pauperum,* 1523-1528.[7] The figure types and costumes are similar, as is the head of Goliath, but the number of figures in the print was sharply reduced and the poses altered. Given these comparisons, the copies listed above must go back to an original painting on glass by Lucas dating from the period 1510-1515.

Cat. C5. *Fall of Man* (Fig. 44)

Location unknown; presumably lost; circa 1517-1520.

Copy: Drawing, by Jan de Bisschop (Fig. 44); location unknown; brush and wash, measurements unknown; signed "L" on rock at lower left. *Lit.:* J. G. Van Gelder, 1971, p. 214, fig. 44.

In this composition by Lucas, Adam is seated on a rock in the left foreground, with Eve on his knee. They look down at an apple in his right hand,

and Eve holds another in her lap. A third dangles from the jaws of the serpent in the large tree at the right.

The long torsos, relatively slender legs, and undeveloped arms point to a date around 1517–1520 for the original, which may have been a print or drawing rather than a painting. Like *The Virgin and Child in the Clouds* (Cat. C17), this work can be closely linked to Lucas's graphic style of the period: the nudes in two other representations by Lucas of the *Fall of Man,* a woodcut of circa 1517 (B.2) and an engraving of 1519 (B.8), are similar in figure type. The serpents are also comparable, as are the large trees with twisted, snakelike roots. The men in the silverpoint drawing *Two Nude Men on a Sphere* in the British Museum, circa 1516, are somewhat thinner counterparts of Adam.[1] The rounded face and sloping shoulders of Eve are closest to female types of Lucas's middle period, as in the engravings of *Christ Appearing to Mary Magdalene* (B.77) and the *Dance of Mary Magdalene* (B.122), both dated 1519. The greater breadth and monumentality of the figures in the *Virgin and Child with Angels* in Berlin, circa 1521 (fig. 11), are not yet evident in this drawn copy.

Cat. C6. *Judgment of Solomon* (Fig. 59)

Location unknown, presumably lost; circa 1526–1531.

Copies: (1) Painting, artist unknown; City of York Art Gallery, inv. no. 746; panel, rounded above, 58.4 x 41.2. *Prov.*: sale Coll. Golton, Berlin (Lepke), May 10, 1921, no. 87 (as Lucas); sale Singewald, Frankfurt (Bangel), October 11, 1927, no. 18 (as Antwerp Master, ca. 1520); sale Cologne (Lempertz), May 2, 1929, no. 5 with illus. (as Antwerp Master, ca. 1520); sale London (Sotheby), May 9, 1934, no. 138 (as Lucas), bought by F. D. Lycett Green; gift of Mr. Green to the Art Gallery, 1955. *Exh.*: Nottingham, Midland Counties Art Museum, 1881; York, City Art Gallery, 1955, no. 21 (as Dutch School or Antwerp Mannerist). *Lit.*: Van Regteren Altena, 1939, p. 227; York, City Art Gallery, 1961, pp. 77–78 (as Flemish School, early sixteenth century; perhaps an old copy after a lost painting by Lucas).

(2) Drawing, attributed to Aertgen van Leyden; Musée du Louvre, inv. no. 22.689; black chalk and pen and ink, 35.8 x 26.3. *Prov.*: sale E. Jabach, March 26, 1671; acquired by the museum in 1886. *Lit.*: Lugt, 1968, p. 33, no. 98, pl. 52 (by Aertgen); Gibson, 1970a, p. 88, n. 12.

(3) Drawing, artist unknown; location unknown; signed "L" at bottom center. *Prov.*: sale Winthrop Newman, New York (Anderson), February 2–3, 1920, no. 129. *Lit.*: D.I.A.L., 1968, 71I31.

(4) Drawing, attributed to Nicolaes de Bruyn or Jan de Bisschop (Fig. 59); in reverse of Copies 1-3; Albertina, inv. no. 7808; pen and ink, brush, and wash, in brown, 27.1 x. 21.4; signed "L" at lower left. *Prov.*:[1] Coll. Tonneman; Coll. M. Oudaan; Coll. J. van der Marck, 1773; Coll. C. Ploos van Amstel, 1800. *Lit.*: Benesch, 1928, p. 39, no. 407 (as Nicolaes de Bruyn, perhaps partially modeled on an earlier composition); Van Regteren Altena, 1939, p. 227; J. G. Van Gelder, 1957, p. 96, no. 11 (as Jan de Bisschop after Aertgen van Leyden); Lugt, 1968, p. 33 (preparatory drawing for an engraving, since the figures are left-handed); Gibson, 1970a, p. 85.

(5) Engraving, by C. Ploos van Amstel, after Copy 4; signed and dated "L.1515." *Lit.*: Van Regteren Altena, 1939, p. 227; Hollstein, 1949-1974, 10:242, no. 61; J. G. Van Gelder, 1957, p. 96; Lugt, 1968, p. 33 (engraved ca. 1780).

In this composition Solomon is seated in a large, canopied throne at the center of a symmetrically arranged interior. The two prostitutes are before him, one kneeling in supplication, and the disputed child lies on the steps of the throne (see 1 Kings 3:16-28). A soldier brings the sword requested by Solomon, and other spectators are grouped in the background.

Both the drawing in the Albertina and the engraving (Copies 4-5) are signed with Lucas's monogram, but Van Gelder suggested that these are after a lost painting by Lucas's contemporary Aertgen van Leyden rather than by Lucas himself.[2] Lugt attributed the rough sketch in the Louvre (Copy 2) to Aertgen, although he and Van Regteren Altena noted that this composition could not be the *Judgment of Solomon* mentioned by Van Mander as Aertgen's last work.[3] The drawing in the Albertina (Copy 4, Fig. 59) has a number of affinities with figure types and poses found in Lucas's late works. The man with the sword is reminiscent of the muscular, thick-legged soldier, also in the costume of a German *landsknecht,* who was originally on the exterior of Lucas's 1531 triptych in Leningrad (Fig. 39, Cat. 26). The cluster of men in the background and certain details of physiognomy and dress are repeated in the Leningrad painting and in *Moses after Striking the Rock* in Boston, dated 1527 (Fig. 24, Cat. 7). The profile head of the woman at the left, with its distinctive nose, heavy jawline, and elaborately coiled braids, is characteristic of Lucas's late period and is found again, for example, in the Boston painting and in several of Lucas's engraved *Virtues* (B.131, 132). Therefore the date of 1515 included in the engraving by Ploos van Amstel (Copy 5) must be incorrect.[4] The original composition, now lost, was probably painted by Lucas circa 1526-1531. The careful, detailed drawing in the Albertina provides a more exact stylistic indication of the original painting than either the sketch in the

Louvre or the rather rude painting in York (Copy 1). It is apparently in reverse, however, and was probably intended as a preparatory study for an engraving.[5]

Cat. 7. *Moses after Striking the Rock* (Figs. 24–25)

Museum of Fine Arts, Boston, inv. no. 54.1432; glue tempera on canvas, 183 x 228.5; signed "L" and dated 1527 on rock in central foreground.

Provenance: Coll. Borghese, Rome, probably since 1657;[1] Coll. Principessa de Piombino, Rome, 1891/2–1900;[2] with Julius Böhler, Munich, 1900; acquired in 1900 by the Germanisches Nationalmuseum, Nuremberg; on loan to Rijksmuseum, 1952; with Schaefer Gallery, New York, 1954; acquired by the museum on December 9, 1954.

Exhibitions: Rome, Galleria Borghese, 1928, no. 5; New York, Metropolitan Museum of Art, 1970, no. 18.

Literature: Scannelli da Forli, 1657, p. 142 (description of a painting in the Borghese collection that must be *Moses,* although its subject is not indicated; see note 1); Burckhardt, 1879, p. 616 (Bode correctly reassigned it from "School of Ferrara" to Lucas); Woltmann and Woermann, 1882, p. 533; Hymans, 1884, p. 151; Piancastelli, 1898 (describes fate of painting after death of D. Marcantonio Borghese in 1888); Dülberg, 1900b (first intensive analysis of the painting's style and history; suggests that it originally hung in the same room with the now-lost *Rebecca* canvas [Cat. 8]); Friedländer, 1900–1901; Bredius, 1901; Friedländer, 1901, p. 4; Dülberg, 1909, p. 15; Nuremberg, Germanischen Nationalmuseums, 1909, p. 28, no. 80; Beets, 1913, pp. 104–6, 128 (influence of Dürer, e.g. *Landscape with Cannon,* B.99; dates *Moses* before Lucas's trip, ca. 1527–28, with Gossaert); Kahn, 1918, pp. 113–14; Conway, 1921, p. 483; Baldass, 1923, pp. 20, 33 (reproduced in reverse, pl. 25); Winkler, 1924, p. 266; Burger, 1925, p. 156 (clear connection with Cornelis Engebrechtsz., especially his *Feeding of the Five Thousand,* formerly in Berlin [Fig. 68]);[3] Hoogewerff, 1928, pp. 119–20; Wescher, 1929, pp. 168–69; Dülberg, 1929, p. 169 (close to Dürer's *Landscape with Cannon,* B.99, and *Martyrdom of the Ten Thousand,* Vienna); Dülberg, 1933, pp. 12–13; Hoogewerff, 1936–1947, 3:304–6 (the painting described by Van Mander, fol. 213v [see Cat. 8], incorrectly interpreted as *Rebecca and Abraham's Servant*); Beets, 1940, p. 57; Beets, 1954, p. 446; D. P. A., 1955 (sold by Nuremberg to raise money for purchase of the Codex Aureus of Otto III); *Art News,* 1955; *Art Quarterly,* 1955; Leymarie, 1956, p. 50; Friedländer, 1963a, pp. 66, 69; Boon, 1964, col. 352; Della

Pergola, 1964, p. 224, no. 86 (listed in the 1693 inventory of the Borghese collection); Boston, Museum of Fine Arts, 1969, pp. 111-12 (incorrectly described as formerly in the Barberini Collection); Friedländer, 1969, p. 126; Von der Osten and Vey, 1969, p. 178 (self-portrait included);[4] Rathbone, 1970, p. 62; Friedländer, 1967-1976, 10:56, 82, no. 116; Silver, 1973 (following the text of Num. 20:1-13, the painting represents the sin of Moses and deals with key Reformation questions of faith and the Sacraments); Bangs, 1974a; Silver, 1974c; Bangs, 1975 (identifies Aaron as the figure to Moses's left; concludes the painting did not refer to Sacramentarian ideas); Silver, 1975; Gibson, 1977, p. 149 (influence on Cornelis Engebrechtsz.); Filedt Kok, 1978, pp. 6, 99-101 (perhaps the same painting described by Van Mander, fol. 213v, as *Rebecca* [see Cat. 8]; or a companion piece); Silver and Smith, 1978, p. 276; Vos, 1978a, p. 122; Vos, 1978c, p. 500, n. 97; Bosshard, 1982, pp. 33, 40; Gibson, 1986, pp. 44-45; Wolfthal, 1989, pp. 79-80, Cat. 77 (well preserved, with some repainting and abrasions and with darkened colors).

This painting depicts Moses and the Israelites shortly after the striking of the rock, as described in Exod. 17:1-7 and Num. 20:2-13. A crowd of men, women, and children fills the foreground, drinking and conversing in small groups and moving to and from the newly created spring with containers for water. In the far left background, the remainder of the Israelites approach with their camels. Moses, Aaron, and eight or nine elders (Exod. 17:5) are placed off-center to the right, behind the foreground figures (see Fig. 25). They are set apart by their stiff vertical stances, the tight clustering of the group, and the eye-catching diagonal of Moses's staff of authority. Moses is clearly recognizable by his central position, his staff, and his horns.

The identification of Aaron, Moses's brother and spokesman, is more problematic. Dülberg, Beets, and more recently Silver have seen him as the figure at Moses's right, dressed in rich brocade.[5] The figure standing on his left, however, matches the biblical description of Aaron as three years older than his brother (Exod. 7:7), and his costume more closely approximates that of the high priest described in Exodus 28. Most obvious is the depiction of the bells, although Lucas showed them across Aaron's chest rather than around the skirt of his mantle (Exod. 28:35). His sword is of a ceremonial rather than a military type because of its ornately decorated hilt and scabbard and should perhaps be considered the sacrificial sword of a priest.[6] A sword is also carried by the strikingly posed figure at the far right of the central panel in Lucas's *Dance around the Golden Calf* in Amsterdam (Fig. 32, Cat. 11) and by the figure behind Moses in Dirk Vellert's drawing of *Moses's Miracle at Mara*, dated 1523 and now in Hamburg.[7] Both of these men might also be identified as Aaron.

Moses after Striking the Rock is one of two extant paintings by Lucas that are signed and dated, the other being the *Virgin and Child with Mary Magdalene and a Donor* in Munich, from 1522 (Fig. 12, Cat. 14). The monogram and date on the *Moses* canvas are undoubtedly original; they correspond to the style of the letters and ciphers used in the 1527 engravings (B.106, 160–61, 165, 167) and in the Munich diptych. Only two other paintings by the master can be securely dated by early documentation, the 1526 *Last Judgment* in Leiden (Figs. 17–19, Cat. 20) and the 1531 *Christ Healing the Blind Man* in Leningrad (Fig. 35, Cat. 25), so this canvas is of considerable importance in the development of a chronological framework for Lucas's painted oeuvre.

Connections can be made between this dated work and the five engravings from 1527. The children in the left corner of the painting have the chubby, awkward proportions, small heads, thickset limbs, and elongated torsos of *Two Children Carrying a Helmet and a Flag* (B.165). The decorative detailing in the painting also has its counterpart in the engravings from the same year. Four of his five dated engravings of 1527 emphasize purely decorative patterns (B.160, 161, 165, 167), and a parallel can be seen between the stylized flowers and acanthus-leaf tendrils in B.160–61 and the curvilinear designs that embellish such forms in *Moses* as the water jugs, the headdress of the woman at the lower left, and the sword of Aaron.

Certain facial types and gestures in this painting also reappear in the engravings of 1527. The juxtaposition of two elderly men, one with a cropped beard and the other with a full-grown one, is found in *Sts. Peter and Paul Conversing* (B.106) as well as in the center background of *Moses*. The distinctive profile of Paul, with the tousled forelock, hooked nose, and long curling beard, is repeated several times in the painting, at the extreme left and again in the figure of Moses. Finally, the speaking gesture of Peter also appears twice in the painting. These comparisons provide useful insights into the relationship between Lucas's prints and paintings—often quite close in details, allowing for stylistic comparisons of this sort, but usually very different in their overall compositional approach.

Cat. 8. *Rebecca and Eliezer at the Well*

Location unknown, presumably lost; tempera on canvas.
Literature: Van Mander, 1604, fol. 213v; Evrard, 1884, p. 640, no. 269; Dülberg, 1900b, p. 163 (identical to *Moses after Striking the Rock,* Boston [Fig. 24, Cat. 7]); Dülberg, 1909, p. 15; Hoogewerff, 1936–1947, 3:306; Silver, 1973,

p. 407; Filedt Kok, 1978, pp. 6, 169, n. 133; Vos, 1978c, p. 500, nn. 94–97; Wolfthal, 1989, p. 17.

This painting is known only through the description by Van Mander: "There is also by Lucas a beautiful watercolor canvas in Leyden, at the house of a distinguished gentleman named Van Sonneveldt, or at the house of Mr. Knotter, being an exceptional lover of art and himself a painter.[1] This is also a very beautiful work, being the History of Rebecca and Abraham's servant, who received a drink from her at the fountain: here there are represented very pleasant little women or maidens, in various poses, drawing water and so forth: also with a beautiful landscape and nice grounds."[2]

This is one of several paintings by Lucas in this medium mentioned by Van Mander (see also Cats. 2 and 27), although none of the works described in *Het Schilder-Boeck* has survived. The only canvas extant, *Moses after Striking the Rock* in Boston (Fig. 24, Cat. 7), was in an Italian collection by the mid-seventeenth century and apparently was not known to Van Mander. Several scholars have suggested, however, that Van Mander did see or hear about the painting of *Moses* and mistakenly identified it as the story of Rebecca.[3] The representation of Eliezer's meeting with Rebecca (Gen. 24:11–27) must indeed have had certain similarities to the canvas in Boston. Van Mander's description suggests resemblances in composition, with many figures in a broad landscape, but it is unlikely that he would have confused the two scenes. There is no well in the Boston painting, and the figure of Moses is clearly designated by his horns and staff. The two works might have been pendants, or part of a series. If so, they would have been similar to the canvas series of the *History of Joseph,* mentioned by Van Mander and now lost (Cat. 2.)

Cat. C9. *Susanna in Her Bath* (Fig. 60)

Location unknown, presumably lost; circa 1526–1531.

Copy: Drawing, by Jan de Bisschop (Fig. 60); destroyed during World War II, formerly in the Kupferstichkabinett, Staatliche Museen Preussischer Kulturbesitz, Berlin-Dahlem, inv. no. 13181; brush and wash; triptych, with upper edges leveled off; center 36 x 29, each wing 36 x 12.9. *Lit.*: Bock and Rosenberg, 1930, 1:39 (copy after a lost triptych by Lucas from his late period); J. G. Van Gelder, 1957, pp. 92 (no. 1), 96, 98 (copy after a lost painting by Lucas); Parshall, 1974, pp. 141–43 (after an original by Lucas, ca. 1525–1527).

In this lost triptych Lucas returned to the *History of Susanna,* a theme that he had represented several times in his youth. In his engraving of circa 1508 (B.33) the emphasis was on the lecherous elders. The painting of *Susanna before the Judge* formerly in Bremen, circa 1512 (Fig. 6, Cat. 3), depicted Daniel's defense of the innocent young woman. Lucas's interest during his late period in the triptych format, or perhaps more properly speaking the interest of his patrons, provided the opportunity for a more extensive representation. Various episodes of the story are shown here in a single setting uniting the three panels. In the left wing the two elders hide behind a rock in the garden (Dan. 13:16). In the central panel the nude Susanna is bathing; she hands her keys to two maids and requests soap and olive oil (13:17). These same servants are represented again in the right wing, leaving the enclosed garden (13:18). The conclusion of the story, involving the judgment of Susanna and Daniel's defense, is depicted in an open hall in the distant background of the central panel (13:28–60). In the left foreground, a statue of Diana provides a mythological parallel to the biblical account. Diana's nudity here suggests the episode of Actaeon's glimpse of the bathing goddess, and the shield she holds aloft for protection against Cupid's arrows is indicative of her role as a personification of chastity.[1]

Susanna's body with its thickset torso is similar to other nudes from Lucas's late period, including those of the *Last Judgment* in Leiden, 1526 (Figs. 17–19, Cat. 20), the engraved *Venus and Cupid* dated 1528 (B.138), and the series of *Virtues* from 1530 (B.127–33). The relatively tall, slender servants, their elaborate headdress, and the active folds of their drapery resemble figures in the *Dance around the Golden Calf,* circa 1529–1530 (Fig. 32, Cat. 11), and the 1529 *History of Adam and Eve* (B.1–6). The rather feathery foliage of the trees in this triptych is also related to that in the 1529 series (for example, B.1, 3). Finally, the decoration of the fountain by Susanna's bath is similar to Lucas's ornamental prints of 1527–1528 (B.161–62, 164). The lost triptych must have been painted in Lucas's late period, around 1526–1531.

Cat. C10. *Meeting of David and Abigail* (Fig. 61)

Location unknown, presumably lost; circa 1528–1531.

Copy: Drawing, by Jan de Bisschop (Fig. 61); Kupferstichkabinet, Museum der bildenden Künste, Leipzig, inv. no. NI2978; brush and brown wash, 32.5 x 43.7;[1] signed "L" on a tablet in the center foreground and dated 1514. *Prov.:* Coll. G. Uilenbroek, 1741; Coll. B. Hagelis, 1762; Coll. J. van der Marck, 1773.

Lit.: J. G. Van Gelder, 1957, pp. 94 (no. 7), 96, 98 (copy by De Bisschop after a lost work by Lucas); Gibson, 1986, p. 48 (close in time to *Christ Healing the Blind Man* in Leningrad).[2]

The meeting of David and Abigail in the wilderness of Paran is represented by the artist in a mountainous landscape. David is shown on horseback in full armor at the center of the composition. He is accompanied by armed men on their way to punish the sheep farmer Nabal, who refused to provide them with food. At the left Nabal's wife, Abigail, kneels before the troops, begging for mercy. Behind her, servants bring gifts of food loaded on camels and asses. David gestures with his scepter toward Abigail as he accepts her offer of reconciliation (1 Sam. 25:1-35).

The drawing by De Bisschop is signed with Lucas's monogram, and Van Gelder is certainly correct in his assumption that it is a copy after a lost painting from Lucas's late period. There are a number of parallels with *Christ Healing the Blind Man* in Leningrad, originally dated 1531 (Fig. 35, Cat. 25). Both compositions are arranged around a centralized scene flanked by groups of onlookers, and in both cases the densely populated foreground is set against a wide, mountainous landscape. Large, multifigured compositions occur much earlier in Lucas's graphic oeuvre, but the 1517 *Calvary* (B.74) and the 1519 *Dance of Mary Magdalene* (B.122) are more diffuse and lack the classical symmetry of the very late paintings. Lucas balanced the figures carefully in the left and right foreground to set the lateral limits of the scene. This geometric design is typical of the *Dance around the Golden Calf* in Amsterdam (Fig. 32, Cat. 11), as well as the Leningrad painting. The date of 1514 lightly drawn at the bottom center of the *Meeting of David and Abigail* is undoubtedly false. The format is characteristic of Lucas's latest works, and the style of the individual figures, fully rounded and amply proportioned, also points to the years 1528-1531.

Cat. 11. *Dance around the Golden Calf* (Figs. 32-34)

Rijksmuseum, inv. no. A3841; panel, triptych; central panel 93 x 67, each wing 91 x 30; circa 1529-1530.

Provenance: private collection in the Calverstraat, Amsterdam, 1604;[1] Coll. Jasper Losschert, Amsterdam; Coll. Woiutiers, Amsterdam, 1671;[2] Coll. Jan Lossert, Amsterdam, 1675;[3] Coll. Jacob Wuytiers, Amsterdam, and bequeathed on April 14, 1679, to Dirck Wuytiers;[4] sale Jacob Cromhout and Jasper Loskart, Amsterdam, May 7-8, 1709, no. 25 (by Lucas), for 1,470 guilders;[5] sale

Marquis du Blaisel, Paris, March 16–17, 1870, no. 78 (by Lucas), bought by M. Sichel for 6,200 francs; Coll. Mme. Bigniez, Paris; acquired in June 1952.

Exhibitions: Amsterdam, Rijksmuseum, 1958, no. 137 (before 1525); Leiden, Stedelijk Museum, 1978, no. 10 (ca. 1530); Amsterdam, Rijksmuseum, 1986, 1:17–18, 2:149–51, no. 37 (ca. 1530, triptych for domestic use).

Literature: Van Mander, 1604, fol. 213v (ruined by dirty varnish);[6] Hoet, 1752–1770, 1:135, no. 25; Descamps, 1753, p. 45; Evrard, 1884, p. 642, no. 274; Moes, 1889, p. 150; Dülberg, 1909, p. 16; Bredius, 1913; Peltzer, 1925, p. 87; Beets, 1952b (ca. 1525); Beets, 1952a (ca. 1524–1525); *Verslagen,* 1952, pp. 12–14 (ca. 1527–1533); Van Schendel, 1953 (ca. 1527–1533); Beets, 1954, p. 446 (ca. 1524); Amsterdam, Rijksmuseum, 1956, pp. 117–18 (late work); Leymarie, 1956, p. 50 (ca. 1525); Müller-Hofstede, 1959, p. 230; Bille, 1961, 1:144; Friedländer, 1963a, p. 69, n. 37; Boon, 1964, col. 352; Meyer, 1964, p. 26; Reznicek-Buriks, 1965, pp. 242, 244 (ca. 1525); Von der Osten and Vey, 1969, p. 179; Wurfbain, 1971 (ca. 1530); Markx-Veldman, 1973, p. 116; Rostworowski, 1973, pp. 25–26; Van Asperen de Boer and Wheelock, 1973, p. 80; Friedländer, 1967–1976, 10:88, add. 179; Silver, 1973, pp. 407–9; Grosjean, 1974, p. 140; Bangs, 1974a; Silver, 1974, p. 310; Parshall, 1974, pp. 134–63 (ca. 1525); Amsterdam, Rijksmuseum, 1976a, p. 345; Freedberg, 1976, p. 35; Gibson, 1977, p. 149 (influence on Cornelis Engebrechtsz.'s *Feeding of the Five Thousand,* formerly in Berlin [Fig. 68]);[7] Kirschenbaum, 1977, pp. 71, 111 (influence on Jan Steen's painting of the same subject in Leiden); Filedt Kok, 1978, pp. 101–14, 117–18, 122–23, 126–27, 137 (ca. 1530; sketchy black chalk underdrawing, including color notations); Kloek, 1978, p. 441; Nikulin, 1978, pp. 306, 308 (ca. 1528); Silver and Smith, 1978, p. 276; Vos, 1978a, p. 499, nn. 92–93; Wurfbain, 1978, p. 210; Gibson, 1986, pp. 44–46.

The *Dance around the Golden Calf* is a small triptych, with imitation red and green marble painted on the exterior of the wings. On the interior, a scene from the book of Exodus representing the folly and idolatry of the Israelites stretches across all three panels. During their flight from Egypt, Moses and his followers made camp in the wilderness at the foot of Mount Sinai (Exod. 19:1–2): their tents and makeshift shelters are shown by Lucas in the middle distance. The main event of the biblical narrative (verse 32) is the idolatry of the golden calf made by Aaron with the help of the Israelites, who had lost patience before Moses's descent from the mountain (32:1–5). In Lucas's representation, however, the idolatrous dance is relegated to the middle distance, and the feast to the Lord declared by Aaron (32:5–6) is shown in the foreground. Although the sacrifices and peace offerings mentioned in the biblical passage are not included in the painting, the description of the Israelites who "sat down to eat and drink, and rose up to play" can be considered the main inspiration for Lucas's work. In the far background of the center panel, Moses is receiving the tablets of the Law, shrouded in a cloud representing the glory of the Lord (Exod. 24:15-18). As he descends from Mount Sinai with his servant Joshua, he witnesses the betrayal of his people and in his anger lifts the tablets to shatter them (32:15-19).

Since its rediscovery in 1952, the triptych has been consistently placed among Lucas's works from the 1520s. In the first important article devoted to the painting, Beets mentioned its similarities to the 1531 *Christ Healing the Blind Man* in Leningrad (Fig. 35, Cat. 25), although he proposed a much earlier date of 1524 1525. Van Schendel suggested that the triptych was painted during Lucas's last years (1527-1533) based on parallels with other late works. Recently Wurfbain, Filedt Kok, and Vos have agreed on a date of circa 1530, but a comprehensive comparative analysis has yet to be published.[8]

A close inspection of Lucas's late prints confirms that the triptych must have been painted around 1529-1530. The inflated figures, with their easy movements and startlingly lifelike action, have little in common with the cramped, overly complex poses in engravings such as the *Murder of Abel* (B.13) or *Lamech and Cain* (B.14), both from 1524. Although the curious drooping head and curved body of the man at the right of the central panel might be compared to Lamech in B.14, the figure has a much looser, more emphatic and space-consuming aspect that is closer to that of figures in the *Murder of Abel* from 1529 (B.5). The anatomy of the bodies in the *Dance* is more accurate than that typical of the prints from 1524-1525. The abrupt twist of neck and wrist and the physical anomalies of the earlier *Murder of Abel* (B.13) and the 1525 *Virgil Suspended in a Basket* (B.136) are replaced here by greater naturalism. In this respect certain figures in the triptych also closely approximate Lucas's late drawing style, a similarity especially evident in the breadth of form found in the British Museum *Virgin and Child* (Fig. 30) and the Hamburg *Adam and Eve*.[9]

The foreground structure of the *Dance*, which links the three panels of the triptych and introduces the viewer to the range of figures and landscape beyond, is similar to that of *Christ Healing the Blind Man*. The landscape settings of the two works are also remarkably close. The trees, rocks, and small-scale figures in the middle distance act as an intermediary between the dominant foreground crowd and the dramatic background of blue mountains. The children cavorting in the foreground of the *Dance* and *Moses after Striking the Rock* in Boston, dated 1527 (Fig. 24, Cat. 7), are strikingly similar in type and placement. Although comparisons are limited by the condition of the paintings and the different media involved, the color range of the Amsterdam triptych seems to be closely linked to that of the late paintings. Red, orange, and yellow play across the surface of these works, highlighted with whites and steadied by deeper tones. The aqueous blue-greens of the *Dance* seem closer to those spotted throughout *Moses after Striking the Rock,* while *Christ Healing the Blind Man* employs a more somber range of grays, blacks, and dark greens.

Details of costume can help to date the *Dance* triptych. The gypsy headdress of the women appears in both *Moses after Striking the Rock* and *Christ Healing the Blind Man.* The feathered berets, intricately tied turbans, and cone-shaped hats worn by the men are also typical of Lucas's late paintings. In addition, the complicated loops and braids of hair, often interwoven with ribbons, are characteristic of Lucas's engravings from 1529–1530 (for example B.131–32). The *Dance around the Golden Calf* should be dated to these years because of its similarity to the prints of this period and to the paintings in Boston and Leningrad.

New Testament Paintings

🙵 Cat. 12. *Virgin and Child with Angels* (Fig. 11)

Staatliche Museen Preussischer Kulturbesitz, Berlin-Dahlem, inv. no. 584B; panel, 77.5 x 46, rounded above; circa 1521.

Provenance: Coll. Posonyi, Vienna;[1] sale A. Hulot, Paris (Galerie Georges Petit), May 9-10, 1892, no. 65 (as Michael Wohlgemuth), bought by the museum.

Exhibitions: Washington, National Gallery, 1948, no. 106; Amsterdam, Rijksmuseum, 1950, no. 65 (youth at left possibly a donor); Schaffhausen, 1951, no. 45 (ca. 1515); Amsterdam, Rijksmuseum, 1958, no. 132 (influence of Dürer on the foreground angels).

Literature: Bode, 1895, p. 118 (young donor at the side probably a self-portrait); Von Frimmel, 1898, p. 65, and 1899, p. 64; Riegel, 1900, p. 110 (according to an old note on the back the man at the left is a self-portrait; striking similarity to the Braunschweig *Portrait* [Fig. 14, Cat. 32]); Bredius, 1901; Berlin, Kaiser Friedrich-Museum, 1906, p. 201 (ca. 1515); Von Frimmel, 1907, p. 40; Dülberg, 1909, pp. 13-14 (ca. 1520; the lute-playing angel derives from Giovanni Bellini); Heidrich, 1910, p. 53; Beets, 1913, pp. 89-90 (ca. 1520-1523); Conway, 1921, pp. 480-81 (probably painted in Antwerp in 1522; influence of Dürer); Friedländer, 1922, p. 131; Baldass, 1923, pp. 22-23, 31 (ca. 1515); Burger, 1925, p. 154 (putti similar to works by Jacob Cornelisz.; Virgin close to prints by Dürer); Sjöblom, 1928, p. 165; Dülberg, 1933, p. 9; Hoogewerff, 1936-1947, 3:279-81 (1522-1525; Italianate putti and architectural details); Knuttel, 1938, p. 130; Beets, 1940, p. 55 (ca. 1520); Toth, 1943, p. 76; Leymarie, 1956, p. 49; Wegner, 1959, p. 8 (influence of Dürer); Friedländer, 1963a, pp. 60-61, 68 (ca. 1519-1520; brocade behind Virgin is similar to the decoration in the engraving of *Emperor Maximilian,* 1520, B.172; Virgin reminiscent of *Christ Appearing to Mary Magdalene,* 1519, B.77); Reznicek-Buriks, 1965, p. 244 (ca. 1520); Friedländer, 1969, p. 125; Friedländer, 1967–1976, 10:54, 83, no. 127 (ca. 1517–1518); Berlin, Staatliche Museen, 1978, p. 230 (ca. 1520); Filedt Kok, 1978, pp. 42–45, 55, 121, 125 (ca. 1520; the thin, closely placed brush lines of the underdrawing are close to the *Card Players,* Wilton House [Fig. 9, Cat. 38], although even finer and more regular); Vos, 1978a, pp. 141, 145, n. 55, 188 (ca. 1520); Vos, 1978c, pp. 500–501, n. 102.

In this composition the Virgin and Child are seated in an elaborate columned hall. The curvilinear embroidery on the tapestry behind them repeats the ornate foliate decoration on the architecture and provides a brilliant foil for the glowing red robe and golden halo of the Virgin. The heavy grape-leaf garland overhead accentuates the strict symmetry of the setting. On a green ledge in the foreground is an apple or pear that, along with the fruit held by the Christ Child, represents the salvation of humanity through the "new Adam."[2] Lucas also included a bunch of grapes symbolizing Christ's blood, the wine of the Eucharist. The grapevine above has a similar meaning derived from Christ's words: "I am the true vine, and my Father is the husbandman" (John 15:1; see also verse 5).

In front of the balustrade are three youthful angels whose figures are cut off by the lower edge of the frame, giving the illusion that they occupy part of the spectator's space. One tunes a lute while his companion plays a flute, and the third reaches back to hand the Christ Child a carnation, signifying divine love.[3] Just behind the ledge to the right two children sing from a sheet of music, while at the far left a young boy looks on. He has been called a self-portrait of the artist, presumably by virtue of his resemblance to the so-called *Self-Portrait* in Braunschweig (Fig. 14, Cat. 32). In 1895, Bode suggested that this youth should be identified as the donor, and his pose, contemporary dress, and hairstyle certainly distinguish him from other figures in the painting.[4] In expression and placement, he is remarkably similar to the worshiping boy or youthful angel in Lucas's engraving of the *Virgin and Child* dated 1523 (B.84). His immaturity makes it unlikely that he commissioned the painting himself, although he could be a young relation of the donor.

Comparison with other works by Lucas points to a date around 1521 for the *Virgin and Child with Angels.* In style and paint technique the panel stands between the *Card Players* in Wilton House, circa 1517 (Fig. 9, Cat. 38), and the *Virgin and Child with Mary Magdalene and a Donor* in Munich, dated 1522 (Fig. 12, Cat. 14). The full forms and the delicacy and polish of the surface paint on the flesh areas indicate that it should be dated closer to the 1522 panel. The facial features of the Virgin in Berlin closely resemble those of the Magdalene in the Munich diptych.[5] The similarity in the highlighting around the eyes of these two figures is especially noteworthy.

The architectural ornamentation in the Berlin *Virgin and Child* is closest to that in works from 1519-1522. The grapevine tendrils that decorate the pot in the engraving *Christ Appearing to Mary Magdalene,* 1519 (B.77), reappear on columns, capitals, and pots in the later painting. The same motif is found on the tapestry hanging behind the Virgin, combined with a stylized fruit form as on the embroidered cloth in the engraving of *Emperor Maximilian,* 1520 (B.172). In both works, Lucas used a vine encircling the top of the column as a sort of secondary capital. The relief carvings on the throne and balustrade in the Munich painting lend a similar sense of sculptural richness to the environs.[6]

This painting has been assigned a range of dates from 1515 to 1525, with the majority of scholars in agreement on circa 1520.[7] It is stylistically close to the painting in Munich, although less convincing in its spatial relationships. Lucas's interest in this traditional theme may have been renewed by contact with Jacob Cornelisz.'s painting of the same subject, which was in Leiden in 1521.[8] More important, perhaps, he surely had the opportunity during his trip south in 1521 to study other representations of the *Virgin and Child with Musical Angels,* including paintings of the Flemish school and the prints and drawings of Dürer. It seems likely that the panel was painted in the brief period between Lucas's trip to Antwerp and his commencement of the Munich diptych in 1522.

Cat. C13. *Virgin and Child with Joseph, Anne, and Two Male Saints* (Fig. 45)

Location unknown, presumably lost; circa 1521.

Copies: (1) Drawing, artist unknown (Fig. 45); Cabinet des Dessins, Musée du Louvre, inv. no. 22686; pen and ink, with wash, 21.3 x 22.6. *Prov.:* bought from E. Jabach, March 29, 1671. *Lit:* Lugt, 1968, p. 32, no. 91 (very close in manner to Lucas).

(2) Engraving, published by H. Cock; inscribed at left "L INVENTOR" and at right "H. COCK EXUDE." *Lit:* Hollstein, 1949-1974, 10:240, no. 27 (engraving after Lucas); Lavalleye, 1967, nos. 185-86 (by Lucas, 1530).

The Virgin and Child are seated in an open portico beside St. Anne, while Joseph leans over the low balustrade to hand a piece of fruit to Jesus. In the left and right foreground are two elderly men in sixteenth-century costume, whom Lugt has tentatively identified as Zacharias, husband of Elizabeth and father of John the Baptist, and Joachim, husband of Anne.[1]

The labored regularity of the hatching and the precision of the technique suggest that Lucas was not the artist of the sketch in the Louvre (Copy 1, Fig. 45). This is most apparent when the work is compared to the lively, varied drawing style of his *Portrait of Maximilian* in the Fondation Custodia, Paris, circa 1520.[2] The figure style is so close to Lucas's middle period, however, that the drawing can be considered a copy after a lost work. The proportions are fuller and the poses more assured than those found in the *Virgin and Child with St. Anne* engraving of 1516 (B.79), but the heavy, rounded forms of the 1523 *Virgin and Child* (B.84) have not yet evolved. The facial characteristics, the awkwardly proportioned and foreshortened arms, and details of the architecture correspond to *Esther before Ahasuerus* of 1518 (B.31) and the Berlin *Virgin and Child with Angels,* circa 1521 (Fig. 11, Cat. 12). The face and short beard of Joseph are repeated in several *Small Passion* engravings of 1521 (for example, B.44–45). The original by Lucas probably dates from the period immediately following his return from Antwerp in 1521.

The second copy, engraved in the same direction as the drawing, was published by Hieronymus Cock of Antwerp. Although the composition is trimmed at the bottom, it shows more of the architecture on the other three sides. Its dimensions (23 x 24.6) are slightly larger than those of the drawing. Only minor changes were made, for example in the turn of Christ's head, the addition of halos for the Virgin and Child, and the decoration of the floor.

Cat. 14. *Virgin and Child with Mary Magdalene and a Donor* (Fig. 12)

Alte Pinakothek, Munich, inv. no. 742; panel, originally a diptych and now joined; 50.5 x 67.8; signed "L" and dated 1522 on the balustrade, inscribed "M" on the pin on Mary Magdalene's bodice.[1]

Cat. 15. *Annunciation* (Fig. 13)

Alte Pinakothek, Munich, inv. no. 7713; panel, originally the reverse of the right wing of Cat. 14; 42.2 x 29.2, trapezoidal above; inscribed on the banderole "AVE GRATIA PLENA DOMI[NUS] TEC[UM]" and on the vase of lilies "M" and "A."

Provenance: Coll. Frans Hooghstraet, outskirts of Leiden, sometime before 1604;[2] Coll. Emperor Rudolf II, Prague, 1604, Coll. Duke Maximilian I of Bavaria, Kammergalerie, Munich, from 1627/28 until his death in 1651;[3] in the storehouse of the Residenz, Munich, 1729; Castle, Schleissheim, 1770, 1775;[4] Hofgartengalerie, Munich, 1781–ca. 1800; Castle, Schleissheim, ca. 1800, 1836;[5] acquired by museum in 1836.

Exhibitions: Rome, Galleria Borghese, 1928, no. 4 (only the *Virgin and Child* panel exhibited); Amsterdam, Rijksmuseum, 1948, nos. 77–78; Amsterdam, Rijksmuseum, 1958, no. 134 (only the *Annunciation* exhibited); Leiden, Stedelijk Museum, 1978, nos. 6–7.

Literature: Van Mander, 1604, fol. 213v;[6] Bullart, 1682, p. 398 (mistakenly described the date as XXII, indicating Lucas painted it when he was twenty-two years old);[7] Le Comte, 1702, p. 321 (signed "L 22," so painted at the age of twenty-two); D'Argenville, 1745, p. 51; Descamps, 1753, p. 45 (made for F. Hoogstraeten); Van Dillis, 1839, p. 193, no. 151; Rathgeber, 1844, cols. 168, 215, nos. 742–43; Michiels, 1847, pp. 129 (no. 14), 130 (nos. 26–27); Munich, Alte Pinakothek, 1859, p. 178, no. 151 (gives incorrect date of 1552; notes that the praying man has been identified as a self-portrait); Kramm, 1860, 4:972 (as *Virgin and Child with St. Christina and St. James the Less*); Waagen, 1860, p. 118; Blanc, 1861, p. 12; Waagen, 1862, p. 152; Förster, 1867, pp. 67–68 (with engraved copy of the *Annunciation* by H. Walde); Marggraff, 1872, pp. 156–57, no. 743; Rosenberg, 1877, p. 8; Taurel, 1881, p. 21; Woltmann and Woermann, 1882, p. 533; Evrard, 1884, pp. 646 (no. 282), 650 (no. 294), 651 (no. 295); Munich, Alte Pinakothek, 1884, p. 37, nos. 148–49; Von Wurzbach, 1885, p. 56; Von Reber, 1892, pp. 25, 42; Dülberg, 1909, p. 14; Beets, 1913, pp. 90–92 (intended for a domestic chapel); Conway, 1921, p. 480 (painted in Antwerp; the donor and his wife dressed as Joseph and Mary Magdalene); Baldass, 1923, pp. 23–24, 31–32; Winkler, 1924, p. 264; Burger, 1925, p. 155; Hoogewerff, 1928, p. 118; Dülberg, 1929, p. 168; Munich, Alte Pinakothek, 1936, pp. 131–32; Hoogewerff, 1936–1947, 3:281–83; Baldass, 1937a, p. 206; Beets, 1940, pp. 55–56; Hirsch, 1948, pp. 130, 132; Leymarie, 1956, p. 49 (painted for the private chapel of a castle; influence of Gossaert); Wegner, 1959, p. 8 (influence of Dürer); Bruyn, 1961, p. 113; Friedländer, 1963a, pp. 60–61; Boon, 1964, col. 352 (traces of Dürer's influence remain); Reznicek-Buriks, 1965, pp. 243–44; Grohn, 1967, pp. 133–34; Friedländer, 1969, p. 126; Von der Osten and Vey, 1969, p. 177 (still shows Dürer's influence); Friedländer, 1967–1976, 10:54, 81–82, no. 114; E. De Jongh, 1974, pp. 166–67; Filedt Kok et al., 1975 (full discussion of the material history and reconstruction of the diptych); Filedt Kok, 1978, pp. 45–56,

118, 121, 123 (underdrawing of the *Virgin and Child* with thin brush and black paint is quite different from the sketchy black-chalk underdrawing of the *Annunciation;* also a broader, livelier paint technique in the *Annunciation*); Vos, 1978a, pp. 81–87, 188; Vos, 1978c, pp. 472–73, 497–98, nn. 82–89; Bangs, 1980, p. 93.

In the *Virgin and Child with Mary Magdalene and a Donor* (Fig. 12) the Virgin, shown in three-quarter length, is seated at the left on an ornately decorated throne.[8] On her lap is the Christ Child, who holds a bunch of grapes symbolizing the wine of the Eucharist (Matt. 26:28–29; see also John 15:1). At the right, Mary Magdalene stands beside a stone balustrade. She is identified by the luxurious dress appropriate to her early wealth and nobility, by the initial *M* on her pin, and by her most familiar attribute, the alabaster box containing the ointment she used to anoint the feet of Christ (Luke 7:37–38). With her right hand she intercedes on behalf of the donor, a middle-aged man kneeling in prayer whom Van Mander mistakenly described as a woman.[9] Filedt Kok has shown that the lilies and carpenter's tools in the arms of the donor were a later addition, thus transforming the portrait into a figure of St. Joseph. His costume has also been overpainted in order to approximate more closely the dress of the saint.[10]

The panel of the *Annunciation* (Fig. 13) shows Mary turning to witness the arrival of Gabriel as she kneels at the prie-dieu in her bedroom. The Archangel's scepter is outstretched, and intertwined with it is a curling scroll on which appear his words "AVE GRATIA PLENA DOMINUS TECUM" (hail, you who are full of grace, the Lord is with you; Luke 1:28). His hair and drapery are swept back, and one long end of his red cloak is held aloft by a cherub who gazes at the heavenly light above. The momentum of his entrance appears to have scattered a number of grape leaves on the floor. Even as the bunch of grapes signifies Christ, the grapevine represents Mary. This is an idea expressed, for example, by the thirteenth-century Dutch poet Jacob van Maerlant: "You are the vineyard, the grape your child."[11] The lilies in the right foreground, symbolizing the purity of the Virgin, are arranged in a vase apparently marked with her name. The letters *M* and *A* appear as decoration on the half visible to the spectator.[12]

These two panels were painted by Lucas as a diptych but have undergone many alterations. The two interior wings, once curved at the top, are now united by fillers to form the rectangular panel of the *Virgin and Child with Mary Magdalene and a Donor.* The join is still clearly visible just to the left of the donor's hands and continuing up by the saint's right elbow. The *Annunciation* was on the reverse of the right wing.[13] The joining of the two wings must have taken place sometime between 1604, when Van Mander described the work as a "closing diptych" (*sluytende kasken*), and 1627, when it appeared in the inventory of Duke Maximilian as one panel with the appropriate measurements.[14] It is not certain whether this was done while it was in the collection of Rudolf II in Prague, or later when it was in Munich, but a likely suggestion is that it was one of a number of works known to have been altered or overpainted by an artist in the court of Maximilian.[15] The figure of the donor was also probably transformed into St. Joseph at this time, and the horizontal strip added to the top to heighten the composition by approximately one third of its original size. A large portion of the upper part of the panel was overpainted to hide the transition between the original composition and the upper strip. The pillar behind the Magdalene was added as a support for the seventeenth-century arcade, and the filler segments in the spandrels of the original arches were painted with a continuation of the mountains at the right, the sky in the middle, and the baldachin and garland at the left. Until 1874 the *Annunciation* was intact on the reverse, but in that year it was sawn off so that the *Virgin and Child* panel could be strengthened with a solid backing. In 1911 the strip at the top was removed (and apparently discarded), and the original condition was approximated by covering the fillers in the upper center and corners with an arched frame.[16] Today the work is exhibited without the frame so that the additions are readily visible, and the *Annunciation* is hung alongside.

The extremely fine, detailed brushwork of the interior contrasts dramatically with the broader, thicker application of paint on the exterior *Annunciation*. Filedt Kok has shown that the style and technique of the underdrawing also vary considerably.[17] The controlled brush lines of the *Virgin and Child with Mary Magdalene* are quite different from the sketchy, summary notations in chalk on the exterior.

Cat. C16. *Christ as Man of Sorrows and Virgin of Sorrows* (Fig. 47)

Location unknown, presumably lost; 1522.

Copies: (1) Paintings, artist unknown; Walker Art Gallery, Liverpool, inv. nos. 1184–85; panel, 32 x 25.3 (*Christ*), 26.6 x 21.2 (*Virgin*). *Prov.*: acquired by the Liverpool Royal Institution between 1859 and 1893; presented to the gallery in 1948. *Lit.*: Liverpool, Walker Art Gallery, 1963, p. 100 (after Lucas;

the type is associated with Albrecht Bouts; the panel of the *Virgin* has been cut down, and is slightly inferior in quality).

(2) Paintings, artist unknown; Rijksmuseum, inv. nos. A1483-84; panel, 26.5 x 21.5 each; *Christ* signed and dated "AD 1511." *Prov.*: sale Amsterdam, December 4, 1888, no. 25 (as Albrecht Dürer). *Lit.*: Amsterdam, Rijksmuseum, 1976a, p. 685.

(3) Paintings, artist unknown; Musée de Dijon, Coll. Chamblanc; panel, 26 x 21 each. *Lit.*: Liverpool, Walker Art Gallery, 1963, p. 100.

(4) Paintings, artist unknown; location unknown; panel, 31.4 x 25.1 each. *Prov.*: Coll. Frank L. Babbott, Brooklyn, 1924-1933.[1] *Exh.*: London, Arcade Gallery, November 1961 (as Lucas). *Lit.*: Friedländer, 1924, p. 42; Liverpool, Walker Art Gallery, 1963, p. 100.

(5) Paintings, artist unknown; location unknown; panel, 29.5 x 23 each. *Prov.*: sale Coll. Roger Erhardt, Paris, February 16, 1939 (attributed to Lucas); sale Paris (Galliera), June 13, 1963, nos. 12-13. *Lit.*: Liverpool, Walker Art Gallery, 1963, p. 100.

(6) Paintings, artist unknown; location unknown; panel, 32 x 25 each. *Prov.*: with Xaver Scheidwimmer, Munich. *Lit.*: *Die Weltkunst* 33 (October 10, 1963): 13, no. 19a (workshop of Lucas).

(7) Paintings, artist unknown; location unknown; panel, 31.7 x 24.8 each. *Prov.*: with Spink & Son, London, 1923.

(8) Paintings, artist unknown; location unknown; panel, 28.5 x 18.5 each. *Prov.*: Coll. Hacker, Munich, 1907; Coll. Manos, Munich, 1912; sale Wetzler, Paris, November 30, 1956. *Lit.*: Liverpool, Walker Art Gallery, 1963, p. 100.

(9) Paintings, artist unknown; location unknown; panel, 26.4 x 20 each. *Prov.*: sale Corstius, Geneva, October 27, 1934. *Lit.*: Liverpool, Walker Art Gallery, 1963, p. 100.[2]

(10) Paintings, artist unknown; location unknown; panel, tondo, 28.6 diameter. *Prov.*: probably from the Liesborn monastery, Westphalia; Caldenhof Gallery, Westphalia; sale Berlin (Lepke), June 8, 1929, nos. 19-20 (in the manner of Lucas). *Exh.*: Münster, 1879, no. 1461 (as parts of an altarpiece). *Lit.*: Liverpool, Walker Art Gallery, 1963, p. 100.

(11) Paintings, artist unknown; location unknown; panel, tondo, 27.3 diameter (*Christ*), 26.97 diameter (*Virgin*). *Prov.*: Coll. Earl of Wemyss, Amisfield, 1771 (nos. 154-55); Gosford House, East Lothian, Scotland (nos. 201-2, as Flemish School after Lucas).

(12) Painting, of the *Virgin* only, artist unknown; Coll. Mr. and Mrs. George J. Nelson, New York, 1975; panel. *Lit.*: Friedländer, 1924, p. 42 (appears to be by Lucas).

(13) Painting, of the *Virgin* only, artist unknown; private collection on the

Tarn River, southern France; panel, 50 x 42. *Lit.*: Liverpool, Walker Art Gallery, 1963, p. 100.

(14) Painting, of the *Virgin* only, artist unknown; location unknown; panel 29.2 x 21. *Prov.*: sale Wagner, London (Christie), January 16, 192?. *Lit.*: Liverpool, Walker Art Gallery, 1963, p. 100.

(15) Painting, of the *Virgin* only, artist unknown; location unknown; panel, 25 x 22. *Prov.*: Coll. Adolf Wollenberg, Berlin, 1925-1932; sale Wollenberg, Berlin (Lepke), March 17, 1932, no. 187 (workshop of Lucas). *Exh.*: Berlin, Kaiser Friedrich-Museum, 1925, no. 214. *Lit.*: Liverpool, Walker Art Gallery, 1963, p. 100.

(16) Painting, of the *Virgin* only, artist unknown; location unknown; panel, 26 x 21.6. *Prov.*: sale Schaefer, New York, 1940. *Lit.*: Liverpool, Walker Art Gallery, 1963, p. 100.

(17) Painting, of *Christ* only, artist unknown; Rijksmuseum Het Catharijneconvent, Utrecht, inv. no. 514; panel, 28.5 x 22.5; signed "L.C." on balustrade. *Prov.*: gift of G. W. van Heukelum. *Lit.*: Benesch, 1970, p. 282, n. 14; Utrecht, Centraal Museum, 1933, p. 248 (as unknown German master; signature added later).

(18) Painting, of *Christ* only, artist unknown; with De Boer, Amsterdam, 1963; panel, 28.2 x 24.2. *Lit.*: Liverpool, Walker Art Gallery, 1963, p. 100.

(19) Painting, of *Christ* only, artist unknown; location unknown. *Exh.*: Leipzig, 1929, no. 82. *Lit.*: Liverpool, Walker Art Gallery, 1963, p. 100.

(20) Etching, attributed to Simon Frisius (Fig. 47); 13 x 18.4; signed and dated at upper right "L 1522." *Lit.*: Nagler, 1845, 4:247, no. 20 (in the manner of Lucas); Passavant, 1860, 3:6-7, no. 175 (by Lucas); Volbehr, 1888, p. 23, no. 81; Friedländer, 1924, p. 42; Hollstein, 1949-1974, 7:35, no. 194 (by Frisius after Lucas), 10:241, no. 34; Amsterdam, Rijksprentenkabinet, 1978, p. 106, n. 176 (attributed to Frisius; probably copied after a lost diptych by Lucas).

(21) Engraving, artist unknown, with an architectural background; 7.8 x 11.2. *Lit.*: Nagler, 1845, 4:247; Passavant, 1860, 3:7, no. 176 (by Lucas); Hollstein, 1949-1974, 10:243, no. 79.

(22) Engraving, artist unknown, with the figures in two medallions; 9.7 x 15.1. *Lit.*: Bartsch, 1803-1821, 7:436-37, no. 2 (in the manner of Lucas); Volbehr, 1888, p. 47, no. 176; Hollstein, 1949-1974, 10:242, no. 77.

(23) Engraving, of the *Virgin* only, artist unknown; 24.7 x 19; signed "L." *Lit.*: Hollstein, 1949-1974, 10:242, no. 78.

(24) Woodcut, of the *Virgin* only, artist unknown. *Lit.*: Lavalleye, 1967, no. 223 (by Lucas, 1519); Amsterdam, Rijksprentenkabinet, 1978, pp. 100-101, 103, 106, n. 176 (copied perhaps after a lost diptych by Lucas, ca. 1520).

These variants of the half-length Man of Sorrows and mourning Virgin probably all go back to a lost devotional diptych by Lucas.[3] There are numerous Flemish diptychs of this subject from the late fifteenth and early sixteenth centuries, and Lucas could well have seen one or more of these during his trip south in 1521.[4] The date of 1522 on the etching (Copy 20, Fig. 47) is appropriate in light of stylistic criteria. The figure types, with their full, rounded torsos and somewhat ill-proportioned arms, are comparable to the Munich *Virgin and Child with Mary Magdalene and a Donor* of the same date (Fig. 12, Cat. 14). The oval face of the Virgin, the long, thin nose, and the small mouth and chin are all characteristic of Lucas's female types from the early 1520s, as in the Munich painting, the Berlin *Virgin and Child with Angels* (Fig. 11, Cat. 12), and the engraving of the *Burial of Christ* of 1521 (B.54). The headdress of the Virgin is also similar to that of the 1521 print. The figure of Christ and the crown of thorns match the representations in the 1521 series of the *Small Passion* (see B.50), and the many angular drapery folds are also close in style to this series (see B.51).

Cat. C17. *Virgin and Child in the Clouds* (Fig. 46)

Location unknown, presumably lost; circa 1522–1523.
Provenance: perhaps in the Coll. Johan Cornelis Backer, The Hague, 1662.[1]
Copies: (1) Drawing, by Jan de Bisschop (Fig. 46); Albertina, inv. no. 7810; pen and ink, brush, and wash, 23.7 x 18; signed "L" at lower left. *Prov.*: Coll. H. Busserus, 1782. *Lit.*: Rathgeber, 1844, col. 215, no. 739; J. G. Van Gelder, 1957, pp. 94 (no. 10), 96, 98 (probably a copy after a lost original by Lucas, ca. 1520–1525).
(2) Lithograph, by L. Bouteiller. *Lit.*: Hollstein, 1949–1974, 10:240, no. 15.

In this composition the *Virgo lactans* (nursing Virgin) is enthroned in the clouds, perhaps a reference to the *Sedes Sapientiae* (seat of wisdom, or throne of Solomon), intended to emphasize Christ's eternal wisdom and the role of Mary as his support. A youthful angel at the right offers an apple, symbol of the redemption of fallen humanity through the Savior. Six angels hover in the clouds around the throne while a host of cherubim appears in the distance. At the center top are the dove of the Holy Ghost and the Hebrew letters spelling Jehovah, which complete the Trinity. At the bottom of the composition a mountainous landscape, divided by a wide body of water with a city on its shore, is seen as if from a great height.

Although the composition is most closely related to Lucas's *Virgin and Child with Angels* in Berlin (Fig. 11, Cat. 12), circa 1521, the throne in the drawing by De Bisschop shows a more developed sense of three-dimensional space. The individual figures in the *Virgin and Child in the Clouds* are massive and weighty and thus closer to the *Virgin and Child with Mary Magdalene and a Donor* in Munich (Fig. 12, Cat. 14), dated 1522, and especially to Lucas's engraving of the *Virgin and Child* from 1523 (B.84). The intricate folds of the headdress are similar to those in a drawing by Lucas from this period, now in the Kupferstichkabinett, Berlin-Dahlem, representing the *Virgin Annunciate*.[2] The *Virgin and Child in the Clouds*, which originally may have been an engraved rather than a painted work, can be dated around 1522–1523 based on these stylistic comparisons. The renewed influence of Dürer's art during this period must also have been important to Lucas's representation of this subject.

Cat. C18. *Adoration of the Magi* (Fig. 55)

Location unknown, presumably lost; 1526.

Copies: (1) Painting, artist unknown; Staatliche Kunsthalle, Karlsruhe, inv. no. 155; panel, 62.5 x 83.5; signed and dated on the stone in the left foreground "L" and "1526."[1] *Prov.*: Grand-Ducal Gallery, Karlsruhe;[2] Badische Kunsthalle, Karlsruhe. *Lit.*: Parthey, 1864, p. 31, no. 8 or 9 (by Lucas); Dülberg, 1909, p. 14 (copy after a lost composition by Lucas, ca. 1520–1525); Beets, 1913, pp. 103–4 (best of the various copies; mannerism characteristic of Lucas's works from the 1520s; composed in the Antwerp style); Karlsruhe, Kunsthalle, 1929, p. 70 (sixteenth-century copy after Lucas); Hoogewerff, 1936–1947, 3:393–96 (weaker replica of the composition in Schleissheim [Copy 3], attributed to Aertgen van Leyden, ca. 1520–1525); Friedländer, 1963a, pp. 71–72 (after an original by Lucas, ca. 1522); Boon, 1964, col. 350 (could well be by Lucas); Karlsruhe, Kunsthalle, 1966, p. 172.

(2) Painting, artist unknown (Fig. 55); Mittelrheinisches Landesmuseum, Mainz, inv. no. 701; panel, 65 x 88; signed "HB" on the sword of the Magus at the right. *Prov.*: legacy J. Schick, 1906. *Exh.*: Spiers, Historisches Museum, 1957, no. 2 (copy after Aertgen, ca. 1520–1530). *Lit.*: Mainz, Mittelrheinisches Landesmuseum, 1911, pp. 42–43 (as North German Master, second half of sixteenth century); Mainz, Mittelrheinisches Landesmuseum, 1925, p. 39 (Hendrik Bles?); Hoogewerff, 1936–1947, 3:395; Friedländer, 1963a, p. 71.

(3) Painting, artist unknown; formerly Staatsgalerie, Schleissheim, inv.

no. 1478 (missing since 1945); panel, 74 x 97.5; signed lower left "L.v.L." *Prov.*: Gemäldegalerie, Mannheim; loan from Nuremberg, 1934. *Lit.*: Schleissheim, Königlichen Gallerie, 1885, p. 4, no. 34 (one of many replicas of this composition after Lucas, probably stemming from an imitation by Goltzius); Schleissheim, Königlichen Gemäldegalerie, 1914, pp. 141–42, no. 3034; Hoogewerff, 1936–1947, 3:393–96; Von Löhneysen, 1956, pp. 304–5; Friedländer, 1963a, p. 71.

(4) Painting, artist unknown; Staatliche Museen Preussischer Kulturbesitz, Berlin-Dahlem, on loan to Landesmuseum, Münster i.W., inv. no. 627; panel, 61 x 87. *Lit.*: Von Lehner, 1883, p. 40 (as Netherlandish School, follower of Patinir); Schleissheim, Königlichen Gemäldegalerie, 1914, p. 141; Karlsruhe, Kunsthalle, 1966, p. 172.

(5) Painting, artist unknown; private collection, Swabia; signed "L" at lower left.[3]

(6) Painting, artist unknown; Coll. Kneppelhout, Sterkenburg.

(7) Painting, artist unknown; location unknown; panel, 65 x 87. *Prov.*: Castle, Sigmaringen, inv. no. 129. *Lit.*: Von Lehner, 1883, p. 40 (Netherlandish, from the time and in the style of Lucas).

(8) Painting, artist unknown; location unknown; panel, 70 x 98.5. *Prov.*: sale Rene della Faille de Waerloos, Amsterdam (Muller), July 7, 1903, no. 17 (school of Lucas).

(9) Painting, artist unknown; location unknown; panel, 70 x 98.5; with Rapp, Stockholm; with Morgan, Stockholm. *Exh.*: Stockholm, Rapps Art Dealer, 1948, no. 32 (by Lucas).

(10) Painting, artist unknown; location unknown; panel, 66 x 93.5. *Prov.*: with C. Benedict, Paris, 1938; sale Luzern (Fischer), October 26, 1946, no. 1362 (by Lucas).

(11) Painting, artist unknown; location unknown; panel, 70 x 92. *Prov.*: with Landry, Paris, 1949 (copy after Aertgen).

(12) Painting, artist unknown; location unknown. *Prov.*: with Wengraf, London (copy after Aertgen); certified by M. J. Friedländer, 1947, as a good replica after Lucas.

(13) Painting, artist unknown; location unknown. *Prov.*: with S. Hartveld, Antwerp, 1940; D.I.A.L. 73B58.

(14) Painting, artist unknown; location unknown; panel, 63 x 88. *Prov.*: sale London (Sotheby), April 14, 1948, no. 108; sale N. Katz, Paris (Charpentier), April 25, 1951, no. 40; sale Paris (Charpentier), December 7, 1954, no. 74 (attributed to Lucas).[4]

A number of copies of this *Adoration* are extant, most of them virtually identical. Poses, costumes, and architecture are so closely repeated in the best versions that it is difficult to distinguish among them, with the only differences being in minor details or in the size and framing.[5] The Virgin and Child are in the center of the composition, seated on a stone bench in a deteriorating structure. They are turned toward the Magus who kneels to their right, while behind him the Ethiopian king hands his hat to his black servant. In the right foreground, the third Magus is in a mannered, half-risen pose. Joseph appears through a doorway in the middle ground, and further back two shepherds peer over a low wall.[6]

The composition has been associated with the style of Aertgen van Leyden as well as with that of Lucas, but the figure types have little in common with paintings attributed to Aertgen.[7] Many points of comparison can be found with Lucas's works of the 1520s. The influence of his brief sojourn in Antwerp in 1521 is evident, not only in the portrayal of the Virgin and Child, a theme that dominated his work in the years following the trip, but also in the style and composition of the painting. Although no direct source has been found, the symmetrical arrangement of the figures around a centralized Virgin and Child appears in earlier works such as Memling's *Adoration* in Madrid and Gossaert's *Adoration* in London.[8] The background figures, one appearing through a doorway and two others leaning over a balustrade, may have been taken from Hugo van der Goes's Monforte Altarpiece, circa 1470. This composition could have been known by Lucas through copies by the Antwerp Master of Frankfurt.[9]

The subject was a favorite of Joos van Cleve and the early sixteenth-century painters known somewhat misleadingly as the "Antwerp Mannerists." Lucas could have been struck by the popularity of the theme in Antwerp, but the extremely cluttered compositions of such works are very different from the open spaces used by the Leiden artist at this time.[10] The rather contorted, exaggerated poses of some of the figures in Lucas's *Adoration* and his *Last Judgment* in Leiden (Figs. 17–19, Cat. 20), as well as other paintings from this period, could be considered a derivation from the same source.[11] Beets noted that the splayed leg of the Magus at the right is similar to that of the Israelite in the same foreground position in *Moses after Striking the Rock* in Boston, from 1527 (Fig. 24, Cat. 7).[12] The twisted, *contrapposto* poses of the two flanking Magi are also repeated throughout the interior and exterior of the *Last Judgment*. The Virgin's broad forehead and small chin are found in female figures in the Boston and Leiden paintings, and Joseph's cocked head and short, square beard reappear in the man carrying the cask to the left of Moses. The lost profile of the kneeling Magus, one of Lucas's favorite motifs, crops up frequently in both the Boston and Leiden paintings as well. The muscular calves, the knobby knees, and the hands with wide palms and short fingers are all characteristic of Lucas's style at this period. Given these points of similarity, the signature and date of 1526 on the Karlsruhe *Adoration* (Copy 1) are probably accurate. Even the best of the many versions, for example those in Karlsruhe and Mainz (Copies 1-2), cannot be considered originals. The labored paint technique, hard contours, and somewhat wooden facial expressions lack the vitality of an original. All seem to be copies from the later sixteenth century.

Cat. C19. *John the Baptist Preaching in the Wilderness* (Fig. 56)

Location unknown, presumably lost; circa 1526-1527.
Copy: Engraving, by Nicolaes de Bruyn (Fig. 56); 39.4 X 54.6; first state signed "Aert van L. In. / Nicolas de Bruyn Sculp."; second state signed "L van Leye Inventor / Nicolas de Bruyn Sculp." *Lit.:* Hollstein, 1949-1974, 4:18, no. 116 (after Lucas; with illustration of the first state).

This work represents John the Baptist seated at the left, counting off the points of his sermon on his fingers as he preaches to a crowd of men and women gathered near the Jordan (Matt. 3:1-12, Mark 1:4-8, Luke 3:1-18, John 1:19-28).[1] As described in the biblical accounts, John wears "a garment of camel's hair, and a leather girdle around his waist"; the bystanders are dressed in sixteenth-century Netherlandish costume, except for one woman at the right who has the *bern* headdress of a gypsy.

The figures have much in common with Lucas's works from the late 1510s and 1520s. The male and female facial types are consistent with those in his prints and paintings from this period, and the motif of the lost profile recurs throughout his career. The square, blocky, frontally viewed male faces are found in the *Dance of the Magdalene,* 1519 (B.122), *Ecce Homo,* 1521 (B.50), and *Moses after Striking the Rock* in Boston, 1527 (Fig. 24, Cat. 7), among others, and the female faces with small mouths, long noses, plump cheeks, and broad foreheads appear in works such as the *Annunciation* in Munich, 1522 (Fig. 13, Cat. 15), the *Virgin and Child with Two Angels,* 1523 (B.84), *Last Judgment* in Leiden, 1526 (Figs. 17-19, Cat. 20), and *Virgin and Child* in Oslo, circa 1527 (Fig. 29, Cat. 23).

The composition is quite close to that of the Boston *Moses:* the protagonist in each case is placed off-center, secondary groups anchor the front corners, and the stately verticals of the standing figures clustered throughout the foreground zone are enlivened by a variety of gestures, tilted heads, and glances outward. Confirmation of a date around 1526-1527 for this work is found in the similarity between the man facing John the Baptist, turned slightly away from us, and the kneeling Magus in the *Adoration of the Magi* from 1526, also known only through copies (see Fig. 55; Cat. C18). The unusual twisted, intertwined tree trunks in the engraving are also found in the background of the *Adoration,* although they do not appear elsewhere in Lucas's oeuvre.

The engraving by Nicolaes de Bruyn is known in two states. In the first the composition is attributed to Aertgen van Leyden, but this is changed to Lucas in the second. The landscape is also different: the densely forested background of the first state is altered in the second to include a more distant view of rocks and mountains behind the Jordan.

Cat. 20. *Last Judgment* (Figs. 17-23)

Stedelijk Museum "De Lakenhal," Leiden, inv. no. 244; panel, triptych; central panel 269.5 x 184.8, bell-shaped above; each wing 265 x 76.5; 1526.

Provenance: commissioned August 6, 1526, in memory of the Leiden timber merchant Claes Dircsz. van Swieten;[1] hung near the baptismal font in the church of St. Peter, Leiden, ca. 1527-1566;[2] probably removed in 1566 to St. Jacob's Hospital for safety;[3] in St. Catherine's Hospital probably from 1572 to 1577; in the burgomasters' chamber in the Leiden Town Hall from 1577 to 1872;[4] moved to the Stedelijk Museum in 1872.

Exhibitions: Amsterdam, Rijksmuseum, 1958, no. 138; Leiden, Stedelijk Museum, 1978, no. 8.

Literature: Van Mander, 1604, fol. 213v (criticism of the sharp-edged outlines of some of the nudes; the exterior better in paint technique than the interior; unsuccessful attempt by a foreign potentate to buy it);[5] Orlers, 1641, p. 361 (excellent condition); Parival, 1669, p. 66; Bullart, 1682, pp. 397-98; Jourdain, 1699, p. 245; Le Comte, 1702, p. 320; Goris, 1712, pp. 159-60; Von Uffenbach, 1754, p. 400 (coloring beautiful and fresh); Tirion, 1742, p. 523; Descamps, 1753, p. 45; Van Mieris, 1762, 1:29 (originally hung in the baptistery of St. Peter's), 2:370 (originally at the high altar; repeats Orlers's account of Rudolf II, with the addition of a laudatory verse); Von Heinecken, 1769, p. 61 (completely overpainted in bright colors);[6] De la Roche, 1783, pp. 61-62 (painted by Jean de Leyde); Volkmann, 1783, pp. 199-200; Watson, 1790, p. 96; Schnaase, 1834, pp. 62-64; Immerzeel, 1842, p. 172; Dodt van Flensburg, 1844, p. 106; Rathgeber, 1844, pp. 16-17, 220, nos. 855-57;

Michiels, 1847, pp. 127, 133 (nos. 68–70), 134 (nos. 83–84); Kramm, 1860, 4:972–73 (painted for the high altar of St. Peter's); Waagen, 1860, pp. 117–18; Blanc, 1861, p. 4; Elsevier, 1862; Kist and Moll, 1862, p. 441; Waagen, 1862, p. 151; K., J., 1865, pp. 208, 210; Kugler, 1867, pp. 573–74; Lennep et al., 1870, no. 40; Wolters, 1874 (a novelistic account of the painting of the triptych and of the events of 1566); Elsevier, 1875 (painted for the high altar; primarily discusses the events of 1566–1577; does not consider the memorial painting cited in the July 12, 1577, document as the *Last Judgment;* reads the date of the commission as March 16, 1526); Rosenberg, 1877, pp. 9–10; Taurel, 1881, pp. 15–18 (ca. 1533, probably for the high altar); Duplessis, 1882, p. 4 (painted for the high altar); Woltmann and Woermann, 1882, p. 531; Blok, 1884a, pp. 279–80; Evrard, 1884, pp. 6, 639, 664–68 (falsely attributed to Lucas, based on a comparison with the engravings; composition foreign to Lucas); Hymans, 1884, p. 143, n. 1 (1533); Von Wurzbach, 1885, pp. 55–56 (1533; exterior figures of Peter and Paul suggest it was painted for the high altar; no Italian influence on the nudes); Leiden, Stedelijk Museum, 1886, pp. 79–80, no. 1000; Van der Burch, 1887; Emile Michel, 1893, pp. 10–11 (1533); Lafenestre and Richtenberger, 1894–1907, pp. 171–72 (follow traditional identification of the elderly man in the center of the left wing as Lucas's father and identify a self-portrait of Lucas in the foreground of the central panel); Pit, 1894, pp. 84–86; Dülberg, 1899a (most detailed study before 1978; painted before 1525; identifies the donors as the elderly man in the left wing and the middle-aged man at the left of the central panel, walking with his wife; other donors perhaps two of the seated males in the central panel); Dülberg, 1899c, pp. 72, 82 (discusses the amount paid for the triptych; refutes the local tradition of a self-portrait in the seated male with praying hands in the central panel); Friedländer, 1901, p. 4; Overvoorde and Martin, 1902, pp. 16–24 (follow Dülberg in the identification of the two standing donors); Dülberg, 1903–1908a, pp. 3, 15–21; Overvoorde, 1907, pp. 141, 143; Dülberg, 1909, pp. 14–15; Heidrich, 1910, pp. 53–54 (more influence of Dürer than of Marcantonio); Beets, 1912a (perhaps influence of Dürer's *Large Fortune*, B.77, on the female at the left of the central panel; disagrees with Dülberg's identification of the donors); Peltzer, 1911–1912, p. 106; Beets, 1913, pp. 92–103, 128 (inspired by Bernard van Orley's *Last Judgment* in Antwerp); De Stuers, 1914 (account of the overpainting of the figure of God the Father, ca. 1832); R., 1915 (report of the diary of M. de la Roche, 1773–1778); Hirschmann, 1916, pp. 40–41 (Goltzius's role in the attempt by Rudolf II to buy the painting); Havelaar, 1918, pp. 102–3; Kahn, 1918, pp. 111–13; Valentiner, 1919, pp. 118–19 (compares the triptych to a *Last Judgment* in the New York Historical Society, attributed by him to Lucas); Conway, 1921, pp. 481-82 (no Italian influence in the forms); Baldass, 1923, pp. 25-29, 33-34 (nudes still northern in type, revealing the influence of Dürer rather than that of Gossaert or Marcantonio); Winkler, 1924, p. 266; Burger, 1925, pp. 155-56 (influence of Van Orley's Antwerp *Last Judgment*); Buchelius, 1928, p. 21; Sjöblom, 1928, pp. 165-69; Bremmer, 1929, pp. 11-15 (influence of Dürer); Dülberg, 1929, pp. 168-69; Wescher, 1929, p. 169; Van Balen, 1930, p. 22; Dülberg, 1930, p. 306; Dülberg, 1933, p. 12; Beets, 1934, p. 153 (many of the nudes show the influence of Marcantonio's *Venus and Cupid*, B.311); Coert, 1935-1936, pp. 76-83 (discussion of the overpainting and cleaning of the figure of God the Father); Hoogewerff, 1936-1947, 3:289-302 (influence of Van Orley's Antwerp *Last Judgment;* probably had an epitaph under the central panel); J. G. Van Gelder, 1938 (no donor portraits); Knuttel, 1938, pp. 126-28 (nudes show the influence of Lucas's meeting with Gossaert); Van de Wetering, 1938, p. 49 (strong influence of Jan van Scorel on the exterior landscape); Beets, 1940, pp. 56-58; Benesch, 1945, p. 85 (influence of Dürer and Gossaert); Korevaar-Hesseling, 1948, p. 33 (Italian influence on the exterior landscape); Pelinck, 1948; Leiden, Stedelijk Museum, 1949, pp. 161-67, no. 244; Bersier, 1951, p. 55; Beets, 1954, p. 450; Leymarie, 1956, p. 50; Von Löhneysen, 1956, pp. 292-94, 298, 301-2, 304, 306; Reznicek, 1956, pp. 75-76 (Jan Muller's role in the attempt by Rudolf II to buy the triptych in 1602); Swillens, 1957, pp. 267-68 (Van Mander's criticism of Lucas's abrupt transitions from light to shadow); Gerson, 1962, pp. 28-29; Friedländer, 1963a, pp. 63-65, 84; Boon, 1964, col. 352 (influence of Dürer); Hoetink, 1966; Grohn, 1967, pp. 134-35 (probably not completed until late 1527, after his return from Flanders); Friedländer, 1969, p. 126; Von der Osten and Vey, 1969, pp. 177-78; Tümpel, 1969, p. 184 (influence of Paul on Rembrandt's Stuttgart *Paul in Prison*); Friedländer, 1967-1976, 10:54-55, 63, 81, no. 113 (influence of Gossaert and Van Scorel); Silver, 1973, pp. 407-9 (the troubled representation of the exterior scene reveals Lucas's concern about current Reformation questions); Bangs, 1974a (disputes Silver's analysis of the exterior); Knipping, 1974, 2:244; Silver, 1974c, p. 310; Bangs, 1975 (information on Claes Dircsz.'s political role in Leiden); Corwin, 1976, pp. 226-27 (influence of Bosch on the Hell wing); Harbison, 1976, pp. 145, 162-63, 179-80, 279, no. 76 (somewhat proto-Protestant triptych); Gibson, 1977, p. 149 (influence on Cornelis Engebrechtsz.'s Paul on the left wing of the *Feeding of the Five Thousand,* formerly in Berlin); Brown, 1978; Von Brussel, Moerman, and Wurfbain, 1978, pp. 9-11; Filedt Kok, 1978, pp. 65-99, 116-18, 121-26, 136-47 (description of the paint technique and underdrawing in brush, wash, and black and red chalk); Silver and Smith, 1978, pp. 275, 278; Vos, 1978a, pp. 115-19, 138-39; Vos, 1978c, pp. 496-97, nn. 79-81; Hermesdorf et al., 1978 (detailed discussion of the material history of the triptych and its 1973-1977 restoration; study by Wurfbain of the iconography, donors, and original location in the church); Parshall, 1978-1979, p. 52; Bangs, 1979a, pp. 68, 113, 137, n. 1 (influence on Aertgen van Leyden's *Last Judgment* in Valenciennes); Renger, 1979, p. 268; Bangs, 1980, p. 95 (believes the top layer of the painting was stripped in the restoration of 1973-1977); Gibson, 1980, pp. 107-9; Leiden, Stedelijk Museum, 1983, pp. 202-4, no. 244; Bangs, 1985, p. 13 (relates the painting to a plaque in Leiden, 1525-1526); Gibson, 1986, pp. 43, 48; Silver, 1986, p. 30.

Copies: (1) Painting, by Pieter de Groot; copy of God the Father made ca. 1809; Leiden, Gemeente Archief, inv. no. 22353; watercolor, on squared paper; 32 x 20. *Lit.*: Hoogewerff, 1936-1947, 3:295; Leiden, Stedelijk Museum, 1949, p. 165; Knipping, 1974, 2:244; Von Brussel, Moerman, and Wurfbain, 1978, p. 9; Hermesdorf et al., 1978, pp. 333-34 and fig. 18.

(2) Drawings, by Abraham Delfos (and assistants?), ca. 1785; copies of the two exterior panels; Leiden, Gemeente Archief, inv. no. 22344; pen and ink and wash. *Lit.*: Dülberg, 1899a, p. 38; Hermesdorf et al., 1978, pp. 331-33.

(3) Drawings, by Abraham Delfos (and assistants?), ca. 1785; copies of the two exterior panels; Leiden, Gemeente Archief, inv. no. 22345; black chalk. *Lit.*: Dülberg, 1899a, p. 38; Hermesdorf et al., 1978, pp. 331-33.

(4) Drawings, by Abraham Delfos (and assistants?), ca. 1785; copies of the two exterior panels; Leiden, Gemeente Archief, inv. no. 22346; watercolor. *Lit.*: Dülberg, 1899a, p. 38; Hermesdorf et al., 1978, pp. 331-33 and fig. 17b.

(5) Drawings, by Abraham Delfos (and assistants?), ca. 1785; copies of the two exterior panels; Leiden, Gemeente Archief, inv. no. 22349; pen and gray ink. *Lit.*: Dülberg, 1899a, p. 38; Hermesdorf et al., 1978, pp. 331-33.

(6) Outline engravings, by Abraham Delfos or Pieter de Mare, ca. 1785-1792; copy after the interior in six sheets. *Lit.*: Kramm, 1860, 3:973 (extremely rare); Leiden, Stedelijk Museum, 1886, p. 80; Dülberg, 1899a, p. 38; Hermesdorf et al., 1978, pp. 331-33 (a number of these engravings have been overdrawn with chalk, sepia, or watercolor; three copies are signed by Delfos and dated 1791 or 1792; see fig. 17a).

(7) Outline engraving, by Pieter de Mare after Abraham Delfos, 1785; copy after the praying man in the foreground of the central panel (believed at that time to be a self-portrait). *Lit.*: Dülberg, 1899a, p. 33; Hermesdorf et al., 1978, p. 331 and n. 101 (perhaps an etching).

The interior of this triptych shows the *Last Judgment* as one continuous scene across all three panels (Figs. 17-19). The Last Judgment, also known in the Bible as "the day" or "the day of our Lord Jesus Christ" (see, for example, 2

Cor. 1:14), is mentioned repeatedly in both the Old and New Testaments. The most detailed accounts are given in Matthew (25:31–46), John (5:27–30), and Revelation (20:11–14), and the traditional schema of Last Judgment representations derives from these passages, particularly the two Gospels. As in Lucas's triptych, the enthroned Christ is typically the upper focal point of the composition. Below, we see the resurrection of the dead, with the righteous being led off to Heaven and the damned being cast into Hell.

The judge is clearly identified in the Bible as Jesus Christ, Son of Man (John 5:27, Rev. 1:18), and as such he appears in the Revelation of John with the sword of retribution: "out of his mouth came a sharp two-edged sword" (1:16; see also Isa. 11:4, 49:2). The sword appears in Lucas's painting in its customary place to Christ's left; to his right is the lily of grace. These two objects, as well as Christ's gestures of salvation and damnation, symbolize his role as judge. In his depiction of the complete Trinity, Lucas followed the biblical emphasis on God the Father as the ultimate authority for Christ's judgment (John 5:30; see also Rom. 2:16 and 1 Cor. 15:24–28). The representation of the Trinity, relatively unusual in fifteenth- and sixteenth-century northern *Last Judgment* scenes, emphasizes a humanized view of Christ. Although he acts as judge, he is also still an intercessor on man's behalf with his Father: "should anyone commit a sin, we have one to plead our cause with the Father, Jesus Christ, and he is just" (1 John 2:1; see also 4:17).[7] For this reason Lucas stresses the gentleness and mercy of Christ the crucified Savior, whose calm pose and expression differ from the aggressive, dynamic Christ in Bernard van Orley's earlier *Last Judgment*, now in Antwerp. His wounds are also not expressly indicated, unlike those in Jan Mostaert's *Last Judgment*, from around 1514, in Bonn, or in a problematic northern Netherlandish panel probably dating from the 1520s, now in the Nationalmuseet in Copenhagen.[8] In Lucas's *Last Judgment*, two golden aureoles above the figure of Christ contain images of the dove of the Holy Spirit (see Mark 1:10) and of God the Father. God, held aloft by six cherubim, is represented as "ancient in years" with a long, forked beard (Dan. 7:9). He wears a variant of the papal crown, which was considered an appropriate symbol of the Lord's omnipotence during the late Middle Ages.[9] The gesture of his right hand echoes Christ's sign of grace.

Further details concerning the day of judgment can be gleaned from other biblical references. Lucas's Christ is seated on a rainbow, derived from the description in Revelation of a rainbow around his throne (4:3; see also Ezek. 1:28). The rainbow was an Old Testament symbol of mercy or grace because of its appearance after the Flood. In fact, Matthew draws a clear parallel between the events of the Flood and the Second Coming of Christ (24:37–41). Christ's feet rest on a large globe, common in Last Judgment representations, symbolizing his power and sovereignty over the world. He is flanked by the twelve apostles (Matt. 19:27–28), and behind him is a host of saints in grisaille. At the head of the group on his right is the Virgin Mary and on the left John the Baptist or John the Evangelist. Lucas broke with the pictorial tradition by dramatically reducing their roles as the primary intercessors and placing the emphasis on Christ.

Below the apostles, Lucas depicted two angels in complex, twisted poses as they blow horns to raise the dead from their graves (1 Cor. 15:51–52, 1 Thess. 4:16). In a vast panorama across all three panels of the triptych, the division of the blessed from the damned takes place (Matt. 13:41–43, 45–50). The saved are led off to Christ's right, some carried heavenward by angels dressed in colorful and often quite fanciful costumes, very different from the white robes described in Rev. 7:13–14. Lucas simplified the image of heaven (Fig. 18), envisioning it as a golden realm of light filled with musical angels rather than the traditional garden or towers of Jerusalem (see Rev. 21:2). The damned are at Christ's left, on the side of his sword, downturned hand, and averted gaze. They are pushed, pulled, and beaten into Hell by a motley crew of demons. Here, Lucas diverged less from the traditional format, depicting Hell as eternal fire (Fig. 19): "the blazing furnace, the place of wailing and grinding of teeth" (Matt. 13:42, 50; see also 3:12, 18:8–9, and Mark 9:47–48). He represented, like many artists before him, a great monster hell-mouth, its fiery jaws spread wide to receive the wicked. Job's description of Leviathan, the sea monster, was borrowed as a fitting image: "Firebrands shoot from his mouth, and sparks come streaming out; his nostrils pour forth smoke like a cauldron on a fire blown to full heat. His breath sets burning coals ablaze, and flames flash from his mouth" (Job 41:19–21).

Missing entirely from Lucas's *Last Judgment* is the *psychostasis,* or weighing of souls by the Archangel Michael (see 1 Thess. 4:16; Dan. 12:1–3). Prominent in most fifteenth-century northern representations, it was also a central motif in several early sixteenth-century *Last Judgment* paintings in Holland. Examples include a work originally decorating the choir of St. Laurenskerk, Alkmaar, and now in the Rijksmuseum, which has been attributed to Jacob Cornelisz. and his workshop and is dated 1518. St. Michael also figures prominently in a lost triptych attributed to Jan Mostaert or Geertgen tot Sint Jans, known only from a nineteenth-century drawn copy in a private collection in Amersfoort. The *psychostasis* was generally reduced in size and importance in the sixteenth century, as in Van Orley's triptych in Antwerp and Joos van Cleve's panel in New York, both painted in the 1520s.[10] Lucas's work is unusual in completely eliminating the Archangel. In other works in which Michael is omitted, the reason is frequently a lack of space, since many *Last Judgment* scenes are crowded with large central figures of Christ, the Virgin, and John.[11] Lucas's representation is different, however, in the remarkably open spacing of the center of the composition.

The exterior panels are also painted as a continuous and unified panorama (Fig. 23). The figures are set against a rocky landscape with the sea as background. On the left panel, which forms the reverse of the interior wing depicting Heaven, Peter is seated in a twisted, contorted pose. He gazes out of the frame to his right while gesturing across his torso to his left. In his left hand he holds a large key, the traditional attribute of Peter, guardian of the gates of Paradise, symbolizing "the keys of the kingdom of heaven" (Matt. 16:13–20). Paul, seated in the foreground of the right panel, turns his body and gazes at the other apostle. He responds to Peter's gesture with his right hand and with his left holds a book, an allusion to his Epistles. Other books lie unopened at his right, while the sword of his martyrdom rests on the ground before him.[12] In the background, Lucas represented Paul's shipwreck near Malta, an episode from Acts 28.

The triptych was commissioned in August 1526 in memory of Claes Dircsz. van Swieten, who probably died the year before. It was thus a commemorative painting and was not placed on one of the altars of the church, as has frequently been claimed.[13] A document of July 12, 1577, in which five descendants of Claes Dircsz. lay claim to the triptych, described the painting as hanging close to the baptismal font. The baptistery was reconstructed after the 1512 collapse of the church tower and situated at the southwest corner of the church, projecting from the side aisle. Since the chapel itself is too small to have housed the triptych, the painting must have been placed close to its entrance on either the south or the west wall. Most likely it hung over the *schepenbank,* a bench for the city magistrates located against the west wall near the baptistery.[14] It is known that Claes Dircsz. had been active in the local government. He was a magistrate (*schepen*) in 1518 and one of the burgomasters in 1523, as well as a churchwarden and a member of the Council of Forty.[15] This location could also explain the large size of Lucas's triptych, unusual in a commemorative panel. It is more than twice the size of Jan Mostaert's *Last Judgment* in Bonn, for example, which was dedicated to the memory of the Van Noordwijk family. The wall space above the magistrates' bench would have been greater than that over an individual tomb, and the importance of the location would also have called for a monumental work. Although the Last Judgment was not one of the more common subjects for a memorial painting, representations of it were frequently used to decorate town halls in northern Europe.[16] The theme was intended to be seen not only as a warning of the justice that will be accorded to everyone on the last day but also as an example for secular officials in their daily judgmental duties. If Lucas's triptych was meant to be read in this way, it would also help to explain the absence of portraits of the Van Swieten family.[17] The omission of particular references universalizes the warning and makes the painting more suitable for its purported location over the bench reserved for government officials.

Three northern Netherlandish memorial panels representing the Last Judgment, dating from the late fifteenth and sixteenth centuries, provide useful comparisons: Jan Mostaert's panel of circa 1514, now in Bonn; the panel in Copenhagen, dating from the 1520s and variously attributed to Mostaert and to the school of Jacob Cornelisz.; and the triptych known only from the drawing in Amersfoort, probably copied after Mostaert or Geertgen. The first two paintings are in bell-shaped frames similar to the central panel of Lucas's triptych, and both include a representation of the Trinity. Certain details point to the possibility that Lucas or the donors knew of one or both of these paintings. For example, in the Copenhagen panel the role of the Archangel is minimized and he is pushed off-center, whereas in Mostaert's *Last Judgment* in Bonn he is not shown at all. Both show the sword of retribution at Christ's left with its end pointed outward, as Lucas portrayed it. This is an iconographic peculiarity, although not unique to these three paintings.[18] The Copenhagen and Bonn works differ significantly from Lucas's, however, in that the dominant foreground position is given over to portraits in both, while the division of the saved from the damned is relegated to the background. In the Amersfoort drawing the central panel is devoted to the representation of the Last Judgment, but donors are portrayed on the wings. The reason there are no donors' portraits in Lucas's triptych seems to be the unusual nature of its original location.

Lucas's painting was influential for several contemporary artists. Cornelis Engebrechtsz.'s figure of Paul on the left wing of his *Feeding of the Five Thousand*, formerly in Berlin (Fig. 68), was based on Lucas's Paul.[19] A Leiden School *Last Judgment* now in the New-York Historical Society and once attributed to Aertgen van Leyden is compositionally derivative. Its central view back into depth, the pose of Christ, the placement of the rainbow and orb, and the two trumpet-playing angels are all comparable, and the group in its left foreground is drawn piecemeal from figures in the Leiden triptych. Lucas's modest female figure in the center background has been shifted forward, and she is flanked by two male figures similar to the profile nudes in the foreground of Lucas's painting.[20] In a triptych in the Bode Museum, East Berlin, Jean Bellegambe made slight alterations to the pose of this same woman and, like the Leiden School artist, placed her in a prominent location at the left. He also seems to have borrowed the rather mannered, pinwheel pose of the man in the left foreground of Lucas's painting, turning and varying the figure.[21]

Cat. C21. *Rest on the Flight into Egypt* (Fig. 57)

Location unknown, presumably lost; 1527.

Provenance: probably in the collection of Duke Maximilian I of Bavaria, ca. 1627–1628 (signed with Lucas's monogram and dated 1527).

Copies: (1) Painting, attributed by the museum to Hans Liefrinck (Fig. 57); Stedelijk Museum "De Lakenhal," Leiden, inv. no. 1725; panel, 76 x 87. *Prov.:* Coll. F. J. Gsell, Vienna; sale Vienna (Künstlerhaus), March 14, 1872, no. 207 (as Hendrick Goltzius), to Georg Plach; sale Montù and others, Berlin (Sachse), November 9, 1891, no. 45 (Hendrick Goltzius); Coll. Rosenau, Berlin, 1923; Coll. Schönfeld, Zurich, 1937;[1] Coll. Alice Schönfeld-Seligson, Berkeley, California; sale Vienna (Dorotheum), May 22, 1973, no. 87 (as Aertgen Claesz.), to museum. *Lit.:* Friedländer, 1963a, p. 72 (after a composition by Lucas); Hiller and Vey, 1969, pp. 64–65 (copy of a lost composition by Lucas, of lesser quality than the Cologne painting [Copy 2]); Friedländer, 1967–1976, 10:83; Filedt Kok et al., 1975, pp. 247, 257, n. 33 (after an original by Lucas, ca. 1527); Leiden, Stedelijk Museum, 1983, pp. 205–6 (in the manner of Lucas; Joseph inspired by the apostles in the sky of Lucas's *Last Judgment;* foreground figures perhaps by Bartholomeus Ferreris, based on similarity of Joseph to drawing of Paul attributed to Ferreris, sale Amsterdam, Mak van Waay, June 9, 1975, no. 17; landscape and background figures perhaps by Hans Liefrinck II; 1595–1598).

(2) Painting, artist unknown; copy of the Virgin and Child only; Kunstgewerbemuseum, Cologne, inv. no. A1075; panel, 64.5 x 52. *Prov.:* gift of Wilhelm Clemens, Munich, 1919 (inv. no. 29, as a school work or copy after Lucas, ca. 1530).[2] *Exh.:* Cologne, Kunstgewerbemuseum, 1963, no. 24 (as Lucas, ca. 1525). *Lit.:* Straus-Ernst, 1921, p. 14 (by Lucas); Friedländer, 1963a, p. 72 (copy after Lucas, ca. 1528); Reznicek-Buriks, 1965, p. 242; Hiller and Vey, 1969, pp. 64–65 (in the manner of Lucas, ca. 1526); Friedländer, 1967–1976, 10:83, no. 125 (original? about 1525); Filedt Kok et al., 1975, p. 257, n. 33 (probably a partial copy of a lost composition by Lucas, ca. 1527); Filedt Kok, 1978, pp. 166–67, n. 117.

(3) Painting, artist unknown;[3] copy of the Virgin and Child; location unknown; canvas, 65 x 53; signed "H" or "A" just to the right of the Virgin's elbow. *Prov.:* acquired 1908 in Würzburg by a private collector, Germany.[4]

(4) Painting, artist unknown; copy of Joseph; location unknown; canvas, 27 cm wide.

These works are probably all copies after a lost painting by Lucas, the work in Leiden (Copy 1, Fig. 57) being the most complete version. The Virgin is shown in half length behind a rocky ledge, and the Christ Child is comfortably ensconced on a pillow in front of her, holding a white rose symbolic of purity. The apple or pear in Joseph's hand complements the rose held by Jesus, referring to salvation from original sin through Christ, the "new Adam." Both Mary and Jesus look at Joseph, to their right, but the Child remains the focus of the inverted-triangle composition. The tilt of the Virgin's head and the line of Joseph's body lead the eye downward to Christ. The background landscape shows the Flight into Egypt; the Virgin and Child ride on a donkey, accompanied by Joseph who walks alongside.

Copies 3 and 4 were originally one painting. The figure of Joseph was later cut off, but part of his shoulder is still visible at the left of copy 3. Although smaller than the panel in Leiden, the work is similar in all foreground details. Only the landscape has been slightly altered, with steeper, more pronounced mountains. This version is the poorest in quality, and its wooden features and hard modeling make it particularly awkward.

The *Virgin and Child* in Cologne (Copy 2) shows a much finer paint technique, with more detailed drapery folds and more carefully applied highlights. In this version, all reference to the Flight has been omitted. Mary and Jesus are set before a neutral dark background, and Christ is seated on a balustrade or table. He looks off to his right as before, but the Virgin looks directly at the spectator, while Joseph is missing from the composition. In all other details there is virtually no distinction among the three versions.

The figures in these sixteenth-century paintings are so clearly reminiscent of Lucas's late style that there can be no doubt that they were copied after an original from this period. The facial types of Mary and Jesus, as well as their compositional grouping, have much in common with the Oslo *Virgin and Child* (Fig. 29, Cat. 23) and with the copies in Norfolk (Fig. 58) and Amsterdam of a lost *Virgin and Child* (Cat. C22). The *contrapposto* pose of the Child is roughly similar to the same figure in the Berlin *Virgin and Child with Angels* (Fig. 11, Cat. 12). The broad hands and rather short fingers are characteristic of Lucas's figures, and the crisp, angular folds of cloth closely resemble his drapery style of 1526–1527, especially on the exterior of the Leiden *Last Judgment* (Fig. 23, Cat. 20). The complex hairstyle of the Virgin is also repeated in other paintings of Lucas's late period: in *Moses after Striking the Rock* in Boston (Fig. 24, Cat. 7) and the *Dance around the Golden Calf* in Amsterdam (Fig. 32, Cat. 11). He used it again in the prints of the *Virtues* (especially B.130–32) and in the preparatory drawing in the British Museum for the Oslo *Virgin and Child* (Fig. 30).[5] The loosely painted, monochromatic figures in the background of the copy in Leiden are comparable in style to those in the *Last Judgment* in the same museum (Fig. 17). Based on stylistic evidence, the original must have been painted around 1526-1528. It may be possible to fix a more precise date of 1527 from the description of a panel in the inventory of Duke Maximilian I of Bavaria: "Our Beloved Lady with the little Child and St. Joseph by Lucas van Leyden from Holland, with the year 1527 and the signature 'L', is very finely and diligently made. In the light [out of the frame?] 2 feet 5½ inches high, and 3 feet broad, No. 32." The descriptions and measurements (74.9 x 91.4) are very close to the *Rest on the Flight* in Leiden, so this seventeenth-century entry may have referred to the original painting by Lucas.

Cat. C22. *Virgin and Child* (Fig. 58)

Location unknown, presumably lost; circa 1528.

Copies: (1) Painting, artist unknown (Fig. 58); The Chrysler Museum, Norfolk, Virginia, inv. no. 71.490; panel, 27 x 22.5. *Prov.*: from Spain;[1] Coll. Joseph Daniels, Zurich, 1952; with Frederick Mont, New York, 1952; Newhouse Galleries, New York, 1953; Coll. Walter P. Chrysler, Jr., New York; gift to Norfolk, 1971. *Exh.*: Portland, Art Museum, 1956, no. 1 (as Lucas, ca. 1520); Provincetown, Chrysler Art Museum, 1958, no. 72 (ca. 1520). *Lit.*: Neugass, 1957 (ca. 1520; strong influence of Dürer); Filedt Kok, 1978, p. 134 (probably not an original by Lucas).

(2) Painting, artist unknown; Rijksmuseum, inv. no. A3739; panel, 35 x 27.5. *Prov.*: with Langton Douglas, London; Coll. Adolphe Schloss, Paris, at least from 1913; taken by the Germans during World War II and recovered in 1947;[2] sale Adolphe Schloss, Paris (Charpentier), May 25, 1949, no. 29 (as Lucas), bought by the museum. *Exh.*: Utrecht, Gebouw voor Kunsten en Wetenschappen, 1913, supp. no. 167; Paris, Orangerie des Tuileries, 1946, no. 75 (ca. 1526); Amsterdam, Rijksmuseum, 1958, no. 135. *Lit.*: Beets, 1913, p. 128; Beets, 1914, pp. 59-60 (ca. 1520); Cohen, 1914, p. 31; Conway, 1921, p. 483, n. 1 (not much earlier than 1528); Friedländer, 1922, p. 131 (after 1522); Baldass, 1923, pp. 23, 31-32 (later than the Berlin *Virgin and Child* [Fig. 11, Cat. 12]); Winkler, 1924, pp. 264-65 (before 1522); Wescher, 1929, p. 169 (late 1510s; influence of Dürer); Hoogewerff, 1936-1947, 3:285-86 (ca. 1523-1524); Beets, 1940, p. 55 (ca. 1520); Amsterdam, Rijksmuseum, 1951, p. 103; Beets, 1952a, p. 183 (ca. 1520); Amsterdam, Rijksmuseum, 1956, p. 117; Leymarie, 1956, p. 49 (influence of Gossaert); Marette, 1961, p. 193, no. 235 (ca. 1520); Gerson, 1962, p. 28 (influence of Gossaert); Friedländer, 1963a, pp. 60-61, 69 (ca. 1521); Reznicek-Buriks, 1965, p. 245 (possibly a school work by a follower or pupil of Lucas); Von der Osten and Vey, 1969, p. 178

(influence of Gossaert); Friedländer, 1967–1976, 10:54 (soon after 1522), 83, no. 126 (ca. 1526); Filedt Kok, 1978, pp. 132–34 (probably a copy of a lost Lucas, from the same period as the Oslo *Virgin and Child* [Fig. 29, Cat. 23]); Renger, 1979, p. 59 (not an original by Lucas).

These two copies of the *Virgin and Child* are virtually identical. In both, Mary is seated before an olive-colored curtain with the Christ Child reclining in her lap. The Child holds a red carnation, symbol of divine love, in his right hand, and with his left he steadies the cross-crowned globe representing his sovereignty over the world. The paintings are similar in color, including the whitish-blue headdress and mantel of the Virgin, her blue overdress, and the red sleeve. The Amsterdam panel is slightly larger, although its composition is more closely cropped at the base and along the right side.[3]

There is a substantial difference, however, in the painting style and quality of the two; the Norfolk version is more carefully executed.[4] The detailed play of light and shadow on the flesh gives the skin a softer blush, as opposed to the dry, sketchy impression given by the other work. The artist of the Norfolk panel displays a greater understanding of anatomy, as in the lines and dimples of the Virgin's hands (especially the roundness of her right hand as it curves under Christ's body). The Virgin's hands in the Amsterdam painting are flattened by the lack of articulation. The artist of the Norfolk panel achieved a convincing sense of space through the careful modeling and the intricate detailing of the drapery, while the other painting lacks depth and precision.

Despite the admirable qualities mentioned above, the Norfolk work cannot be considered an original by Lucas. Although it is similar to the Oslo *Virgin and Child* (Fig. 29, Cat. 23) in composition and in Mary's massive body, round, small-featured face, and broad dimpled hands, the modeling of the flesh and the contours and articulation of her hands exhibit the hard and exaggerated style of a copyist.[5] Both the Norfolk and Amsterdam panels must be copies after a lost work by Lucas, painted by two different artists working in the first half of the sixteenth century. Given the copies' similarities to the Oslo painting and the *Betrothal* in Strasbourg (Fig. 26, Cat. 44), the original was probably painted around 1528.[6] Perhaps the copyist of the Amsterdam version attempted to "improve" what must have been the three-quarter-length composition of the original, reproduced in the Norfolk panel and also seen in the Oslo *Virgin and Child*. He concentrated the image into a more stable, centralized composition closely bound by the Virgin's elbows and knees. In the Amsterdam painting the emphasis is on the Virgin, whereas the Christ Child seems to have been the focus of the original composition. Also in the original, now known only secondhand through the Norfolk version, the greater amplitude of the composition allowed a full expansion of the monumental forms, unrestricted by a closer framing.

Cat. 23. *Virgin and Child* (Fig. 29)

Nasjonalgalleriet, Oslo, inv. no. 1390; panel, 24.5 x 21.5; circa 1528.

Provenance: Coll. R. von Kaufmann, Berlin; sale Von Kaufmann, Berlin (Cassirer), December 4-5, 1917, pt. 2, no. 117 (as Lucas); acquired in 1917 by Christian Langaard, Oslo; presented to the museum in 1923.

Exhibitions: Utrecht, Gebouw voor Kunsten en Wetenschappen, 1913, no. 39; Delft, Prinsenhof, 1952, no. 143 (ca. 1528); Amsterdam, Rijksmuseum, 1958, no. 136; Leiden, Stedelijk Museum, 1978, no. 9.

Literature: Colvin, 1893, p. 169, no. 9 (dates the drawing in the British Museum [Fig. 30] ca. 1525 but does not relate it to the Oslo painting); Friedländer, 1906, p. 39 (ca. 1528); Dülberg, 1909, p. 16 (influence of Italian art); Beets, 1913, pp. 106-8 (influence of Gossaert; considers the British Museum drawing a correction of the painting for a later version of the same subject; date of 1528 confirmed by the etching of a *Virgin and Child* [Fig. 31] after a similar composition by Lucas); Beets, 1914, pp. 59-60; Cohen, 1914, p. 31; Friedländer, 1917, p. 228, no. 117 (ca. 1525); *Cicerone,* 1918, p. 26, no. 117; Conway, 1921, p. 483 (inferior in design to the British Museum drawing; an example of Lucas's failing powers); Friedländer, 1922, pp. 131-32; Baldass, 1923, pp. 24, 33 (pure Romanism, through the intermediary of Gossaert; ca. 1523-1526); Winkler, 1924, p. 264; Dülberg, 1929, p. 169 (possibly ca. 1527, during trip with Gossaert); Wescher, 1929, p. 169 (dates painting and drawing ca. 1525); Popham, 1932, pp. 30-31, no. 10; Hoogewerff, 1936-1947, 3:285-86 (ca. 1526-1527); Wegner, 1959, p. 8 (ca. 1520); Friedländer, 1963a, pp. 60-61, 69 (ca. 1528); Reznicek-Buriks, 1965, p. 244, no. 16 (ca. 1528); Von der Osten and Vey, 1969, p. 178; *Der Grossen Galerien,* n.p. (ca. 1528; influence of Dürer); Friedländer, 1967-1976, 10:54 (soon after 1522), 83, no. 124 (ca. 1528); Oslo, Nasjonalgaleriet, 1973, pp. 295-96, no. 657 (ca. 1528); Brown, 1978, p. 782 (associated in style and technique with the Leiden *Last Judgment* [Figs. 17-19, Cat. 20]); Vos, 1978a, p. 130 (ca. 1527); Filedt Kok, 1978, pp. 40-41, 66, 117, 119, 126 (ca. 1528, by comparison with the dated print by Simon Frisius [Fig. 31]; suggests possibility of an intermediate drawing between the one in the British Museum and the painting); Vos, 1978c, p. 500, n. 102 (perhaps referred to by Van Mander, fol. 214r); Parshall, 1978-1979, p. 52 (late 1520s).

In this painting, the Virgin is wedged into a shallow space between the deep blue background curtain and the cloth-covered ledge on which the Christ Child stands. Christ holds an apple, symbolic of the Fall and the hope of redemption through Mary and her son, the "new" Adam and Eve.[1] The Virgin looks at the Child, whom she holds with her right hand, while with her left she presses her bared breast. This variation of the *Virgo lactans* (nursing Virgin) composition, in which Mary readies her breast before it is suckled, is based on an earlier tradition popularized in the north by the Master of Flemalle in his *Salting Madonna*. The half-length format and its subject, an intimate moment between mother and child prior to feeding, suggest that the panel was intended for domestic use.[2] This abbreviated format became customary for private devotional images not only because of its smaller, less expensive size, but also because of its popular motifs. The pose of the Virgin at a window, frequently indicated by a balustrade or parapet in the foreground, is a reference to the heavenly window "through which God shed the true light on the world."[3] The plant in the right foreground of Lucas's painting has not been conclusively identified, but its small white flowers and its location are comparable to the lilies in Joos van Cleve's *Virgin and Child* in Cambridge, and it probably serves a similar symbolic function.[4]

An etching by the early seventeenth-century Dutch artist Simon Frisius, signed with Lucas's monogram and dated 1528 (Fig. 31), bears a close resemblance to the Oslo *Virgin and Child*.[5] Differences in pose, dress, and attributes suggest that the print was modeled on a lost variant of the Oslo composition, but the similarities confirm a date of circa 1528 for the painting. The amplitude of the Virgin's form in the Oslo panel parallels the development in Lucas's engravings of 1528–1530 toward a greater plasticity and corporeality of the figures. But the Child is closer in type to the awkwardly proportioned figures of the 1527 *Two Putti with a Coat of Arms* (B.167) or 1528 *Venus and Cupid* (B.138) than to the Raphaelesque putti in the 1530 series of the *Virtues* (B.127-33). Comparison of both figures with the women and children in the late paintings places the Oslo panel between *Moses after Striking the Rock* in Boston, dated 1527 (Fig. 24, Cat. 7), and the *Dance around the Golden Calf* in Amsterdam, circa 1529–1530 (Fig. 32, Cat. 11). Although the Oslo Virgin is similar to the massive Israelite woman in the foreground of the *Dance,* the Christ Child does not yet show the easy movement and convincing anatomy of the child in the later panel.

A signed preliminary black-chalk drawing for the composition is in the British Museum (Fig. 30). Filedt Kok has shown that there is a great difference between the sketchy chalk underdrawing of the painting itself, mainly limited to rapid suggestions of figural contours, and the more careful, detailed style of the preliminary drawing. Although this drawing is the only surviving preliminary study for a painting by Lucas, it typifies the contrast in styles during his late period between his independent drawings and the underdrawing of his paintings.[6] At this time Lucas seems to have relied more heavily on separate studies as a means of determining compositional and figure types, no longer feeling the need for the detailed preparatory work of his early panels. The British Museum drawing, as a working sketch, showed a number of variations from the painted image, including changes in dress, the tilt of the Virgin's head, and the pose of the Christ Child, whereas the cursory lines of the underdrawing simply served as an indicator of the final form of the composition, with one exception: the only change that occurred during the painting process itself was his decision to show the head of the Child in three-quarter rather than profile view.

Van Mander's description of a small, sweet painting of the Madonna in the collection of Bartholomeus Ferreris, Leiden, might have referred to this work, but it could also have described the other *Virgin and Child* by Lucas, in Berlin (Fig. 11, Cat. 12), or several variants known only from copies (see Cat. C22).[7]

❦ Cat. C24. *Christ Healing the Lepers* (fig. 63)

Location unknown, presumably lost; circa 1529–1531.

Copies: (1) Painting, artist unknown; California Palace of the Legion of Honor, San Francisco, inv. no. 1958-100 (as Lucas); panel, fragment, 76 x 102. *Prov.*: Coll. Sir Alec Martin; sale Viscountess d'Abernon and others, London (Christie), June 27, 1952, no. 33 (as Lucas; 76 x 100.5). *Lit.*: Leiden, Stedelijk Museum, p. 71 (North Netherlandish, ca. 1545).

(2) Drawing, by Jan de Bisschop (Fig. 63); Stedelijk Museum "De Lakenhal," Leiden, inv. no. 1135; pen in brown ink, and brown wash, 29 x 41.9. *Prov.*: Coll. R. Begeer, Voorschoten; acquired 1963. *Exh.*: Florence, Istituto universitario olandese di storia dell' arte, 1971, no. 28. *Lit.*: Leiden, Stedelijk Museum, 1983, p. 71 (after lost painting by Lucas); Gibson, 1986, pp. 44, 48 (perhaps copied after an original by Lucas in tempera on linen, painted a few years earlier than the Leningrad *Christ Healing the Blind Man* [Fig. 35, Cat. 25]).

Christ is the central focus of this composition; he stands in profile with his arms upraised, blessing the ten lepers at the right (Luke 17:11–14). Behind him at the left are the disciples and followers who accompanied him on his journey to Jerusalem. In the foreground, a woman rests at the roadside with her two children, while a dog explores their basket of food. A sequel to the episode is depicted in the background. The cured lepers exit to the right; one turns back in order to thank the Savior (17:15) and is shown again at the left as he kneels before Christ and receives his blessing (17:16–19).

The painting in San Francisco (Copy 1) shows only the left half of the composition and has been reduced along the upper and lower edges. The figure of Christ is cut off at midshin, and the landscape ends just above the scene in the background. Otherwise it is close to the drawing, with only slight variations in the *staffage,* but the modeling is very hard and the figures are more elongated and ill proportioned than those in the copy by De Bisschop. The museum's attribution of the painting to Lucas is certainly incorrect, and it appears to be a later sixteenth-century copy.

The composition of the drawing (Copy 2, Fig. 63) must go back to an original by Lucas from his late period. The layout is extremely close to that of Lucas's *Christ Healing the Blind Man* in Leningrad, from 1531 (Fig. 35, Cat. 25). It is also comparable to a lost representation of the *Meeting of David and Abigail,* known from a drawing by De Bisschop (Fig. 61, Cat. C10). The figures are typical of Lucas's later style. The affected, splayed-leg poses reappear in the painting in Leningrad and in *Moses after Striking the Rock* in Boston, dated 1527 (Fig. 24, Cat. 7). The figure of Christ, with his thin face and voluminous drapery, is echoed in the Leningrad panel and also related to the figure of God the Father in Lucas's engraving *God Forbids the Eating of the Fruit* from 1529 (B.2). The woman in the foreground is similar in appearance and function to the woman with her children in the drawing of the *Baptism of Christ* in the Louvre, and her profile and hairstyle are especially reminiscent of *Justicia* in Lucas's engraved series of the *Virtues,* 1530 (B.131).[1] Given these comparisons, the original by Lucas would seem to have been painted around 1529–1531.

Cat. 25. *Christ Healing the Blind Man* (Figs. 35, 37–38)

The Hermitage, Leningrad, inv. no. 407; canvas, transferred from panel; joined center and wings 115.7 x 150.3; signed "L" on rock in central foreground; 1531.

Cat. 26. *Shield-Bearers* (Fig. 39)

The Hermitage, Leningrad, inv. no. 407; canvas, transferred from panel, originally the exterior of the wings of the triptych; 89 x 33.5 each.

Provenance: commissioned by Jacob Florisz. van Montfoort and Dirckje Boelensdr. van Lindenburgh;[1] acquired from Leiden by Hendrick Goltzius, Haarlem, 1602;[2] Coll. Pierre Crozat, Paris, 1740 to 1772;[3] acquired by Catherine II for The Hermitage in 1772; exterior wings sold at 1854 auction, The Hermitage; Coll. M. A. Kauffmann, St. Petersburg;[4] acquired again by the museum in 1886.

Exhibition: Amsterdam, Rijksmuseum, 1986, pp. 151-53, no. 38.

Literature: Van Mander, 1604, fols. 212v-213r (acquired 1602 by Goltzius; dated 1531 on exterior of wings; probably Lucas's last painting); Orlers, 1641, pp. 359-61 (copied from Van Mander's account); Bullart, 1682, p. 397; Le Comte, 1702, p. 320; Descamps, 1753, p. 44 (mostly taken from Van Mander; adds that the colors are very fresh, and the paint is easily and rapidly applied); Rathgeber, 1844, col. 218, nos. 800-802; Michiels, 1847, pp. 115-16; Waagen, 1864, p. 120; Kugler, 1867, p. 574; Leningrad, Hermitage, 1870, pp. 16-17, no. 468; Rosenberg, 1877, p. 12 (exterior figures probably the donors); Woltmann and Woermann, 1882, p. 534; Evrard, 1884, pp. 658-59 (nos. 319-20), 693-94 (no. 395, authenticity not proven); Semenov, 1885-1886, p. 39; De Somof, 1899, pp. 259-60; De Somof, 1901, pp. 198-99, no. 468; Friedländer, 1901, p. 4; Greve, 1903, pp. 151-52; Kiewning, 1903, pp. 142-44 (first publication of letter from the court painter Johann Tilmann to Count Simon zur Lippe, Amsterdam, June 7, 1603, mentioning the poor condition of a highly priced painting by Lucas in Goltzius's collection);[5] Rooses, 1903, p. 16; Jan Veth, 1906, p. 42 (influence on Rembrandt's 100 Guilder Print, B.74); *Catalogues de ventes,* 1909, pp. 5, 87, no. 338; Dülberg, 1909, pp. 16-17; Wrangell, 1909, pp. xi, 67; Beets, 1910 (identifies coats of arms on exterior as those of Jacob Florisz. van Montfoort and Dirckje Boelensdr. van Lindenburgh; perhaps the bearded, cloaked nobleman and the woman beside him in the right foreground of the interior are the donors; probably owned by Jacob's eldest son Dirck until 1602); Heidrich, 1910, p. 54; Kekule von Stradonitz, 1910 (agrees with Beets in identifying coats of arms); Kekule von Stradonitz, 1911; Peltzer, 1911-1912, p. 106 (concerning the attempt by Rudolf II to buy the triptych); Réau, 1912, p. 472; Beets, 1913, pp. 113-18 (probably commissioned for a hospital in Leiden); Wrangell, 1913; Hirschmann, 1916, pp. 39-40 (reprints 1603 letter of Johann Tilmann and suggests he exaggerated the bad condition of the painting); Kahn, 1918, pp. 114-16; Conway, 1921, p. 484 (perhaps earlier than 1531); Baldass, 1923, pp. 20-23 (no Italian influence on the figures); Winkler, 1924, pp. 266, 268; Burger, 1925, p. 156; Peltzer, 1925, p. 87; Dülberg, 1929, p. 169 (perhaps influence of Jan van Scorel in the combination of figures with landscape); Gavell, 1929, p. 398; Wescher, 1929, p. 169; Dülberg, 1933, pp. 12-13;

Hoogewerff, 1936-1947, 3:306-12 (central panel originally had a semicircular top); Knuttel, 1938, pp. 130-31 (Italianizing landscape influenced by Van Scorel); Van de Wetering, 1938, p. 50 (landscape painted completely in the style of Van Scorel); Beets, 1940, pp. 57-58; Toth, 1943, p. 77; Münz, 1952, 2:101; Beets, 1954, pp. 447, 450 (influence on exterior figures of Dürer's *Four Nude Women,* B.75); Leningrad, Hermitage, 1955, pp. 16-17; Leymarie, 1956, p. 50; Von Löhneysen, 1956, pp. 289-91, 301; Leningrad, Hermitage, 1958, p. 24; Jaeger, 1960, p. 94; Gerson, 1962, p. 28; Nikulin, 1962, pp. 28-29; Friedländer, 1963a, pp. 67-68; Boon, 1964, col. 352; Nikulin, 1964 (sees a self-portrait of Lucas in the man wearing the red hat in the left background and points out its similarity to Dürer's silverpoint drawing in Lille [Fig. 70]); Nikulin, 1965 (studies the history and condition of the painting; probably originally in a frame similar to that of the *Dance around the Golden Calf* in Amsterdam [Fig. 32, Cat. 11]); Lewinson-Lessing, 1965, no. 57; Stuffmann, 1968, p. 93, no. 302; Friedländer, 1969, p. 126; Von der Osten and Vey, 1969, p. 179; Descargues, n.d., pp. 88-89; Nikulin, 1972, pp. 111-19, no. 56 (detailed information on physical changes during the nineteenth century and present condition; suggests influence on the exterior figures of Dürer's *Triumphal Arch of Maximilian,* B.138); Filedt Kok, 1978, pp. 115-18, 122, 126 (summary, careless underdrawing, probably in black chalk); Kloek, 1978, p. 458; Nikulin, 1978 (a reworking of his 1965 article); Silver and Smith, 1978, p. 276; Vos, 1978a, pp. 88-92; Vos, 1978c, p. 494-96, nn. 68-77 (mistakenly describes the medium as tempera rather than oil); Bangs, 1979a, p. 137, n. 1 (*Shield-Bearers* perhaps influential for Aertgen van Leyden's figures holding coats of arms on the exterior of the Valenciennes *Last Judgment*); Gibson, 1986, pp. 47-48.

Copies: (1) Painting, artist unknown (Fig. 36); copy in triptych format of the interior; Suermondt Museum, Aachen, inv. no. G. K. 472; panel, central panel 114 x 84; each wing 114 x 32. *Prov.:* bequest Weber-van Houtem, 1886. *Exh.:* Utrecht, Gebouw voor Kunsten en Wetenschappen, 1913, no. 52 (modified repetition by Lucas); Utrecht, Aartsbisschoppelijk Museum, 1962, no. 52 (circle of Jan van Scorel). *Lit.:* Aachen, Suermondt Museum, 1902, p. 81, no. 40 (copy after Lucas); Dülberg, 1909, p. 17 (attributed by many to Van Scorel); Beets, 1914, p. 59; Cohen, 1914, p. 31 (very close technically to Leningrad painting); Aachen, Suermondt Museum, 1932, p. 157 (circle of Van Scorel); Jaeger, 1960, p. 94, no. 47 (by Van Scorel after Lucas); Grimme, 1963, p. 212, no. 113 (circle of Van Scorel); Nikulin, 1972, p. 116 (Van Scorel; different man in place of the Leningrad self-portrait); Filedt Kok, 1978, p. 135; Vos, 1978a, p. 93; Amsterdam, Rijksmuseum, 1986, 2:151-52.

(2) Painting, artist unknown; copy, on two panels, of the exterior figures;

location unknown; panel, each 90 x 34. *Prov.*: sale Oehler, Frankfurt am Main (Heinrich Hahn), June 27, 1934, no. 77 (illustration on cover of catalogue; perhaps by Jörg Breu the Elder).

(3) Drawing, by Gabriel de Saint Aubin, 1771-1772; copy of the united interior, with the exterior wings in separate frames attached to the sides; chalk; in margin of *Catalogues de ventes,* 1909, p. 5. *Lit.*: Nikulin, 1978, p. 301 and fig. 3.

The center of *Christ Healing the Blind Man,* both thematically and compositionally, is the representation of Christ healing the blind beggar Bartimaeus (Mark 10:46-52, Luke 18:35-43). Lucas depicted the moment just prior to the miracle, as the beggar stumbles forward with his eyes closed. The main group is limited to three figures, Christ, Bartimaeus, and the beggar's youthful guide. As narrated in the gospels, Christ is accompanied by his disciples and a large crowd. These figures are placed to the left and right in two roughly symmetrical groups, extended without interruption onto the original wings of the triptych. Nine disciples are shown behind Christ, and the rest of the crowd is composed of Pharisees, well-dressed townspeople, and four or five adults in gypsy costume accompanied by children. Two *coulisses* at the far left and right lead to distant towns, the one at the left presumably Jericho. The central landscape is formed of a dense growth of trees.

The middle ground is populated by two groups. Above Christ's head several figures, including a woman dressed as a gypsy, converse among themselves. On the winding road at the upper right Lucas shows an event from the following day. After leaving Bethany with his disciples, Christ turned to a fig tree for nourishment, but finding no fruit, he cursed the tree and condemned it to sterility (Mark 11:12-14). This simple and seemingly meaningless event is recalled later in the narrative as an exhortation to faith. The next day, as the disciples passed the tree again, they noticed that it had withered because of Christ's curse. Jesus responded with a call for faith that parallels the central theme of the healing of Bartimaeus (see Mark 10:51-52 and 11:20-24).

On the exterior wings, now detached from the front, two monumental figures emerge from shallow niches (Fig. 39). In elaborate costumes and active poses, they present the coats of arms of the donors Jacob Florisz. van Montfoort and Dirckje Boelensdr. van Lindenburgh. According to Van Mander, the exterior of the triptych was dated 1531.[6] This date was probably painted on the upper section of one of the two wings, which were shortened by approximately twenty-seven centimeters sometime before 1755.[7]

Although the triptych format was traditionally associated with a church setting, it could well be that this painting, like Lucas's *Dance around the Golden*

Calf triptych (Fig. 32, Cat. 11), was intended for domestic use by the Van Montfoort family. A large number of triptychs during this period seem to have served no church function.[8]

Nikulin has described the changes the painting suffered in the eighteenth and nineteenth centuries. Today the surface is badly worn and repainted, especially on the exterior wings, and the original triptych format is difficult to detect. The most substantial alterations took place between 1740 and 1755, while the painting was in the Crozat collection. The inner and outer wings were sawn apart and the inner wings attached to the central panel to form one continuous composition. Additions to the upper corners were probably made at this time to form a regular rectangle. The outer wings were framed separately and attached to each side of *Christ Healing the Blind Man*. The joins between the original central and side panels are conspicuous: the one at the left separates the red-robed apostle leaning toward Christ and the seated man turning away from him; the one at the right divides the two elegantly dressed men, one in red hose and the other in yellow, facing in opposite directions. Although Lucas intended the three inner panels to be viewed as a continuous scene, he was clearly aware of the importance of representing a well-framed composition within each unit. In 1848, the united interior was transferred from panel to canvas, and in 1850 the same procedure was carried out for the exterior wings.[9]

The slightly smaller sixteenth-century painting in Aachen (Copy 1, Fig. 36) retains the triptych format, although Lucas's *Shield-Bearers* are not reproduced on the exterior of the wings. The interior foreground is a relatively faithful reproduction of the original, especially the number and positions of the figures. One of the few changes in the foreground group occurs in the man in the red hat at the far left, who was identified by Nikulin as a self-portrait. This figure in the Leningrad painting does bear some resemblance to Dürer's silverpoint drawing of circa 1521, now in Lille and supposedly of Lucas (Fig. 70). In 1972, Nikulin suggested that the supposed self-portrait had become an entirely different man in the Aachen copy, but a close examination reveals that the basic facial structure of both figures is the same.[10] The alterations to the Aachen figure were superficial—the addition of a dark mustache, the hair turned gray, the eyes lowered, and the hat slightly altered—and such variations are also found in other figures in the copy. For example, among the apostles in the Aachen panel are found an added beard, a change of hair color, and a shifted glance. There is no reason to believe the "self-portrait" was treated in some special way by the copyist.

Details of the background landscape were significantly altered in the Aachen triptych, although the general location of trees, mountains, and architecture remained the same. Almost all of the middle-ground *staffage* was eliminated, and only the distant figure of Christ remained, shifted to the left. Some of the most obvious variations occurred in those areas in the upper corners that were added at a later date in the Leningrad triptych. It seems that the copyist simplified to a rectangle the shape of the original, which was probably curved at the top, and then filled in the upward extension of the landscape. He seems to have been influenced in his representation of landscape and background architecture by the circle around Jan van Scorel.[11]

The painted copy of the exterior *Shield-Bearers* (Copy 2) is quite close in pose and costume to the original. The architectural setting was reduced on all sides and greatly simplified. The walls flanking the niches were stripped of decoration, and the foreground flight of stairs was reduced to one shallow step. The rather dainty appearance of the figures suggests the copy was executed by an eighteenth-century artist. If so, these panels would give no clue as to when the original wings were cut down.

Saints

Cat. 27. *History of St. Hubert*

Location unknown, presumably lost; tempera on canvas; circa 1506.
Provenance: commissioned by the Lord of Lochorst, Leiden.
Literature: Van Mander, 1604, fol. 211v; Evrard, 1884, pp. 36–37, 671; Beets, 1913, pp. 80–81; Vos, 1978c, p. 483, nn. 21–24; Bangs, 1979a, p. 95; Wolfthal, 1989, p. 17.

The painting of St. Hubert is known only from Van Mander's description: "When he was a child twelve years old, he painted a canvas with water-color, being the history of St. Hubert, that was a very wonderful thing and made him very well-known. This piece was made for the Lord of Lochorst, who gave him as many gold guilders for it as the years of his age."[1]

Lucas probably represented St. Hubert's conversion, which took place on a hunting trip when he was confronted by a stag with the image of the crucified Savior between its antlers. Hubert's conversion is almost identical to that of St. Eustace, also an officer in the Roman army, and Vos has suggested that Lucas's composition was influenced by Dürer's engraving of *St. Eustace* from circa 1500 (B.57).[2] The subject would have provided an ideal exercise in landscape, which was an abiding interest for Lucas from the time of his early prints. The painting was made for the Lochorst family, wealthy inhabitants of the castle Gravensteen, and was probably commissioned by Gerrit, who was Lord of Sliedrecht as early as 1497. He was later a member of the Council of Forty and Sheriff of Leiden before his death in 1548.[3]

Lucas made several paintings in tempera on canvas, although the only one extant is *Moses after Striking the Rock* (Fig. 24, Cat. 7). The technique seems to have been common in the Netherlands at that time as a way of decorating walls less expensively than with tapestries. All of Lucas's known paintings from his early period are very small (34 x 46 or smaller), but given the medium, this painting would probably have been somewhat larger.[4] It was apparently made in 1506, calculating from the birth date of 1494 cited by Van Mander. In this case, it would be the earliest known painting by Lucas.

Cat. 28. *St. Andrew* (Fig. 8)

Staatliche Kunsthalle, Karlsruhe, inv. no. 1478; panel, 21.8 x 16.8; circa 1512–1517.
Provenance: acquired in 1925 from the Coll. Von Eichler, Karlsruhe.
Exhibitions: Rotterdam, Museum Boymans–van Beuningen, 1936, no. 85 (ca. 1511); St. Gallen, Kunstmuseum, 1947, no. 56.
Literature: Karlsruhe, Kunsthalle, 1929, p. 70, no. 1406; Wescher, 1929, p. 169; Hoogewerff, 1936–1947, 3:247 (shortly after 1512); Baldass, 1937a, p. 128; Lauts, 1957, pp. 34, 44, no. 39 (ca. 1511–1512); Friedländer, 1963a, p. 57 (ca. 1516; probably a fragment); Reznicek-Buriks, 1965, p. 244 (ca. 1516); Karlsruhe, Kunsthalle, 1966, p. 172 (ca. 1511–1512); Friedländer, 1967–1976, 10:83, no. 130 (ca. 1511); Gibson, 1977, p. 193 (influence of the stylized rock formations of the Lamentation Master);[1] Filedt Kok, 1978, pp. 56–57 (a fragment, probably from the right wing of a triptych; the direct paint technique would suggest a late date, but the forms and coloring point to ca. 1515–1520; unusual lack of underdrawing); Vos, 1978a, p. 187, no. 201 (ca. 1518).

This small panel represents the half-length figure of the apostle St. Andrew with a distant view of a rocky landscape. He is reading a book, here a symbol of the New Testament, and rests one arm on a cross. Medieval accounts record his martyrdom by crucifixion in Greece, and legend has it that he asked to die on the X-shaped cross, feeling unworthy of imitating Christ.[2]

X-radiographs reveal that the painting is a fragment of a larger panel that was cut down on the upper, lower, and right sides. The panel was originally rounded at the upper left, but a small piece was added to fill in the corner, presumably at the same time as the other alterations. The curved line marking the addition is apparent in the illustration (Fig. 8). Filedt Kok suggests the painting formed the inside right wing of a triptych, the most likely hypothesis given the direction in which the saint is turned. If the figure had belonged to the left exterior panel, he would have been looking away from the compositional center.³

In its original state, the panel probably showed St. Andrew in full length unaccompanied by any other figures. There would scarcely have been room for a kneeling donor, although there is a chance that a second saint was depicted to the right of Andrew.⁴ Netherlandish triptychs frequently show saints on the wings, flanking a devotional image in the center. The size of the *St. Andrew* panel suggests that the original triptych was a small altarpiece, designed for a domestic setting or private chapel. It was perhaps similar in measurement and intent to Jan Provost's triptych in the Mauritshuis, with a half-length Virgin and Child on the central panel and full-length saints on the wings. It is not unusual to find paintings of saints that were later cut down to a half-length format in order to increase their salability as private devotional images.⁵

The panel must have been painted in the 1510s, although an exact date is difficult to determine. It has been placed circa 1511–1512, but its figure style is clearly more mature than that of *Potiphar's Wife Accusing Joseph* (Fig. 4, Cat. 1) or *Susanna before the Judge* (Fig. 6, Cat. 3). Andrew's head is smaller in relation to his body, and there is a greater sense of volume in the form beneath the heavy drapery. Scholars have dated it later in the decade than the Wilton House *Card Players* (Fig. 9, Cat. 38), but the carefully delineated hair and beard of the saint are closer to earlier works.⁶ Although the thick, broad brushwork is very different from the thin, flowing style of *Potiphar's Wife Accusing Joseph* and the later *Card Players* in Wilton House, the unusual technique may be due to the panel's original purpose and location on the inside right wing of a triptych, as a contrast to the finer work in the center panel.⁷ *St. George* (Fig. 43, Cat. C29) may have been the counterpart to *St. Andrew* on the left wing, both probably the donor's patron saints, and the panels should be dated between *Potiphar's Wife Accusing Joseph,* circa 1510–1511, and the *Card Players,* circa 1517.

Cat. C29. *St. George* (Fig. 43)

Location unknown, presumably lost; circa 1512–1517.

Copy: Drawing, by Jan de Bisschop (Fig. 43); British Museum; pen and ink in sepia and sepia wash; 22.7 x 17.8. *Prov.:* acquired from the Coll. Sir Peter Lely, 1874. *Lit.:* Hind, 1926, p. 39, no. 4 (copy after some unidentified painting, apparently by Lucas); J. G. Van Gelder, 1957, pp. 94 (no. 8), 96, 98 (probably after a lost work by Lucas; influence of Dürer).

The drawing by Jan de Bisschop shows St. George in three-quarter length, holding a banner and dressed in armor covered by a tunic and cloak. The cross emblazoned on the tunic is one of his attributes, since this young tribune of the Roman army is best known for killing, in the name of Christ and under the sign of the cross, a dragon that was terrorizing the countryside.[1] The head of the slain beast lies in the bottom left corner of the composition.

The drawing is probably a copy after a lost work by Lucas, which must have been painted close in time to *St. Andrew* in Karlsruhe, circa 1512–1517 (Fig. 8, Cat. 28), and the *Card Players* in Wilton House, circa 1515–1517 (Fig. 9, Cat. 38). The saint's facial features, the representation of his ear, and the style of his hat are all similar to the card-playing man at the center of the Wilton House panel. The composition is closest in feeling to the painting of *St. Andrew*, now a fragment, which probably belonged to the inner right wing of a triptych. The similarities between the two compositions are striking, and the drawing by De Bisschop may well have been copied after some portion of the inner left wing of the same lost triptych. This could only be the case if alterations had already been made to the panel, as with *St. Andrew*. It is possible that this hypothetical triptych by Lucas was dismantled (sometime between 1517 and 1650), its wings cut down, and their curved upper edges filled in to make rectangular panels that would have been salable as devotional images of individual saints.

The two compositions are in certain respects mirror images. The saints are posed in opposite directions, so both would have faced the purported central panel when the wings were open. The long, diagonal staff of George's banner exactly matches in size and placement the arm of Andrew's X-shaped cross. The landscapes are also comparable, with a group of trees in the left foreground and a more distant view of mountains at the right. Finally, the costumes of the two saints are close in design, and the broad curves of the mantels echo each other around the arms. In both works the drapery is formed of broad, rather simplified areas with a few deep folds. Although tunics and cloaks give the figures a sense of bulk, the bodies beneath them are somewhat frail. This is especially clear in the thin forearms, similar to those in the Wilton House *Card Players*.

Thus, the original after which De Bisschop's drawing was copied may once have formed part of the inner left wing of a triptych dating from the middle years of the second decade. St. George frequently appeared in Netherlandish paintings in his role as the patron saint of soldiers and as a namesake.[2] Because of its similarities in style and composition, the painting of *St. Andrew* in Karlsruhe could well have been the counterpart of *St. George* on the right wing of the same triptych.

Cat. C30. *St. James the Greater Raising a King and Queen of Spain* (Fig. 48)

Location unknown, presumably lost; circa 1522-1527.
Copy: Engraving, by Nicolaes de Bruyn (Fig. 48); 57.1 x 44.5; signed and dated at the top "Nicolaes de Bruyn Sculptor 1600," with a variant of Lucas's monogram in the foreground, and entitled "MIRACVLA SANCTI IACOBI." *Lit.*: Hollstein, 1949-1974, 4:17, no. 115 (after Lucas).

The apostle St. James the Greater (Jacobus Major in Latin, Santiago in Spanish) was martyred in Jerusalem, but medieval legends elaborated on the facts of his life to include a journey to Spain and a subsequent burial of his relics in Compostella. From the thirteenth century on he was often dressed as a pilgrim, as in this engraving, where he is identified by his attribute of the scallop shell.[1] In the foreground the saint raises a king and queen of Spain from the dead, while behind them various animals are brought for sacrifice. The figure types are similar enough to Lucas's style to warrant attribution to him, although the monogram is slightly different in its hooked top from Lucas's usual signature. One can compare the men at the left to those in the engravings of *St. Jerome*, 1521 (B.114), *St. Christopher*, 1521 (B.109), and *Sts. Peter and Paul*, 1527 (B.106), for example, or to Peter and Paul on the exterior of the Leiden *Last Judgment*, 1526 (Fig. 23, Cat. 20), and to figures in *Moses after Striking the Rock* in Boston, 1527 (Fig. 24, Cat. 7). Similar parallels can be drawn between the resurrected queen and the Virgin Mary in Lucas's engravings of *The Crucifixion* from 1516 and 1521 (B.75 and B.52) and in the lost painting of *Christ as Man of Sorrows and Virgin of Sorrows*, 1522 (Fig. 47, Cat. C16).

The background architecture is more clearly Italianate than in the early engravings from 1510 of *Ecce Homo* (B.71) and *The Return of the Prodigal Son* (B.78), pointing to a date for this composition in the 1520s. A later date can be verified by the fact that the decorative details are closest to the ornamental prints of 1527-1528 (for example, B.161, 162, 164, 167). The capitals formed from faces are particularly reminiscent of the mask in B.167. The overall layout of the background scene is found again in two other late works, also known only through copies: *Judgment of Solomon* (Fig. 59, Cat. C6) and *Susanna in Her Bath* (Fig. 60, Cat. C9), both circa 1526-1531. Other details supporting an attribution to Lucas include the foreground zone with steps and ledges (compare B.19, 23, 31, 43, 133) and the plants in the right corner (compare B.1, B.84, and Figs. 44 and 60).

Although the king and queen are centrally placed, the composition is arranged asymmetrically along a diagonal into depth. The balanced classicism of Lucas's latest paintings is not evident here, and the design should probably be placed closer to the engraving of *Virgil Suspended in a Basket* from 1525 (B.136). The subject may have been inspired by Lucas's trip to Antwerp and was perhaps intended to commemorate the close association between Flanders and Spain: Charles V was raised a Fleming, became king of Spain in 1516, and enjoyed his first protracted stay there from 1522 to 1529.

Portraits

Cat. 31. *Portrait of a Man Aged 38* (Fig. 10)

National Gallery, London, inv. no. 3604; panel, 46.5 x 40.5; inscribed "38" on a paper held in the sitter's hand; circa 1521.

Provenance: perhaps owned by Claes Adriaensz. van Leeuwen, Leiden, 1604; Coll. Cornelis van Doeswerff, Leiden, 1686;[1] sale Coll. Alexandre le Breton van Doeswerff, Leiden, July 31, 1775, no. 1 (as a self-portrait of Lucas); bought by the art dealer Abraham Delfos, Leiden;[2] sale Leiden, August 26, 1788, no. 79 (as a self-portrait of Lucas, 1521);[3] acquired by Lewis Fry, Bristol, ca. 1850 (as a Holbein);[4] presented to the museum in memory of Lewis Fry by his children, through the National Art-Collections Fund, 1921.

Exhibitions: London, Royal Academy of Arts, 1902, no. 157 (by Holbein); Leiden, Stedelijk Museum, 1978, no. 5 (by Lucas, ca. 1521).

Literature: Friedländer, 1902, p. 146 (by Lucas, ca. 1520); Dülberg, 1909, p. 13; Beets, 1913, pp. 88-89 (ca. 1521, by comparison with the portrait drawings); Gleadowe, 1922 (ca. 1521); Baldass, 1923, pp. 14, 31-32 (composition but not technique reminiscent of Dürer); Winkler, 1924, p. 268; Burger, 1925, p. 155 (somewhat later than 1517); Dülberg, 1929, p. 168; London, National Gallery, 1929, p. 190 (mistakenly described as painted on canvas); Hoogewerff, 1936-1947, 3:274-75 (incorrectly described as painted on canvas); Barnes, 1937, p. 213; Beets, 1940, pp. 59-60; Beets, 1954, p. 448; Leymarie, 1956, pp. 48-49; Gerson, 1962, p. 28 (influence of Dürer, ca. 1521); Friedländer, 1963a, pp. 61-62, 69 (probably painted ca. 1520-1521 in Antwerp, under the influence of Joos van Cleve; gives incorrect measurements); Boon, 1964, cols. 351-52; Reznicek-Buriks, 1965, p. 244; Davies, 1968, pp. 79-80; Bruyn, 1969, p. 46, n. 27 (ca. 1515-1517); Friedländer, 1969,

p. 126; Friedländer, 1967-1976, 10:54, 84, no. 138 (ca. 1520); London, National Gallery, 1973, p. 392; Brown, 1978, p. 782; Filedt Kok, 1978, pp. 58-60 (probably ca. 1520-1525; only a few chalk lines as underdrawing in the flesh areas); Kloek, 1978, p. 429 (closely linked to the portrait drawings from 1521); Vos, 1978a, pp. 14-15, 188; Vos, 1978b, p. 4; Filedt Kok, 1979, p. 511.

 This portrait was sold in 1775 as a painting by Lucas and was acquired by Lewis Fry seventy-five years later as the work of Hans Holbein the Younger. It was exhibited as a Holbein in 1902, but in his review of the exhibition Friedländer reattributed it to Lucas.[5] Although it is one of only two known painted portraits by the artist, it can be dated by comparison with a group of portrait drawings from around 1521. The similarities to Lucas's *Portrait of a Man* in Leiden, drawn in black chalk and dated 1521, have been noted.[6] The intricate embroidery around the neck of the shirt, the pose of the head, the set of the mouth, and the glance of the eyes are repeated. Although Bruyn prefers a date of circa 1515-1517 for the painting, its technique is most reminiscent of other works from 1520-1522.[7] The precise detailing of the face is not found in either the *Card Players* at Wilton House, circa 1517 (Fig. 9, Cat. 38), or late works such as the *Betrothal* in Strasbourg (Fig. 26, Cat. 44) and the *Virgin and Child* in Oslo (Fig. 29, Cat. 23). The plastic modeling of the face is similar to that of the Berlin *Virgin and Child*, circa 1521-1522 (Fig. 11, Cat. 12), and is closest to the Munich *Virgin and Child with Mary Magdalene and a Donor*, dated 1522 (Fig. 12, Cat. 14). These religious paintings and the Leiden portrait drawing show the same carefully drawn eyes as the man in the portrait, with emphatic and elongated tear ducts and the molded ridges of flesh around the eye sockets.

 The identity of the sitter, dressed in a dark green gown with black collar and cap, is unknown. Although the work was described as a self-portrait of Lucas in the sale of 1775, the man bears no resemblance to any known portraits of the artist. The number 38 on the slip of paper in his right hand must refer to the age of the sitter, which is often included in German portraits, although usually written in the background and accompanied by the words *Aetatis Suae* (his/her age). This sort of information is not often found in Netherlandish portraits, but one exception, memorable for its trompe-l'oeil effect, is Jan van Scorel's *Portrait of a Man* in the Rijksmuseum.[8] There the date of the painting (1529) and the age of the sitter appear on a painted scrap of paper seemingly attached to the simulated frame at the base of the panel. Blank scrolls or pieces of paper are held by the sitter in a number of northern portraits, but the depiction of the sitter's age on the paper is more unusual.

Two examples are Quinten Massy's *Portrait of a Man* (Coll. Reinhart, Winterthur), which has a complete inscription on the paper, and a *Portrait of a Man* in the Louvre incorrectly attributed to Van Scorel.[9] The choice of a scroll as a prop for his sitter might have been suggested to Lucas by portraits by Dürer and Jan Gossaert. Dürer's *Bernhard von Riesen* portrait in Dresden, painted during the artist's trip to the Netherlands, and Gossaert's *Portrait of a Man* in New York, circa 1520-1525, recall Lucas's painting in composition, pose, and the use of an inscribed paper. Lucas could also have seen and studied Joos van Cleve's portraits on his trip south, including Van Cleve's *Portrait of a Man* in Vaduz, which has marked similarities to this *Man Aged 38*.[10]

Cat. 32. *Portrait of a Man* (so-called *Self-Portrait*) (Fig. 14)

Herzog Anton Ulrich-Museum, Braunschweig, inv. no. 160; panel, 28.9 x 21.4;[1] circa 1525-1527.

Provenance: acquired 1777 by the Fürstliche Bildergalerie, Salzthalen, near Braunschweig (as a self-portrait by Hans Holbein);[2] carried to Paris by Marechal Denon in 1807; returned to Braunschweig in 1815.[3]

Exhibitions: Rotterdam, Museum Boymans–van Beuningen, 1936, no. 79; Amsterdam, Rijksmuseum, 1952, no. 84 (ca. 1518-1519, according to the costume); Amsterdam, Rijksmuseum, 1958, no. 128; Delft, Prinsenhof, 1964-1965, no. 72 (ca. 1511); Leiden, Stedelijk Museum, 1978, no. 1; Braunschweig, Herzog Anton Ulrich-Museum, 1980, no. 2 (self-portrait from the late 1520s; the physiognomic differences from Dürer's drawing of Lucas in Lille [Fig. 70] must be explained by the difference in age).

Literature: Pape, 1836, pp. 75-76, no. 202 (by Hans Holbein the Younger); Pape, 1849, pp. 75-76, no. 202 (by Maarten van Heemskerck); Blasius, 1868, p. 13, no. 108 (by Van Heemskerck); Colvin, 1882, pp. 134-35 (by Lucas; source of Stock's engraving [Copy 6, Fig. 16]); Riegel, 1882, 2:145-49 (a self-portrait by Lucas, by reference to the Stock engraving [Copy 6], but the inscription on the print is wrong in that it seems to represent a man about thirty rather than fifteen years old); Scheibler, 1883, p. 191 (possibly by Lucas, although the attribution is not unassailable); Evrard, 1884, pp. 703-4 (no. 414), 795-96 (an original by Lucas or an old copy of Stock's engraving; ca. 1510); Riegel, 1885, p. 25, no. 25; Dülberg, 1899c, pp. 77-78 (self-portrait of Lucas in his twenties, dating from the late 1510s); Riegel, 1900, p. 110, no. 160; Von Frimmel, 1907, pp. 38-39; Waetzoldt, 1908, p. 395; Dülberg, 1909, pp. 1, 13 (ca. 1517); Bock, 1910 (soon after 1510; must be separated by at least a decade from the portrait by Dürer in Lille); Heidrich, 1910, p. 54; Ring, 1912-1913, pp. 31, 71, 112-13 (ca. 1510); Beets, 1913, pp. 17 (ca. 1510-1511), 84 (ca. 1509-1510); Vermeulen, 1915 (earliest possible date is 1518, because of the type of smocked shirt collar represented; the misleading inscription in Stock's engraving must be due to poetic license); De Jonge, 1916 (ca. 1519; minor corrections of Vermeulen's analysis of the costume); Kahn, 1918, p. 2 (probably late 1510s, by comparison with the Berlin *Virgin and Child* [Fig. 11, Cat. 12]); Conway, 1921, pp. 464-66 (not a self-portrait; uses measurements to show that a different man is represented than in Dürer's drawing in Lille); Gleadowe, 1922, p. 180 (apparently a self-portrait, but a different type than in Dürer's portrait in Lille); Baldass, 1923, pp. 13, 31, 39 (probably painted when Lucas was about twenty years old); Winkler, 1924, p. 268; Burger, 1925, p. 155; Dülberg, 1929, p. 168; Gavelle, 1929, p. 43 (perhaps the same portrait mentioned by Van Mander);[4] Wescher, 1929, p. 169 (Stock unreliable as a source of information); Friedländer, 1930, p. 498 (1509); Dülberg, 1933, p. 7 (datable between ca. 1510 and 1516); Beets, 1934, p. 57; Goldscheider, 1936, p. 23 (questionable as a self-portrait because of differences from Dürer's portrait in Lille); Hoogewerff, 1936-1947, 3:269, 271-72 (represents Lucas at about twenty years, ca. 1515-1516; Stock's inscription is surely incorrect and perhaps was a mistake on the plate); Baldass, 1937b, p. 206; Beets, 1940, pp. 6, 8 (painted when Lucas was about eighteen); Benesch, 1945, p. 85; Boon, n.d., p. 19; Pelinck, 1949, p. 194; Müller-Hofstede, 1951, p. 243; Leymarie, 1956, p. 48; Müller-Hofstede, 1959 (presents the findings of the restoration by H. Wernicke begun ca. 1951, in particular the removal of eight layers of varnish and paint in the background to reveal what he considered to be the original red tempera; ca. 1521-1522, under the influence of his meeting with Dürer); Bruyn, 1960, p. 61 (skeptical of the reliability of the Stock engraving compared with Dürer's drawing in Lille); *Braunschweiger Presse*, 1963 (discussion of Wernicke's restoration); Friedländer, 1963a, pp. 10, 53, 69 (stylistically closer to ca. 1511 than 1509); Van Hall, 1963, p. 186, no. 1 (ca. 1509-1519); Nikulin, 1964, pp. 17-18 (agrees with an early dating, by comparison with the portrait of Lucas by Dürer and a self-portrait he identifies in the Leningrad *Christ Healing the Blind Man* [Fig. 35, Cat. 25]); Boon, 1964, col. 351 (ca. 1508); Reznicek-Buriks, 1965, p. 244 (ca. 1512); Friedländer, 1967-1976, 10:47, 52-53, 84, no. 135; Schubert, 1973, p. 27; Gibson, 1977, p. 144; Filedt Kok, 1978, pp. 58-60, 145 (no underdrawing apparent; the last layer of green tempera in the background was probably original and wrongly considered a later overpainting; difficult to date because of the damaged condition, but probably ca. 1525-1530 by comparison with the Leiden *Last Judgment* [Figs. 17-19, Cat. 20]); Vos, 1978a,

p. 21; Brown, 1978, p. 782 (ca. 1512–1515); Vos, 1978b, p. 3; Parshall, 1978–1979, p. 52 (certainly by Lucas, but probably incorrectly identified as a self-portrait; perhaps painted in the late 1510s); Filedt Kok, 1979, p. 510.

Copies: (1) Painting, artist unknown; location unknown. *Prov.*: with Norbert Fischman Galleries, London. *Lit.*: *Burlington Magazine* 83 (November 1943): ii, with illus. (portrait of Lucas); Van Hall, 1963, p. 186, no. 1 (ca. 1800).

(2) Drawing, by Peter Paul Rubens (Fig. 15); Fondation Custodia, Institut Néerlandais, Paris; brush and bister, 27.9 x 20;[5] inscription in reverse on banderole around lower frame of the oval: "Illustrat Fama Labores" (Labor crowned by fame); inscription on simulated stone at base: "Lucas Leydanus / Sculptorum Columen, Lux, Lunaq[ue], Solq[ue], penelli" (Lucas van Leyden, prince of engravers, the light, the moon, and the sun of the art of painting).[6] *Prov.*: Coll. Pierre-Jean Mariette, Paris; sale Mariette, Paris, November 15, 1775, no. 1016 (by Rubens),[7] bought by Abbé Charles de Tersan; sale Tersan, November 8–30, 1819; Coll. Marquis de Lagoy; Coll. A. Danby Seymour; sale Coll. Miss Seymour, London (Sotheby), April 26, 1927, no. 32, bought by F. Lugt, Paris (inv. no. 2889). *Exh.*: Antwerp, Koninklijk Kunstverbond, 1927, no. 7; Rotterdam, Museum Boymans–van Beuningen, 1938, no. 401; Paris, Institut Néerlandais, 1959, no. 3; Delft, Prinsenhof, 1964–1965, no. 153; London, Victoria and Albert Museum, 1972, no. 81. *Lit.*: Rooses, 1886–1892, 5:267, no. 1511; Lugt, 1943, pp. 100–103; Held, 1959, pp. 151–52, no. 149 (ca. 1630–1635); Müller-Hofstede, 1959, pp. 235–37; Van Hall, 1963, p. 186, no. 1; Vos, 1978a, p. 21; Vos, 1978b, p. 3 (ca. 1630); Braunschweig, Herzog Anton Ulrich-Museum, 1980, p. 43.

(3) Drawing, by D. P. G. Humbert de Superville (1770–1849); Prentenkabinet, Kunsthistorisch Instituut der Rijksuniversiteit, Leiden, inv. no. PK479; pencil, pen and brown ink; inscribed in pencil, lower right, "Effigies Luca Leidensis propria manu / incidere" (portrait of Lucas van Leyden engraved by his own hand). *Prov.*: Kneppelhout legacy. *Lit.*: Van Hall, 1963, p. 186, no. 1.

(4) Drawing, artist unknown; location unknown; pen and brush. *Prov.*: with N. Beets, Amsterdam. *Lit.*: Müller-Hofstede, 1959, p. 236, n. 18; London, Victoria and Albert Museum, 1972, p. 108, n. 5.

(5) Drawing, by Jan de Bisschop; Albertina. *Prov.*: Coll. J. Goll van Franckenstein, 1833. *Lit.*: J. G. Van Gelder, 1957, p. 96, no. 13 (after the painting or Stock's print [Copy 6]); Eisler, 1967 (after Stock's print).

(6) Engraving, by Andries Jacobsz. Stock (Fig. 16); signed on banderole below the portrait "L. de Leyde Pincit" and "And. Stokius fecit"; inscribed on same banderole: "Effigies Lucae de Leyda, Pictoris et sculptoris Incomparabilis, / dum esset annor[um] XV ad ectypum propria ipsius manu depictum / Obyt Lugd [uni] Batav[orum] anno MDXXXIII Aetat suae XXXIX"

(Portrait of Lucas van Leyden, the incomparable painter and engraver, when he was 15 years old, after the painting by his own hand. He died in Leiden in 1533, at the age of 39). *Lit.*:[8] De Marolles, 1666, pp. 37–38; Le Comte, 1702, p. 319; Muller, 1853, p. 159, no. 3320c; Van Someren, 1888–1891, 2:412, no. 3353; Buchelius, 1928, p. 88.

(7) Engraving, in reverse, by De Larmessin; in Isaac Bullart, 1682, 2:395; inscribed "LUCAE LEIDANO PICTORI" and signed "De Larmessin, scul."

(8) Engraving, in reverse, artist unknown; in D'Argenville, 1745, p. 47; inscribed "LUCAS DE LEIDEN" on the shell frame.

The subject of this bust-length portrait is a young man wearing an olive-green cloak and a brownish-black hat. The dark colors and broad, loose brushwork of the costume are a dramatic foil for the finely painted face. The inscription at the base of a seventeenth-century copy engraved by Andries Stock (Copy 6, Fig. 16) describes the painting as a self-portrait by Lucas at the age of fifteen—according to the birth date of 1494 given by Van Mander, the original would have been painted in 1509.[9] But these assertions were made about the work approximately a century after its painting, and both the identification as a self-portrait and the dating of 1509 are now highly controversial. In light of Stock's dubious reliability as a source of information, his inscription should be reexamined with an eye to other material as corroborative evidence.

Although Stock's date of 1509 is frequently questioned by modern scholars, few have challenged the identification of the painting as a self-portrait. Conway and Goldscheider voiced doubts on the grounds that the facial type is irreconcilable with Dürer's silverpoint drawing in Lille, supposedly a portrait of Lucas made in 1521 (Fig. 70). Recently, similar reservations were expressed by Filedt Kok, Vos, and Parshall.[10] Vos, who has published doubts about all of the so-called portraits of Lucas, has opened the way for a reconsideration of the problem. I provide a full discussion of this issue in the Appendix, concluding that there is insufficient evidence for considering the painting a self-portrait.

Since its reappearance as a work by Lucas, the portrait has been assigned a number of dates, which reflect primarily the different criteria used. Few have adhered to the date of 1509 given by Stock. Datings based on estimates of the age of the sitter have ranged from 1508–1512, when Lucas was in his mid-teens, to 1524, when he was thirty.[11] Methods of dating based on an analysis of the costume and on stylistic comparisons with other known works by the same artist are more reliable, considering the uncertainty of the sitter's identity. A study of his dress led Vermeulen to conclude that the earliest possible date for the portrait was 1518. Vermeulen showed that the type of smocked collar worn by the man in the portrait was not seen in Germany until the late

1510s, from where it spread via Antwerp to the northern Netherlands. De Jonge arrived at roughly the same date of around 1519, although by different means. He identified the type of collar as a simpler ruffled style that had been popular throughout the second decade of the sixteenth century but had not appeared before 1510. He seems to follow Dülberg in his assertion that Stock mistakenly cited Lucas's age in the engraved inscription as XV (painted in 1509) rather than XXV (in 1519).[12] Numerous comparisons were cited by both Vermeulen and De Jonge, but it remains difficult to determine the exact type of collar worn by the man in the portrait given the rather imprecise, loose painting of that area.

The style of the hat worn by the sitter may prove more useful for dating the portrait. The cushion-like crown, the broad band at the base hugging the sides and back of the head, and the long earflaps usually worn tied together at the top are all characteristics of a type rarely seen in Lucas's early work. The hat worn by one of the men at the far right in the 1509 engraving of the *Conversion of Paul* (B.107), for example, is quite different from this one. Closer parallels are found in works dating from the late 1510s and 1520s. Hats very similar to the one in the portrait are included in Lucas's woodcut *Tavern Scene*, circa 1517–1519 (B.20), in two portrait drawings of 1521, and in the 1525 engraving *Virgil Suspended in a Basket* (B.136), where the hat is seen in a rear view in the right background.[13]

The utility of dating the portrait by means of the costume is clearly limited. A more precise time frame can only be established by an analysis of the paint technique and style. Unfortunately the surface of the paint in the background and along the contours of the figure has been so badly damaged that its original condition is difficult to determine. The restoration in the early 1950s did more to confuse the issue than to clarify it. Müller-Hofstede reported in 1959 that eight layers of background varnish and paint were removed in the restoration, clearing away all later additions and leaving a red background. During this process the restorers removed a layer of green tempera that is now generally thought to have been part of the original background. This green layer of paint had covered a thin strip approximately one centimeter in width, running the length of the man's back; it lent an illusory slenderness to the torso, an effect considered "unbalanced" by Wernicke and Müller-Hofstede. Müller-Hofstede argued that the "restoration" of the proper balance between head and body by the removal of the green layer also resulted in a more harmonious color balance between the green costume and the red background. The thinner silhouette of the torso produced by this layer of green paint is clearly evident in Stock's engraving from the early seventeenth century (Fig. 16), so Müller-Hofstede dated the overpainting of the red background to the second half of the sixteenth century. He observed that the red layer must have been exposed for at least twenty years, to judge from its weathered appearance. On the other hand, Filedt Kok has suggested that the background of the portrait was originally similar to that of the *Portrait of a Man* in London (Fig. 10, Cat. 31): an underpainting of red covered by a glaze and finally an upper surface of green. He contradicts Müller-Hofstede's claim, arguing that the green layer was added soon after the painting of the red background. He based this assertion on the fact that the green was so closely bonded to the layer of paint beneath it that it was removed only with difficulty.[14]

A final resolution of this issue is probably impossible. It should be noted, however, that one characteristic of tempera is that it will bind closely with any paint on which it is laid, regardless of the time elapsed between the application of the layers. Thus Filedt Kok's argument about the bond cannot help in pinpointing the time of the overpainting. The chief restorer at the museum recently noted that there are still traces of green paint, especially on the left side, covering small gaps or damaged areas in the red layer. This supports the idea that the red background must have been left uncovered for some time before it was overpainted.[15] Although red backgrounds are unusual in Netherlandish portraits of the fifteenth and early sixteenth centuries, Lucas could have been influenced by German portraits. Dürer's *Portrait of Bernhard von Riesen* in Dresden was painted during his trip through the Netherlands and might well have been known to Lucas. The bust-length format without hands is also uncommon in Netherlandish painting of the period and has more affinities with German portrait types.[16]

This portrait has often been assigned to Lucas's early and middle periods, from 1508 to 1521, but stylistic evidence seems to support a later date of 1525–1527. Compared to youthful works such as the Berlin *Chess Players* (Fig. 1, Cat. 34), the Rotterdam *Potiphar's Wife Accusing Joseph* (Fig. 4, Cat. 1), or even the *Card Players* in Wilton House (Fig. 9, Cat. 38), the portrait displays a more convincing portrayal of three-dimensional form. The stiffness of the early figures is gone, and the head now turns and tilts easily on its axis. The fleshy rolls of the neck and drooping folds of the eyelids enhance the sense of corporeal solidity. The highlighting of the facial area gives a glow to the flesh and a delicate sheen to the whites of the eyes. This subtle use of highlighting is remarkably advanced compared to the overemphasized and rather crudely modeled *Chess Players*. The closest parallels can be found in two of Lucas's large, multifigured compositions from around 1526–1527: the Leiden *Last Judgment* (Figs. 17–19, Cat. 20) and the Boston *Moses after Striking the Rock* (Fig. 24, Cat. 7).[17] Figures such as the man looking out at the spectator in the middle left of the Boston painting exhibit a similar ease of movement and spontaneity of expression. The individual strokes of white highlighting overlaid on the flesh areas in the portrait panel (for example, across the bridge of the nose and in the whites of the eyes) are comparable to the modeling of the main figures in *Moses* and of the apostles flanking Christ and the seated man in profile in the center foreground of the *Last Judgment*. Despite marked differences in size, purpose, and technique among these three works by Lucas, the stylistic similarities suggest a date of circa 1525–1527 for the Braunschweig portrait.

History Painting

🙰 **Cat. C33.** *Procession of the Holy Sacrament* (Fig. 62)

Location unknown, presumably lost; circa 1527–1531.

Copies: (1) Drawing, by Jan de Bisschop (Fig. 62); Musées Royaux des Beaux-Arts, Brussels, inv. no. 311; pen and ink, with gray wash, 18.9 x 29.5; signed at lower left "L." *Prov.:* Coll. P. Blusse van Zuidland en Velgersdijk, 1870; Coll. De Grez. *Lit.: Inventaire,* 1913, no. 311; J. G. Van Gelder, 1957, pp. 94 (no. 3), 98 (by Jan de Bisschop, perhaps after a lost predella by Lucas); Eisler, 1967 (probably copied after a drawing from the circle of Lucas, now in The Hermitage [Copy 2]).

(2) Drawing, artist unknown; The Hermitage, Leningrad, inv. no. 15127 (as Netherlandish, circle of Lucas); pen and ink, with wash, 13.5 x 27.3; signed at lower right "L." *Prov.:* Coll. I. I. Betzkoy. *Lit.:* Jaffe, 1965, pp. 25–26 and pl. 18a (repaired and reworked by Rubens); Eisler, 1967.

Two monks in the center of this composition carry a chest or reliquary on a decorative stretcher. In the left foreground a couple of men in ragged clothes, one a cripple, remove their hats as a sign of respect. Other poverty-stricken and lame figures kneel as the sacred object passes by. A number of women, apparently nuns by their dress, lead the way in the left background, and at the right a group of well-to-do men talk among themselves as they follow the procession.

Both drawings are signed with Lucas's monogram, and the layout of the scene and style of the figures are very close to his late period. The centralized composition—flanked by a man seen from the rear at the left and a group of citizens at the right—is similar to that of *Christ Healing the Blind Man* in Leningrad, from 1531 (Fig. 35, Cat. 25). In both compositions a child is placed in the lower foreground in order to lead the eye upward, and similar tall hats are worn by men at the right in both. The representation of a number of figures grouped before a distant mountainous landscape is characteristic of many of Lucas's late paintings, such as *Christ Healing the Blind Man, Moses after Striking the Rock* in Boston (Fig. 24, Cat. 7), and *Dance around the Golden Calf* in Amsterdam (Fig. 32, Cat. 11). The large fully rounded figures are also analogous, as are the easy, exaggeratedly graceful poses. The drawings appear to be copied after a painting from Lucas's late period, circa 1527–1531.

Allegorical Genre Paintings

Cat. 34. *Chess Players* (Fig. 1)

Staatliche Museen Preussischer Kulturbesitz, Berlin-Dahlem, inv. no. 574A; panel, 27 x 35; circa 1508.

Provenance: Coll. Baron Werther, Vienna;[1] Coll. Suermondt, Aachen; acquired in 1874 from Suermondt.

Exhibitions: Washington, National Gallery, 1948, no. 105; Amsterdam, Rijksmuseum, 1950, no. 64 (ca. 1508); Schaffhausen, 1951, no. 46; Amsterdam, Rijksmuseum, 1958, no. 124 (ca. 1510).

Literature: Waagen, 1862, pp. 152–53; Kugler, 1867, p. 575; Rosenberg, 1877, pp. 4–6 (earlier attributed to Lucas, but recently recognized as a work by Cornelis Engebrechtsz.); Berlin, Königliche Museen, 1880, p. 72 (style of Lucas; probably by the master himself); Woltmann and Woermann, 1882, p. 533; Berlin, Königliche Museen, 1883, pp. 238–39 (early work by Lucas); Hymans, 1884, p. 151 (by Lucas); Von Frimmel, 1898, pp. 64–65, 204–5 (identified as the gaming scene in the Vienna Schatzkammer [see note 1]); Friedländer, 1901, p. 3 (ca. 1510); Dülberg, 1909, p. 12 (ca. 1510); Heidrich, 1910, p. 52; Berlin, Kaiser Friedrich-Museum, 1911, pp. 410–11; Beets, 1913, pp. 81–82 (ca. 1510); Kahn, 1918, pp. 2, 24 (ca. 1508–1510); Conway, 1921, p. 472; Baldass, 1923, pp. 14–15, 29–30, 33 (ca. 1508, but because of its confident technique not Lucas's first painting); Demonts, 1923, p. 129 (very different from the Louvre *Fortuneteller* of ca. 1510 [Fig. 2, Cat. 35]; perhaps a German adaptation of a lost painting by Lucas); Winkler, 1924, p. 264; Burger, 1925, p. 154; Dülberg, 1929, pp. 167–68 (perhaps before 1511); Friedländer, 1930, p. 494 (not earlier than 1508); Sterling, 1930, pp. 110–12; Berlin, Staatliche Museen, 1931, p. 249 (ca. 1508); Dülberg, 1933, p. 6

(ca. 1510); Fritsch-Estrangin, 1936; Hoogewerff, 1936–1947, 3:228 (ca. 1508); Baumgart, 1939, pp. 502–3; Beets, 1940, p. 45; Toth, 1943, p. 77; J. A., 1951, pp. 92–94 (identifies the game as courier, a variant of chess); Beets, 1954, p. 445; Pittsburgh, Carnegie Institute, 1954, p. 11; Leymarie, 1956, p. 48; Wichmann, 1960, p. 300, no. 82; Niemeijer, 1961, p. 19; Gerson, 1962, p. 27; Murray, 1962, p. 484; Friedländer, 1963a, pp. 47–48 (ca. 1508); Boon, 1964, p. 351 (ca. 1508); Poch-Kalous, 1965, p. 7; Reznicek-Buriks, 1965, p. 244 (ca. 1508); Held, 1966, p. 447; Schuyer, 1968, p. 26; Friedländer, 1969, p. 125 (ca. 1510); Van Marle, 1971, 2:65, n. 2; Friedländer, 1967–1976, 10:50–51, 61, 84, no. 140 (ca. 1508); Parshall, 1974, pp. 98, 106–9 (ca. 1508); Berlin, Staatliche Museen, 1978, p. 229 (ca. 1508); Filedt Kok, 1978, pp. 19–26, 120–21, 123, 125 (ca. 1508–1510; careful, detailed underdrawing with thin brush and black paint); Kloek, 1978, p. 439; Vos, 1978a, pp. 104–5 (ca. 1508); Wurfbain, 1978, p. 202–4 (ca. 1510); Washington, National Gallery, 1979–1980, p. 114.

Copies: (1) Painting, artist unknown; location unknown; panel. *Prov.:* Coll. Bernard, Lyon.[2] *Lit.:* Berlin, Königliche Museen, 1891, p. 143; Sterling, 1930, p. 111, n. 1.

(2) Painting, artist unknown; location unknown; panel, 33.5 x 43. *Prov.:* Coll. Conte Salasco, Vicenza.[3]

(3) Painting, artist unknown; location unknown; panel, 28 x 36. *Prov.:* Coll. Crespi, Milan (no. 83, as sixteenth-century Flemish school).

Twelve figures represented in three-quarter length are tightly packed into this small painting. In the center foreground a young man and woman are seated at a table playing a variant of the game of chess called courier.[4] The woman is in the process of making a move, aided by an elderly adviser, while her opponent seems to react in surprise or puzzlement as he scratches his head. In the left foreground a man is seen from the rear, pointing to the competition. The background is filled with seven men and a woman.

This panel is dated almost without exception to 1508–1510. There are a number of close parallels to Lucas's engravings and drawings of around 1508. As in *Mohammed and the Monk Sergius* (B.126) and *David Playing the Harp before Saul* (B.27), the male faces in the *Chess Players* are square in shape, with emphatic, angular jawlines. Details of the painting, such as the slight unevenness of the eyes, the slitted lids of some of the figures, and the occasional indication of teeth behind parted lips, recur in these engravings. Also comparable are the small hands with short fingers. The obtrusive, ridged joints of the hand in the center background of the painting are repeated in the left hand of the monk Sergius (B.126). The simple folds of the drapery are closely related to these two prints of 1508. The broad faces and relatively short, thickset figures are also typical of Lucas's drawings of this period: for example, the silverpoint sketch of the *Head of a Young Man Looking Upward* in Berlin and the chalk drawing in the British Museum of the *Head of a Young Man with a Fur Hat*.[5] The heart-shaped faces of the women with their high, broad foreheads compare closely to those in the engraving of *Abraham Renouncing Hagar,* circa 1507 (B.17). By 1509-1510, the figures in Lucas's engravings were taller and lankier and the faces generally thinner. The painting of the *Chess Players* appears to date circa 1508.

Cat. 35. *The Fortuneteller* (Fig. 2)

Musée du Louvre, inv. no. RF 1962-17; panel, 24 x 30.5; circa 1508.

Provenance: Coll. Luzarche d'Azay, Azay le Féron, Indre, France; Coll. Mme. Pierre Lebaudy (née Luzarche d'Azay); acquired in 1962 through a Lebaudy bequest.

Exhibitions: Leningrad, The Hermitage, 1965, p. 27 (doubtful attribution, probably completed by an unknown imitator); Paris, Orangerie des Tuileries, 1967-1968, no. 389 (ca. 1508; earliest known painting by Lucas).

Literature: Demonts, 1923 (copy of a lost painting of ca. 1510 by Lucas); Sterling, 1930, pp. 110-12 (perhaps an original, although differences in technique from the *Chess Players,* Berlin [Fig. 1, Cat. 34], suggest a partial repainting; ca. 1510, and still under the strong influence of Cornelis Engebrechtsz.); Fritsch-Estrangin, 1933 (ca. 1510, contemporary with the Berlin *Chess Players*); Beets, 1934, pp. 49-51, 56 (an original by Lucas, ca. 1510); Pigler, 1936, p. 184 (probably a copy after a lost original); Hoogewerff, 1936-1947, 3:229; Beets, 1954, pp. 445-46; Bergström, 1958, p. 89; Friedländer, 1963a, p. 48 (copy of a lost original of ca. 1508); Reznicek-Buriks, 1965, p. 245 (probably an original of ca. 1515-1517, by comparison with the Wilton House *Card Players* [Fig. 9, Cat. 38]); Laclotte, 1967, pp. 332, 335; Friedländer, 1967-1976, 10:87, supp. 172 (*A Party;* a replica of approximately equal merit as the version in Nantes [Copy 1, Fig. 3]), p. 95; Parshall, 1974, p. 100, n. 2 (not an autograph work by Lucas); Cuzin, 1977, p. 25 (ca. 1508?); Filedt Kok, 1978, pp. 23, 25-26 (ca. 1510-1512; close to the *Chess Players* in paint technique, coloring, and forms, but the thin brush lines of the underdrawing are closer to *Potiphar's Wife,* Rotterdam [Fig. 4, Cat. 1]); Vos, 1978a, p. 106 (ca. 1509); Wurfbain, 1978, pp. 204-5 (somewhat weaker in composition and execution than an original by Lucas; signed "H" in lower left corner, so possibly by

Huygh Jacobsz. in imitation of Lucas);[1] Parshall, 1978-1979, p. 53 (needs to be examined next to more firmly attributed works); Washington, National Gallery, 1979-1980, p. 114.

Copies: (1) Painting, artist unknown (Fig. 3); Musée des Beaux-Arts, Nantes, inv. no. 476; panel, 24 x 31. *Prov.*: Coll. François Cacault, Nantes (as Jan van Eyck); acquired in 1810 with the Coll. Cacault (as unknown Netherlandish artist). *Lit.*: *Magasin Pittoresque,* 1842, p. 324 (attributed to Jan van Eyck and believed to represent Philip the Good consulting a fortune-teller); Nantes, Musée des Beaux-Arts, 1846, p. 110, no. 487 (by Jan van Eyck); Nantes, Musée des Beaux-Arts, 1876, p. 126, no. 541 (as German School, *The Marriage Proposal*); Willshire, 1876, pp. 15-16; Nicolle, 1913, pp. 176-77 (as anonymous sixteenth-century artist); Hargrave, 1930, p. 160; Sterling, 1930, pp. 110-12 (sixteenth-century copy after a lost original of ca. 1510 by Lucas); Beets, 1934, p. 50 (copy); Pigler, 1936, p. 184 (copy); Hoogewerff, 1936-1947, 3:229 (weak copy); Van Rijnberk, 1947, p. 24; Benoist, 1953, p. 141 (replica of the composition by Lucas in Paris); Friedländer, 1963a, p. 48 (considers this painting better than the Paris version, although both are probably copies after a lost original); Reznicek-Buriks, 1965, p. 245, n. 9 (somewhat weaker than the panel in Paris); Bielefeld, Deutsches Spielkarten Museum, 1972, p. 8 (circle of Lucas; representation of the *Prodigal Son*); Friedländer, 1967-1976, 10:84, no. 143 (original?), p. 95; Taylor, 1973, p. 454 (costume from the time of Charles VIII, 1483-1498); Parshall, 1974, p. 100, n. 2 (not an autograph work by Lucas).

(2) Wood engraving, artist unknown; published in *Magasin Pittoresque,* 1842, p. 324 (as Jan van Eyck).

In this small painting, a young woman is seated at a table with a deck of cards. A well-dressed young man stands beside her at the left, doffing his hat as they exchange a flower. In the background another woman offers a fool a cup of wine, which she has apparently just poured from the tankard on the table. The spaces around these figures are packed with eight or nine elderly males, whose heads overlap in a planar frieze.

The painting in Nantes (Copy 1, Fig. 3) is an exact copy but is much weaker in execution. The modeling in the facial areas is harder, and the dominant, decorative pattern of the drapery folds competes jarringly with the main action. There has been some doubt as to whether the Louvre panel is an original by Lucas or a copy after a lost painting from his early period.[2] The composition is remarkably similar to that of the *Chess Players* in Berlin (Fig. 1, Cat. 34). Both are tightly packed with a crowd of three-quarter-length figures in a dark and airless interior, with the foreground table providing the only spatial relief. The facial types are also comparable: the pale, heart-shaped faces of the women contrast with the ruddier faces of the men, with their angular jawlines and diagonally accented cheekbones. In both paintings dark tones dominate—somber browns and deep blue-greens—relieved only occasionally by a rich shade of red or the white headdress of the women. Filedt Kok has also shown that the thin brush lines of the underdrawing are close in style to those of the *Chess Players* and *Potiphar's Wife Accusing Joseph* in Rotterdam (Fig. 4, Cat. 1).[3]

Compared to the *Chess Players,* the paint on the Louvre panel is more loosely and thickly applied. The pasty pigment is swirled on in long, free strokes in the drapery folds—a great contrast to the meticulous hatching of the folds in the Berlin panel, although the loose brushwork on the white fabric of the undersleeves is handled in a similar manner. The bold highlighting of the right sleeve of the youth with the flower is close to the handling of the knotted belt of the female chess player. The more careless technique of the *Fortuneteller* tends to flatten the forms in places (as in the midriff of the woman in the foreground and the left forearm of her companion at the right), but this is a problem of draftsmanship frequently encountered in Lucas's early engravings (for example, B.17, 85, and 149). The highlighting of the facial areas is at times less well integrated and clearly more hastily painted than that of the Berlin panel, but it essentially seems only a variation of the technique used there.

Given the overall similarities to the *Chess Players* in composition, coloration, figure type, and underdrawing, these differences in the application of the paint should perhaps be seen not as the result of a copyist's work but rather as the experimentation of an imaginative and talented young artist. The *Fortuneteller* appears to have been painted in the same period as the panel in Berlin, around 1508.

Cat. C36. *The Betrothal* (Fig. 40)

Location unknown, presumably lost.

Copy: Painting, artist unknown (Fig. 40); location unknown; panel. *Prov.*: with Fiegl, Prague, 1932; with Schatzker, Vienna.[1]

This painting represents five bust-length figures closely confined by the frame. Only the suggestion of a landscape, including the foliage of trees and some clouds, is visible at the top. In the immediate foreground, a young man and woman look at each other and hold hands; at the right stands a fool who points at the couple.² Just behind them are two older men, one of whom looks directly at the spectator. Although the clumsy execution of the figures clearly points away from an attribution to Lucas, the painting is related in many ways to works of his early style. The cramped, airless composition is reminiscent of Lucas's earliest paintings, the *Chess Players* in Berlin (Fig. 1, Cat. 34) and *The Fortuneteller* in Paris (Fig. 2, Cat. 35). Lucas's youthful manner of filling gaps with half-seen faces is particularly noticeable. The facial types are also roughly similar to those of Lucas's early period, as are the fur collar of the young man and the fur-cuffed costume of the woman. Her white headdress is so close to that of the fortune-teller in the Louvre that it might be a line-for-line copy. The painting might therefore be a later sixteenth-century pastiche of early works by Lucas, or a copy after a lost painting or drawing from his early period.

Cat. 37. *Card Players* (Fig. 7)

Coll. Thyssen-Bornemisza, Villa Favorita, Lugano-Castagnola, inv. no. 164A; panel, 29.8 x 39.5; inscribed "FM" on the woman's bodice;[1] circa 1513–1515.

Provenance: Coll. Sir John Philipps (d. 1736), Picton Castle, Pembrokeshire, Wales; Coll. Sir Richard Philipps, Lord Milford (d. 1857); Coll. Sir Charles Edward Gregg Philipps; Coll. Sir Henry Erasmus Edward Philipps; Coll. Mrs. Randall Plunkett, Lady Dunsany (daughter of Sir Henry), Dunsany Castle, Ireland; sale Lady Dunsany, London (Christie), November 26, 1971, no. 72, to G. B. Huiskamp, The Hague; acquired in 1971.

Exhibitions: London, Royal Academy of Arts, 1952–1953, no. 20 (as Lucas); Amsterdam, Rijksmuseum, 1958, no. 130 (probably an early work, although later than the *Chess Players,* Berlin [Fig. 1, Cat. 34]); Washington, National Gallery, 1979–1980, no. 24 (1521; see note 1).

Literature: Beets, 1954, p. 445 (a good repetition of the copy, then in Eindhoven, which he attributed to Lucas, ca. 1510–1512); Friedländer, 1963a, p. 52 (by Lucas; mistakenly gives the measurements, in reverse, of the Eindhoven copy); Reznicek-Buriks, 1965, pp. 242, 244 (ca. 1515 or somewhat earlier); *Connoisseur* 79 (March 1972): 220–21, no. 2 (sold for £105,000 at Christie's); Friedländer, 1967–1976, 10:88 (Add. 181), 94; Parshall, 1974, pp. 98–99, 109 (ca. 1512, by comparison with Lucas's engravings of the *History of Joseph,* B.19–23); Utrecht, Gemeentelijke Archiefdienst, 1976, p. 104, no. 55 (by Lucas, ca. 1520); Eisler, 1977, p. 86, n. 8 (incorrectly identifies the *Card Players* as two paintings, one owned by Lady Dunsany and the other by Miss Randall Plunkett); Stewart, 1977, pp. 68, 174 (nos. 87–88; ca. 1512);[2]

Filedt Kok, 1978, p. 36 (a weak and heavily restored painting by Lucas, ca. 1515; similar to the *Card Players,* Wilton House [Fig. 9, Cat. 38], in coloring, figure types, and underdrawing); Vos, 1978a, pp. 110-11, 187 (ca. 1515); Wurfbain, 1978, p. 202, n. 7 (attributed to Frans Minnebroer because of the initials FM; see note 1); Parshall, 1978-1979, p. 53 (needs to be examined next to more firmly attributed works); Eisler, 1989, pp. 216-19, cat. 31 (after Lucas, ca. 1520).

Copy: Painting, artist unknown;[3] location unknown; panel, 42 x 51. *Prov.:* with N. Beets, Amsterdam, 1935; Coll. A. F. Philips, Eindhoven. *Lit.*: Beets, 1940, pp. 45, 47 (considered an original by Lucas, somewhat earlier than the *Chess Players,* Berlin [Fig. 1, Cat. 34]); Beets, 1954, p. 445 (an original by Lucas); Amsterdam, Rijksmuseum, 1958, p. 109; Friedländer, 1963a, p. 52 (a replica of the panel in the Coll. Thyssen); Friedländer, 1967-1976, 10:87, supp. 171 (by Lucas, ca. 1512); Parshall, 1974, pp. 98-99, n. 2 (a poor copy); Stewart, 1977, p. 175, no. 89 (after Lucas, ca. 1512).

The three figures playing cards in this painting are seated at a round table in a wooded landscape. The woman in the center has apparently just laid a jack of spades and some coins on the table. She looks at the fashionably dressed young man to her left, who is showing a king of spades. To the right, an elderly man pulls an eight of spades from the stack of cards.

The painting is in poor condition—overpainted and retouched in a number of places.[4] Despite these alterations, it is possible to classify the work as an original by Lucas from around 1513-1515. The parallels to his *Card Players* in Wilton House, circa 1515-1517 (Fig. 9, Cat. 38), go beyond general similarities of composition and figure type. The hands are extremely close in form and description, and the careful detailing of the eyes (with their emphatic tear ducts and delicately painted triangular bags under the lower lids) is also comparable. The thin brush lines of the underdrawing are visible beneath the flesh areas, as in the Wilton House panel. Also characteristic of Lucas's style are the careful outlining of the woman's upper lip and the short vertical strokes describing the lip of the elderly man.[5] Certain colors also reappear—bright red details are important unifying elements in both compositions, and the mustard-orange robe boldly edged with black, worn by several men in the Wilton House painting, recurs in slightly varied form on the card-playing young man. The figures are closer in proportion, however, to the paintings of 1510-1512. Their relatively large heads match those in *Potiphar's Wife Accusing Joseph* in Rotterdam (Fig. 4, Cat. 1) and *Susanna before the Judge,* formerly in Bremen (Fig. 6, Cat. 3). The panel was probably painted during 1513-1515, after these works and not long before the *Card Players* in Wilton House.

Cat. 38. *Card Players* (Fig. 9)

Collection Earl of Pembroke, Wilton House, Salisbury; panel, 34.7 x 47.5; circa 1515-1517.

Provenance: at Wilton House before 1730, probably bought by Thomas, 8th Earl of Pembroke.

Exhibitions: London, British Institution for Promoting the Fine Arts, 1849, no. 137; Manchester, 1857, no. 422; London, Burlington Fine Arts Club, 1892, no. 59 (signed);[1] London, Royal Academy of Arts, 1929, no. 30; Rotterdam, Museum Boymans-van Beuningen, 1936, no. 82; Bristol, Red Lodge, 1946, no. 7; London, Eugene Slatter, 1949, no. 19; Leiden, Stedelijk Museum, 1978, no. 4 (ca. 1515).

Literature: Passavant, 1833, p. 141; Rathgeber, 1844, col. 224, no. 946; Michiels, 1847, p. 136, no. 101; Waagen, 1854, p. 152; Kramm, 1860, 4:974; Waagen, 1860, p. 118; Waagen, 1862, pp. 152-53; Kugler, 1867, pp. 137-38; Woltmann and Woermann, 1882, p. 531; Evrard, 1884, pp. 679-80, no. 369; Tschudi, 1893, pp. 108-9 (close in time to the Berlin *Chess Players* [Fig. 1, Cat. 34], although richer in color and more fluid in execution); Wilkinson, 1907, pp. 157-58, no. 98 (strong influence of Quinten Massys); Dülberg, 1909, p. 13 (ca. 1519); Heidrich, 1910, pp. 52-53; Beets, 1913, pp. 112-13 (ca. 1530, based on the costumes and hairstyles; compares figure types to *The Sermon*, Rijksmuseum, which he attributes to Lucas, ca. 1530); Conway, 1921, p. 480 (probably painted slightly before Lucas's trip to Antwerp, 1521); Baldass, 1923, pp. 16, 31, 33 (ca. 1520; represents the game of Hazard); Winkler, 1924, p. 264; Burger, 1925, pp. 154-55 (from Lucas's middle period); Sjöblom, 1928, pp. 165, 172-73 (ca. 1530); Dülberg, 1929, p. 168 (ca. 1515-1520); Wescher, 1929, p. 169 (presumably from the Royal Collection Charles I);[2] Friedländer, 1930, p. 494; Dülberg, 1933, pp. 6-7 (ca. 1516); Hoogewerff, 1936-1947, 3:258-59 (ca. 1515-1518); Baumgart, 1939, pp. 502-3; Beets, 1940, p. 51 (ca. 1530); Toth, 1943, p. 77; Beets, 1954, p. 445; Marlier, 1954, p. 221; Leymarie, 1956, p. 48; Von Löhneysen, 1956, pp. 295, 303; Friedländer, 1963a, pp. 56-57, 68 (ca. 1515); Reznicek-Buriks, 1965, p. 244 (ca. 1517); Sidney, 1968, pp. 44-45, no. 116 (ca. 1514); Friedländer, 1969, p. 125; Van Marle, 1971, 2:68; Friedländer, 1967-1976, 10:54, 84, no. 141 (ca. 1513-1514); Parshall, 1974, pp. 99, 110-11 (ca. 1518); Eisler, 1977, pp. 85-86 (possibly represents the game of primero); Brown, 1978, p. 782 (ca. 1515); Filedt Kok, 1978, pp. 32-36, 120, 125 (ca. 1515-1518; detailed brush underdrawing); Vos, 1978a, pp. 106, 109, 187 (ca. 1517); Wurfbain, 1978, p. 205; Filedt Kok, 1979, p. 511; Washington, National Gallery, 1979-1980, p. 114.

Copies: (1) Painting, artist unknown;[3] Coll. Earl of Haddington, Tyninghame, East Lothian, Scotland; panel, 34 x 47. *Prov.:* in the possession of the Earls of Haddington since 1833. *Exh.:* Edinburgh, Royal Scottish Academy, 1833, no. 534 (as Quinten Massys). *Lit.:* Gray, 1833, p. 8 (attributed to Massys, but probably at least designed by Lucas); London, Burlington Fine Arts Club, 1892, p. 26 (a very good old copy); Wilkinson, 1907, p.157 (a good sixteenth-century copy); Sidney, 1968, p. 45 (probably a sixteenth or early seventeenth-century copy); Parshall, 1974, p. 99, n. 1 (seventeenth century?).

(2) Painting, artist unknown; National Museum, Warsaw, inv. no. Nieb. A134; copper, 35 x 46. *Prov.:* Coll. M. H. Radziwill, Nieberow. *Lit.:* Warsaw, National Museum, 1969, p. 227, no. 667 (copy of the painting in Wilton House).

In this painting, two men and two women sit at a table playing cards and betting with gold coins, while five other figures observe the play. A young man and woman sit on opposite sides of the table, the latter momentarily uninterested in the game as she glances out of the picture frame. An elderly couple standing in the right background also dissociate themselves from the action taking place before them, in contrast to a young man who leans over the shoulder of a woman player and suggests her next play. The game takes place in a stark, undecorated interior, relieved only by a view through an open window of a green and gently rolling landscape.

Although this panel has been universally accepted as an original by Lucas, the dating has varied from 1513 to 1530.[4] Most scholars tend to place the panel in Lucas's middle period, 1515–1520. The figures are still far removed from the massive forms of the Munich *Virgin and Child with Mary Magdalene and a Donor,* dated 1522 (Fig. 12, Cat. 14). The range can be narrowed even further by comparing the relatively thin, flat drapery in the *Card Players* with the much richer and more complex profusion of folds in Lucas's engravings of *Esther before Ahasuerus* of 1518 (B.31) and the *Dance of Mary Magdalene* of 1519 (B.122). When attempting to fix the earliest possible date for the painting, it is useful to compare this work with *Susanna before the Judge,* formerly in Bremen and datable to circa 1512 (Fig. 6, Cat. 3). Although there are similarities in figure type and placement, the composition in Wilton House is more spacious and loosely organized. Furthermore, several details of the costumes recur in the engraving of the *Triumph of Mordecai,* 1515 (B.32). The relatively wide circular hat with an upturned and decoratively spotted brim, at the far left in the print and in the right foreground in the painting, does not reappear in any of Lucas's other prints. The grouping of the figures is reminiscent of the loose clusters in Lucas's *Calvary* of 1517 (B.74), and the drapery, the slim proportions, and the somewhat stiff poses of the individual figures are also comparable. The most likely date for this *Card Players* is circa 1515–1517.

Cat. C39. *Card Players* (Fig. 53)

Location unknown, presumably lost; circa 1522–1525.
Copies: (1) Painting, artist unknown (Fig. 53); Museum of Fine Arts, Budapest, inv. no. 923; panel, 28.2 x 41.2.[1] *Prov.*: perhaps in the Weltliche Schatzkammer, Vienna, 1747–1750; Pressburg Castle, Hungary, 1770;[2] Hofkammerpräsidium, Buda; Nationalmuseum, Budapest, 1848, *Lit.*: Pigler, 1936 (an original by Lucas, ca. 1515–1520); Hoogewerff, 1936–1947, 3:229, n. 2 (Dirck Huyghensz.?; by the same hand as the *Allegory of Transience* [Fig. 50]); Pigler, 1954, p. 316 (by Lucas, ca. 1515–1520); Pigler, 1968, pp. 378–79 (school of Lucas); Parshall, 1974, p. 99 (later copy of an original by Lucas, ca. 1520).

(2) Painting, by Duncan Macalester (1751–1812); Collot d'Escury Foundation on loan to the Museum Mr. Simon van Gijn, Dordrecht; panel, 37 x 44. *Prov.*: Coll. Baron Collot d'Escury, Paris; on loan to the Rijksmuseum, from 1904. *Exh.*: Dordrecht, 1893. *Lit.*: Tschudi, 1893, pp. 108–9 (by Lucas; the players are identified in the exhibition as Cornelis van Bleyenburg [1450–1521], Antwerp, and his first wife Catharina Schoyts [?–1487]; unlikely because the painting was not made before 1515, and the man is youthful); Amsterdam, Rijksmuseum, 1905, p. 198, no. 1453a (seventeenth-century copy, probably after Lucas); Ring, 1912–1913, p. 162 (copy after a lost painting in the style of Lucas).

In the painting in Budapest (Copy 1, Fig. 53) a young couple, shown in three-quarter length, is seated at a table playing cards. Behind them an older man and woman look on and seem to offer advice, and in the background a fool peers from behind a curtain.[3]

Parshall's identification of this panel as a copy after a lost painting by Lucas is probably correct. It is certainly not an original, as Pigler first suggested.[4] The modeling is extremely hard and wooden, the faces are flattened by sharp outlining, and the drapery folds are crudely painted. The large, heavy figures indicate a date for the original of circa 1522–1525, close in time to the two *Vanitas* allegories (Figs. 50–52, Cats. C41–C42) and slightly earlier than the *Card Players* in Washington (Fig. 54, Cat. C43). The broad expanses of the drapery with its thick folds are close to the *Virgin and Child with Mary Magdalene and a Donor* in Munich, dated 1522 (Fig. 12, Cat. 14), as are the somewhat stiff poses. But the greater amplitude of form and more confident use of foreshortening suggest that the painting was made in the following few years.

This copy in Budapest may be by the artist of the *Allegory of Transience* (Fig. 50) and the *Temptation of a Young Man* (Fig. 52), previously mentioned, although it is difficult to judge from the available photographs. The type of drapery fold, the hard outlining of the eyelids, and the dark divisions between the fingers are all characteristic of this artist's style. The *Allegory of Transience* is more rapidly painted, however, and shows less of the hard, wooden qualities apparent in the other two works.[5]

Cat. C40. *A Family Surprised by Death* (Fig. 49)

Location unknown, presumably lost; 1523.

Copy: Engraving, artist unknown (Fig. 49); 10.2 x 13.5; signed and dated at upper right "15L23." *Lit.*: Bartsch, 1803–1821, 7:434–36 (doubtful as Lucas; perhaps designed by him); Rathgeber, 1844, col. 224, no. 948; Beets, 1913, p. 122 (by the same impostor who signed an etching after a drawing by Dürer with Lucas's monogram; see Bartsch, 1803–1821, 7:433, no. 173); Bock and Rosenberg, 1930, p. 39 (copy after Lucas); Hollstein, 1949–1974, 10:244, no. 98 (after Lucas).

This engraving shows two couples—one young, the other elderly—and two children grouped around a table set under trees. To their right is a figure of Death, wrapped in a white shroud and carrying an hourglass. The woman next to him is wreathed in laurel and holds a skull, while a putto hovers overhead, aiming his bow and arrow at the young couple. As in the *Allegory of Transience* (Figs. 50–51, Cat. C41), the theme concerns the brevity and vanity of human life.[1]

The date of 1523 is stylistically appropriate, since the figure types are comparable to those in other works by Lucas from this period. The crone is repeated in two prints from 1524 and 1525 (B.155 and 136), and the young women are similar in facial type and build to those in the three engravings of 1523 (B.82, 84, 157). This work is probably copied after a lost painting from that year.

Cat. C41. *Allegory of Transience* (Figs. 50–51)

Location unknown, presumably lost; circa 1523–1525.

Copies: (1) Painting, artist unknown (Fig. 50); location unknown; panel,

36.5 x 49. *Prov.*: sale Mme. Du B . . . de L . . . (Paris), Amsterdam (F. Muller), November 25, 1924, no. 20 (attributed to Lucas); with De Laborderie, Paris, 1924-1927; sale Cologne (Lempertz), June 3, 1930, no. 55 (school of Lucas); sale Marczell von Nemes, Munich (Hugo Helbing), November 2, 1933, no. 55 (by Lucas); with P. de Boer, Amsterdam, 1936; Coll. H. Schoen, Amsterdam; with Paech, Amsterdam. *Lit.*: Bock and Rosenberg, 1930, p. 39, no. 11842 (related to the Berlin drawing [Copy 2, Fig. 51], but not by Lucas); Hoogewerff, 1936-1947, 3:229, n. 2 (by the same hand as the *Card Players,* Budapest [Fig. 53, Cat. C39]); Friedländer, 1963a, p. 72, no. 6 (in the manner of Lucas).

(2) Drawing, artist unknown (Fig. 51); Kupferstichkabinett, Staatliche Museen Preussischer Kulturbesitz, Berlin-Dahlem, inv. no. 11842; pen and brown ink, 10 x 13.3. *Prov.*: acquired in 1923. *Lit.*: Bock and Rosenberg, 1930, p. 39 (the *Prodigal Son;* by Lucas?); Friedländer, 1963a, p. 72, n. 39 (Winkler; copy of the painting in Amsterdam [Copy 1]).

The painting (Copy 1, Fig. 50) and drawing (Copy 2, Fig. 51) differ only in minor details.[1] The scene is a wooded landscape, and the figures are grouped around a table set with fruit and cups. The focal character, a young man, sits behind the table at the left. He is embraced by a young woman, while another looks on at the right. The allegorical figure of Death, in the form of a shrouded skeleton brandishing an hourglass and barb, peers from behind a tree in the background. A young woman enters from the left carrying a tray with a skull. In the foreground, two children observe the scene, an elderly couple flees to the right, and a fool points mockingly at the young couple.

It has been suggested that the scene represents the temptations of the prodigal son, as in Lucas's woodcut *Tavern Scene* (B.20). It is more likely that both were intended as generalized moralizing scenes, as Filedt Kok has already pointed out in reference to the print.[2] Both show fools ridiculing reckless lifestyles and in this way are comparable to Lucas's gaming scenes (especially Fig. 53, Cat. C39) and to the *Dance of Mary Magdalene* (B.122). In the *Allegory of Transience* Lucas intensifies the moral by including the image of Death (the *Tavern Scene* contains the warning "watch how it turns out"). Like Lucas's engraving of the *Young Man with a Skull* (B.174), the central message is memento mori: the contemplation of death leads to an understanding of the transience of life and the vanity of earthly existence.[3]

The composition has a number of stylistic affinities with Lucas's middle period. The heavy figures, especially evident in the painted copy, are analogous to those in the engravings of 1523-1525 (for example, B.84, 136). The full, rounded faces of the women also recall the engravings, as do the children. Most of the drapery is formed of broad, simple areas with a few thick, angular folds and is comparable to costumes in these engravings. The faces of the older men and women—almost grotesque, with their hooked noses and prominent chins and cheekbones—are also close to types found in the prints of these years (see B.136, 155-57). The two copies appear to be after a lost original by Lucas from circa 1523-1525.

Cat. C42. *Temptation of a Young Man* (Fig. 52)

Location unknown, presumably lost; circa 1525.

Copy: Painting, artist unknown (Fig. 52); location unknown; canvas, transferred from panel, 33 x 48. *Prov.:* Coll. Count Limburg Stirum, The Hague; with François Kleinberger, Paris, 1906-1911; sale Paris (Kleinberger), 1911, no. 85 (by Lucas); Coll. Paul Ganz, Basel; sale Luzern (Fischer), November 21-25, 1972, no. 2544 (attributed to Lucas). *Exh.:* Bruges, Stedelijk Museum, 1907, no. 228 (by Lucas). *Lit.:* Bock and Rosenberg, 1930, 1:39 (similar to the drawing *Allegory of Transience* in Berlin [Fig. 51], but not by Lucas); Friedländer, 1963a, p. 72, no. 7 (in the manner of Lucas; [incorrectly] described as probably a copy of the *Allegory of Transience* [Cat. C41, Figs. 50-51]).

This painting is close to Lucas's composition and figure style. It may be a later work in the manner of Lucas but is most likely a copy after a lost painting by him dating from the 1520s. Five figures are represented in a portico, with the background landscape partially obscured by a wide curtain. A well-dressed young man is seated at a table with an hourglass suspended above his head. He is flanked on his right by a fool dressed in yellow and on his left by a personification of Virtue, in the form of a young woman in classical garb crowned with a laurel wreath.[1] In the left foreground a richly cloaked man with demonic horns spreads a tempting pile of gold coins on the table. He is balanced on the right by a shrouded figure of Death, who points to the skull he carries. The book on the table is perhaps an attribute of Death, containing the roll of the dead. The youth, tempted by the Devil, stares straight ahead and holds steadfastly to Virtue.

The sale catalogue of 1911 identifies the four figures from left to right as Riches, Pleasure, Love, and Memento Mori and suggests the book symbolizes the future. The catalogue for the auction of 1972 calls the scene an allegorical representation of Virtue, the Vices, and Transience. Friedländer called it a Vanitas Allegory, with personifications of the Devil and Death. As in the *Allegory of Transience* (Figs. 50-51, Cat. C41), the work's function as a memento mori is emphasized. The two compositions, which are of comparable size, might well have been pendants. In the *Allegory* the youth squanders his life on the pleasures of the flesh; here warnings about the brevity of earthly existence are heeded. The heavyset figures, full, rounded faces, and broad hands may indicate a slightly later date for the *Temptation* (circa 1525) or may be evidence of the copyist's style. These two allegories may be by the same copyist as the *Card Players* in Budapest (Fig. 53; see Cat. C39).

Cat. C43. *Card Players* (Fig. 54)

Location unknown, presumably lost; circa 1525–1527.

Copy: Painting, artist unknown (fig. 54); National Gallery of Art, Washington, inv. no. 1387 (K1854); panel, 56.4 x 60.9. *Prov.:* with Van Diemen, Berlin, 1923; sale London (Christie), May 20, 1926, no. 269 (as Lucas), to Asscher; with Julius Böhler, Munich, 1929; with Tomas Harris, London, 1935; with Frederick Mont, New York; Coll. Samuel H. Kress, 1951; on loan to museum from the Kress Foundation, from March 17, 1956; given to museum in 1961. *Exh.:* London, Tomas Harris, 1935, no. 19 (as Lucas); Basel, Kunstmuseum, 1945, no. 43 (as Lucas). *Lit.:* Art News 29 (May 16, 1931): n.p. (by Lucas); Fell, 1935, p. 171 (by Lucas, probably ca. 1520); Hoogewerff, 1936–1947, 3:258–59 (by Lucas, ca. 1520); Suida and Shapley, 1956, pp. 118–19, no. 45 (the latest of Lucas's gaming scenes); Morehead, 1957, pl. 2 (by Lucas, ca. 1525; probably the French game *pair et séquence*); Judson, 1961, p. 347 (probably a late sixteenth-century copy); Friedländer, 1963a, pp. 62–63 (by Lucas, ca. 1525), n. 28 (Winkler: probably a copy); Reznicek-Buriks, 1965, pp. 244–45 (not an original); Washington, National Gallery, 1965, p. 78 (by Lucas, ca. 1520); Held, 1966, p. 447 (old copy); Simon, 1966, p. 70; Friedländer, 1967–1976, 10:54, 84, no. 142 (by Lucas, ca. 1520); Parshall, 1974, pp. 99–100, 110–11 (close copy of an original by Lucas, ca. 1525; possibly a heavily overpainted original); Silver, 1974a, pp. 113–14; Washington, National Gallery, 1975, p. 202 (by Lucas, ca. 1520); Amsterdam, Rijksmuseum, 1976b, p. 152; Eisler, 1977, pp. 85–86 (a copy after a lost Lucas, or a painting in the style of Lucas; identifies the game as primero); Filedt Kok, 1978, pp. 128–32 (copy after a lost Lucas or a painting in the style of Lucas; possibly by a German artist); Vos, 1978a, p. 106 (copy after a lost Lucas); Washington, National Gallery, 1979–1980, p. 114 (after Lucas).

This panel shows two couples playing cards around a table. Four other figures—three men and a woman—observe the game with interest, several acting as advisers. The group is well dressed, and the background still life of flowers, fruit, and a few containers adds to the sense of middle-class prosperity.

The painting was at one time accepted as an original by Lucas. Judson questioned its authenticity in 1961, and it is now generally considered a copy after a lost composition by Lucas.[1] The modeling of the flesh areas is hard and linear, and the drapery folds are flat and schematic in places.[2] It has been suggested that the copy might have been painted in Spain, given the extensive still life in the background that includes Spanish *mazapan* boxes. Still lifes are uncommon in Lucas's oeuvre, but a similar arrangement appears in his woodcut *Jael Killing Sisera,* circa 1517 (B.7). He might have been influenced by paintings seen during his trip to Antwerp in 1521. Joos van Cleve, among others, often included still-life representations in his paintings, and similar flat, round containers are found in other Flemish works. For example, the still life in the background of Quinten Massys's *Banker and His Wife* in the Louvre, dated 1514, has several objects in common with the *Card Players.*[3]

The figure types are characteristic of Lucas's style of the mid to late 1520s. The women's faces, for instance, are comparable to those in two panels from around 1527, the *Betrothal* in Strasbourg (Fig. 26, Cat. 44) and the *Virgin and Child* in Oslo (Fig. 29, Cat. 23). The jutting noses and strong chins that distinguish the men reappear in *Moses after Striking the Rock* in Boston, dated 1527 (Fig. 24, Cat. 7). The dresses and necklaces of the two women in the background are close to those in *The Betrothal,* while the gloves worn by the woman at the left are found again in *Moses.* Friedländer noted that the work has features in common with Lucas's engraving of *Virgil Suspended in a Basket* of 1525 (B.136). Although the painting is frequently dated circa 1520, the forms are more robust and expansive than those found in the engravings of *The Promenade* (B.144) or *Young Couple Seated in a Landscape* (B.148). Given these comparisons, a date of circa 1525–1527 for the lost original seems most likely.[4]

Cat. 44. *The Betrothal* (Fig. 26)

Musée des Beaux-Arts, Strasbourg, inv. no. MNR445; panel, 28 x 33.5; circa 1527.

Provenance: acquired in 1951 by the Deposit des Musées Nationaux.[1]

Exhibitions: Amsterdam, Rijksmuseum, 1958, no. 131 (probably cut down on the upper and lower edges); Paris, Petit Palais, 1965–1966, no. 187 (ca. 1519–1520; superior to the version in Antwerp [Copy 1]; examination of the panel shows that it has not been cut down); Leiden, Stedelijk Museum, 1978, no. 3 (1513?, ca. 1520?; the panel was originally larger, ca. 56 x 75).

Literature: Wegner, 1959, p. 8 (ca. 1520); Parshall, 1974, p. 100; Brown, 1978, p. 782 (ca. 1517; background appears overpainted); Filedt Kok, 1978, p. 63 (ca. 1527; paint technique and coloring are similar to the Leiden *Last Judgment* [Figs. 17-19, Cat. 20]; very summary underdrawing in red chalk; upper and lower edges have been cut); Vos, 1978a, pp. 111-12, 190 (ca. 1527); Wurfbain, 1978, pp. 206-7; Parshall, 1978-1979, p. 52 (from Lucas's last period); Filedt Kok, 1979, pp. 510-11.

Copies: (1) Painting, artist unknown; Koninklijk Museum voor Schone Kunsten, Antwerp, inv. no. 202; panel, 30.3 x 32.3. *Prov.:* Van Ertborn bequest, 1841. *Lit.:* Antwerp, Musée d'Anvers, 1849, p. 76, no. 54 (by Lucas); Blanc, 1861, p. 12 (by Lucas); Antwerp, Musée Royal des Beaux-Arts, 1905, p. 153, no. 202 (after an engraving in the manner of Lucas); Beets, 1913, p. 122; J. G. Van Gelder, 1957, p. 96; Antwerp, Musée Royal des Beaux-Arts, 1958, p. 124; Paris, Petit Palais, 1965-1966, p. 143; Filedt Kok, 1978, p. 167, n. 120.

(2) Drawing, by Jan de Bisschop (Fig. 27); Museum Teyler, Haarlem, inv. Qx, no. 43; pen and ink, and wash, in bister, with incised contours; 16.3 x 12.2. *Prov.:* Coll. J. M. Cok, 1771; Coll. J. van der Marck, 1773; Coll. Count van Neale, 1774; Coll. H. van Maarseveen, 1793; Coll. B. Hagedoorn, 1869.[2] *Lit.:* Scholten, 1904, p. 228 (after Lucas); J. G. Van Gelder, 1957, p. 94, no. 6 (pricked for a print [see Copy 4]); Paris, Petit Palais, 1965-1966, p. 143 (similar to the print [Copy 4], but independent of it); Filedt Kok, 1978, p. 167, n. 120.

(3) Drawing, by Jan de Bisschop; Musées Royaux des Beaux-Arts, Brussels, inv. no. 303; pen and ink, and wash, in sepia; 16.3 x 9.4. *Prov.:* Coll. J. Goll van Franckenstein, 1833; Coll. de Grez. *Lit.: Inventaire,* 1913, no. 303 (after Lucas); J. G. Van Gelder, 1957, p. 92, no. 2; Paris, Petit Palais, 1965-1966, p. 143 (similar to the print [see Copy 4], but independent of it); Filedt Kok, 1978, p. 167, n. 120.

(4) Etching, in reverse, attributed to Simon Frisius; 16.7 x 13.3; signed "L" at lower left. *Lit.:* Bartsch, 1803-1821, 7:437, no. 3 (in the manner of Lucas); Rathgeber, 1844, col. 225, no. 966; Volbehr, 1888, p. 47, no. 179 (by Lucas); Beets, 1913, pp. 121-22; Hollstein, 1949-1974, 7:36, no. 195 (as Simon Frisius), 10:241, no. 35 (after Lucas); J. G. Van Gelder, 1957, p. 94 (rejects attribution to Frisius); Amsterdam, Rijksmuseum, 1958, p. 109 (this composition suggests the Strasbourg panel was cut down on the upper and lower edges); Paris, Petit Palais, 1965-1966, p. 143 (probably by Frisius; because of its dimensions, it must correspond to a version other than the Strasbourg panel); Filedt Kok, 1978, p. 167, n. 120.[3]

In this painting two figures are shown in half length. A man slips a ring on the left index finger of his fiancée, while she rests her other hand on his shoulder. The setting is restricted, and the neutral dark background is relieved only by a green curtain pulled back at the left.[4] The panel appears to have been cut down at the upper and lower edges, so it is possible that in its original state it looked like the three seventeenth-century copies (Copies 2–4; Fig. 27).[5] The two drawings by Jan de Bisschop and the etching attributed to Simon Frisius are almost exact copies of the painting in Strasbourg. They show slightly more of the man's sleeve at the bottom, however, and an arched niche or alcove at the top. Jacques Foucart considers the trompe-l'oeil architecture uncharacteristic of Lucas and concludes that it must have been added by the copyists, but the flattened arch was a favorite motif of Lucas's, although not in the exact form shown here. It appears in his engravings (B.22, 63, 71, 136, and 156), woodcuts (B.7, 20), and drawings, so it seems reasonable that the panel in Strasbourg originally included the arch as shown in the copies.[6]

The Betrothal has been attributed to Lucas since its relatively recent appearance in the 1950s. It has been dated by some scholars to Lucas's middle period, circa 1517–1520, but it shows little stylistic relationship to Lucas's works of this time. Wegner, for example, compares the painting to the engravings *Christ Appearing to Mary Magdalene* of 1519 (B.77) and *Young Couple Seated in a Landscape* of 1520 (B.148).[7] The figures in *The Betrothal* are much heavier, however, and the hands and the woman's face are broader. The drapery folds are also simpler and less agitated. A number of prints from around 1520 are thematically related to *The Betrothal*, and the painting in Strasbourg might be a reworking from the late 1520s of this earlier idea.[8]

The rounded face and broad torso of the woman closely match those of the *Virgin* in Oslo (Fig. 29, Cat. 23). The plump jawline and neck reappear in the angel at the left of the central panel in the Leiden *Last Judgment* (Fig. 17, Cat. 20), and the same summary red-chalk underdrawing is found in all three works.[9] The heavy, columnar drapery folds are also similar to those of the angels in the Leiden triptych. The hands of the man in *The Betrothal*, with his knuckles highlighted with double brushstrokes, are treated in the same manner as those of Peter on the exterior of the *Last Judgment* (Fig. 23) and of Moses in *Moses after Striking the Rock* in Boston (Fig. 25, Cat. 7). The dimpled fingers of the woman recall the hands of the *Virtues* of 1530, particularly *Spes* and *Prudencia* (B.128, 130). Brown suggested that the man's profile appeared to have been altered by overpainting, but this three-quarter lost profile is common in Lucas's oeuvre—from the early *Chess Players* in Berlin (Fig. 1, Cat. 34) through his last painting, of *Christ Healing the Blind Man* in Leningrad (Fig. 35, Cat. 25). Very close parallels to this face in lost profile are found among the apostles in the *Last Judgment* and the Israelites in *Moses after Striking the Rock*. Given these comparisons, Filedt Kok's date of circa 1527 seems reasonable.[10]

ALLEGORICAL GENRE PAINTINGS / 179

⚜ Cat. C45. *The Betrothal* (Fig. 28)

Location unknown, presumably lost; circa 1527.

Copy: Painting, artist unknown (Fig. 28); Coll. M. Q. Morris, London, in 1959; panel, 56 x 75; signed and dated "L 1513" at bottom right;[1] inscribed on banderole "het es haest ghetrowt dat langge rowt" (marry in haste, repent at leisure).[2] *Prov.:* with Thomas Agnew, London, 1920; Coll. Louis C. G. Clarke, Cambridge, 1920–1921; with W. E. Duits, London, 1943; with P. de Boer, Amsterdam, 1948–1952; with W. E. Duits, London. *Exh.:* London, Burlington Fine Arts Club, 1920, no. 2 (as Lucas, 1513); Nottingham, Midland Counties Art Museum, 1945, no. 39 (as Lucas, 1513); Amsterdam, De Boer, 1948 (as Lucas); Delft, Prinsenhof, 1949 (as Lucas). *Lit.: Burlington Magazine* 83 (November 1943): iv (by Lucas); Engelman, 1949 (by Lucas); J. G. Van Gelder, 1957, p. 96; Hobhouse, 1959, no. 5 (by Lucas); Wegner, 1959, p. 8; Paris, Petit Palais, 1965–1966, p. 143 (copy of a lost original, ca. 1519–1520; the signature and date are suspect); Parshall, 1974, p. 100, n. 4 (apparently by the artist of the *Card Players* in Budapest [Fig. 53, Cat. C39]);[3] Brown, 1978, p. 782 (ca. 1517); Vos, 1978a, pp. 110–11 (unknown artist; partial copy after the Strasbourg panel).

This composition is an elaboration of *The Betrothal* in Strasbourg (Fig. 26, Cat. 44). The panel is enlarged to include a fool peering from behind the curtain at the left. Out of the mouth of his *marotte,* or jester's wand, appears a banderole, curling above the betrothed couple and inscribed with a warning for those who marry in haste.[4] Otherwise the two paintings are similar, with only minor variations in details of costume and pose. Because of the close relationship between the two works, the lost original of the enlarged version should also be dated circa 1527. The panel in the Morris Collection is carefully painted, but the stiff, hard contours and rather crude modeling lack the vitality of Lucas's *Betrothal* in Strasbourg.

⚜ Cat. C46. *Fluteplayer* (Fig. 64)

Location unknown, presumably lost; 1530.

Copies: (1) Painting, artist unknown; location unknown; panel, 32 x 26. *Prov.:* Private Collection, Castle Herdringen, Westphalia. *Exh.:* Düsseldorf, Kunstverein, 1928, no. 42 (after a lost painting from 1530 by Lucas). *Lit.:* Bruyn, 1983, p. 220.

(2) Engraving, by Bartholomeus Dolendo, in reverse of the painting [Copy

1] (Fig. 64); 18.5 x 14.3; signed and dated on wall to the left of the head "1530 L" and "B Dol. fe."; inscribed on the window frame "Hh ex." (published by Hendrick Hondius) and on the strip at the far left "Wel lustih fluyterken, wilt mynen lust coelen / fluyt met v luytken, dat ickt mach voelen" (Lusty little flute-player, if you want to cool my desire / play the flute with your little lute, so that I can feel it) and "34." *Lit.*: Le Blanc, 1854, p. 135, no. 12 (as Dolendo after Lucas); Nagler, 1845, 1:771, no. 1771; Evrard, 1884, p. 797, no. 3 (self-portrait of Lucas); Von Wurzbach, 1910, 1:412, no. 13; Beets, 1913, p. 121 (after an original by Lucas; misread the date as 1531); Burchard, 1913 (in the manner of Lucas); Hollstein, 1949–1974, 5:259, no. 42, and 10:241, no. 30; Brussels, Palais des Beaux-Arts, 1971, p. 175; Kettering, 1977, p. 34; Braunschweig, Herzog Anton Ulrich-Muscum, 1978, p. 51; Bruyn, 1983, pp. 219–20 (considered a copy after a lost painting by the Pseudo-Heemskerck, based on similarities in the representation of the hands to the *Portrait of a 42-year-old Man* in the Coll. Von Wied, Schloss Waldheim).

In this composition from Lucas's late period a young man, shown in three-quarter length and holding a flute in his hands, is seated in an interior. Although the work might be a portrait, with the flute a reference to the sitter's occupation or avocation, a sexual metaphor is conveyed in the inscription. The flute was known as an attribute of Dionysus and frequently used as a phallic symbol, while the lute mentioned in the poem suggests the female organs because of its shape.[1]

The number 34 in the second state is difficult to explain. Although it might refer to the date 1634, Dolendo's last dated print is from 1629, and it is thought that he died soon after that. If the work is a portrait, the number inscribed by the man's shoulder could indicate his age. A number without any accompanying words is almost certainly a reference to the sitter's age in Lucas's *Portrait of a Man* in London (Fig. 10, Cat. 31), where it appears on a piece of paper held in the man's hand; in two pendant portraits of a man and a woman in Brussels, sometimes attributed to Cornelis Engebrechtsz.; and in a *Portrait of a Man* (Cat. A14) formerly given to Lucas.[2] If Lucas painted this work as a portrait of a specific man, the inscription must have been added later by Dolendo in an attempt to make the print more salable. On the other hand, if the inscription is by Lucas, it was apparently painted originally on the frame and transferred by the copyist.

The large eyes and heavy, fleshy features are reminiscent of the *Portrait of a Man* in Braunschweig (Fig. 14, Cat. 32). The thickset torso and broad, dimpled hands are similar to those of the Strasbourg *Betrothal* (Fig. 26, Cat. 44) and the late *Christ Healing the Blind Man* in Leningrad (Fig. 35, Cat. 25). There is little reason, therefore, to question the date of 1530 given in the engraving.

Erroneous Attributions

Cat. A1. *Lot and His Daughters*

Musée du Louvre, inv. no. RF1185; panel, 58 x 34.
Provenance: acquired in July 1900 from M. P. Cooper.[1]
Exhibitions: Paris, Musée des Arts Decoratifs, 1936, no. 55 (attributed to Lucas); Paris, Musée Cernuschi, 1958–1959, no. 374a.
Literature: Nicolle, 1901, p. 192 (early Dutch school); Dülberg, 1903–1908c, p. 1, no. 12 (by Lucas, ca. 1513–1515); Dülberg, 1909, pp. 12–13 (by Lucas, ca. 1512–1514); Beets, 1913, p. 85 (ca. 1514); Demonts, 1922, p. 63, no. 2640A (attributed to Lucas); Baldass, 1923, pp. 19–20, 32 (ca. 1521–1522, under the influence of Antwerp Mannerism); Briere-Misme, 1924, pp. 4–5; Winkler, 1924, p. 268 (from Lucas's late period); Burger, 1925, p. 156; Edouard Michel, 1926, pp. 92–93; Vogelsang, 1927 (a late variant by Lucas of the composition in the Coll. N. Tellander [Cat. A2, Copy 1]); Dülberg, 1929, p. 169 (ca. 1527); Gavelle, 1929, pp. 308–10 (ca. 1519, based on the type of sleeve depicted); Wescher, 1929, p. 169 (school repetition); Friedländer, 1930, p. 498 (ca. 1508); Dülberg, 1933, p. 7; Beets, 1934, pp. 51–53, 158–61 (ca. 1514; probably by a master in Lucas's immediate circle, e.g., Jan de Cock; influence of Marcantonio Raimondi on the female in the left foreground); Hoogewerff, 1936–1947, 3:238–41 (later repetition of the composition in Rotterdam [Cat. A2]; ca. 1520, perhaps during Lucas's stay in Antwerp; or perhaps by Lucas's brother Dirck Huyghensz.); Baldass, 1937a, p. 128; Knuttel, 1938, p. 129; Van de Wetering, 1938, pp. 49–50 (1509); Bersier, 1951, p. 52; Edouard Michel, 1953, pp. 155–56 (by Lucas, from his early period); Hoogewerff, 1954, p. 59; Leymarie, 1956, p. 51; Artaud, 1960; Marette, 1961, p. 193, no. 234 (by Lucas, ca. 1509); Friedländer, 1963a, pp. 48–50 (ca. 1509); Poch-

Kalous, 1965, p. 7 (ca. 1509); Breustedt, 1966, 1:209-12, 2:62-63, no. 143 (early work by Lucas); Held, 1966, p. 447 (landscape conceived entirely in Patinir's manner and cannot have been painted by Lucas; figures might be by Lucas); Friedländer, 1967-1976, 10:51-52, 82, no. 115 (ca. 1509); Corwin, 1976, pp. 228-30, no. 32 (probably by an Antwerp Mannerist with Leiden influence, ca. 1530s); Filedt Kok, 1978, p. 161, n. 71 (differs from Lucas's work in both composition and technique); Silver and Smith, 1978, p. 255 (attributed to Lucas); Clark, 1979, pp. 78, 80 (school of Lucas, from a design by him); Renger, 1979, p. 58 (not by Lucas); Bangs, 1985, p. 2 (possibly by one of Lucas's family members or by another Leiden painter; ca. 1512, given the reference to the collapse of the tower of St. Peter's, Leiden).

Cat. A2. *Lot and His Daughters*

Museum Boymans-van Beuningen, Rotterdam, inv. no. 2456; panel, 32.5 x 45.

Provenance: acquired in Italy in 1933 by N. Beets, Amsterdam; Coll. D. G. van Beuningen, Rotterdam; acquired by the museum in 1958.

Exhibitions: Rotterdam, Museum Boymans-van Beuningen, 1936, no. 78 (as Lucas); Paris, Petit Palais, 1952, no. 56 (as Lucas).

Literature: Beets, 1934, pp. 52-57 (first attributed to Lucas by Hoogewerff in Rome; ca. 1510-1512; perhaps painted in Antwerp in 1511, under the influence of Bosch; influence of Dürer on the landscape); Beets, 1935b, pp. 198-99 (ca. 1510-1512); Hoogewerff, 1936-1947, 3:235-37 (ca. 1510); Veth, 1936, p. 290; Baldass, 1937a, p. 128; Beets, 1940, pp. 40, 43 (ca. 1511-1512); Hoogewerff, 1954, pp. 58-59; Rotterdam, Museum Boymans-van Beuningen, 1962, pp. 77-78 (ca. 1510-1512); Friedländer, 1963a, pp. 49-50 (the best of the repetitions after the Louvre panel [Cat. A1]; a second conception by Lucas); Breustedt, 1966, 2:63-64, no. 144 (by Lucas); Friedländer, 1967-1976, 10:87, supp. 168 (a free replica of the Louvre painting); Corwin, 1976, pp. 231-32, no. 34 (probably by an Antwerp Mannerist with Leiden influence, ca. 1530s); Bangs, 1985, p. 2 (possibly by one of Lucas's family members or by another Leiden painter; ca. 1512, given the reference to the collapse of the tower of St. Peter's, Leiden).

Copies: (1) Painting, artist unknown; Coll. N. Tellander, Monnaz s/Morges, Switzerland, in 1970; panel, 31 x 41. *Prov.:* with J. Goudstikker, Amsterdam; Coll. A. H. Kleiweg de Zwaan, Amsterdam and Neerlangbroek, 1952; with P. de Boer, Amsterdam. *Exh.:* Amsterdam, Rijksmuseum, 1939, no. 11a (as

Lucas); Delft, Prinsenhof, 1952, no. 17 (as Lucas). *Lit.*: Vogelsang, 1927 (an original by Lucas from his early period; the Louvre painting [Cat. A1] is a later variant by Lucas); Beets, 1934, p. 53 (perhaps also by Lucas, although inferior to the Rotterdam panel in quality); Hoogewerff, 1936-1947, 3:237-38 (a weaker replica or old copy of the Rotterdam panel); Paris, Petit Palais, 1952, p. 32 (one of three versions of the subject by Lucas); Friedländer, 1963a, pp. 49-50 (copy of the Rotterdam panel); Friedländer, 1967-1976, 10:87, supp. 168 (a free replica of the Louvre painting); Corwin, 1976, pp. 294-95, no. 82 (gives measurements as 27.5 x 40; attributed to Lucas Gassel, ca. 1550-1570).

(2) Painting, artist unknown; location unknown; panel, 18 x 23. *Prov.*: with Schatzker, Vienna, 1937. *Lit.:* Ehrenstein, 1923, p. 162, no. 15 (by the Brunswick Monogrammist); Friedländer, 1963a, pp. 49-50 (copy of the Rotterdam panel).

(3) Painting, artist unknown; with Robert Finck, Brussels, at least from 1968 to 1972; panel, 20 x 26. *Prov.*: with J. Gans, The Hague, 1940. *Exh.*: Brussels, Finck, 1968, no. 3 (replica of the Rotterdam painting). *Lit.*: Corwin, 1976, pp. 232-33, no. 35, pl. 54 (replica of the Rotterdam panel).

(4) Painting, artist unknown; Bonnefantenmuseum, Maastricht, inv. no. 529, on loan from the Dienst voor 's Rijks Verspreide Kunstvoorwerpen, no. 1958; panel, 26.4 x 39.6. *Exh.*: Hasselt, Provincial Begijnhof, 1955, no. 15 (southern Netherlandish follower of Lucas, second quarter of the sixteenth century); Amsterdam, P. De Boer, 1937, no. 9 (by Herri met de Bles). *Lit.*: Maastricht, Bonnefantenmuseum, 1958, p. 38.

In the painting in Paris (Cat. A1) the elderly Lot is seated before his tent, fondling one of his daughters while another pours wine at the left. On the bridge in the background, Lot's wife is changed into a pillar of salt as she disobediently turns to see the destruction of Sodom (Gen. 19:23-26, 30-36). This work is in a tall, vertical format; the other paintings are in a horizontal format (Cat. A2). The figures in the left background of the Rotterdam painting (Cat. A2) are arranged in the same relationship to each other, to the tent and tree, and to the background view of Sodom as in the Louvre panel. Their poses differ slightly, however, and a number of landscape details have also been changed: notably, the bridge in the right middle-ground has been transformed into a dirt road flanked by a cottage. Copies 1-3 are all close duplicates of the Rotterdam panel, although of lesser quality. Copy 4 is more loosely related to the others: the three figures before the tent are in the right foreground and are so much smaller than the landscape they inhabit that they are almost reduced to the status of *staffage*.

Even apart from the question of style, the Paris and Rotterdam panels have more compositional affinities to the Flemish school of Joachim Patinir than to the landscapes of Lucas. A standard practice of Patinir's workshop was to fill half the background with steep rocky outcroppings, featuring fantastic architecture and caves, and then add a distant view of a river or harbor to the other side. The composition of *Lot and His Daughters* is much closer to this Flemish format than to any of Lucas's works. Other details also point to the school of Patinir: the tall, spindly foreground tree, the rickety bridge built on pilings, and the winding road painted in streaks of dark and light. The tangled, imaginative vegetation in the foreground of the Louvre panel is quite different from Lucas's carefully detailed and naturalistically observed foliage (see his 1509 print of the *Temptation of St. Anthony* [B.117]). The flamelike representation of the tree stump at the right also has close counterparts in Patinir's paintings. Even the two salamanders in the Rotterdam panel (which Beets correctly associated with Dürer's woodcut of the *Flight into Egypt* [B.89]) are features of Patinir's *St. Christopher* in the Escorial.[2]

The figure types in both the Paris and Rotterdam versions have frequently been compared to early engravings by Lucas. Lot's daughter pouring wine in the left foreground has been associated with the females in *Abraham Renouncing Hagar* (B.17), the *Milkmaid* (B.158), and *Pyramus and Thisbe* (B.135).[3] These *contrapposto* figures have only a general resemblance to Lot's daughter, however; Lucas's female types lack her elegant grace and decorative silhouette. The delicate features and extremely soft, almost blurred modeling in the faces of the Paris and Rotterdam paintings are not executed in Lucas's style, nor is the smooth, polished glaze of the paint surface. In conclusion, none of the six paintings of *Lot and His Daughters* can be attributed to Lucas, nor should they be considered copies after a lost composition by him. They show little, if any, relationship to the Leiden School and should probably be assigned to the Flemish circle of Patinir.[4]

Cat. A3. *Lot and His Daughters*

National Gallery, London, inv. no. 3459; panel, 32.4 x 22.9.

Provenance: sale London (Christie), December 20, 1902, no. 92 (as early Flemish school), bought by T. Blake Wirgman; purchased by the museum in 1919 from Mr. Wirgman.

Literature: London, National Gallery, 1929, p. 106 (Dutch School, ca. 1510; perhaps an early work by Lucas); Beets, 1934, pp. 57–59 (earliest known painting by Lucas, ca. 1507); Beets, 1940, pp. 11, 38, 40, 43 (by Lucas); Friedländer, 1963a, p. 52 (early work by Lucas); Davies, 1968, pp. 80–81 (in the style of Lucas, but an early pastiche after engravings or a lost drawing; costumes ca. 1520); Friedländer, 1967–1976, 10:87, supp. 169 (possibly by Lucas, ca. 1509); London, National Gallery, 1973, p. 392 (style of Lucas); Corwin, 1976, pp. 230–31, no. 33 (probably by an Antwerp Mannerist with Leiden influence, ca. 1530s); Renger, 1979, p. 58 (not by Lucas); Bangs, 1985, p. 2 (possibly by a member of Lucas's family or by another Leiden painter, ca. 1512).

This painting was assigned to Lucas's early period around 1507–1509 by both Beets and Friedländer, and it includes features similar to those found in his engravings from this time.[1] A group of figures seated before a central, tree-covered hillock appears here and in the *Rest on the Flight* (B.38), for example, and the trees and facial types are repeated in early engravings of the *Holy Family* (B.39, 85).

The panel is very crudely painted in parts. The hands are drawn in a rudimentary fashion, the highlighting of the faces is rough and broad, and the landscape is flat and undetailed. Beets suggested that the painting was executed by Huygh Jacobsz. or even Cornelis Engebrechtsz., but it has no stylistic affinities to the oeuvre of Engebrechtsz. or to any of the paintings tentatively assigned to Lucas's father. Davies's hypothesis that the work is an early pastiche in the style of Lucas seems reasonable.[2]

Cat. A4. *Job and His Three Friends*

Courtauld Institute Galleries, Lee Collection, London, inv. no. 44; panel, 40 x 31.

Provenance: Coll. Viscount Lee of Fareham, Richmond.

Literature: Van de Wetering, 1938, p. 50 (by Lucas, ca. 1510); Hoogewerff, 1936–1947, 3:241 (by Lucas; similar to *Lot and His Daughters,* Paris [Cat. A1]); Friedländer, 1963a, pp. 55–56 (by Lucas, ca. 1512); Poch-Kalous, 1965, p. 6; Friedländer, 1967–1976, 10:82, no. 117 (by Lucas, ca. 1510).

In this small painting Job is seated nude on a rock in a landscape, surrounded by his three friends (Job 2:11–13). They are portrayed as musicians, "to condole with him and comfort him" (2:11), and are dressed in costumes of the early sixteenth century.[1]

The figure types are those of the early Leiden School, but the brushwork is more delicate and precise than that of Lucas. The hard, sharply delineated contours of the figures and drapery folds are also foreign to Lucas's style. The background landscape is decoratively painted, with soft, blurred foliage that lacks the detail of Lucas's plants. The tonal recession in the foliage of the trees—with dark masses played off against lighter areas—and the subtle atmospheric perspective of the distant landscape suggest that the panel was painted by a later sixteenth-century artist in the style of the early Leiden School.

Cat. A5. *Angel*

Busch-Reisinger Museum, Cambridge, Mass., inv. no. 1965.24; panel, 35.5 x 27.9.

Provenance: Coll. Sir Robert Abdy; with Mrs. Sterner, New York; Coll. Grenville L. Winthrop, New York (as School of Patinir); bequeathed by him to Fogg Museum of Art, Cambridge, in 1943 (inv. no. 1943.98); transferred to the Busch-Reisinger in 1965 (as Lucas).

Literature: Rosenberg, 1943, pp. 48–49 (early work by Lucas, ca. 1508; probably a fragment from the upper left corner of an *Annunciation*); *Art News* 42 (January 1944): cover; *The Portfolio and Art News Annual* 4 (1961): cover and p. 2.

This panel, which shows an angel on a hill with his wings spread, has been cut down on the bottom and along the right. Rosenberg's suggestion that it was originally part of an *Annunciation to the Shepherds* or *Annunciation to Joachim* is probably correct.[1] Although the angel's features reveal affinities with Lucas's manner (as in the upturned nose and wide-set eyes with heavy, slitted lids), the stylistic differences are even more striking. The elegant and graceful pose, the long, lithe body, and the relatively easy foreshortening of the right arm are very different from Lucas's figures. The delicate complexity of the drapery folds and the miniaturistic detailing of the elongated, tapering wings are more typical of the Flemish style. The coarse realism of the angel's face contrasts with the precision of the rest of the painting. While the drapery is characteristic of works of the early Netherlandish period, the subtle atmospheric recession of the landscape in the right background is more advanced. The work may be a fragment of a later sixteenth-century copy after some unknown Netherlandish artist.

Cat. A6. *Adoration of the Magi*

The Art Institute, Chicago, inv. no. 33.1045; panel, 28.6 x 35.7.
Provenance: Spanish Gallery, London; sale Berlin (Boehler & Steinmeyer), May 25, 1914; Coll. Mr. & Mrs. Martin A. Ryerson, Chicago; on loan to the museum from at least 1916; bequeathed to the museum in 1932.
Exhibitions: Chicago, Art Institute, 1933, no. 43 (as Lucas); 1934, no. 121; 1938 (ca. 1510; probable influence of Gerard David); 1938–1939, no. 2577a; 1954 (ca. 1510).
Literature: Valentiner, 1919, p. 119 (by Lucas); Conway, 1921, pp. 471–72 (ca. 1510); Baldass, 1923, pp. 18–19, 29–30 (ca. 1510); Winkler, 1924, p. 264; Burger, 1925, p. 155 (influence of Cornelis Engebrechtsz. in the background); Friedländer, 1928 (early work by Lucas deriving from a composition by Gerard David); Dülberg, 1929, p. 168 (ca. 1515–1520); Friedländer, 1930, p. 498 (compositional format from Bruges, probably from a manuscript illumination); Dülberg, 1933, p. 7 (some influence of Gerard David on the Magi and of Cornelis Engebrechtsz. on the secondary figures); Rich, 1933; *Art News*, 1935, p. 13; Tietze, 1935, p. 335, no. 146 (ca. 1510); Hoogewerff, 1936–1947, 3:233 (ca. 1510; background completely in the style of Cornelis Engebrechtsz.; foreground figures show influence of the Bruges School and of Albrecht Dürer); Beets, 1940, pp. 51–52; Chicago, Art Institute, 1961, pp. 259–60 (ca. 1510); Bruyn, 1962 (attributed to Cornelis Cornelisz. Kunst); Friedländer, 1963a, p. 50 (ca. 1509; perhaps copied in Bruges by Simon Bening and Ambrosius Benson [see Copies 1–2], but relationship to Bruges also explained by attribution to Cornelis Cornelisz.); Reznicek-Buriks, 1965, p. 245 (problematic for its dependence on the Bruges School); Held, 1966, p. 447 (not by Lucas; favors attribution to Cornelis Cornelisz.); Friedländer, 1967–1976, 10:51, 82, no. 120 (ca. 1509–1510); Gibson, 1977, p. 219, n. 92; Filedt Kok, 1978, p. 161, n. 71 (similarities to Bruges miniatures make the attribution to Lucas unlikely; landscape and some figures related to the style of Cornelis Engebrechtsz.); Renger, 1979, p. 58 (not by Lucas).
Copies: (1) Painting, attributed to Ambrosius Benson; location unknown; panel, 28 x 33. *Prov.*: Coll. E. Pidal, Madrid; Coll. Léon Somzée, Brussels; Coll. Sir Robert Hatfield, London; with Tomas Harris, London, 1935; Coll. Louis and Mildred Kaplan, New York, 1950. *Exh.*: London, Tomas Harris, 1935, no. 8 (Friedländer: by Ambrosius Benson; same composition as the Chicago painting). *Lit.*: *Art News*, 1935 (by Benson); Valentiner and Wescher, 1950, intro. and Cat. 1 (exact copy by Benson after Lucas); Friedländer, 1963a, p. 50 (in the style of Benson).
(2) Painting, attributed to Simon Bening; the Louvre, Dépôt de la Fonda-

tion de France (as Simon Bening); panel, 33 x 25. *Prov.*: Coll. Léon Somzée, Brussels, 1902; with Leegenhoek, Paris; gift to the Dépôt from Salavin-Fournier. *Exh.*: Bruges, Stedelijk Museum, 1902, no. 246 (as follower of Gerard David). *Lit.*: Friedländer, 1930, p. 498 (similar composition, but not a copy of the Chicago painting); Friedländer, 1963a, p. 50 (Bruges school, ca. 1515), n. 17a (Winkler: by Simon Bening).

(3) Painting, artist unknown; location unknown; panel, 28 x 33. *Prov.*: sale Cologne (Lempertz), June 1976, no. 6 and pl. 20.

This small painting depicts the Adoration with three-quarter-length figures arranged in a narrow foreground zone. The Virgin and Child are seated at the left, with Joseph leaning against a ledge in the ruins behind them. The eldest Magus kneels before the Child, offering his gift. Behind him stand the two other wise men and their servants. In the distant background a long procession of travelers, apparently the retinue of the Magi, winds through the mountainous landscape.

Up until the 1960s, this *Adoration* was generally thought to be a work by Lucas from his early period. The figure types, drapery, and composition, however, seem unrelated to early works by Lucas such as the *Chess Players* in Berlin (Fig. 1, Cat. 34), *Potiphar's Wife* in Rotterdam (Fig. 4, Cat. 1), and the engraved *Adoration* (B.37, 1513). The hard, bright colors of the *Adoration* are uncharacteristic of Lucas. Its brush underdrawing is harsh and routinely descriptive in comparison to the lively, varied underdrawing of the Berlin and Rotterdam works.[1] Although this painting is not by Lucas, it should be associated with the early sixteenth-century Leiden School. Bruyn's attribution of the panel to Cornelis Cornelisz. Kunst, one of Cornelis Engebrechtsz.'s three sons, is plausible.[2]

A few of the figures in the foreground are strongly reminiscent of the Bruges School, a similarity first recognized by Friedländer.[3] The closest parallels to the thin, delicate features and extremely soft, almost blurred modeling of the Virgin, Child, and second Magus are found in the works of Gerard David and Adriaen Isenbrant (see David's *Adoration* in the National Gallery, London, and Isenbrant's triptych of the same subject, location unknown). The compositions of these three works are similar, with a restricted foreground separated from the background landscape by a low wall set parallel to the picture plane.[4] A relationship to the Bruges School is confirmed by the existence of two copies by Bruges artists. The one attributed to Ambrosius Benson (Copy 1) is virtually identical to the Chicago panel, lacking only the stone pillar along the right edge. Copy 2 has been given to Simon Bening and reveals a number of minor changes as a result of its vertical format. But the panel in

Chicago is clearly the work of a Leiden rather than a Bruges artist, as demonstrated by the style of the secondary figures and the background landscape. The rather slack modeling of the faces in the right foreground and the sharp, linear drapery folds are very close to those of Cornelis Engebrechtsz.'s triptych of *Naaman Bathing in the River Jordan,* in Vienna.[5] The *staffage* and mountains of the background are also reminiscent of *Naaman.*

No works by Engebrechtsz.'s son Cornelis are identifiable, although Van Mander described several of them in detail.[6] In *Het Schilder-Boeck* he mentioned that Cornelis Cornelisz., who was born in Leiden, lived in Bruges for short periods because of the activity of the art market there. As a Leiden artist strongly influenced by the style of his father and a frequent traveler to Bruges, Cornelis Cornelisz. Kunst seems the most likely painter of this *Adoration of the Magi*. It may have been copied after a lost painting or miniature in Bruges, and the versions by Benson and Bening probably also derive from the same source.

Cat. A7. *Adoration of the Magi*

Barnes Foundation Museum of Art, Merion, Pa., inv. no. 443; panel, triptych, rounded above; central panel 76 x 45, each wing 76 x 18.

Provenance: with P. Cassirer, Berlin; Coll. Albert C. Barnes, Philadelphia; acquired from Cassirer in 1928.[1]

Literature: Friedländer, 1928 (by Lucas, ca. 1510); Wescher, 1929, p. 168; Friedländer, 1930, p. 498 (before 1511); Dülberg, 1933, p. 7; Hoogewerff, 1936-1947, 3:233-35 (somewhat later than 1510); Barnes, 1937, pp. 204, 213, 492 (by Lucas); Van Regteren Altena, 1955, p. 111 (early work by Lucas; influenced in several details by the Master of the St. John Panels, whom he identifies as Huygh Jacobsz.); Gerson, 1962, p. 27 (a few years later than 1508); Friedländer, 1963a, pp. 54-55 (ca. 1509), 69 (1512); Boon, 1964, col. 350 (attributed to Lucas's early period); Poch-Kalous, 1965, pp. 6-7 (ca. 1519); Reznicek-Buriks, 1965, p. 245 (probably an early work by Lucas, but shows weak draftsmanship); Held, 1966, p. 447 (superficially related to Lucas but by another artist); Friedländer, 1967-1976, 10:52, 81, no. 110 (by Lucas, ca. 1510); Filedt Kok, 1978, p. 161, n. 71 (not by Lucas; similar to the *Last Supper,* Aachen); Vos, 1978a, pp. 32-33 (ca. 1505, by an unknown artist, possibly Huygh Jacobsz.); Renger, 1979, p. 58 (not by Lucas).

In this small triptych the arrival, adoration, and departure of the Magi are spread across three panels. The painting was first assigned to Lucas's early period in 1928. Since then many scholars have accepted this attribution, despite the work's unusually loose paint technique. Held raised doubts about the attribution in 1966, and several recent publications have removed the triptych from Lucas's oeuvre.[2] Details such as the heart-shaped face of the Virgin are reminiscent of Lucas's early and middle style, but in general the broad, summary brushwork and careless draftsmanship are quite different from Lucas's.

The *Adoration* can be assigned to a group of paintings by the same artist that includes the triptychs of the *Last Supper* in Aachen and the *Feeding of the Five Thousand* in Koblenz.[3] The comparison between the *Adoration* and the *Last Supper* is particularly close. The awkward poses and small hands of the unnaturally proportioned figures and the drapery with hard, intricate folds are all similar. To judge from photographs, these are also characteristics of the later triptych in Koblenz. Also analogous is the depiction of the trees and the bare, rolling hills that overlap each other without achieving a convincing depth. In all three works the horizon is relatively high, although this is much more apparent in the left wing of the Aachen triptych than in the more convincing landscape setting of the *Feeding of the Five Thousand*.[4] The artist found it difficult to show a head in lost profile, as seen in the black servant in the foreground of the left wing of the Merion triptych and the figure in the middle-ground of the right wing in the Aachen work. The children in all three paintings are similar, and male types are repeated from one triptych to another. The lean face of the elderly man with a long beard in the middle ground of the right wing in Koblenz is related to physiognomies in the right wings of the other two works. The high cheekbones, slanted eyes, and grim, downturned mouth of the male servant in the *Last Supper* are features of the man following the black Magus in the *Adoration*. The same face (with minor variations) appears in *John the Baptist Preaching, with Christ and His Disciples* in Philadelphia (Fig. 67), a work by the Master of the St. John Panels, Huygh Jacobsz.[5] The landscape backgrounds of these triptychs are also remarkably close to those of the *St. John* panels, as discussed in Chapter 1.

The paintings in Merion, Aachen, and Koblenz should be assigned to the early sixteenth-century Leiden School—more specifically, to an artist closely related to the studio of Huygh Jacobsz. There is no firm evidence to support an attribution of these paintings to Lucas's older brother Dirck, but it would not be unreasonable, given their similarities to the works of Huygh and Lucas.[6]

ERRONEOUS ATTRIBUTIONS / 191

Cat. A8. *Salome Receiving the Head of St. John the Baptist*

John G. Johnson Collection, Philadelphia, inv. no. 413; panel, 30.8 x 23.2.[1]

Provenance: Coll. Léon Somzée, Brussels, in 1892; Coll. C. and G. de Somzée, Brussels; purchased from Gaetan de Somzée, July 23, 1902, by Thomas Agnew, London; purchased from Agnew, January 20, 1905, by John G. Johnson.

Exhibitions: London, Burlington Fine Arts Club, 1892, no. 25 (as Lucas); Paris, Exposition Universelle, 1900, no. 12 (as Lucas); Bruges, Stedelijk Museum, 1902, no. 272; Toledo, Museum of Art, 1935, no. 17; New York, World's Fair, 1939, no. 223 (ca. 1515).

Literature: Tschudi, 1893, p. 109 (early work by Lucas; similar to his engraving of the same subject, B.111); Friedländer, 1903, p. 170 (ca. 1512); Dülberg, 1909, p. 13; Beets, 1913, pp. 82-83 (ca. 1511-1512, following a visit to Antwerp); Valentiner, 1913, 2:54 (ca. 1512); Conway, 1921, p. 474 (influence of the Antwerp School on Salome's costume); Baldass, 1923, pp. 18, 29, 33 (ca. 1509); Winkler, 1924, p. 264 (from period of the Berlin *Chess Players* [Fig. 1, Cat. 34]); Burger, 1925, p. 154 (reminiscent of Jacob Cornelisz. in the foliage and Renaissance ornament); Dülberg, 1929, pp. 167-68 (perhaps before 1511); Wescher, 1929, p. 168 (before the Berlin *Chess Players*); Fritsch-Estrangin, 1933; Beets, 1934, p. 54 (Antwerp influence); Hoogewerff, 1936-1947, 3:232, 241 (mirror image of Lucas's engraving, B.111; possibly by Lucas's brother Dirck Huyghensz.); Beets, 1940, pp. 40, 43-44 (ca. 1511-1512); Von Löhneysen, 1956, p. 303; Bier, 1957, pp. 215-21; Friedländer, 1963a, pp. 50-51, 68; Reznicek-Buriks, 1965, p. 245 (probably not an original Lucas because of its uninventive relationship to two of Lucas's engravings, B.111 and B.117); Friedländer, 1969, p. 125; Philadelphia, John G. Johnson Collection, 1972, pp. 50-51; Friedländer, 1967-1976, 10:83, no. 129 (ca. 1510).

This small painting has been attributed to Lucas's early period since its first appearance in 1892, until in 1965 Reznicek-Buriks expressed doubts about the identification of the artist. Tschudi was the first to note the work's similarity to Lucas's engraving the *Beheading of John the Baptist* (B.111). Hoogewerff described the painting as a mirror image of the print, and Reznicek-Buriks based her rejection of the panel on its uninventive relationship to this composition.[2] It may be, however, that this comparison has been exaggerated. In both works, Salome is seen in profile receiving the head of the Baptist. The legs of St. John are roughly comparable in the painting and engraving, but otherwise there is little to connect the two. The mannered, pinwheel stance of the executioner can be seen as a feature of the Flemish tradition, and other details link the painting with the southern Netherlands (including the crossed arms of John and the style of the costumes).³

The painting should be rejected primarily on the basis of style and technique. Although it contains facial types resembling these in the left background of *Susanna before the Judge,* ca. 1512 (Fig. 6, Cat. 3), the flesh of the figures has a hard, wooden quality. The manner of painting the hands is also quite different from that of Lucas's early period, and the color combinations are harsh and unnatural. The plants in the foreground are stylized in comparison to Lucas's rich foliage in engravings such as the *Temptation of St. Anthony,* 1509 (B.117). Finally, although the background architecture has affinities with that in *Susanna before the Judge,* the careful detailing of each stone creates a complex linear pattern foreign to Lucas's style.

Two other works can be tentatively attributed to the artist of this painting: a half-length *Salome* formerly with Schaefer in New York (Cat. A9) and a representation of *Fortuna* in Strasbourg (Cat. A19).

Cat. A9. *Salome with the Head of St. John the Baptist*

Location unknown; panel, 28 x 23.

Provenance: Coll. Don Tomás de Verí, Majorca; Coll. Condé de Sallent, Majorca; Coll. Marquis de Arianij, Madrid; with N. Beets, Amsterdam, 1926–1936; with Agnew, London, 1939; with Schaefer, New York, 1963.

Exhibitions: Amsterdam, Rijksmuseum, 1929, no. 84 (as Lucas, ca. 1512); Rotterdam, Museum Boymans–van Beuningen, 1936, no. 78a (as Lucas).

Literature: Dülberg, 1929, p. 168 (ca. 1515–1520); Dülberg, 1933, p. 8; Beets, 1935b, pp. 197–98 (details of costume and facial type are similar to the Strasbourg *Fortuna* [Cat. A19]); Cornelis Veth, 1936, p. 290; Hoogewerff, 1936–1947, 3:233 (early work); Beets, 1940, pp. 43–44; Friedländer, 1963a, p. 72 (perhaps an original, ca. 1520); Reznicek-Buriks, 1965, p. 242; Friedländer, 1967–1976, 10:83, no. 128 (ca. 1510).

This small panel shows a half-length figure of Salome holding a salver with the head of the Baptist.¹ Formerly given to Lucas, the attribution was first doubted by Friedländer. Since 1963, however, the painting's whereabouts have been unknown. The pale, rounded face, high forehead, and small mouth and chin resemble Lucas's female facial type, but the hard contours of the thinly painted face are unlike his softer and more careful modeling. The representation of the costume is also uncharacteristic of Lucas, particularly in the decorative detailing of the headdress, the tangle of necklaces, and the confusing, somewhat arbitrary folds of the sleeves.

This painting has a number of similarities to two other works once attributed to Lucas, *Salome Receiving the Head of John the Baptist* in Philadelphia (Cat. A8) and *Fortuna* in Strasbourg (Cat. A19). All three may have been painted by the same artist. The severed head of the Baptist in the Philadelphia panel is close in facial type to that in the painting of *Salome,* especially the long, narrow ears.[2] The paintings also resemble one another in the faces of the two Salomes, the emphatic outlining, the highlighting of the metal salvers, the hard, crisp drapery folds, and the complexity of the costumes. The thin arms of the figures in these two paintings differ from the full, round forms of the Strasbourg *Fortuna,* but certain details suggest that *Fortuna* may be a later work by the same artist. The necklaces worn by the allegorical figure are almost identical to those in the half-length *Salome*.[3] The hands, with their carefully delineated fingernails, are also comparable, and the tight, sharp folds of Fortuna's drapery match those in the two earlier works. The modeling of her legs and the shape of her knees are similar to the executioner's right leg in the Philadelphia panel. The identity of this artist is unknown, although he seems to have been familiar with Lucas's oeuvre.

Cat. A10. *St. Jerome Penitent*

Staatliche Museen Preussischer Kulturbesitz, Berlin-Dahlem, inv. no. 584A; panel, 27.7 x 31.8.

Provenance: acquired in 1872 from the estate of S. G. Liesching, Stuttgart.

Literature: Rosenberg, 1877, p. 11 (by Lucas; probably soon after his engraving of the same subject, dated 1516, B.113; the print is probably a study for the painting); Berlin, Königliche Museen, 1880, p. 72 (one of the few true paintings by Lucas); Berlin, Kaiser Friedrich-Museum, 1906, p. 201 (by Lucas, ca. 1512); Dülberg, 1909, p. 13 (ca. 1515); Heidrich, 1910, p. 53; Beets, 1913, pp. 85–86 (ca. 1515); Conway, 1921, p. 476 (ca. 1516); Baldass, 1923, pp. 19, 30 (ca. 1512–1513); Winkler, 1924, p. 264; Burger, 1925, p. 154; Sjöblom, 1928, pp. 164–65; Dülberg, 1929, p. 168 (ca. 1515–1520); Hoogewerff, 1936–1947, 3:247–52 (ca. 1514–1515); Beets, 1940, p. 54; Friedländer, 1963a, pp. 59–60, 68 (ca. 1520); Reznicek-Buriks, 1965, p. 244 (ca. 1516); Friedländer, 1969, p. 125; Friedländer, 1967–1976, 10:54, 83, no. 132 (ca. 1515–1516); Berlin, Staatliche Museen, 1978, pp. 229–30 (ca. 1515–1516); Filedt Kok, 1978, pp. 127–28, 137 (underdrawing and paint technique are dissimilar to those of Lucas's other paintings); Parshall, 1978–1979, p. 53 (stylistically closer to Antwerp).

There are many points of comparison between this painting of the penitent St. Jerome and other works from Lucas's middle period. The most striking parallels occur with an engraving by Lucas of the same subject, dated 1516 (B.113). The saint's kneeling pose is similar in both, although the placement of his arms differs slightly. The engraving reverses the figure of St. Jerome and shows him in full length as opposed to the closer, three-quarter-length view in the panel. The wooded settings of these works, with their distant views at the side, are also close. The connection between the two works is undoubted, and while the artist of the panel certainly borrowed some details of landscape, figure type, and pose from the engraving, it does not necessarily follow that Lucas painted the panel.

Some details of the painting are indeed reminiscent of Lucas's style. The carefully delineated foliage and the type of drapery fold in the painting resemble those in the *Virgin and Child* panels in Berlin and Munich, both from the early 1520s (Figs. 11–12, Cats. 12, 14). The clouds are also very close in form and technique to those of the Berlin *Virgin and Child.* Although depicted in a less detailed and draftsmanlike manner, the shape of Jerome's ear is virtually identical to ears in the Wilton House *Card Players* (Fig. 9, Cat. 38).

The painting style itself is problematic, particularly in the very long, flowing brushstrokes of the flesh areas. The loose, broad application of paint on the torso and arms, for example, flattens the forms in a way quite foreign to Lucas's meticulous style. Even in the Wilton House *Card Players,* with its relatively liquid and flowing technique, the individual brushstrokes are short and precise and are used to define more limited areas. The technique of *St. Jerome* also differs from the lively, painterly style of Lucas's *St. Andrew* in Karlsruhe (Fig. 8, Cat. 28). Although rather hastily described, Andrew's hands are built up from a number of small daubs and strokes. In contrast, the long, rapid streaks of paint give Jerome's flesh a slack, flat appearance. The landscapes of the two panels are dissimilar, although both could be described as painterly. The background of *St. Jerome* seems thin and flat compared to the thick, juicy description of forms in *St. Andrew.* Finally, the fine detailing of Jerome's hair and beard is almost miniaturistic. Andrew's hair is also carefully drawn, but the effect is one of fullness and depth rather than of delicate linearity. Despite its numerous similarities to Lucas's works from around 1516 to 1522, the paint technique of *St. Jerome* is so different from Lucas's usual style that the panel must be assigned to another artist who was familiar with his work. This reattribution was first made by Filedt Kok in 1978, before which it was accepted as a Lucas.[1] The painting is not a direct copy of Lucas's engraving (B.113) but was probably made under its influence soon after 1516.

Cat. A11. *St. Paul*

Yale University Art Gallery, New Haven, Conn., inv. no. 1961.52; panel, 32.9 x 24.2; inscribed on banderole: "PAVLVS."

Provenance: with E. A. Silberman, New York, 1907; sale Berlin (Lepke), May 25, 1911, no. 134 (attributed to Albrecht Dürer); Coll. D. H. Lijversberg, Cologne; Coll. Paul Esch, Cologne; with Stern, Düsseldorf, 1936; with P. de Boer, Amsterdam, 1936; with E. A. Silberman, New York; Coll. Chester Dudley Tripp, Chicago; given by the latter to the museum in 1961–1962.

Exhibitions: Cologne, Kunstverein, 1922, no. 46; Düsseldorf, Kunstverein, 1928, no. 41; Rotterdam, Museum Boymans–van Beuningen, 1936, no. 84 (ca. 1515); New York, World's Fair, 1939, no. 224; Grand Rapids, Art Gallery, 1940, no. 98; Indianapolis, John Herron Art Institute, 1950, no. 46 (perhaps originally part of the wing of a triptych); New York, E. and A. Silberman Galleries, 1955, no. 14.

Literature: Baldass, 1923, pp. 24–25, 31 (ca. 1515; strong influence of Dürer); Cohen, 1928, pp. 55, 57; Wescher, 1929, p. 169; Gerson, 1936, p. 137; Hoogewerff, 1936–1947, 3:283, 285 (ca. 1523–1524); Vaughan, 1939, pp. 11–13; Beets, 1940, pp. 54–55; Gerson, 1962, p. 28 (example of Lucas's later style); Ritchie, 1962; Friedländer, 1963a, p. 63 (ca. 1526; Winkler, n. 29, compares it to a woodcut of *St. Philip* by H. B. Grien);[1] Reznicek-Buriks, 1965, p. 245 (probably an original Lucas, ca. 1516); Friedländer, 1967–1976, 10:87, supp. 170 (ca. 1520; a fragment?); Filedt Kok, 1978, pp. 56, 165, n. 104 (by Lucas? ca. 1520?); Parshall, 1978–1979, p. 53 (loose handling of paint supports the elimination from Lucas's oeuvre).

St. Paul is seen in two-thirds length, holding in his left hand a book symbolic of his Epistles and in his right hand the sword of his martyrdom. He is clothed in a voluminous white robe that contrasts dramatically with the salmon-colored book and the deep reddish brown background. A banderole curving across the upper background and inscribed with the Latin form of his name (*Paulus*) was uncovered in 1936 during restoration.[2]

The painting is in poor condition. There are brown stains spotting the robe, some paint loss in the lower left and right corners, and inpainting in the beard, hair, and along the edges of the panel.[3] The facial area and drapery are thinly painted, revealing rough, sketchy, rather crude underdrawing. Although the panel has been attributed to Lucas since the early 1920s, recent scholarship has cast doubts on its authenticity.[4] In addition to the underdrawing, which at times seems purposeless, the eyes are dull and lackluster and the drapery folds are flat and unconvincing. The perspective is slightly askew, and the left hand in particular is painted in a clumsy, wooden manner.

The pose of the figure—with the torso placed at a forty-five-degree angle and the head tilted forward slightly—is related to poses in Lucas's engraving of *Peter and Paul with Veronica's Veil* (B.105), dated 1517. The facial features, the decoration of the sword hilt, and even the metal boss on the book cover also have affinities with this work. The sword and book, with only minor variations, reappear on the exterior of the Leiden *Last Judgment* (Fig. 23, Cat. 20), and other parallels between *St. Paul* and this triptych can be drawn, especially with the style of underdrawing. The lines used to indicate the folds are sometimes emphasized by repeated scoring, and the ends are usually marked off with angular hooks. Also, the shadowed areas of the drapery are covered with long, roughly parallel hatching. This can be seen in the drapery beneath Paul's left wrist, to both the left and the right. Paul's furrowed brow is a feature of the same figure in Leiden, with a telling detail apparent in the underdrawing of both panels: just off-center to the right above the noses of both saints are two short, vertical hatching lines used to mark the wrinkled forehead.[5] Paul's hands in the Yale *St. Paul* show several characteristics of Lucas's style. The long joints of the fingers, the awkward connection between the fingers and the hand, the carefully outlined nails, and the parallel lines of highlighting used to indicate the joints are all found in the Munich *Virgin and Child with Mary Magdalene and a Donor* (Fig. 12, Cat. 14), dated 1522, and in the exterior figures of the Leiden triptych.

St. Paul appears to be the work of an artist closely associated with Lucas's workshop. It may be a copy after a lost painting by the master or simply a work painted in his manner. The panel shows the artist's familiarity with Lucas's art of 1523–1527. The forceful, volumetric figure style of the *Last Judgment* is not a feature of this work, but *St. Paul* is similar to the *Last Judgment* in aspects of the underdrawing and in details of the face and hands.

Cat. A12. *Portrait of Claes van Isendoren*

Doncaster Museum and Art Gallery, South Yorkshire (loan from the British Rail Employees Superannuation Fund Art Collection); panel, 36 x 28, rounded above; inscribed on border of shirt: "CLAES VAN ISEN."

Provenance: Coll. F. Lepeletier, Saint-Fargeau, France;[1] Das Gothische Haus, Wörlitz, inv. no. 1316; Coll. Duke of Anhalt-Dessau, Castle Dessau; with

J. Goudstikker, Amsterdam, 1928-1936; Coll. Mrs. J. Goudstikker, New York; Coll. D. von Sahervon Halbau, Bilthoven.

Exhibitions: Bruges, Stedelijk Museum, 1907, no. 227 (by unknown artist of the northern Netherlands, ca. 1525-1530; probably Lucas, although formerly attributed to Hans Holbein); Amsterdam, Goudstikker, 1928, no. 22 (by Lucas?); Amsterdam, Rijksmuseum, 1929, no. 85 (by Lucas?); London, Royal Academy of Arts, 1929, no. 15 (by Lucas?); Rotterdam, Museum Boymans–van Beuningen, 1936, no. 87 (by Lucas); Amsterdam, Goudstikker, 1936-1937, no. 31.

Literature: Dülberg, 1909, p. 13 (very close to Lucas in style, but inferior in quality); Bremmer, 1932, no. 89 (by Lucas); Hoogewerff, 1936-1947, 3:276-78 (by Lucas, under the influence of Gossaert); Baldass, 1937b, p. 208 (by Lucas).

The young man in this portrait wears a black hat and cloak over a brown jacket and is seated before a green background. He is identified by the embroidered inscription around the neckline of his thin smocked shirt.[2]

Once attributed to Hans Holbein the Younger, the painting was first tentatively associated with Lucas in the Bruges exhibition of 1907. It was hesitantly accepted by a number of scholars earlier in the century—the most notable exception being Friedländer, who did not mention the portrait in any of his works. In the last forty years the panel has been virtually forgotten. Although it is not by Lucas, it deserves notice as a finely painted sixteenth-century portrait. The strongly outlined eyes are flattened by the harsh modeling of the lids, which is quite different from the London *Portrait of a Man* (Fig. 10, Cat. 31) and the chalk drawing in Leiden. The artist lacks Lucas's ability to build up the face and neck through subtle shading. There is little underdrawing in Lucas's painted portraits, but here the finely hatched lines are liberally used for contours and shading.[3]

Baldass noted the similarity of this portrait to the Rotterdam *Portrait of a Woman* (Cat. A18), but it is not possible that the same artist worked on both.[4] The face of the man has a certain vibrancy resulting from the fine network of lines drawn beneath the thin paint layer, which is in direct contrast to the thick, enamel-like surface and heavy highlighting of the *Portrait of a Woman*.

Cat. A13. *Portrait of a Man*

Groninger Museum, Groningen, inv. no. 2384; panel, 24 x 15, rounded above.

Provenance: early possession of the "Ubbenagasthuis" (Ubbena hospital); given to the museum in 1910 by the governors of the hospital.

Literature: Groningen, Groninger Museum, 1910, p. 10, no. 26 (first half of the sixteenth century; perhaps by Lucas; possibly a portrait of Johan Lubbers);[1] Hoogewerff, 1936–1947, 3:53 (the poor condition makes an attribution difficult); Baldass, 1937b, p. 206 (by Lucas); Reznicek-Buriks, 1965, p. 242; Friedländer, 1967–1976, 10:no. 136, p. 84 (by Lucas, ca. 1512), p. 94.

This portrait with its sharp, linear contours could not be by the artist of the carefully modeled *Portrait of a Man Aged 38* in London (Fig. 10, Cat. 31). It has been dated circa 1512 but is worked in a manner uncharacteristic of Lucas's style at that time. This is readily apparent from comparison of the panel with *Potiphar's Wife* in Rotterdam (Fig. 4, Cat. 1) and *Susanna before the Judge,* formerly in Bremen (Fig. 6, Cat. 3). A number of details suggest that it is an early work by the artist who painted the fragmentary *Portrait of a Man* in the Coll. Thyssen-Bornemisza, also formerly attributed to Lucas.[2] The linear definition of the cheek, jaw, and facial features is similar in both works, although the Thyssen portrait is more loosely painted. The long brushstrokes of white highlighting, especially around the nose and mouth, are also comparable, as are the dotted highlights in the irises and the double curved lines of the upper eyelid. The hair of both men is broadly painted and accented by thick linear strands. If these two works are by the same artist, a considerable development took place in his style during the interval between their painting.

Cat. A14. *Portrait of a Man Aged 25*

Location unknown; panel, 36.8 x 25.7, rounded above; inscribed at left center "25" and dated on frame at bottom center, "1518" (?).[1]

Provenance: with Leonard Koetser, London, 1954; Coll. Sir Claude Alexander; sale Paris (Charpentier), January 29, 1957, no. 23 (as Lucas);[2] Private collection, Germany, 1958.

Exhibitions: Delft, Antiques Fair, 1954; Stuttgart, Staatsgalerie, 1958–1959, no. 110 (self-portrait by Lucas, by comparison with the so-called self-portrait in the *Sermon,* Rijksmuseum).

Literature: Connoisseur, 1954, pp. lxxi (by Lucas, dated 1518), 287; *Connaissance des Arts,* 1957 (by Lucas, dated 1518).

In this little-known portrait, a young man wears a black hat and a dark green cloak over his black jacket. In the 1950s Friedländer and Valentiner certified the painting as a well-preserved painting by Lucas, circa 1520-1525, but it was lost to scholarship when it became part of a German private collection.³ It bears no resemblance to the so-called portrait of Lucas in a painting formerly attributed to him, the Rijksmuseum *Sermon,* as the catalogue for the 1958-1959 exhibition in Stuttgart tried to show, nor is it similar to any of the other supposed portraits of the artist. The painting should be excluded from Lucas's oeuvre on the basis of the harsh modeling and contouring of the facial area and the clumsy, rigid drapery folds.

The number 25 painted on the green background to the left of the man's head almost certainly refers to his age.

Cat. A15. *Portrait of a Man*

Coll. Mrs. G. E. Naylor, London; panel, 26 x 21.
Provenance: Coll. Viscount Lee of Fareham, Richmond.
Exhibition: London, Royal Academy of Arts, 1952-1953, no. 17 (as Lucas).
Literature: Hoogewerff, 1936-1947, 3:278 (late work by Lucas); *Burlington Magazine* 95 (1953): 33-34 (according to J. G. Van Gelder, by Jan Swart van Groningen); Friedländer, 1967-1976, 10:84, 100, n. 85, no. 137 (by Lucas, ca. 1530).

Friedländer and Hoogewerff thought this portrait belonged to Lucas's late period, but details of paint technique and draftsmanship suggest otherwise.¹ The extremely linear representation of the eyelids is unlike that in Lucas's portraits in London and Braunschweig (Figs. 10, 14, Cats. 31-32), which are also meticulously painted but much more convincing in their rendition of plastic form. The heavy contours along the tip of the man's nose and his right cheek are uncharacteristic of Lucas, as are the heavy, flat locks of hair. Van Gelder's attribution to Jan Swart van Groningen may be correct, although it is difficult to judge from the available comparative material.²

Cat. A16. *Portrait of a Man in a Red Hat*

Six Collection, Amsterdam; panel, hexagonal, 9 x 7.5.

Cat. A17. *Portrait of a Man in a Three-Cornered Hat*

Six Collection, Amsterdam; panel, hexagonal, 9 x 7.5.
Provenance: Coll. Six, Amsterdam, 1900; sale Coll. Six, Amsterdam (Muller), October 16, 1928, no. 19 (as a *Portrait of a Humanist* and *Portrait of a Magistrate,* by Lucas); sale London (Sotheby), June 10, 1937, no. 78; reacquired by Coll. Six.
Exhibition: Amsterdam, Rijksmuseum, 1900, nos. 56, 57.
Literature: Beets, 1913, pp. 86–87 (probably by Lucas, ca. 1517); *International Studio* 91 (October 1928): 92, 94; Fritsch-Estrangin, 1933 (no scholarly agreement on the attribution); Hoogewerff, 1936–1947, 3:272, 382–83 (close in style to Lucas, but even closer to Lucas Cornelisz.).

These small, bust-length portraits are both of elderly men set against a light greenish background. One is shown almost in profile wearing a wide-brimmed red hat with a medallion pinned to it and a medallion necklace. The other, in a more frontal presentation, wears a three-cornered black hat and a dark robe with a fur collar.

Beets's date of 1517 for these portraits is based on his comparison of the man in the red hat with a man similarly dressed in the background of Lucas's engraving *Esther before Ahasuerus,* 1518 (B.31). This does not prove conclusively either an attribution to Lucas or a precise date, and in fact these portraits seem unrelated to Lucas's painting style, although they are still given to Lucas in the Six collection. The eyes in both panels lack any sense of depth or vitality, especially compared to Lucas's London and Braunschweig portraits (Figs. 10, 14, Cats. 31–32). The eye sockets are not built up with the careful detailing and modeling Lucas used to achieve the illusion of three-dimensionality. Hoogewerff's assignment of the two paintings to Cornelis Engebrechtsz.'s son Lucas Cornelisz. is not without problems either. These two portraits are very different from another *Portrait of a Man* (formerly with the dealer N. Beets, Amsterdam) that Hoogewerff attributed to this artist.[1]

Cat. A18. *Portrait of a Woman*

Museum Boymans–van Beuningen, Rotterdam, inv. no. 2457; panel, 26 x 24, rounded above.
Provenance: with Goudstikker, Amsterdam; Coll. D. G. van Beuningen, Rotterdam, from 1936; acquired in 1958 with the Coll. van Beuningen.

Exhibitions: Rotterdam, Museum Boymans–van Beuningen, 1936, no. 86 (as Lucas); Rotterdam, Museum Boymans–van Beuningen, 1938, no. 11; Rotterdam, Museum Boymans–van Beuningen, 1949, no. 17; Amsterdam, Rijksmuseum, 1952, no. 85 (ca. 1520; similar to Lucas's portrait drawings of 1521); Paris, Petit Palais, 1952, no. 55; Bruges, Stedelijk Museum, 1953, no. 70 (ca. 1521); Amsterdam, Rijksmuseum, 1958, no. 129 (ca. 1520).

Literature: Bremmer, 1936, no. 1 (by Lucas); Hoogewerff, 1936–1947, 3:278 (ca. 1520); Veth, 1936, p. 290; Baldass, 1937b, pp. 206–7 (similar to the woman in the *Chess Players,* Berlin [Fig. 1, Cat. 34]); Friedländer, 1949, p. 145 (seems to have been painted by Lucas in Antwerp, ca. 1520); Hannema, 1949, p. 31, no. 17; Wegner, 1959, p. 8 (influence of Dürer); Rotterdam, Museum Boymans–van Beuningen, 1962, p. 78 (ca. 1520); Friedländer, 1963a, p. 62; Reznicek-Buriks, 1965, p. 244, no. 11 (ca. 1521); Friedländer, 1967–1976, 10:88, supp. 173 (editor's note: attribution to Lucas probably correct; ca. 1518?); Parshall, 1978–1979, p. 53 (not by Lucas).

In this bust-length portrait a young woman wears a transparent white headdress and a gown with a black bodice and red sleeves. Since the panel's appearance at the Rotterdam exhibition of 1936, it has been accepted as a Lucas by most scholars and dated circa 1520–1521. It has affinities with the portraits Lucas drew on his journey to Antwerp in 1521 and is particularly close to the *Portrait of a Young Woman* drawing in Weimar, especially in the pose, the style of the headdress, and the treatment of the face.[1]

The heavy-handed paint technique betrays this as the work of a less-accomplished master, one unable to match the fine detailing of the *Portrait of a Man Aged 38* in London (Fig. 10, Cat. 31). The harsh, crudely drawn outline of the woman's forehead and right cheek, edged by flat shadows, contrasts sharply with the delicate, sensitive contour of the London panel.[2] The folds of her chemise are more thickly highlighted than the folds of the clothing in the *Portrait of a Man,* and this heavy-handed touch also distorts her eyes. The convincing modeling of the eye sockets and virtuoso rendering of the reflected windows in the eyes of the man in London are unmatched by the flat, unintegrated daubs of highlighting in this work. This *Portrait of a Woman* should be attributed to an early sixteenth-century Dutch artist.

Cat. A19. *Fortuna*

Musée des Beaux-Arts, Strasbourg, inv. no. 84; panel, 31 x 20.

Provenance: sale Spitzer, Paris, April 17–June 16, 1893, no. 3331, bought by the museum.

Exhibition: Amsterdam, Rijksmuseum, 1958, no. 139 (as Lucas).

Literature: Strasbourg, Musée des Beaux-Arts, 1899, p. 22, no. 60 (unknown artist, ca. 1530); Beets, 1935b (an original by Lucas from the late 1520s; influence of Dürer's prints, especially *Four Nude Women*, B.75); Hoogewerff, 1936–1947, 5:74 (by Lucas); Strasbourg, Musée des Beaux-Arts, 1938, p. 65, no. 84 (by Lucas, ca. 1520–1530); Beets, 1940, pp. 44–45, 57–58.

This painting represents a full-length nude figure of *Fortuna*, standing on a sphere or globe and holding a smaller cross-topped sphere in her right hand. A Greek cross hangs from one of her necklaces. Other than these chains, her only ornament is an elaborate headdress tied with a long, rose-colored scarf that curls about her body. Beets suggested that the pose derives from one of the nudes in Dürer's engraving of *Four Nude Women* (B.75), dated 1497. Beets also found parallels between *Fortuna* and Eve in Lucas's 1529 print of the *Fall of Man* (B.3) and the female *Shield-Bearer* originally on the exterior of *Christ Healing the Blind Man* in Leningrad (Fig. 39, Cat. 26).[1] The figure type with small, high breasts, a thick torso, and long, relatively slender legs is reminiscent of the female nudes in the *Last Judgment*, circa 1526 (Figs. 17–19, Cat. 20), and even her rib cage forms a pattern similar to that used by Lucas in the *Last Judgment:* a semicircle bifurcated by a vertical line. The face is also characteristic of Lucas's high-browed, small-featured female types. These general similarities do not argue convincingly for an attribution of the painting to Lucas. The modeling of the flesh is harder and the contours more pronounced than those in Lucas's works, and the eyes and nose are more sharply drawn. Fortuna's right forearm is almost grotesquely misshapen, and her left arm is curiously segmented at the elbow and wrist. Even in his late period Lucas had problems drawing arms and hands, but his mistakes were never so pronounced as those in this panel. The long scarf is also quite different from the one worn by the *Shield-Bearer* in Leningrad. In *Fortuna* the folds are tight and angular, seeming thin and lifeless in comparison with the looser, broader, and more lively folds in the *Shield-Bearer.* This small panel must have been painted by an artist familiar with Lucas's oeuvre and able to approximate but not match his style. Although an identification of the artist is impossible, several other paintings formerly attributed to Lucas can be included in his oeuvre; see Cat. A9 for the similarities to *Salome,* formerly with Schaefer in New York, and *Salome Receiving the Head of John the Baptist* in Philadelphia.

ILLUSTRATIONS

Fig. 1.

Lucas van Leyden, *Chess Players* (Cat. 34).
Staatliche Museen Preussischer Kulturbesitz,
Gemäldegalerie, Berlin. Panel, circa 1508.

Fig. 2.

Lucas van Leyden, *The Fortuneteller* (Cat. 35).
Musée du Louvre, Paris. Panel, circa 1508.

Fig. 3.

Artist unknown, *The Fortuneteller* (Cat. 35, Copy 1). Musée des Beaux-Arts, Nantes. Panel. Copy after Fig. 2.

ILLUSTRATIONS / 207

Fig. 4.

Lucas van Leyden, *Potiphar's Wife Accusing Joseph* (Cat. 1). Museum Boymans–van Beuningen, Rotterdam. Panel, circa 1510–1511.

Fig. 5.

Artist unknown, *Potiphar's Wife Accusing Joseph* (Cat. 1, Copy 2). Engraving. Copy after Fig. 4.

Fig. 6.

Lucas van Leyden, *Susanna before the Judge* (Cat. 3). Destroyed during World War II; formerly Kunsthalle, Bremen. Panel, circa 1512.

Fig. 7.

Lucas van Leyden, *Card Players* (Cat. 37). Thyssen-Bornemisza Collection, Lugano, Switzerland. Panel, circa 1513–1515.

Fig. 8.

Lucas van Leyden, *St. Andrew* (Cat. 28). Staatliche Kunsthalle, Karlsruhe. Panel, circa 1512–1517.

Fig. 9.

Lucas van Leyden, *Card Players* (Cat. 38). Collection Earl of Pembroke, Wilton House, Salisbury. Panel, circa 1515–1517.

Fig. 10.

Lucas van Leyden, *Portrait of a Man Aged 38* (Cat. 31). Reproduced by courtesy of the Trustees, The National Gallery, London. Panel, circa 1521.

Fig. 11.

Lucas van Leyden, *Virgin and Child with Angels* (Cat. 12). Staatliche Museen Preussischer Kulturbesitz, Gemäldegalerie, Berlin. Panel, circa 1521.

Fig. 12.

Lucas van Leyden, *Virgin and Child with Mary Magdalene and a Donor* (Cat. 14). Alte Pinakothek, Munich. Panel, 1522.

Fig. 13.

Lucas van Leyden, *Annunciation* (Cat. 15).
Alte Pinakothek, Munich. Panel, 1522.

Fig. 14.

Lucas van Leyden, *Portrait of a Man* (so-called *Self-Portrait*) (Cat. 32). Herzog Anton Ulrich-Museum, Braunschweig. Panel, circa 1525–1527.

Fig. 15.

Peter Paul Rubens, *Portrait of a Man*, so-called *Portrait of Lucas van Leyden* (Cat. 32, Copy 2). Fondation Custodia (Collection F. Lugt), Institut Néerlandais, Paris. Drawing. Copy after Fig. 14.

ILLUSTRATIONS / 217

Fig. 16.

Andries Jacobsz. Stock, *Portrait of a Man*, so-called *Portrait of Lucas van Leyden* (Cat. 32, Copy 6). Engraving. Copy after Fig. 14.

Fig. 17.

Lucas van Leyden, *Last Judgment* (Cat. 20), center panel. Stedelijk Museum "De Lakenhal," Leiden. Panel, 1526.

Figs. 18 and 19.

Lucas van Leyden, *Last Judgment* (Cat. 20), left and right wings.

Fig. 20.

Lucas van Leyden, *Last Judgment* (Cat. 20), underdrawing of the head of the female in the right wing.

Fig. 21.

Lucas van Leyden, *Last Judgment* (Cat.20), detail of center panel.

Fig. 22.

Lucas van Leyden, *Last Judgment* (Cat. 20), underdrawing of part of the group in Fig. 21.

ILLUSTRATIONS / 221

ILLUSTRATIONS / 223

Fig. 23.

Lucas van Leyden, *Sts. Peter and Paul* (Cat. 20), exterior of *The Last Judgment*.

Fig. 24.

Lucas van Leyden, *Moses after Striking the Rock* (Cat. 7). William K. Richardson Fund. Courtesy, Museum of Fine Arts, Boston. Glue tempera on linen, 1527.

Fig. 25.

Lucas van Leyden, *Moses after Striking the Rock* (Cat. 7), detail of group with Moses and Aaron.

ILLUSTRATIONS / 225

Fig. 26.

Lucas van Leyden, *The Betrothal* (Cat. 44). Musée de Strasbourg. Panel, circa 1527.

226 / ILLUSTRATIONS

Fig. 27.

Jan de Bisschop, *The Betrothal* (Cat. 44, Copy 2). Museum Teyler, Haarlem. Drawing.

Fig. 28.

Artist unknown, *The Betrothal* (Cat. C45, Copy).
Collection M. Q. Morris, London. Panel.

ILLUSTRATIONS / 229

Fig. 29.

Lucas van Leyden, *Virgin and Child* (Cat. 23). Nasjonalgalleriet, Oslo. Panel, circa 1528.

Fig. 30.

Lucas van Leyden, *Virgin and Child*. Reproduced by courtesy of the Trustees of the British Museum, London. Drawing, preliminary study for Fig. 29.

Fig. 31.

Simon Frisius, *Virgin and Child*. Engraving.

Fig. 32.

Lucas van Leyden, *Dance around the Golden Calf* (Cat. 11). Rijksmuseum, Amsterdam. Panel, circa 1529–1530.

Fig. 33.

Lucas van Leyden, *Dance around the Golden Calf* (Cat. 11), detail of center panel.

Fig. 34.

Lucas van Leyden, *Dance around the Golden Calf* (Cat. 11), detail of right wing.

Fig. 35.

Lucas van Leyden, *Christ Healing the Blind Man* (Cat. 25). The Hermitage, Leningrad. Canvas, transferred from panel, 1531.

Fig. 36.

Artist unknown, *Christ Healing the Blind Man*
(Cat. 25, Copy 1). Suermondt-Ludwig-Museum,
Aachen. Panel. Copy after Fig. 35.

Fig. 37.

Lucas van Leyden, *Christ Healing the Blind Man* (Cat. 25), detail of Christ and the blind man.

Fig. 38.

Lucas van Leyden, *Christ Healing the Blind Man* (Cat. 25), detail of spectators.

Fig. 39.

Lucas van Leyden, *Shield-Bearers* (Cat. 26). Exterior wings of *Christ Healing the Blind Man* (Fig. 35). The Hermitage, Leningrad. Canvas, transferred from panel, 1531.

Fig. 40.

Artist unknown, *The Betrothal* (Cat. C36, Copy). Location unknown. Panel.

Fig. 41.

Artist unknown, *Triumphal Entry of David into Jerusalem* (Cat. C4, Copy 1). Galleria della Biblioteca Ambrosiana, Milan. Glass.

ILLUSTRATIONS / 241

Fig. 42.

Jan Saenredam, *Triumphal Entry of David into Jerusalem* (Cat. C4, Copy 10). Engraving.

242 / ILLUSTRATIONS

Fig. 43.

Jan de Bisschop, *St. George* (Cat. C29, Copy). Reproduced by Courtesy of the Trustees of the British Museum, London. Drawing.

Fig. 44.

Jan de Bisschop, *Fall of Man* (Cat. C5, Copy). Location unknown. Drawing.

Fig. 45.

Artist unknown, *Virgin and Child with Joseph, Anne, and Two Male Saints* (Cat. C13, Copy 1). Musée du Louvre, Département des Arts Graphiques, Paris. Drawing.

Fig. 46.

Jan de Bisschop, *Virgin and Child in the Clouds* (Cat. C17, Copy 1). Albertina, Vienna. Drawing.

Fig. 47.

Simon Frisius, *Christ as Man of Sorrows and Virgin of Sorrows* (Cat. C16, Copy 20). Etching.

Fig. 48.

Nicolaes de Bruyn, *St. James the Greater Raising a King and Queen of Spain* (Cat. C30, Copy). Engraving.

Fig. 49.

Artist unknown, *A Family Surprised by Death*
(Cat. C40, Copy). Engraving.

Fig. 50.

Artist unknown, *Allegory of Transience* (Cat. C41, Copy 1). Location unknown. Panel.

Fig. 51.

Artist unknown, *Allegory of Transience* (Cat. C41, Copy 2). Kupferstichkabinett, Staatliche Museen Preussischer Kulturbesitz, Berlin. Drawing.

Fig. 52.

Artist unknown, *Temptation of a Young Man* (Cat. C42, Copy). Location unknown. Canvas, transferred from panel.

Fig. 53.

Artist unknown, *Card Players* (Cat. C39, Copy 1). Museum of Fine Arts, Budapest. Panel.

Fig. 54.

Artist unknown, after Lucas van Leyden, *Card Players* (Cat. C43, Copy). National Gallery of Art, Washington; Samuel H. Kress Collection. Panel.

Fig. 55.

Artist unknown, *Adoration of the Magi* (Cat. C18, Copy 2). Mittelrheinisches Landesmuseum, Mainz. Panel.

Fig. 56.

Nicolaes de Bruyn, *John the Baptist Preaching in the Wilderness* (Cat. C19, Copy). Engraving.

Fig. 57.

Attributed to Hans Liefrinck, *Rest on the Flight into Egypt* (Cat. C21, Copy 1). Stedelijk Museum "De Lakenhal," Leiden. Panel.

Fig. 58.

Artist unknown, *Virgin and Child* (Cat. C22, Copy 1). The Chrysler Museum, Norfolk, Virginia. Panel.

Fig. 59.

Nicolaes de Bruyn or Jan de Bisschop, *Judgment of Solomon* (Cat. C6, Copy 4). Albertina, Vienna. Drawing.

Fig. 60.

Jan de Bisschop, *Susanna in Her Bath* (Cat. C9, Copy 1). Destroyed during World War II; formerly Kupferstichkabinett, Staatliche Museen Preussischer Kulturbesitz, Berlin. Drawing.

Fig. 61.

Jan de Bisschop, *Meeting of David and Abigail* (Cat. C10, Copy). Kupferstichkabinett, Museum der bildenden Künste, Leipzig. Drawing.

256 / ILLUSTRATIONS

ILLUSTRATIONS / 257

Fig. 62.

Jan de Bisschop, *Procession of the Holy Sacrament* (Cat. C33, Copy 1). Musées Royaux des Beaux-Arts de Belgique, Brussels (inv. 4060/311, Collection de Grez). Drawing.

Fig. 63.

Jan de Bisschop, *Christ Healing the Lepers* (Cat. C24, Copy 2). Stedelijk Museum "De Lakenhal," Leiden. Drawing.

Fig. 64.

Bartholomeus Dolendo, *Fluteplayer* (Cat. C46, Copy 2). Engraving.

Fig. 65.

Artist unknown, *Crucifixion*. Galleria Sabauda, Turin. Archivio Fotografico della Soprintendenza per i Beni Artistici e Storici del Piemonte. Panel.

Fig. 66.

Master of the St. John Panels, *Flight of Elizabeth*. Museum Boymans–van Beuningen, Rotterdam. Panel.

Fig. 67.

Master of the St. John Panels, *John the Baptist Preaching, with Christ and His Disciples.* John G. Johnson Collection, Philadelphia. Panel.

Fig. 68.

Cornelis Engebrechtsz., *Feeding of the Five Thousand*. Destroyed during World War II; formerly Staatliche Museen Preussischer Kulturbesitz, Gemäldegalerie, Berlin. Panel.

Fig. 69.

Artist unknown, *Feeding of the Five Thousand*. Location unknown, formerly Collection Bührle, Zurich. Panel.

Fig. 70.

Albrecht Dürer, *Portrait of Lucas van Leyden (?)*. Musée des Beaux-Arts, Lille. Drawing.

ILLUSTRATIONS / 263

 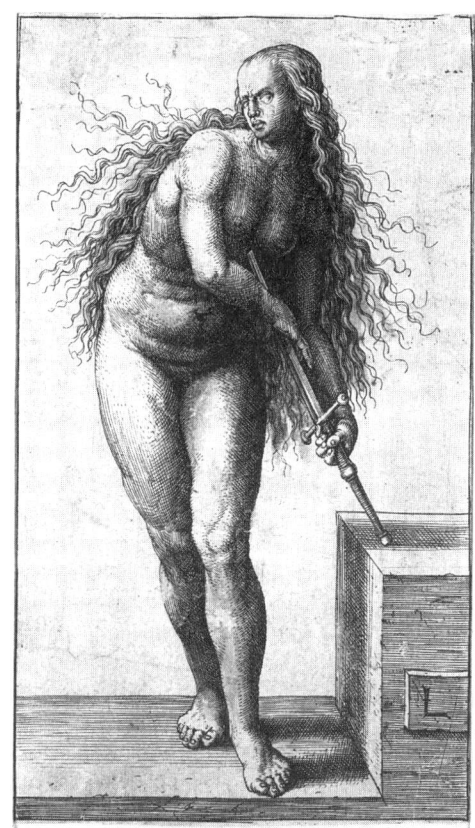

Fig. 71.

Marcantonio Raimondi, *Lucretia*. Engraving.

Fig. 72.

Lucas van Leyden, *Lucretia*. Engraving.

Fig. 73.

Marcantonio Raimondi, *Venus and Cupid*. Engraving.

Fig. 74.

Marcantonio Raimondi, *Massacre of the Innocents*. Engraving.

Fig. 75.

Marcantonio Raimondi, *Judgment of Paris*. Engraving.

ILLUSTRATIONS / 265

Fig. 76.

Marcantonio Raimondi, *Orpheus and Eurydice*. Engraving.

Fig. 77.

Artist unknown, *Card Players*. Historisches Museum, Basel. Tapestry, de

ILLUSTRATIONS / 267

Fig. 78.

Martin Zasinger, *Ball of Duke Albert IV of Bavaria*.
Engraving.

268 / ILLUSTRATIONS

Fig. 79.

Master of the Housebook, *Card Players*.
Engraving.

Fig. 80.

Artist unknown, *Card Players* from
Das Narrenschiff. Woodcut.

APPENDIX

Lucas van Leyden's Appearance

In 1521 Lucas was described in a firsthand account by Dürer as "a small little man," and this was confirmed in *Het Schilder-Boeck* of 1604: "Lucas was on the short side and rather slight."[1] Van Mander went on to mention that Lucas's engraving of *A Young Man with a Skull* (B.174) was a self-portrait, but it is not at all similar to the most likely portrait of the artist: Dürer's silverpoint *Portrait of a Man* in Lille (Fig. 70), made during his journey through the Netherlands in 1521. Dürer noted in his diary that he had drawn a silverpoint likeness of Lucas.[2] Unfortunately, none of his extant drawings from 1520–1521 is inscribed with Lucas's name, although it was not unusual for Dürer to note the name or occupation of his sitter on these works. The sketch in Lille was first identified as a portrait of Lucas in 1572, when an engraved copy of the drawing appeared in a collection of artists' portraits by Domenicus Lampsonius. The copy was accompanied by a laudatory verse in Latin describing Lucas as almost the equal of Dürer.[3] The fact that more than fifty years elapsed between the creation of the drawing and the engraving tends to weaken the authority of the identification, but the sitter does seem to have been "a small little man."

An engraving signed with the initials of Hendrick Hondius and dated 1598 is labeled as a portrait of Lucas: it gives the age of the sitter as thirty-seven and includes the inscription "Lucas Leydanus Pictor. Aerearum Excelentissimus" (The painter Lucas van Leyden, most excellent worker in copper). Although it was at one time thought that Hondius's print was an entirely original representation, it is actually a modified copy in reverse of the 1572 print.[4] The sitter here is shown in bust length, the hat is omitted, and the decoration of the costume has been altered slightly, but the face is virtually identical. If we accept that Lucas was born in 1494 and that he was thirty-seven when he sat for this portrait, then the original would have been made in 1531. Perhaps Hondius mistakenly engraved "37" instead of "27."

Lucas's *Portrait of a Man* in Braunschweig (Fig. 14, Cat. 32) is identified as a self-portrait on the basis of an inscription in a seventeenth-century copy, although the face is very different from the one in Dürer's drawing. The engraved copy by Andries Jacobsz. Stock (Fig. 16) includes an inscription on a banderole that proclaims it a "portrait of Lucas van Leyden, the incomparable painter and engraver, when he was 15 years old, after the painting by his own hand." But during the late eighteenth and nineteenth centuries the painting was given to Hans Holbein and Maarten van Heemskerck; it was reattributed to Lucas in 1882 as a self-portrait.[5] It has enjoyed this status, with few exceptions, ever since. Many scholars have noted the differences between the faces in the Braunschweig panel and in the silverpoint drawing in Lille, but some have accounted for these by placing the two portraits as far apart in time as possible. Others consider these discrepancies the result of the different stylistic vocabularies of the two artists. Cornelis Müller-Hofstede, for example, speaks of the lofty idealism of Dürer's portrait style as opposed to Lucas's physiognomic and psychological realism.[6] But a close study of the two faces leaves no possibility that they are the same man. A weak, receding chin (as in the Braunschweig panel) cannot change, even over a period of years, into a dominant one, nor can fleshy, pendulous lips grow so much thinner. The two noses are of completely different types: the man in the Braunschweig portrait has a nose that is curved and tilted up, while the man in Dürer's drawing has one with a bony bridge and heavy, globular tip.[7]

Given that these two portraits cannot be of the same man, it remains to determine which, if either, is an image of Lucas. The inscription on Stock's print is not fully reliable. The information he included in other portrait engravings has been questioned on at least one other similar occasion, and his date for the painting (1509, when Lucas would have been fifteen) has been proved wrong.[8] The direct glance of the sitter in the Braunschweig painting, closely engaging the viewer, has also been cited as a reason to identify the work as a self-portrait. This "look out of the picture," as Erwin Panofsky terms it, is characteristic of many northern self-portraits, including ones by Dürer, Joos van Cleve, and Jacob Cornelisz. van Oostsanen. But this glance outward was also often a feature of late fifteenth- and early sixteenth-century commissioned portraits, used perhaps to create a bond between sitter and spectator.[9] Its appearance should never be the sole basis for identifying a work as a self-portrait. Finally, since the only sixteenth-century works reputed to be portraits of Lucas are direct descendants of Dürer's silverpoint, it seems more likely that this drawing rather than the Braunschweig panel faithfully represents Lucas's physiognomy.

A drawing in the British Museum has also been attributed to Dürer and called a portrait of Lucas. Done in black chalk and charcoal, it shows a rather thin, sharp-featured, bust-length young man wearing a wide-brimmed hat. Inscribed at the lower left as a portrait of Lucas, it is signed with Lucas's monogram and dated 1525. These notations are apparently not by the same hand that drew the portrait, and traces of Dürer's monogram and the date 1521 are said to be visible beneath these later additions.[10] There is an etched copy in reverse of this drawing, also signed with Lucas's monogram and dated 1525. The inscription reads "Effigies Lucae Leidensis propria manu incidere" (Portrait of Lucas van Leyden engraved by his own hand). Although long accepted as a print by Lucas, it is now considered a seventeenth-century copy of the chalk study in the British Museum. But the question remains whether the drawing is a portrait of Lucas. There are some points of similarity with the silverpoint in Lille—including the bony face, the thin lips, and the hairstyle— but the difference in the shape of the nose makes it unlikely that both works represent the same man.[11]

In 1600, a fourth edition of Lampsonius's collection of artists' portraits was published by Theodoor Galle in Antwerp. The only important change was the replacement of the engraved copy of Dürer's silverpoint drawing of Lucas (as in the 1572 edition) with a weak, gray impression of Lucas's *Young Man with a Skull* (B.174).[12] The choice of this particular engraving is puzzling, since it bears little resemblance to the man in either Dürer's drawings or the Braunschweig painting. It may be possible to explain the substitution by the fact that it includes a skull, which was an attribute of some sixteenth-century self-portraits. In Pieter Coecke van Aelst's *Self-Portrait with His Wife*, for example, the artist has one hand on a skull, the symbol of death and transience. In the seventeenth century the association of the *vanitas* theme with an artist's self-portrait became more common, and in 1610 four of the representations in Hendrik Hondius's compendium of portraits showed an artist holding a skull.[13] Theodoor Galle, in his update of Lampsonius's work, must have been struck by the suitability of this image from Lucas's graphic oeuvre. Galle's transformation of this allegory into a portrait of the artist influenced not only Hondius but also Carel van Mander. In 1604, Van Mander described this engraving as a self-portrait by Lucas, and in his publication of 1610 Hondius used a simplified copy in reverse of the same print.[14] The feathers on the hat are omitted and the background is altered, but otherwise the image is the same.

A great deal has been written about the painting of the *Sermon* in the Rijksmuseum, formerly attributed to Lucas, then to Aertgen van Leyden, and more recently simply to the Leiden School Master of the Sermon. The man fifth from the right in the foreground, who looks directly out at the spectator, has often been called a self-portrait of Lucas. This assertion is primarily based on a comparison with the silverpoint drawing by Dürer, and there are indeed a number of resemblances. The face of the man in the *Sermon* is more elongated, but the wide-set eyes, bulbous nose, and thin lips have much in common. Those who have attributed the painting to Aertgen have tended to retain the idea that this man is a portrait of Lucas.[15]

Certain men in Lucas's paintings have also been singled out as possible self-portraits. His *Portrait of a Man Aged 38* in London (Fig. 10, Cat. 31) was listed as a self-portrait in two eighteenth-century sales, although it is unrelated to any of the other supposed portraits of the artist. According to a note attached to the back of the Berlin *Virgin and Child with Angels* (Fig. 11, Cat. 12), the youth at the far left is a self-portrait. In some respects this man resembles the Braunschweig portrait, especially in the round face, pug nose, fleshy lips, and receding, dimpled chin, but the color of the hair is completely different and the age is irreconcilable. A local tradition in Leiden, with no basis in fact, identifies the man seated with folded hands in the foreground center of the *Last Judgment* (Fig. 17, Cat. 20) as a portrait of the artist. Recently, Von der Osten claimed to have found a self-portrait in the painting *Moses after Striking the Rock* in Boston (Fig. 24, Cat. 7). Nikulin similarly identified a figure in a red hat at the far left of *Christ Healing the Blind Man* in Leningrad (Fig. 35, Cat. 25), pointing out the resemblance of this man to Dürer's silverpoint drawing.[16] He also assigned the Braunschweig "self-portrait" to Lucas's early period, based on its differences from the man in the Leningrad painting. It is possible to draw points of comparison between Dürer's drawing in Lille and the men in the Leningrad *Healing* and the Rijksmuseum *Sermon*, but the Braunschweig panel is too dissimilar to warrant consideration as a self-portrait.[17]

NOTES

Preface

1. Van Mander, 1604, fols. 211v, 212v, 213v, 214r. No original paintings on glass by Lucas are now known, but such works are mentioned in early inventories (see Hymans, 1884, p. 147; Bredius, 1913, p. 206, and 1915–1922, 2:566; and Obreen, 1976, pp. 303–4, 315). For the suggestion that some of Lucas's engravings, especially the *Round Passion* (B.57–65), served as models for glass painters, see Van Mander, 1604, fol. 211v; Dülberg, 1933, p. 5; Beets, 1954, p. 448. Attributions to Lucas of glass paintings have been made by Dülberg, 1909, p. 10; Beets, 1913, pp. 71–73; Seligman, 1923; Hoogewerff, 1936–1947, 3:312–18; Friedländer, 1963a, p. 69; and Ritz, 1972, p. 154, no. 10. Numerous works from the circle of Lucas or from the early Leiden school exist in various collections—see Gibson, 1970a (but cf. Caviness, 1989, pp. 210–11, who questions Gibson's attribution); Kloek and Filedt Kok, 1983, pp. 16–17; and a group of roundels in the Stedelijk Museum "De Lakenhal," Leiden, described there as very similar to early works by Lucas (inv. nos. 6030, 7679–84). Bangs, 1979a, p. 5, notes that Cornelis Engebrechtsz. also designed glass roundels.

It has been suggested that Lucas also made designs for tapestries; see D'Argenville, 1745, p. 51, and Evrard, 1884, pp. 71, 76–77, among others. Duverger, 1957–1958, mentions tapestries copied after engravings and paintings, but concludes that Lucas probably never designed cartoons specifically for tapestries. Bangs, 1976, p. 31, and 1979a, p. 104, considers it possible that both Cornelis Engebrechtsz. and Lucas designed tapestries, since large numbers were produced in Leiden at that time.

2. See Rathgeber, 1844, col. 225, nos. 958–60, and Taurel, 1881, p. 19, for

painted copies that were still accepted as originals; and more recently, Antwerp, Musée Royal des Beaux-Arts, 1958, pp. 124-25; and Pigler, 1968, p. 379.

3. Waagen, 1862, p. 150, and 1864, p. 120. Michiels, 1868, p. 117; for the 110 paintings attributed by him to Lucas, see 1847, pp. 127-37. Evrard, 1884, pp. 636-39, considered none originals (not even the *Last Judgment* in Leiden, which he believed was painted by another artist named Lucas van Leyden). Of the ten accepted by Rathgeber, 1844, cols. 16-17, 210-26, 439, only one is now accepted: the *Virgin and Child with Mary Magdalene and a Donor* in Munich (Cat. 14); col. 215, no. 743. The *Card Players* in Wilton House (Cat. 38) is included among the hundred false attributions. The *Last Judgment* in Leiden (Cat. 20) and *Christ Healing the Blind Man* in Leningrad (Cat. 25) seem to be accepted as compositions by Lucas by virtue of their descriptions in Van Mander, although Rathgeber did not consider them originals.

4. Beets, 1913, pp. 83-84, 89; Friedländer, 1967-1976, 10:60-64; and Hoogewerff, 1936-1947, 3:318-19.

5. Friedländer, 1963a, pp. 68-69.

Chapter 1. A Biographical Account

1. Van Mander, 1604, fols. 211r-215r.

2. Ibid., fols. 211v (for Lucas's birth date) and 214v (for Lucas Dammesz.). Fol. 234v gives a specific birth date for Jan van Scorel, born August 1, 1495; see also Utrecht, Centraal Museum, 1955, p. 19. In the biography of Jacob Cornelisz., Van Mander admitted he was unable to determine when the artist was born (fol. 207r). For Lucas Dammesz. de Hoey as the probable source for Van Mander's information, see Dülberg, 1899c, p. 74, n. 2.

3. Van Mander, 1604, fols. 211v, 212r, and 212v. English translations of Van Mander's life of Lucas are by Gary Schwartz from Vos, 1978c, pp. 463-79.

4. The first serious doubts about the 1494 birth date were expressed by Gavelle, 1929, pp. 29-33, but Gavelle's conflation of the two trips mentioned in *Het Schilder-Boeck* is problematic, as discussed in the section on Lucas's travels. Likewise, Pelinck's proposed birth date of 1489 presupposes that Lucas's grandson could remember the time of the year when Lucas was born but not the year itself (1949, esp. pp. 193-94). His suggestion that Van Mander misunderstood the chronology given by Lucas Dammesz. is highly conjectural, and his argument is weakened by efforts to pinpoint Lucas's age in a number of so-called portraits of the artist.

5. Van Mander, 1604, fols. 214r-v. No mention of such a trip is found in Van Mander's biography of Gossaert. For Gossaert's activities in the late 1520s, see Rotterdam, Museum Boymans-van Beuningen, 1965, pp. 30, 377-79.

6. Scholars who have suggested that the trip in 1521 was identical to the trip taken when Lucas was thirty-three include Bruyn, 1969, p. 44; Bangs, 1979a, pp. 11-12, n. 35, and p. 127, n. 54; and Van Brussel, Moerman, and Wurfbain,

1978, p. 6. For information on Gossaert during 1517–1523, see Rotterdam, Museum Boymans–van Beuningen, 1965, p. 26; Amsterdam, Rijksprentenkabinet, 1978, pp. 44–45; and Vos, 1978c, p. 480, n. 9. For Dürer's entry, see Rupprich, 1956, 1:162. Nonetheless, Dürer never mentioned a meeting with Quinten Massys or Joos van Cleve, Antwerp's foremost artists at the time, although he did visit Massys's house to see some paintings (Brussels, Palais des Beaux-Arts, 1977, pp. 97, 154–56). M. Mende, co-author of the Brussels exhibition catalogue, considers it unlikely that Gossaert would not have made an effort to meet Dürer in Antwerp (p. 155).

7. See Koning, 1959, pp. 82–85, for information on the annuity. The age of majority in Leiden in the late fifteenth and early sixteenth centuries appears to have varied depending on circumstances. One document of 1475 indicates it was twenty-one, while other references present legal emancipation in specific cases at seventeen or eighteen (see Hamaker, 1873, p. 177). In 1545, people younger than twenty-five were considered minors in certain court cases, and this could well have been the practice earlier (p. 380). In correspondence of May 12, 1981, J. Bangs noted that it would not have been necessary for Lucas to have attained the age of majority in order to sign for the payment.

8. Gibson accepted the earlier birth date, adding new reasons based on his suggested date of 1508–1509 for Lucas's apprenticeship with Cornelis Engebrechtsz. (1970b, p. 98, and 1977, pp. 161–62). There is little evidence in Lucas's work of a shift in tutelage from Huygh Jacobsz. to Cornelis, and Gibson considers it unlikely that an artist as young as fourteen or fifteen would have been unaffected by the style of his new master.

Bangs has provided the most recent argument for moving back Lucas's birth date. He found archival evidence revealing that Lucas's father remarried sometime between October 1494 and December 1495, following the death of his first wife, Lucas's mother (1979a, p. 94). This would leave only four or five months from Lucas's birth in May or June to the earliest possible remarriage date in October 1494. It should be no surprise, however, that the father of five young children would quickly woo and wed a second wife.

Recent scholars who seem to agree with the birth date of 1494 given by Van Mander include Vos, 1978a, p. 27, and 1978c, p. 480, n. 9; and Filedt Kok, in Amsterdam, Rijksprentenkabinet, 1978, p. 16 (although he is more hesitant in his 1978 article, p. 5). See also the comments by G. Lemmens in Friedländer, 1967–1976, 10:94.

9. Van Mander, 1604, fol. 211v.

10. Koning, 1959, p. 82; see also Vos, 1978a, fig. 31. A sixth child named Dirck, who also became a painter, was born ca. 1475. Apparently he was not named in the document of 1500 because he was either already of age or married. For more information, see Van Brussel, Moerman, and Wurfbain, 1978, p. 4, and Bangs, 1979a, p. 94.

11. For the annuity payment, see Vos, 1978a, p. 26, fig. 32. Information on the

guild memberships of Lucas, Huygh, and Cornelis is found in Bangs, 1979a, pp. 12-13, n. 45; Gibson, 1977, p. 14; and Dülberg, 1899c, p. 67.

12. Dülberg, 1899c, p. 72, n. 2; also Bijl, 1948, p. 27. Marijtgen's marriage to Dammes Claesz. de Hoey, a painter from Utrecht (ca. 1510-1568/69), produced several children. Among them were Lucas Dammesz. (1533-1604) and Jan de Hoey (1545-1615), both of whom also became painters; Bijl, 1948, p. 27, and Dülberg, 1899b, pp. 158-59. For further information on these three painters, see "Hoey," 1924, pp. 230-32; also Van Brussel, Moerman, and Wurfbain, 1978, p. 4, for Dammes Claesz.

13. Van Mander, 1604, fols. 212v and 214v. According to Van Mander, Lucas believed that he had been poisoned by a jealous artist. Vos, 1978c, pp. 504-5, nn. 124-25, suggests Lucas may have been infected with malaria during this trip and reports that Dürer also became ill after his trip to Zeeland. For the Boschuysen family, see Dülberg, 1899c, pp. 71-72, and for Lucas's marriage, see Koning, 1959, pp. 86-89, and Bangs, 1974a, no. 2 (also Bangs, 1979a, p. 40, for more information on Elysabeth).

14. Bangs, 1979a, p. 1 and n. 5. On June 10, Dammes Claesz. de Hoey, husband of Lucas's illegitimate daughter, Marijtgen, brought a suit against the newly widowed Elysabeth demanding that she make an inventory including all real estate, money, "silverwork, clothing, jewels, armor, weapons, [engraving] plates, pictures, paintings, prints, instruments, paints, money owed and money owing." Information concerning this suit was first published by Elsevier, 1869, p. 21. Even though all of Lucas's possessions were the property of his widow, Dammes presumably wanted the inventory to insure a proper settlement of the goods after her death. According to Lucas's will, following his death and the death of his wife, half of his goods were to go to his father and half to Marijtgen. The ruling made by the magistrates on July 27 was in favor of Marijtgen (Blok, 1884b, pp. 361-63).

15. See Dülberg, 1899c, pp. 68, 73; Hoogewerff, 1936-1947, 3:220-21; and Van Brussel, Moerman, and Wurfbain, 1978, p. 4. It is unclear whether the four siblings wanted 300 Carolus guilders apiece, in which case half of the estate would have amounted to 1,200 guilders, or a total of 300 to be split four ways. Also, it is not apparent if this was the amount left by Lucas in 1533 or the balance after his widow had drawn on the inheritance for four or five years. Dülberg further noted that in Leiden in 1514 approximately 100 of roughly 1,100 families listed had 600 pounds, about 200 had more, and 800 had less (1899c, pp. 72-73; also H. E. Van Gelder, 1976, pp. 46-59, and Bangs, 1979a, pp. 55-58). For reference, 1 gold guilder = 28 stuivers = 1.40 Flemish pounds = 1.40 Carolus guilders.

16. The Mariënpoel convent paid almost three times more for Huygh Jacobsz.'s *Virgin* than for Lucas's *Flight into Egypt* (Bangs, 1979a, p. 58). Bangs also observes that the price for Huygh's painting was more than six times the purchase price of an artisan's house in Leiden at the time. Bernard Van Orley was paid nearly three times the amount paid for Lucas's *Last Judgment* for his triptych of the same subject

in Antwerp, painted ca. 1525 and slightly smaller than Lucas's work. This Flemish artist also received twenty-eight pounds for a single full-length portrait (Hoogewerff, 1936-1947, 3:290-91, and Dülberg, 1899c, p. 72). See Friedländer, 1967- 1976, 8:no. 87, for Van Orley's *Last Judgment* in Antwerp. These comparisons reinforce the fact that Lucas's primary activity and renown seem to have been as a printmaker (Vasari, 1906, 5:406-11, and Van Mander, 1604, fol. 212v). For the prices of Lucas's prints, see Van Mander, 1604, fol. 212v. For information on earnings in other professions, see Blok, 1884a, p. 399, and for the amounts paid for Lucas's prints as opposed to Dürer's, see Dülberg, 1899c, p. 72, and Vos, 1978c, p. 489, n. 56.

17. Vasari, 1906, 7:589 (translation from Vos, 1978c, p. 490, n. 58), and Van Mander, 1604, fol. 212v. Gavelle, 1929, pp. 121-23, suggests the journey might have been made ca. 1510-1511.

18. Rupprich, 1956, 1:174-175; Vasari, 1906, 5:406-7 (translations from Vos, 1978c, p. 489, n. 56, and p. 491, n. 62), and Van Mander, 1604, fol. 212v (a slightly longer description is given in Van Mander's life of Dürer, fol. 209v, but no mention is made there of a trip by the German artist to Leiden).

19. Friedländer, 1924, pp. 23-24, associates this trip with Lucas's experimentation with the technique of etching. All six of Lucas's etchings date from 1520, but his etching style, and even the use of a copper rather than an iron plate, differs from Dürer's prints in this medium (see Amsterdam, Rijksprentenkabinet, 1978, pp. 76-77).

20. Beets, 1935a, p. 50; also Gibson, 1977, p. 206. The guild entry is cited in Rombouts and Van Lerius, p. 99; see also Vos, 1978c, p. 491, n. 62. For information on Lucas standing bail, see Dülberg, 1899c, p. 70, n. 2.

21. Van Mander, 1604, fols. 210r and 211v; also Vos, 1978c, pp. 481-82, nn. 12-13. Huygh was still alive at the time of the suit in 1534 and had died sometime before the second suit of 1538; Blok, 1884b, p. 363, and Dülberg, 1899c, pp. 67-68.

22. For the St. Peter's commission, see Bangs, 1979a, pp. 3, 92-95; also Boon, 1983b, pp. 46-47, for other archival references to Huygh's life in Leiden and Gouda. The Latin entry in Buchelius, 1928, p. 40, reads "Hugo Leidensis Goudae vel Gandae." Later, in Petrus Opmerus's *Opus chronographicum* (1611), fol. 406, the artist is described as "Hugo quoque Leydensis deinde Goudensis" (Hugo from Gouda, also Leiden). See Dülberg, 1899c, p. 68, n. 5, for the full quote, and p. 69 for the suggestion that "Goudensis" might have been a typographical error for "Gandensis" (from Ghent).

I have noted Huygh's association with Ghent. According to Marcus van Vaernewijck, a panel in a chapel of St. Peter's abbey in Ghent was "made here earlier by Master Hugo of Leyden in Holland" (*Den spieghel der Nederlandsche autheyt* [Ghent, 1568]). See Michiels, 1847, p. 108, n. 1; Dülberg, 1899c, p. 68; and Vos, 1978c, pp. 480-81, n. 10. Boon, 1983b, p. 47, notes that Van Vaernewijck confused Huygh with Hugo van der Goes, as clearly seen in *Van die Beroerlicke Tijden in de Nederlanden en voornamelijk in Gendt, 1566-1568,* ed. F. Vander Haegen (Ghent, 1872), p. 169.

23. He seems to have painted works for Hieronymusdal, since in 1482 he received payments for "Hugo, our painter" (Bangs, 1979a, p. 93). Much later, in 1523, he was probably the painter of a panel representing the Virgin for the convent of Mariënpoel, near Leiden (Bangs, 1979a, p. 21; see also Dülberg, 1899c, p. 69, and Gibson, 1970b, p. 91).

Beets, 1954, p. 443, considers Huygh the painter of the *Works of Charity* from the Alkmaar church, now in the Rijksmuseum. However, these panels have no convincing parallels with the early Leiden school. See also Van Brussel, Moerman, and Wurfbain, 1978, p. 2 (with illustration), where the *Allegory of Transience* in the Rijksmuseum is tentatively attributed to Huygh, ca. 1505. These writers have identified a monogram *H* at the lower right of the panel. Also, the four monks have been identified as four rectors from the Mariënpoel cloister near Leiden. There is little relationship between this panel and the early works of Lucas, as they also observed.

24. Hymans, 1884, pp. 1, 151, attributed the Turin triptych to Lucas. Boon, 1953, pp. 211-15, groups a number of other paintings around these two *Crucifixions*. The *Lamentation* formerly in the Coll. Meeus, Brussels (Boon's fig. 3), and *Christ and the Samaritan Woman,* sold in Berlin in 1953 as Amsterdam School, ca. 1500 (his fig. 5), are undoubtedly by the same hand. The link with the other paintings he cites is less clear in photographs. Gibson, 1970b, p. 91, accepts all of these into the oeuvre of Huygh Jacobsz. Boon, 1953, p. 211, also associates the *Lamentation* with a lost composition by Hugo but sees no relationship between any of these paintings and the works of Lucas. He disagrees with the attribution to Huygh.

25. Gibson, 1970b, pp. 91, 93-96; Dülberg, 1903-1908b, pp. 15-17 (Leiden Master of ca. 1510, Huygh Jacobsz.?); Hoogewerff, 1928, p. 113, and 1936-1947, 3:209-12. Friedländer, 1967-1976, 5:no. 66VI, gives the Turin *Crucifixion* to the Master of Delft(?); see his 10:nos. 13 and 64, for similar centurion figures in paintings by Jan Mostaert and by the circle of the Master of Delft.

Numerous examples of similar figures could be cited, although none is identical in pose to Lucas's figure. See Washington, National Gallery, 1967-1968, figs. 53-57 (Schongauer), 135 (Master I.A.M. of Zwolle), and 186-87 (I. van Meckenem; bystanders peering through a window at the scene, as mentioned by Gibson, also appear here); also Dürer's woodcuts in the *Albertina Passion* (Kurth, 1963), nos. 94-95, and his engraving of *Hercules at the Crossroads* (B.73). Gibson's other points of comparison can be similarly refuted. The petal-like cuts decorating the costumes in Turin and in some prints by Lucas are imported from German fashions (see Dürer's engraving B.80 and his woodcut B.11). The children in the foreground of the triptych frequently appear in northern art to enliven, and sometimes to introduce, the main scene (e.g., Dürer's woodcuts B.9 and B.77; also Friedländer, 1967-1976, 10:nos. 13, 60-61).

Boon, 1973, p. 171, suggests the Master of the Turin Crucifixion was an eclectic painter who borrowed motifs from various artists, including his contemporary, Lucas. See also Filedt Kok, 1978, p. 38.

26. The two panels in Rotterdam (inv. nos. 2117-18) measure 132 x 95 and 133 x 95 respectively. The Philadelphia panel (inv. no. J347) measures 122 x 95.6; see Philadelphia, John G. Johnson Collection, 1972, p. 58. Hannema, 1937, suggests they originally formed part of one altarpiece. Van Regteren Altena, 1955, pp. 110-15, tentatively connects the paintings with the altarpiece dedicated to John the Baptist and once in St. John's, Gouda (known through a reference in Walvis, 1714, p. 23). See Châtelet, 1981, pp. 157-60, for illustrations.

27. Friedländer, 1967-1976, 5:36 and no. 37, placed the St. John panels in the 1480s and described the artist as active in Gouda because of parallels with woodcuts in the *Chevalier délibéré*. Valentiner, 1913, 2:19, agreed with Friedländer in attributing the Philadelphia panel to the Dutch School, ca. 1490. The *Birth of John the Baptist* was published for the first time by Hannema, 1937, who also followed Friedländer. Van Regteren Altena (1955, pp. 110-15) was the first to attribute these panels to Huygh Jacobsz., ca. 1500, on the basis of similarities with early works by Lucas. More recently Boon, 1968, pp. 5-6, accepted the attribution to Huygh and returned to Friedländer's association of the paintings with the woodcuts in the *Chevalier délibéré*. De la Marche's 1898 facsimile includes the woodcut illustrations; Boon, 1968, pp. 3-5, 11, n. 1, describes the publication, illustrations, and dating of this book; and Kahn, 1918, pp. 42-43, discusses the influence of the woodcuts on Lucas's early style. Most recently, Châtelet (1981, pp. 160-63) considers them to be a collaboration by several artists, possibly under French influence and also possibly related to the work of Huygh Jacobsz.

Van Regteren Altena, Boon, and Châtelet have enlarged the oeuvre of the St. John Master with a number of paintings. Only one of these is close enough in style to warrant the attribution. *St. Anne with the Virgin and Child, Saints and Donors* in the Rijksmuseum may be an earlier work by the same hand or a school-piece; see Boon, 1968, pp. 6-7, 9, and fig 8, and 1983b, pp. 43-45, and Châtelet, 1981, no. 149. The *Entombment* in Budapest and *Christ Carrying the Cross* on loan to the Museum Boymans–van Beuningen, Rotterdam, were both probably painted in the circle of the Master of Delft (Friedländer, 1967-1976, 5:pl. 108, supp. 117-18 respectively). The *Entombment* should be associated with a fragment of a *Crucifixion* showing the Virgin and John, formerly in the Coll. Kessler, Brussels (Rotterdam, Museum Boymans–van Beuningen, 1936, no. 74, as the Master of Delft, and fig. 48).

Châtelet also tentatively attributed the *Entombment* and *Christ Carrying the Cross* mentioned above to Huygh (1981, pp. 157-58, 238-39). Following Van Regteren Altena he considers it likely that the small triptych of the *Adoration of the Magi*

(Zurich, Coll. Schafrl; fig. 239) is a late work by Huygh, but it is difficult to see the relationship to the Rijksmuseum *St. Anne,* much less to the St. John panels.

28. For the association with the windows of St. John's, which were destroyed by fire in 1552, see Walvis, 1714, pp. 88-89. Friedländer, 1963a, p. 77, reversed his earlier attribution to Lucas (1967-1976, 10:58-59), and his doubts were well founded. As Kloek, 1978, p. 456, observes, there are "too few similarities" to Lucas's known works. Boon, 1973, pp. 163-73, 1978, pp. 118-21, and 1983b, p. 48, reviewed the literature concerning these drawings and assigned them to Huygh's workshop; later (1983a, pp. 440-42), he assigned them to Pieter Cornelisz. Kunst's youthful period. See also Beets, 1913, pp. 70-71, who dates the drawings ca. 1515, and Hoogewerff, 1936-1947, 3:312-13, who places them later in the 1520s.

29. Van Regteren Altena, 1955, p. 110; he also compares the small hands and the grouping of heads in clusters of three. Châtelet (1981, p. 157) notes similarities between these paintings and Lucas's early engravings, in particular the figure types, the depiction of figures seen from behind, and the bare, simplified landscape foregrounds.

30. Van Regteren Altena, 1955, p. 111 (with illustrations).

31. Filedt Kok, 1978, pp. 38, 40, agrees that the identification of Huygh as the Master of the St. John Panels is probably correct, primarily because of similarities in figure type and composition. He concludes, however, that Huygh could have had little influence on the actual training of Lucas as a painter.

32. Van Mander, 1604, fol. 210v (see also 211v). Greve, 1903, p. 208, identifies this painting as the *Adoration of the Magi* in Leiden, Stedelijk Museum (1886, no. 1031). No. 1031 in this catalogue is actually listed as the *Lamentation,* however, and correspondence with M. L. Wurfbain at the museum confirmed that there was never a painting of the *Adoration* matching Van Mander's description in the Leiden museum. For parallels between the two artists' work, see Gibson, 1970b, pp. 97-98; for the dating of the early engravings see Filedt Kok in Amsterdam, Rijksprentenkabinet, 1978, pp. 19-20. See also Kahn, 1918, p. 24, and Friedländer, 1963a, p. 9, for a comparison of the works of Cornelis and Lucas.

33. Bangs, 1979a, p. 50; also Vos, 1978a, pp. 35-37, and Busch, 1982, p. 119. None of Cornelis's paintings from 1500-1510 is similar to Lucas's early panels (see Gibson, 1977, figs. 5-15).

34. Filedt Kok, 1978, pp. 38, 40-41, and figs. 37-38, and Gibson, 1980, p. 108. Sjöblom in 1928 (p. 162) mentioned the influence on Lucas of Cornelis's use of coloring. For a detailed study of Cornelis's underdrawing, see Van Asperen de Boer and Wheelock, 1973.

35. Gibson, 1970b, p. 98; see also Friedländer, 1963a, p. 70.

Chapter 2. Stylistic Development of the Paintings

1. The important studies of Lucas's graphic style and development are Kahn, 1918; Friedländer, 1924; Filedt Kok (Amsterdam, Rijksprentenkabinet, 1978); and Jacobowitz and Stepanek (Washington, National Gallery, 1983). I have also used Lucas's drawings for comparison, although they are less useful than the prints for this purpose: there are far fewer of them, and only five are dated (see Kloek, 1978, nos. 12–15, 19; nos. 21 and 23 are also fairly easily dated because of their close relationship to two dated engravings). In using prints or drawings for comparative purposes, I have had to consider their different functions and techniques, both of which affect the style.

2. Houbraken, 1753, 3:212–13. For more on De Bisschop, see J. G. Van Gelder, 1957 and 1971, esp. pp. 214–16. He also copied works attributed to Jan van Scorel, Frans Floris, Pieter Bruegel, Hans Holbein, Raphael, Giorgione, Titian, and others.

3. Van Mander, 1604, fol. 211v. It has been suggested that Lucas's work could have been influenced by Dürer's early engraving of *St. Eustace* (B.57), since Eustace's conversion was virtually indistinguishable from that of Hubert (Vos, 1978c, p. 483, n. 22).

4. Friedländer, 1930, pp. 493–94, and 1963a, p. 46.

5. Vasari, 1906, 5:410, and Van Mander, 1604, fol. 212r.

6. As an examination of the *Chess Players* revealed, three of these heads were not planned in the underdrawing and were added only during the last stages of the painting process (Filedt Kok, 1978, pp. 21–22).

7. Beets, 1934, p. 50, n. 3. See Parshall, 1974, p. 106, for further discussion.

8. See Ringbom, 1965, pp. 179–88, and Panofsky, 1971a, pp. 114–16; also Parshall, 1974, p. 131, on the similarities between Dürer's painting and Lucas's *Chess Players* and *Susanna before the Judge*.

9. For the influence of Massys and Bosch, see Burger, 1925, p. 154, and Dülberg, 1929, p. 167; also Parshall, 1974, pp. 122–27, for the relationship between Massys and Lucas.

10. The underdrawing was still relatively unchanged from *Chess Players* to *Potiphar's Wife*. See Filedt Kok, 1978, pp. 27–31, for a comparison of the brush underdrawing in the two works; most of my analysis of paint technique draws on this important study. The best description of the colors in *Susanna*, which was destroyed during World War II, is found in Hurm, 1892, pp. 48–50.

11. Réau, 1956, 1:163–65, notes that these two scenes were commonly used as pendants beginning in the sixteenth century. Parshall, 1974, pp. 128–29, dates *Susanna* slightly later than *Potiphar's Wife* for reasons similar to mine.

12. For example, B.17, 24, 33, 42, 78, 85, and 123. Parshall, 1974, pp. 198–203, suggests the influence of Gerard David on Lucas's use of this compositional formula (cf. Kahn, 1918, pp. 10–12, 30–34, who traces it back to Geertgen tot Sint Jans).

13. Van Mander, 1604, fol. 214r.
14. Filedt Kok, 1978, pp. 56–57.
15. Friedländer, 1967–1976, 9b:no. 122.
16. See B.74, 113, 122. Jacobowitz and Stepanek, in Washington, National Gallery, 1983, p. 21, saw the development of landscape as a primary concern of Lucas as printmaker, beginning with his earliest engravings and culminating in 1517–1519.
17. The eight known variations include five engravings dating from ca. 1506 to 1530 (B.3, 7–10), two woodcuts from the 1510s (B.1–2), and a chalk drawing in Hamburg, ca. 1528–1530. See Vos, 1978a, pp. 70–79; Amsterdam, Rijksprentenkabinet, 1978, pp. 50–53; and Kloek, 1978, p. 455, no. 26.
18. For example, Lucas's engraving of the *Nude Woman with a Hind* (B.153, 1509) is clearly a reworking of Dürer's *Fortuna* (B.78) and *Nemesis* (B.77), and the *Triumph of Mordecai* (B.32), 1515, is derived from the *Knight, Death, and Devil* (B.98), dated two years earlier. See Beets, 1911, pp. 11–12, and 1913, pp. 43–46; Kahn, 1918, pp. 45–59; and Held, 1931, pp. 18–28. For an overview of the economic, intellectual, and artistic activities in Antwerp at this time, see Voet, 1973; De Bosque, 1975, p. 46–52; Brussels, Palais des Beaux-Arts, 1977, pp. 95–98, 151–57; and Silver, 1974b, pp. 13–14 (and p. 22, n. 39, for a more detailed bibliography).
19. Amsterdam, Rijksprentenkabinet, 1978, pp. 43–44, 63. For the influence on Netherlandish artists of Dürer's painting of *St. Jerome*, 1521, in Lisbon, see Brussels, Palais des Beaux-Arts, 1977, pp. 42, 66, 165–67; also Panofsky, 1971a, pp. 211–13. Lucas's drawing is in the Ashmolean Museum (Kloek, 1978, p. 449, no. 19).
20. Kloek, 1978, p. 446, no. 13, and Brussels, Palais des Beaux-Arts, 1977, pp. 58–59, 61, and 63.
21. Numerous early Netherlandish examples could be cited, from Rogier van der Weyden's *Lionello d'Este* to Jan Gossaert's *Portrait of a Man with a Scroll*, both in the Metropolitan Museum (see Friedländer, 1967–1976, 2:no. 23 and 8:no. 63). For examples of Joos van Cleve's portraits, see 9a:nos. 79–80. The portrait style of Massys is more varied, but there are a few in this more old-fashioned format (for example, see 7:no. 47). The influence of Netherlandish portraits on Dürer can be seen in his *Portrait of Bernhard von Riesen* in Dresden and *Portrait of a Man* in Madrid (Panofsky, 1971a, pp. 210–11, and figs. 259–60).
22. Friedländer, 1967–1976, 7:nos. 25, 27, 81, 131, add. 203, and supp. 188. A number of paintings of this sort were produced earlier in the studios of Hans Memling, Gerard David, and Dirk Bouts (for example, see 3:no. 17, 6a:no. 9, and 6b:no. 165).
23. Friedländer, 1967–1976, 8:no. 2, dates Gossaert's altarpiece ca. 1511 (p. 90). See Glück, 1945, pp. 123–24, for the Bruges influence on the Palermo triptych. Friedländer, 1969, p. 102, gives the provenance of this triptych by Gos-

saert. The copies by Isenbrandt were formerly in the collections of Frau von Pannwitz, Hartekamp, Netherlands, and Baron de Rothschild, Paris (Friedländer, 1969, p. 102, and 1967–1976, 11:no. 134).

It is also possible that Lucas was inspired by Jacob Cornelisz.'s *Virgin and Child with Angels,* now in Berlin: Jacob's cherubs, singing and playing instruments, are similar to the type portrayed by Lucas. Friedländer dates this triptych ca. 1518 (1967–1976, 12:no. 241, and p. 114). Of course, earlier versions of the theme were painted by minor northern Netherlandish artists, but they have little in common with Lucas's painting (see Rotterdam, Museum Boymans–van Beuningen, 1936, fig. 46). Cf. a panel included in the same exhibition (fig. 50), then with P. de Boer, Amsterdam, and dated ca. 1490, that might have influenced Jacob's representation.

24. For examples of Bellini's work, see Wilde, 1974, figs. 28, 33, and 41. For Dürer, see Panofsky, 1971a, pp. 225–29, and figs. 148, 285–88. Several scholars have seen the influence of Dürer on the Berlin *Virgin and Child* (e.g., Burger, 1925, p. 154, who also noted a relation to the putti in works by Jacob Cornelisz., and Wegner, 1959, p. 8).

25. Cf. also the Oxford *Lamentation* by the Master of Delft, ca. 1510; for these works, see Friedländer, 1967–1976, 10:no. 64, pp. 31–32, and no. 73. See 10:41 for his dating of ca. 1520 for the *Crucifixion,* which is dated ca. 1515 by Gibson, 1977, p. 89.

26. Friedländer, 1967–1976, 6a:no. 64, 9b:no. 178, 2:nos. 28–30, 39–40, and 6a:no. 14.

27. Koch, 1965, and Washington, National Gallery, 1983, p. 192.

28. See Panofsky, 1971b, 1:254 and 2:pl. 172, for Rogier's *Annunciation,* and Friedländer, 1967–1976, 6b:no. 266, for the Bruges Master of the Legend of St. Ursula (Convent of the Brompton Oratory, London), which also includes a banderole inscribed with Gabriel's greeting. See Friedländer, 1967–1976, 9a:no. 25, for Van Cleve's panel in the Friedsam Collection, Metropolitan Museum.

29. Friedländer, 1967–1976, 3:pls. 74–77, 92–93, 6a:pls. 91–92, and 7:pl. 12.

30. This was first observed by Beets, 1913, p. 45. See Vos, 1978a, ch. 6, for more on the relationship between Lucas and the Italians.

31. Friedländer, 1967–1976, 8:no. 44 (1521), and 12:no. 362 (ca. 1530–1535); Krönig, 1936, pp. 142–43; and Oberheide, 1933, pp. 143, 144, 148, and pls. 20, 28.

32. See Amsterdam, Rijksprentenkabinet, 1978, pp. 46–48; Silver and Smith, 1978, esp. pp. 240–41; and Washington, National Gallery, 1983, pp. 23, 134, for the relationship between these engravings and the Italian style.

33. Rathgeber, 1844, pp. 16–17, and Pit, 1894, p. 84, among others, faulted the composition. Schnaase, 1834, p. 63, described it as an unfinished study. Rathgeber, 1844, p. 17, criticized the paleness of the palette. Others have attributed the unusual coloring to an early restoration (e.g., Waagen, 1862, p. 151,

n. 1, and Rosenberg, 1877, p. 10). See Dülberg, 1899a, pp. 38-39, for a summary of nineteenth-century opinions.

34. See Friedländer, 1967-1976, 6a:no. 8, for Memling's work; 8:no. 87 for Van Orley's triptych; and Salinger, 1941, for Van Cleve's panel.

35. See Filedt Kok, 1978, pp. 65-97, for a detailed account of the paint technique and underdrawing of this triptych. In the nineteenth century the exterior figures were more highly praised, in agreement with Van Mander's judgment (1604, fol. 213v); see Schnaase, 1834, p. 64, and Rosenberg, 1877, p. 10. For the Munich diptych, see Filedt Kok, 1978, pp. 48-55. Gibson, 1980, p. 107, points to a comparable distinction between the underdrawing styles on the interior and exterior of altarpieces by Bosch, Engebrechtsz., and Van Scorel. See also Lucas's lost triptych with *St. Andrew* (Cat. 28).

36. Beets is the major exception (especially his 1934 article, pp. 151-62). Friedländer, 1963a, p. 86, commented generally on this Italian influence: "Dürer was a dangerous model for him, and Marcantonio a pernicious one." The lack of Italian influence is mentioned by Baldass, 1923, pp. 27, 34, among others. For the influence of Gossaert, see, e.g., Bersier, 1951, p. 55.

37. M. L. Wurfbain, in Hermesdorf et al., 1978, p. 317.

38. See Jan Mostaert's *Last Judgment* in Bonn (Amsterdam, Rijksmuseum, 1958, fig. 49), Joos van Cleve's *Last Judgment* in New York (Salinger, 1941), and Dürer's woodcut of *Christ in Limbo* (B.41), 1511.

39. Wurfbain, in Hermesdorf et al., 1978, p. 317.

40. Gibson, 1986, pp. 48-49.

41. For illustrations see Hoogewerff, 1936-1947, 2:figs. 264-67. This work, now in the Rijksmuseum, was apparently once dated 1518 and has been attributed to the workshop of Cornelis Buys or Jacob Cornelisz. Dülberg, 1899a, pp. 44-46, was the first to note the similarities between these two representations; see also his 1900a, pp. 203-6; Hoogewerff, 1936-1947, 2:531-38; and Beets, 1908, pp. 63-64.

42. Friedländer, 1967-1976, 8:no. 35. This painting has been dated ca. 1527 by Weisz, 1913, pp. 58ff., and ca. 1525-1530 by Von der Osten, 1961, p. 466. See also Rotterdam, Museum Boymans-van Beuningen, 1965, pp. 163-64. The affinities between these two works were mentioned most recently in Amsterdam, Rijksmuseum, 1986, 2:142-43, no. 29. The similarities are more evident in the Oslo painting itself than in Lucas's preliminary drawing in the British Museum (see my Figs. 29, 30).

43. Friedländer, 1967-1976, 8:no. 39a; see also nos. 34 and 36.

44. See Dürer's early painting of the *Virgin and Child* in Washington (Walker, 1975, p. 149) or his 1520 engraving, B.38; but compare the tightly framed, volumetric figures and the energetic pose of the Child in such paintings by Dürer as the *Virgin and Child* in Vienna (Anzelewsky, 1971, fig. 149). Lucas and Gossaert, both clearly dependent at times on Dürer, were apparently influenced by

different stylistic strains in his art (see Baldass, 1936, pp. 256-57, for this same idea).

45. The comparison with the *Large Cannon* was made by Beets, 1913, p. 105, and Dülberg, 1929, p. 169, who also noted the similarity to the Vienna painting. See Panofsky, 1971a, p. 205, for the fact that Dürer took artworks with him to the Netherlands.

46. Rotterdam, Museum Boymans–van Beuningen, 1965, no. 18 (ca. 1520–1525) and no. 25 (ca. 1525–1530).

47. Filedt Kok, 1978, pp. 101–14.

48. The triptych in Berlin was attributed by Dülberg, 1923, and Knuttel, 1938, p. 124, to Cornelis Engebrechtsz.; by Beets, 1952a, pp. 189–90, to Cornelis Cornelisz. Kunst; and by Gibson, 1977, pp. 144–51, to Engebrechtsz., with the background painted by the same artist whose hand is evident in parts of the *Crucifixion* in Basel (Gibson's fig. 17). Beets and Gibson noted similarities between this painting and Lucas's *Dance;* see especially Gibson, 1977, pp. 17, 149–50. See also his 1986 article, p. 46. For general information on the theme of the Feeding of the Five Thousand in Netherlandish art, see Glück, 1942, and Utrecht, Aartsbisschoppelijk Museum, 1962, pp. 90–92, 126–27.

49. E.g., Jacopo's *Flagellation* and *Beheading of John the Baptist* in the British Museum sketchbook and his drawings of the same subjects in the Louvre (Moschini, 1943, pls. 19, 21, 29, and 33; also Gilbert, 1952, pp. 208–9). For Lucas's use of inversion, see Parshall, 1978, pp. 220–21, 228–29, and figs. 21, 27; also Grosjean, 1974, p. 140, and Moxey, 1977, pp. 12–13, 34–37, for other artists' experimentation with compositional technique.

50. Other figures in *Dance* seem Italianate in pose, although the specific sources are more difficult to determine. The closest graphic parallel to the running, pointing man in the right background of the central panel is found in the background of Marcantonio's *David and Goliath* (B.10). This type of pose recurs frequently in the works of Raphael and his school, however (e.g., the *Meeting of Leo X and Attila* in the Stanza d'Eliodoro, the cartoon for the tapestry of the *Conversion of Saul,* and a variation in Agostino Veneziano's *Two Men at a Cemetery,* B.407). Parshall, 1974, p. 135, n. 2, compared this figure to the man entering at the left of Raphael's *School of Athens.* The woman running with her right arm outstretched in the middle ground of the right wing is comparable in pose to a figure in Raphael's *Fire in the Borgo* in the Stanza dell'Incendio. It is impossible to say whether the similarity is coincidental. Finally, the cloaked man at the right of the central panel, pointing toward the main scene, serves a compositional function similar to that of the figure of Vulcan in the left background of Mantegna's *Parnassus* in the Louvre. The combination of this figure with the ring of dancers in the foreground of Mantegna's panel is particularly suggestive when compared to Lucas's work. Perhaps Lucas knew of this painting through Dürer, although by 1497 it was already hanging in the Castle of St. George, Mantua.

51. Gibson, 1986, pp. 46–50. The cartoons were in Brussels in the 1520s, and Lucas might have seen them there during his travels. See White, 1972, figs. 3–5, and pp. 3–4 for the early history of the cartoons.

52. See Silver and Smith, 1978, pp. 239–44, 265, 278, for their theory of moralizing content allied with classicizing form in Lucas's late engravings.

53. Friedländer, 1967–1976, 12:no. 317, and Bruyn, 1954, pp. 51–52. For brief comparisons between Van Scorel's landscapes, influenced by Venetian painting, and those of Lucas, see Dülberg, 1929, p. 169; Van de Wetering, 1938, pp. 49–50; Friedländer, 1963a, p. 68; and Nikulin, 1972, p. 115. Friedländer, 1963a, p. 70, and Meyer, 1954, p. 192, have suggested a link between Van Scorel's fluid and painterly technique and Lucas's *Last Judgment* triptych. Meyer also cites Van Mander's (1604, fols. 135v and 164r) comparison of the sharply defined figures of both artists.

54. Compared to the extremely detailed underdrawing of the early paintings, the sketchy, summary lines in the late works are used only to indicate the location of the main forms; see Filedt Kok, 1978, pp. 116–20.

Chapter 3. Iconographic Concerns

1. For an interpretation of Lucas's gaming scenes as pure genre, see Friedländer, 1967–1976, 10:61 (but cf. p. 50) and 1963a, pp. 47–56; and Knuttel, 1938, p. 129. The objective nature of the *Chess Players* is also emphasized by Marlier, 1954, pp. 270, 290, Leymarie, 1956, p. 48, and Boon, 1964, p. 351. Other authors have downplayed the significance of the game, seeing it only as an excuse for a study of certain formal problems (e.g., Baldass, 1923, p. 15). Elsewhere Baldass described the works of Lucas and Quinten Massys as satirical-didactic genre paintings (1923–1925, p. 42). A useful discussion of modern uses of the term *genre* in relation to Netherlandish painting is found in Renger, 1970, pp. 9–16.

2. See Van der Linde, 1874, 1:140–41, for Damiani's letter, and 144 and n. 11, for evidence of chess as a legal game in towns in Italy, France, and Germany; also his 1875, p. 69, for an ordinance in Delft, probably from the first half of the fifteenth century. For Neckam, see Murray, 1962, pp. 500–503, and pp. 497–99 for the eleventh-century Einsiedeln Poem known in a Latin manuscript from southern Germany. Chess was described in a fourteenth-century French transcription of the Latin romance *Vetula* as a noble game when played in moderation, without dice. In an early fifteenth-century German work entitled *Destructorium vitiorum*, it is classified as an "honest" game: "genus ludorum socialis honestatis" (Murray, 1963, pp. 507–8, 534). For the condemnation of chess in Paris, see Lacroix, 1871, p. 256; also Wichmann, 1960, pp. 33–37, for further examples in the thirteenth and fourteenth centuries.

3. Lehrs, 1969, fig. 440. See Murray, 1962, pp. 529–30, for the *Quaedam*

moralitas de scaccario; pp. 537-40 for De Cessolis's *Liber de moribus hominum et de officiis nobilium super ludo scacorum;* and p. 548 for a Dutch version of this work, entitled *Dat Scaecspel* and printed in Gouda in 1479 and Delft in 1483. For Melanchthon, see Van der Linde, 1874, 1:153; also Sebastian Brant's *De periculoso scacorum ludo* (Zarncke, 1964), pp. 153-54.

4. Detailed synopses of the poem are given by Sieper, 1898, esp. pp. 117ff., and 1903, 2:59ff.; and Galpin, 1920, pp. 283ff. For *Huon de Bordeaux,* see Murray, 1962, p. 738. He also notes that chess as an allegory of love was popular among the minstrels and troubadours of the time (p. 753, with examples from the thirteenth century).

5. Schuyer, 1968, p. 17 and fig. 3 for the Manesse manuscript miniature. See Kohlhaussen, 1928, pp. 75, 96, and pls. 24, 26, and 36, for the representation of chess games on the ivory panels of boxes from the fourteenth century; also Koechlin, 1924b, pp. 181-84, and 1924a, pp. 381-89, nos. 1042-56 and pl. 180.

6. For the Basel tapestries, see Kurth, 1926, 1:223-24, no. 75/76, and 2:pls. 75/76. Other tapestries with chess scenes are illustrated in her no. 77 and Göbel, 1923-1934, pt. 1, 2:fig. 196. The grisaille window is discussed by Bégule and Bertaux, 1906, with an illustration on p. 409. See Weigand, 1959, p. 32, fig. 8, for the miniature of *Arabel and Willehalm Playing Chess* from the Willehalm Codex, Landesbibliothek, Kassel, and Amsterdam, Rijksprentenkabinet, 1985, fig. 58, for the engraving by Master E. S.

7. Kiefer, 1958, illustration on p. 218. For more examples of the amorous glance, see Fig. 77 and the engraving by Master E. S. cited in note 6. The pastime of dancing is associated in *Das Guldin Spil* with idleness and devotion, and chess with pride and humility (Schröder, 1882, p. 1 of the text, and Murray, 1962, p. 554). This work, published in 1472, was written in Strasbourg earlier in the century, ca. 1432-1433. Information on the Garden of Love as a popular pictorial theme in the fifteenth and sixteenth centuries is found in Bliss, 1928, and Van Marle, 1971, 2:426-32. The engraving by the Master of the Berlin Passion is illustrated in Geisberg, n.d., pl. 65.

8. On the less exclusive nature of chess as a pastime in the fifteenth century, and its decreasing popularity as the middle class turned to card games and dice, see Niemeijer, 1961, p. 16.

9. Weller, 1940, and Wehle, 1947. Another fifteenth-century *cassone* by a north Italian artist is painted with a Garden of Love in which one of the couples plays chess (formerly Coll. Leon Somzée, Belgium; Niemeijer, 1961, p. 16).

10. On the frequency of fur-lined cloaks among Leiden's more-well-to-do burghers, see Bangs, 1979a, pp. 133-34.

11. For the woman as loser, see Koechlin, 1924a, pl. 180, and Wichmann, 1960, pls. 62, 79; cf. pl. 60, in which the outcome of the game is apparently still undecided. That the gesture of the woman's upraised hand should not be interpreted as one of triumph is evident from the smile on the man's face in some of

the representations (e.g., Koechlin, 1924a, p. 382, no. 1043; see also Wehle, 1947, p. 153).

12. The most detailed explanation in English of courier chess is given by Murray, 1962, p. 483; see also Van der Linde, 1874, 1:313, and Crow, 1944, p. 34.

13. Parshall, 1974, pp. 116–17; see also Held, 1966, p. 447. On the Power of Women as a literary theme, see Maurer, 1963, pp. 224–48. The artistic tradition is treated by Fuchs and Kind, 1913; Van Marle, 1971, 2:479–96; Schneider, 1960; and Smith, 1978. See also Davis, 1975. Lucas's interest in the theme is discussed in relation to his prints by Filedt Kok (Amsterdam, Rijksprentenkabinet, 1978, pp. 48–50); Silver and Smith, 1978, pp. 251–55; and Washington, National Gallery, 1983, pp. 102ff.

14. Maurer, 1963, p. 245.

15. See Lehrs, 1969, figs. 533 and 649, for the engravings by Master bg and Van Meckenem. For images of the Battle for the Britches, see Randall, 1966, p. 200 and fig. 576; Kraus, 1975, pp. 25–31 and fig. 16; and Gibson, 1976, pp. 9–15.

16. See Schreiber, 1937, pp. 62–64, for a discussion of the interest in cards shown by the nobility of Brabant, Flanders, and Holland. The earliest extant printed cards seem to date from ca. 1440; Hind, 1963a, pp. 20–21, and 1963b, 1:84–89. By 1521, Dürer was able to buy six decks in Antwerp for seven stuivers (Taylor, 1973, p. 146). In the sixteenth century Antwerp was the leading city in the Netherlands for the manufacture and export of cards (Meyer, 1970, p. 162).

17. See Schreiber, 1937, pp. 64–65, for the Leiden ordinance of 1397; for comparable prohibitions around Europe in the late fourteenth century, see Trumpf, 1958, p. 11. The government of Amsterdam prohibited dice in 1395 but expressly named chess and cards as exceptions to this ban (Janssen, 1965, p. 63). For the kinds of bets made, see Lacroix, 1871, p. 252; Semrau, 1910, pp. 5–6; and Knappert, 1908, p. 12. Bartlett, 1969, p. 117, and Taylor, 1973, pp. 218–19, cite the Duke of Savoy's decree; other fifteenth-century ordinances are mentioned by Burckhardt, 1893, pp. 22–25, and Hamaker, 1873, pp. 235–36 (for a Leiden ordinance of 1450).

18. Burckhardt, 1893, pp. 26–27. Some enterprising churchmen devised new games of religious or educational content to be played with a pack of cards; see Trumpf, 1958, p. 22, and Taylor, 1973, p. 188. See Grupp, 1973, p. 44, Schreiber, 1937, pp. 63–64, and Sporham-Krempel, 1958, p. 28, for fifteenth-century sermons against gaming, and Trumpf, 1958, for an illustration (opposite p. 16) of Schäufelein's woodcut. At that time the entire population of Nuremberg was less than thirty thousand.

19. Semrau, 1910, pp. 9–10; cf. a late medieval French poem that states "the girl who loves gaming leaves the service of God" (p. 3). A Leiden decree of 1397, for example, specifies that no man or woman ("ghien man of wijf") is allowed to play cards; Schreiber, 1937, p. 64; also p. 7.

20. The suit of hearts is also found in Quinten Massys's *Ill-Matched Pair* in the National Gallery, Washington, which shows a young woman fondling a lascivious old man while she surreptitiously hands his money to her accomplice, dressed as a fool (Silver, 1974a, fig. 1 and pp. 113–14). For the meaning of the suit of hearts, see Amsterdam, Rijksmuseum, 1976b, pp. 151–52; for the Basel tapestry, see Gysin, 1947, p. 14, and Kurth, 1926, 1:223–24.

21. Hall, 1974, p. 196, and Steele, 1978, p. 71. For an illustration, see Lehrs, 1969, fig. 102.

22. Schröder, 1882, pp. 61–69. For the engraving by the Housebook Master, see Hutchison, 1972, no. 73.

23. Brant, 1944, pp. 255–56.

24. Erasmus, 1971, pp. 90, 124–25. A cardplaying fool in Pieter Bruegel's *Netherlandish Proverbs*, dated 1559 and now in Berlin-Dahlem, illustrates the dictum "The fool gets the card." See Hanckel, 1952, p. 155, and Fraenger, 1923, p. 143.

25. For Theunissen's print, see Armstrong, 1990, fig. 21 and p. 69; also Renger, 1970, figs. 28, 50, and 52. Aldegrever's work is illustrated in Meyer, 1970, p. 89.

26. Renger, 1970, esp. p. 143. See also his figs. 41 and 43 and pp. 71–95 and 120–28 for a discussion of the idea that one consequence of drink was unchaste love. For the Brunswick Monogrammist, see fig. 68, pp. 101–8. For the *Spiegel des Sünders*, see Schreiber, 1937, p. 9.

27. See Hutchison, 1972, no. 73 and p. 62. A drawing by the same artist (Kupferstichkabinett, Wolfegg) shows a personification of the planet Venus riding on horseback in the sky. Various activities of her children are represented on the earth below: singing, dancing, playing music, and lovemaking. A game of cards is included, in which a young woman takes on two youths (Waldburg-Wolfegg, 1957, fig. 17).

28. See Stewart, 1977, pp. 68, 173–78. Lucas's 1520 print of *An Old Fool Embracing a Young Woman* (B.150) indicates his continuing interest in the theme.

29. The cards have been completely changed in another version of this composition painted in the late eighteenth or early nineteenth century. Owned by the Collot d'Escury Foundation, it is now on loan to the Museum Mr. Simon van Gijn, Dordrecht (Cat. C39). In this crudely painted copy, the two observers at the sides have been omitted and the background oculus has been changed into a rather sketchy landscape. Spades are being played, and the man now holds a card in the suit of hearts. This would seem to rule out the moralizing Power of Women theme so prevalent in most of Lucas's other gaming scenes. The Budapest version is probably a more accurate reflection of the original.

30. Lehrs, 1969, fig. 547. The "idle hands" motif is discussed in detail by Koslow, 1975, in relation to Frans Hals's *Fisherboys;* see esp. pp. 421–23 for other examples in the fourteenth through the sixteenth centuries. The use of this figure

in Lucas's painting as a personification of laziness was noted earlier by Vos, 1978a, p. 106.

31. Eisler, 1977, p. 85. Various rules are given by Nares, 1859, pp. 687–88; Morehead, 1957, pp. 20–21; and Taylor, 1973, pp. 267–71. See Hargrave, 1930, p. 160, for an early sixteenth-century reference to French and Spanish games known in the Netherlands. Morehead, 1957, pl. 2, identified the game as *pair et sequence,* which developed from primero. Parshall, 1974, p. 110, suggested the same game was being played in the Washington and Wilton House panels. This is unlikely, since each hand in the former painting consists of three cards.

32. Vos, 1978a, p. 113; also Parshall, 1974, pp. 112–13, and esp. pp. 119–21, where he suggested that such paintings were used as betrothal or marriage gifts. See also Stewart, 1977, p. 120, for a discussion of patronage for the theme of the Ill-Matched Pair. For the Leiden ordinances, see Knappert, 1908, pp. 12–13, and Hamaker, 1873, p. 313, no. II. Although these laws were enacted primarily against dicing, they also banned any "game, with which one can win or lose money."

33. One exception is Bielefeld, Deutsches Spielkarten Museum, 1972. In that exhibition on fortune-telling cards the painting is identified as a representation of the Prodigal Son among the courtesans, playing cards and losing his fortune.

34. For the *Loszbuch,* see Bielefeld, Deutsches Spielkarten Museum, 1972, pp. 7, 24. Later works on cartomancy, such as a *Losbuch* printed in Strasbourg in 1520 or Francesco Marcolino da Forli's *Le Sorti* (Venice, 1540), are also unhelpful in deciphering Lucas's representation; Bielefeld, Deutsches Spielkarten Museum, 1972, pp. 7, 26, and Sporham-Krempel, 1958, p. 72. Other guides to divination published in the fifteenth and sixteenth centuries did not mention the use of cards; Bielefeld, Deutsches Spielkarten Museum, 1972, p. 9, and Van Rijnberk, 1947, p. 24. In modern divination, the four of diamonds refers to an unfaithful friend or a secret betrayed; Morehead, 1957, p. 136. There is no way of knowing, however, whether this idea was current in the sixteenth century. See Cuzin, 1977, pp. 16–18, for the representation of palm reading, which was also the most popular method portrayed in the later sixteenth and seventeenth centuries; and pp. 19–21, 27–38, where Caravaggio's *Fortuneteller* in the Louvre is discussed in relation to other paintings of the period.

35. Cuzin, 1977, p. 17, and Gibson, 1972, p. 73, discuss the meaning of Bosch's fortune-teller. For Maffi's *Commentaires,* see Van Rijnberk, 1947, p. 45, and for the Strasbourg *Losbuch,* Sporham-Krempel, 1958, pp. 72–73.

36. Semrau, 1910, p. 10. See also the chapter "Of Gluttony and Drunkenness" in the *Gesta Romanorum,* in which drunkenness is condemned as leading to lust (Swan, 1872, 2:390–93). Silver, 1974b, pp. 234–35, mentions the criticism of excessive drink in didactic poems written by early sixteenth-century "rederijkers" (rhetoricians).

37. Bergström, 1958, p. 89 and fig. 38 (Stadsbibliotheek, Bruges, Ms. 437, fol. 395), and Lugano-Castagnola, Villa Favorita, 1977, pp. 33–34, no. 63. For more

information on betrothal portraits, see Mercier, 1937; Westhoff-Krummacher, 1965, pp. 60–61; and Levi d'Ancona, 1977, p. 80–81. The interpretation given here is close to that of Cuzin, 1977, p. 25; Vos, 1978a, p. 106; and Wurfbain, 1978, p. 205. It has been suggested that the scene takes place in a brothel (Sterling, 1930, p. 112; Cuzin, 1977, p. 25) or tavern (Demonts, 1923, p. 124), but the identification of this work as the *Prodigal Son among the Courtesans* (Benoist, 1953, p. 141) seems less convincing.

38. An exception is a slightly different compositional and iconographic type, that of the engraved or painted family tree. The *Family Tree of the Pfeffinger Family*, painted in 1516, includes ancestors dating back to 1217. The couples are arranged in a variety of ways, those of 1437 and 1467 being roughly similar to Lucas's composition. For an illustration of this painting in the Bayerisches Nationalmuseum, Munich, see Hinz, 1974, p. 154, figs. 15–16.

39. An exception must again be drawn from outside the traditional betrothal format, in Lucas Cranach's painting of the *Ill-Matched Pair* in Vienna, ca. 1530–1540; Stewart, 1977, p. 160, no. 53. Steele, 1978, p. 77, discusses the close relationship between the paintings by Lucas and Cranach.

40. See Amsterdam, Rijksprentenkabinet, 1978, p. 72.

41. Panofsky, 1971b, 1:294 and 479, n. 16.

42. Gibson, 1978, pp. 673, 677–79, and fig. 5. For more on the theme of the Battle for the Britches, see Warburg, 1932; Gibson, 1975, pp. 10–13, and 1978, pp. 677–79; Van Marle, 1971, 2:472–76; and Dresen-Coenders, 1977, pp. 34–35 (who connects the theme to a change in marriage patterns). A chapter on representations of marriage in the sixteenth century is included in Moxey, 1989, ch. 5. See also Randall, 1966, p. 200, and fig. 576, and Lehrs, 1969, figs. 533 and 649.

43. Erasmus, 1971, p. 76; also pp. 89, 93. Comparable sentiments are expressed by Brant in *The Ship of Fools* (*Das Narrenschiff*, 1944, p. 213). For Reformation attitudes toward marriage, see Douglass, 1974, pp. 313–14; Wyntjes, 1977, p. 173; and Ozment, 1983, among others.

44. Van Mander, 1604, fol. 214r. See Vos, 1978a, p. 502, nn. 108–9; Washington, National Gallery, 1983, p. 220; and Silver, 1983, p. 133.

45. Parshall, 1974, pp. 119–20.

46. For an illustration and discussion of this painting in the Schlossmuseum, Gotha, see Buchner, 1953, pp. 178–79; Ringbom, 1966, pp. 80–85; and Hinz, 1974, pp. 160–61 and fig. 22. The personalization of a generalized couple through the addition of coats of arms is found in one of the copies after a lost original by Lucas of *Card Players* (see Cat. C39, Copy 2).

47. Reznicek, 1956, p. 100, fig. 22; cf. also fig. 23. For Muller's engravings after Lucas, see Hollstein, 1949–1974, 10:241, nos. 42–57.

48. Silver, 1974a, fig. 1. These images could serve, then, as visual equivalents to Erasmus's description in the *Praise of Folly* of women who "fancy they've found an easy road to wealth by cultivating childless old men" (1971, p. 142); cf. p. 109,

where an old man "is crazy about a girl and outdoes any young man in his amorous silliness." See also ch. 52, "Marrying for the Sake of Goods," in Brant's *Das Narrenschiff,* where a rich old woman is seduced by a young man. More on the theme can be found in Van Marle, 1971, 2:476-79; Stewart, 1977; and Silver, 1974a (esp. pp. 115-16 for examples of other literary parallels).

49. Davis, 1975, p. 124.

50. Kloek, 1978, p. 455, no. 26. Phillips, 1984, p. 111, and Talbot, 1981, p. 28, refer to the fact that crossed limbs were suggestive of physical involvement.

51. Leendertz, 1845, 1:119. See Silver, 1974b, p. 235, for the prejudicial view of women in the early sixteenth-century didactic poems of the rhetoricians. Silver and Smith, 1978, p. 253 (for the St. Jerome quote), and Augustine, *The City of God,* book XIII, ch. 13.

52. Schröder, 1882, p. 68, and Brant, 1964, p. 228. Dante placed Potiphar's wife in the eighth circle of his *Inferno* because she bore false witness (Canto 30:97).

53. See Parshall, 1974, p. 127; Silver and Smith, 1978, pp. 263-64 and nn. 105-6; and Wurfbain, 1978, p. 206, for comparable interpretations of these reliefs. Although Wurfbain accepted the possibility that the figure at the left was Eve, he first identified her as Temperance. He described her as pouring water, a detail not visible to me. There might be an object in her left hand, but it is unrecognizable. Part of a nude figure, perhaps Adam, is visible at the edge of the panel, but this may be a later addition. The engraved copy made in 1820 (Fig. 5; Cat. 1, Copy 2) shows the panel extended behind Potiphar's wife, which makes the whole composition seem unbalanced. In addition, the upper view through the window was transformed from a cityscape into a landscape, the figure of the nude in the relief was changed slightly in pose, and a second nude, apparently male, was added (see also Cat. 1, Copy 1).

54. Princeton, Art Museum, 1969, pp. 27-28; Silver and Smith, 1978, pp. 263-64; and Washington, National Gallery, 1983, p. 240.

55. A discussion of the multiple meanings assigned to this story in the Early Christian period is found in Schlosser, 1966, pp. 244-46. The story of Susanna and Daniel was considered an example of the triumph of justice and the salvation of the faithful by the grace of God. It was also repeatedly used in Early Christian art and literature as an account of divine intervention in human affairs. See the *Ordo commendationis animae,* a prayer for the dying: "Deliver, Lord, the spirit of your servant from all dangers of hell and from the traps of punishment and from all tribulation . . . Deliver, Lord, the spirit of your servant just as you delivered Susanna from false accusation" (Réau, 1956, 1:394, and Migne, 1844-1864, p. 988). See also Schlosser, 1966, pp. 246-48, and Popelka, 1963-1965. The Chevalier's 1371 treatise is mentioned by G. S. Taylor, 1930, p. 88, and *Der Minnen Loep* is discussed by Leendertz, 1845, 1:213-17.

56. Parshall, 1978, and Gibson, 1983, pp. 127-29.

57. Schröder, 1882, p. 61.

58. Patristic as well as fifteenth- and sixteenth-century attitudes toward danc-

ing are discussed by Clive, 1961 (see p. 315, for the dance manual *Orchesographie* by Thoinot Arbeau, published in Langres in 1588). See also Brant, 1944, pp. 204–5.

59. See, e.g., the engraving of *Chess Players* by the Master of the Berlin Passion, with a frame showing a hunting scene (both pursuits probably intended to be read as metaphors of love). For the symbolism of feathers, see Silver, 1983, p. 131, and Armstrong, 1990, pp. 62–63 and fig. 25d.

60. Wurfbain, 1971, p. 17a (also 1978, p. 210); Silver and Smith, 1978, p. 276; and Amsterdam, Rijksmuseum, 1986, 2:150.

61. Silver, 1983, p. 132. For the jug or open flagon as a symbol of female sexuality, see E. De Jongh, 1968–1969, pp. 45–47; Amsterdam, Rijksmuseum, 1976b, p. 216; and Braunschweig, Herzog Anton Ulrich-Museum, 1978, p. 49. The erotic overtones of Lucas's painting were repeated in a seventeenth-century painting of the same subject by Jan Steen, now in the North Carolina Museum of Art, Raleigh. Steen was clearly influenced by Lucas's triptych and emphasized the wanton behavior of the Israelites. See Kirschenbaum, 1977, fig. 85, pp. 71–73, 111, esp. p. 72, for a discussion of Steen's use of sexual gestures and symbols.

62. See, e.g., Lucas's woodcuts of the Fall from ca. 1514 and ca. 1517 (B.1 and B.2) and his engraving from 1529 (B.3). Also comparable in the way in which compositional dominance takes on a metaphorical meaning are his engravings of the *Temptation of St. Anthony*, 1509 (B.117), *Lot and His Daughters*, 1530 (B.16), and *Mars, Venus and Cupid*, 1530 (B.137).

63. Brant, 1944, p. 97. Warnings against the lustful behavior of women and their guiles are found repeatedly in *Das Narrenschiff*; Brant, 1944, pp. 90–91, 178–79, 215. For *Lot and His Daughters*, see Washington, National Gallery, 1983, p. 238, and Silver, 1983, p. 133. In some of the bibles used for study purposes in the fifteenth century there were notations restricting private reading of parts of this episode of Lot and his daughters; Hindman, 1977, p. 102.

64. Van Mander, 1604, fol. 213v.

65. These quotes are from *La Cosmographie universelle* by Sebastian Münster and *Paradoxes sur l'incertitude des sciences* by Agrippa of Nettesheim; see Clébert, 1963, pp. 49 and 75 (also pp. 32–33, 76–77). For more information on the early gypsies, see Macfie, 1943, pp. 65–70; Vaux de Foletier, 1961, pp. 40–45; and Cuttler, 1984, pp. 419–23.

66. Crofton, 1909, pp. 219–27; Vaux de Foletier, 1961, figs. 1, 9–10, and 1966, pp. 165–66; and Cuttler, 1984, fig. 1.

67. Cuzin, 1977, p. 17; Gibson, 1972, p. 73; and Cuttler, 1984, pp. 430–34.

68. Clébert, 1963, p. 76, and Bangs, 1979a, p. 81, n. 36.

69. Krahn, 1968, pp. 41–42. For Zevertsz., who later returned to Leiden where he died in 1534, see Knappert, 1908, pp. 69–77; Kronenberg, 1924, pp. 1–33; Bangs, 1977, and 1979a, p. 64.

70. Knappert, 1908, pp. 94–105; Blok, 1884a, pp. 227–28; and Bangs, 1974a, no. 10, and 1979a, p. 64.

71. Some scholars have seen signs of Lucas's awareness of religious disturbance

much earlier. Parshall, 1987, pp. 166-67, considers the possibility of a proto-Reformation attitude in Lucas's engraving of *Abraham and Hagar,* ca. 1506-1507 (B.17), based on what he sees as a literal interpretation of the biblical narrative akin to what Luther would emphasize. Harbison, 1979, p. 79, sees aspects of Lucas's engraved *Baptism of Christ,* ca. 1508-1510, as "a sign of the increasing religious unrest in the Netherlands." See also Harbison, 1984, pp. 117, 125-27, who discusses Lucas's images of the Magdalene as "revealing the sometimes suddenly shifting perspectives on religious issues found in the early sixteenth century."

72. A discussion of Dürer's conversion to Lutheranism is found in Panofsky, 1971a, pp. 198-99. See Lutz, 1961, p. 175, suggesting that this passage was inserted at a later date. For the burning of books by Hieronymus Aleander, papal legate, see Lindsay, 1925, p. 229.

73. Knappert, 1908, pp. 81-82.

74. For Lucas's woodcut designs for Zevertsz., see Amsterdam, Rijksprentenkabinet, 1978, pp. 89-92; Van de Waal, 1952, pp. 141-47; and Bangs, 1979b, pp. 228, 241-42. The early business relationship between Lucas and Jan Zevertsz. does not warrant an assumption that the artist was later introduced to Lutheran ideas by the printer; see Bangs, 1975. But it does provide useful background information for Lucas's supposed knowledge of Reformation ideas in the later 1520s.

75. Holl, 1959, p. 149, and Spelman, 1951, pp. 166, 172. For further discussion of Reformation attitudes toward images, see David Freedberg, "Art and Iconoclasm, 1525-1580," in Amsterdam, Rijksmuseum, 1986, 2:69-70.

76. Lindsay, 1925, p. 228, n. 2; also Lucas, 1934, p. 503, and Busch, 1982, esp. pp. 113-20. For Erasmus's criticism, see Lucas, 1934, p. 500, and Panofsky, 1969. On the Catholic cult of Mary in the Netherlands at this time, see Bangs, 1979a, ch. 6.

77. Parshall, 1974, pp. 150-51; Silver, 1973, pp. 408-9; and Silver and Smith, 1978, pp. 275-76.

78. Lucas, 1934, pp. 374, 499, for the critical satires of Sebastian Brant and Erasmus; and Knappert, 1908, pp. 50-54, for evidence of the decreasing respect for the priesthood in Leiden in the fifteenth and early sixteenth centuries. On the rise of anti-clericalism and the inclusion of sinful monks in scenes of the Last Judgment, see Harbison, 1976, pp. 36, 40, 148, 212-16.

79. Harbison, 1976, pp. 142-43, 162. Examples of the prominence given to Peter and Paul in representations of the Last Judgment include Rogier van der Weyden's polyptych in Beaune (Friedländer, 1967-1976, 2:pl. 23) and Jan Mostaert's memorial panel in Bonn (Amsterdam, Rijksmuseum, 1958, fig. 49). Both saints also repeatedly warned their correspondents of the coming of the Last Judgment, as noted by Wurfbain (in Hermesdorf et al., 1978, p. 323). See 1 Cor. 15:51-58, 2 Cor. 5:10, 1 Thess. 4:15-18, 1 Peter 4:17, and 2 Peter 3:3-13. The church was dedicated to Peter and Paul by Bishop Godebald in 1121; Over-

voorde, 1915, 1:iii. The martyrdom of the two saints is described in *The Golden Legend* (Ryan and Ripperger, 1948, pp. 337–38, 342). For representations of Peter and Paul with Veronica's veil, see the prints by the Master E. S., 1467 (Shestack, 1967, no. 69), Dürer, 1510 (B.38), and Lucas, 1517 (B.105).

80. Panofsky, 1971a, pp. 230–35, esp. p. 234, and figs. 294–95. For Luther on Paul and Peter, see Lucas, 1934, pp. 430–31, 441; also Krahn, 1968, p. 42, who notes that a report about this debate was printed by Jan Zevertsz. of Leiden.

81. The idea that Lucas's figures were meant as allusions to differing religious views has been suggested by Silver, 1973, pp. 408–9; Parshall, 1974, pp. 150–51; Harbison, 1976, pp. 258–59; and Silver and Smith, 1978, pp. 275–76. See also Washington, National Gallery, 1983, p. 224. For an opposing view to Silver, 1973, see Bangs, 1974a, no. 8.

82. Bornkamm, 1969, pp. 149 and 203; see also Van Moorsel, 1966, pp. 9–12, 22.

83. Bangs, 1975. The typological association between Moses's water and Christ's blood is detailed by Silver, 1973, pp. 403–4. See also Berve, 1969, pp. 66–71, for this association in the *Biblia pauperum* and in other early writings.

84. Silver, 1973, pp. 401–6. A close inspection of the painting shows that all three of the main figures stare at the rod and cannot be construed as looking at the rock, as Bangs, 1975, p. 148, has suggested. Contrary to Bangs's analysis, Silver's suggestion that Lucas illustrated the version of the story given in Numbers rather than in Exodus seems convincing.

85. Popham, 1932, p. 43, no. 6; this drawing is undoubtedly later than Lucas's painting but must still date from the second quarter of the century.

86. Dülberg, 1900b, p. 163; Hoogewerff, 1936–1947, 3:306.114; and Van Mander, 1604, fol. 211v and 213v. Silver, 1973, p. 407, suggested this work was intended for a private home. It should be noted, however, that there were a variety of functions for fifteenth- and sixteenth-century Netherlandish canvases; Wolfthal, 1989, p. 30. See also W. S. Talbot, "Lucas van Leyden, *Moses Striking the Rock in the Wilderness*" (master's thesis, New York University, 1963), pp. 3–4, 68–70 (cited by Wolfthal, 1989, p. 80), suggesting that the technique, the large scale, and the flat style indicate it was a tapestry cartoon. A list of surviving early Netherlandish canvases is given by Schöne, 1938, pp. 82–83, n. 1. A number of canvases, now lost, are mentioned in early documents; see Van Mander, 1604, fol. 237r, Bosshard, 1982, and Wolfthal, 1989, esp. p. 30. For the fragility of such canvases, see Van Mander, 1604, fol. 213v and 214r, and for their use in place of tapestries, fol. 203r–v.

87. Van Mander, 1604, fol. 213v. Dülberg, 1909, p. 15, considered that the *Moses* and *Rebecca* canvases were part of a series. Filedt Kok (1978) has suggested that *Moses* was either identical to *Rebecca* (n. 133) or a companion piece (p. 6); see also Vos, 1978c, n. 97, and Silver, 1973, p. 407.

88. Silver, 1973, p. 409.

89. Wurfbain, 1971, for the identification of Jorisz. Filedt Kok, 1978, pp. 111 and 113, deciphered these letters with the use of infrared reflectograph as *zof*. A correction was offered by Bangs (see Gibson, 1980, p. 108), who read the letters as *rot* or *red*.

90. Silver, 1973, pp. 407–8, and especially Silver and Smith, 1978, pp. 276–78, although no specific connections are given. See Amsterdam, Rijksmuseum, 1986, 2:150, where this connection with the Sacramentarians is considered unconvincing. For Parshall's view, see 1974, pp. 144–56; also pp. 138–44, for his discussion of the unusual appearance of a didactic Old Testament subject on a triptych (this was noted earlier by Van Schendel, 1953, p. 6). See also Markx-Veldman, 1973, p. 116, and David Freedberg, "Art and Iconoclasm, 1525–1580," in Amsterdam, Rijksmuseum, 1986, 2:79.

91. H. A. Enno Van Gelder, 1959, p. 13, discusses the iconographic continuity in Lucas's prints and concludes that his art did not exhibit any important changes under the influence of Luther. He further describes Lucas's attitudes as close in spirit to those of Erasmus (see also Havelaar, 1918, p. 3).

92. See Lankheit, 1959, pp. 23–26.

93. This was proposed by Van Schendel, 1953, p. 7, and Silver, 1973, p. 409. Cf. Bangs, 1974a, who notes the marbled exterior of the small triptych of the *Adoration of the Magi* in the St. Annahof Chapel, Leiden. There is no evidence for Wurfbain's suggestion that the painting originally hung in one of the courtrooms for heresy trials in the Leiden City Hall (1971, p. 17b); see Bangs's rejection of this theory, 1975, p. 148.

It should be remembered that not all triptychs painted during this period were intended for sacred settings. Bosch's triptychs of the *Haywain* and the *Garden of Earthly Delights*, e.g., were probably not hung in a church or monastery but were painted instead for sophisticated noble patrons; Gibson, 1972, p. 99. Amsterdam, Rijksmuseum, 1986, 2:151, also suggests a domestic location rather than a church or chapel for Lucas's *Dance*.

94. Parshall, 1974, pp. 150, 156, and Silver, 1973, p. 409; see also Friedländer, 1963a, p. 91, and Gibson, 1983, p. 129.

95. Silver and Smith, 1978, pp. 270–75; see also Silver, 1973, p. 409.

96. Knappert, 1908, p. 39. In 1527 Pieter Cornelisz. made twelve paintings of Leiden coats of arms to be used in a procession of the Sacrament (Elsevier, 1858, p. 245, n. 6; Gibson, 1977, p. 28, n. 36; and Bangs, 1979a, pp. 87–88).

97. Knappert, 1908, pp. 39–46. J. G. Van Gelder, 1957, p. 98, mentions this work in connection with a procession of the miraculous Host in Amsterdam. He further suggests that the original painting by Lucas might have been the predella of an altarpiece representing the life of a saint or the miracles attributed to the Host.

Conclusion

1. Friedländer, 1963a, p. 46. He accepted more than thirty-four paintings as originals by Lucas, compared to the seventeen extant originals cited here.
2. See Gibson, 1986, pp. 49-50, for a discussion of the difference between Lucas's and Van Scorel's uses of Italian art.
3. Filedt Kok, et al., 1975, p. 245 and p. 256, n. 28.
4. Amsterdam, Rijksmuseum, 1986, 2:33, 329, no. 208, for Aertgen's *Last Judgment*.
5. Ibid., pp. 36-37.
6. See Gibson, 1977, pp. 127, 148-50. The Leiden School paintings of the *Feeding of the Five Thousand* are in Koblenz (see Van Regteren Altena, 1955) and formerly in the Coll. Bührle, Zurich (Fig. 69).
7. See Renger, 1970, esp. pp. 23-24, for the importance of Lucas's woodcut *Tavern Scene* (B.20).
8. This compositional format was also used in German and Italian prints and drawings of the period, however, and it is impossible to speak of the direct influence of Lucas's works on the later Netherlandish artists. See Moxey, 1977, pp. 34-39.
9. Vasari, 1906, 5:406-7.
10. Vos, 1978a, ch. 6.
11. Buchelius, 1928, p. 80; see also Von Löhneysen, 1956, pp. 289-91.
12. For the passage in *Het Schilder-Boeck,* see Van Mander, 1604, fol. 212v. His *Dance around the Golden Calf* was painted in 1602 (illustrated in Haarlem, Frans Hals Museum, 1969, cat. 204b, pl. 10).
13. For a detailed account see Cats. 14, 20, and 25; also Van Mander, 1604, fol. 213v.
14. Van Mander, 1604, fol. 212v; see also fol. 214r.
15. Ibid., fol. 237v (for Goltzius's ownership of works from the Leiden School) and fols. 284v-285r (for reference to Goltzius's master prints). The other engravings classified as Goltzius's master prints (B.15-20) are modeled after works by Dürer, Raphael, Parmigianino, Jacopo Bassano, and Federico Barocci; see Hirschmann, 1919, pp. 27, 72, 79. Beets, 1913, pp. 120-21, gives a short account of Lucas's influence on the artists of this period. See Reznicek, 1961, 1:317, no. 199 (and pp. 113-15, 126), for the Oxford sketch. In 1586, Lucas's *Christ Healing the Blind Man* was still in Leiden and not yet in Goltzius's Leningrad collection. For the influence of Lucas on Goltzius, see also Von Löhneysen, 1956, pp. 271-72.
16. Illustrations of these works are found in Haarlem, Frans Hals Museum, 1969, pls. 10 and 17, and Amsterdam, Rijksmuseum, 1976a, p. 120, no. A3746. Cornelis van Haarlem owned a large collection of prints by Lucas as well as other earlier sixteenth-century artists (Van Thiel, 1965, p. 128). Lucas's painting was mentioned by Van Mander, 1604, fol. 213v, as being in a private collection in Amsterdam, so it was presumably accessible to these artists.

17. Kirschenbaum, 1977, figs. 85 and 88. Rembrandt's knowledge of Lucas's style was garnered almost exclusively from his prints, and it is known that his collection included many of Lucas's engravings and woodcuts (Clark, 1968, pp. 193–209, for a transcription of the 1656 inventory of Rembrandt's possessions; see also Lavalleye, 1967, p. 11, for Rembrandt's purchase of prints by Lucas). Rembrandt's high regard for Lucas is confirmed by his repeated use of his prints as inspiration for his own work (see, e.g., Van Rijckevorsel, 1932, pp. 181–224; Münz, 1952, 2:86–91, 101–8; and Forssman, 1976). Several of Lucas's paintings have also been cited as influential for Rembrandt, but the relationship is minimal, at best. Tümpel, 1969, p. 184, observed that Lucas's figure of Paul on the exterior of the *Last Judgment* (Fig. 23) probably served as the model for Rembrandt's *Paul in Prison* in Stuttgart (Gerson, 1968, pl. 22). Jan Veth, 1906, p. 42, drew a parallel between Lucas's *Christ Healing the Blind Man* and the 100 Guilder Print (B.74); cf. Münz, 1952, 2:101.

18. See Nicolson, 1958, cat. A50, and Judson, 1961, p. 347 (and pp. 346–48 for other examples of Lucas's influence on this artist). In Judson's studies of the Utrecht school, Lucas emerges as a less "distant inheritance" than first supposed by Nicolson, 1958, p. 4; see Judson, 1961, p. 342, and 1959, pp. 43, 75, 79. For a brief discussion of the influence of northern art on Caravaggio's early paintings, see Walter Friedländer, 1974, pp. 81–82; also Judson, 1959, p. 72.

Cat. 1. *Potiphar's Wife Accusing Joseph*

1. Müller, 1820, p. 20, no. 57 (as Lucas, *Susanna before the Judge*). At this time the panel measured approximately 26.7 x 41.9; a strip widening the composition behind the figure of Potiphar's wife is visible in the engraving in Müller's fig. 5 as well as in the painted copy. A painting of the same subject by Lucas is cited by Parthey, 1864, p. 30, no. 1, in the Amalienstift, Dessau, but the dimensions are different (29.2 x 37.5).

2. This information comes from a note on the back of an old photograph in the Rotterdam museum files. It is accompanied by a certificate of authenticity from M. J. Friedländer.

3. Hannema mentions that this panel was reproduced in a seventeenth-century Flemish painting of a collector's gallery (also cited in Paris, Petit Palais, 1952, p. 31). A photograph of this Flemish painting was in Friedländer's possession, but no further information is available.

4. Both copies are similar in this extension of the original composition. The landscape seen through the window is also slightly altered. Before the restoration of 1930, the panel in Rotterdam had further additions not shown in either copy. It was about 5 cm higher, with the landscape more than doubled in height and with an extra decorative relief. It was also 6 cm broader, with curtains painted on the side extensions.

5. Beets, 1940, p. 49.

6. Haussherr, 1973, pl. 18.

7. Gibson, 1970b, p. 93, and Parshall, 1974, p. 128, date it ca. 1508, while Filedt Kok, 1978, p. 26, and Vos, 1978a, p. 32, place it ca. 1512.

8. See Filedt Kok, 1978, pp. 26–31, for a description of the paint technique and style of underdrawing in this panel. He also concludes that it must be later than *Chess Players*.

Cat. 2. *History of Joseph*

1. Van Mander, 1604, fols. 213v–214r.

2. Rosenberg, 1877, p. 8, doubts that Lucas would have painted the same subject that he treated in an engraving, and therefore questions Van Mander's accuracy. Colvin, 1882, p. 137, saw a painting (now lost) in tempera in the Coll. Lord Methuen, Corsham House. It was in bad condition and represented *Joseph Interpreting the Pharaoh's Dreams*.

3. Lucas's painted series could have been similar in scope to the six circular panels by the Master of the Joseph Sequence, an artist active in Brussels ca. 1494–1500. The scenes he depicted include Joseph hidden in a well, sold by his brothers, introduced into Potiphar's house, solicited by Potiphar's wife, interpreting dreams, and married to Asenath. See Friedländer, 1967–1976, 4:nos. 79A–F.

4. Van Mander, 1604, fols. 203r–v. See also Cats. 7–8 for the possibility of another series by Lucas in tempera and for more information on the use of tempera on canvas in the early sixteenth century.

5. See Silver, 1973, p. 407, and Bangs, 1974a, for information on brewing.

Cat. 3. *Susanna before the Judge*

1. The catalogue also noted that this area was in bad condition and perhaps overpainted. Pauli, 1907, p. 24, said the alleged "Hoey" signature was indecipherable.

2. See Antonucci, 1929, pp. 6–7.

3. Di Lentaglio, 1929, p. 18. The staff in Lucas's panel is only a long stick, quite different from the decorative wands carried by judges in other Netherlandish scenes of *Susanna,* but it is probably meant to be seen as a type of scepter (Ferguson, 1976, p. 180; cf. a similar staff held by the judge in the engraving after Maarten van Heemskerck's *Susanna and Daniel;* Hollstein, 1949–1974, 8:247, no. 525). It is possible that Lucas conflated the royal scepter with the staff of authority, formerly a shepherd's rod, as used by Moses and Aaron (Exod. 4:17). The scroll probably refers to the judge's role as writer and scholar; Ferguson, 1976, p. 180.

4. Friedländer, 1967–1976, 6b:no. 222 (Bruges, Groeninge Museum). Cambyses is said to be numbering Sisamnes's crimes on his fingers by Von Simson, 1977,

p. 352. See also Janssens de Bisthoven, 1959, p. 18, and pl. 53 for a detail of the *computat digitis*. Leonardo described the partially open mouth and gestures of the orator in his *Trattato della Pittura* (Tabarrini, 1890, p. 127). Cf. the description of this gesture in Quintilian's *Institutes of Oratory* (J. S. Watson, 1902, 2:372), and Bulwer's *Chirologia, or the Natural Language of the Hand* (Cleary, 1974, pp. 204-5):

> The right index if it marshall-like go from finger to finger (to note them out with a light touch), it doth fit their purpose who would number their arguments and, by a visible distinction, set them all on a row upon their fingers.... This gesture of the hand is not to be used unless the distinctions and distributions be substantial and weighty, being things of great moment which we desire should fix and take deep impression in the minds of men, and of which we are accurately and subtly to dispute.

The gesture appears as early as the middle of the fourteenth century in Italian art, in the fresco of the *Church Militant and the Church Triumphant* in the Spanish Chapel, Sta. Maria Novella, Florence. It continued to be a popular notation of scholastic argument in the fifteenth century, in scenes such as the *Dispute of St. Catherine* and *Christ among the Doctors,* and appeared as the attribute of a reasoning man in three of Joos van Ghent's portraits, painted ca. 1472-1475 for the Duke of Urbino's library (e.g., *Thomas Aquinas* in the Louvre). For illustrations and discussion of the gesture, see Chomentovskaja, 1938. Parshall, 1974, pp. 129-30, mentions the popularity of half-length disputation scenes in the early sixteenth century.

5. This early sixteenth-century painting is now lost, and the composition is known only through a drawing in the 1627 catalogue of the Venetian art collection of Andrea Vendramin. For the popularity of such narratives, see Parshall, 1974, pp. 129-30, and Popelka, 1963, p. 46. Examples of the *Presentation in the Temple,* the *Circumcision,* and *Christ and the Adulteress* abound in the art of northern Italy at this time (Ringbom, 1965, figs. 26-38, 158-61).

6. Ringbom, 1965, pp. 179-92, and Parshall, 174, pp. 130-31. The popularity of such half-length religious narratives had spread as far as Germany by 1532, to judge from a painting of *Christ and the Adulteress* by Lucas Cranach in Budapest (Ringbom, 1965, fig. 160). This would postdate Lucas's early development. A painting of *Christ and the Adulteress* (Coll. Countess Reder, Berlin) described by Friedländer, 1963a, p. 72, as possibly a damaged original by Lucas is unfortunately untraceable. A search by the staff of the Frick Art Reference Library, New York, and the Rijksbureau voor Kunsthistorische Documentatie, The Hague, turned up no information or photograph. If and when it comes to light, it may provide evidence of a link between Lucas and the north Italian school, of which one early example is a painting of the same subject attributed to Marco Marziale, dated 1507 and now in the Accademia Carrara, Bergamo (Ringbom, 1965, fig. 158).

Cat. C4. *Triumphal Entry of David into Jerusalem*

1. "One also sees here and there his pieces on glass, that are worthwhile things to keep. Among others there is a little piece on glass owned by Goltzius, who is fond of his works: [it represents] the dance of the women coming to meet David, treated very beautifully, and it also appears in a print very well engraved by Jan van Saenredam."

2. The inventory of the Schatz- und Kunstkammer, Prague, December 6, 1621, no. 866, lists: "A small panel of the maidens receiving David into Jerusalem, Lucas van Leyden, a poor copy." See Zimerman, 1905, p. xxxix.

3. No. 1771 in the posthumous catalogue of works owned by Rubens is described as the triumph of David after his defeat of Goliath, by Lucas; John Smith, 1842, p. 361 (also Denuce, 1932, p. 64, where it is listed as no. 176).

4. Rathgeber and Michiels mention a 1636 copy by Jean Gleggler, in the ducal gallery, Gotha. The Schlossmuseum in Gotha has no record of the painting, however (correspondence I. Scholz, February 13, 1981). Evrard, 1884, p. 643, also noted a copy sold in Paris, 1867.

5. Copies 7 and 8 may be after the original painting, which the engraving by Saenredam presumably reverses, or they may be after the print published by De Jode (Copy 15). There are several variations between the engraving by Saenredam and these paintings. The woman singing from a sheet of music wears a dark-toned costume in the paintings, compared to the light dress in the print, and the woman at the left in the engraving has been changed into a black woman in both paintings. Hoogewerff, 1936–1947, 3:317, cites these variations to argue that there must have originally been two works by Lucas, the glass painting in Milan and a painting in reverse, of which only a fragment is preserved (Copy 8). Study of the photographs leaves no doubt that all of the paintings listed here are copies.

6. A painting in the collection of the Prince of Liechtenstein, Schloss Vaduz, Liechtenstein (inv. no. 716; panel, 30 x 40), is also composed in breadth with David entering from the left. It appears to be a later pastiche, however, with numerous variations from the copies listed here. All the poses are altered to some degree, and the head of Goliath is in David's left hand rather than held aloft on the sword. The artist was also influenced by Lucas's engraving of 1513–1514 (B.26). For the literature on this painting, see Vienna, Liechtenstein Collection, 1780, p. 48, no. 116 (by an early German painter); Hymans, 1884, p. 147, n. 5; Vienna, Liechtenstein Collection, 1885, p. 96 (by Lucas?); Stiassny, 1888, p. 391 (a free copy after the Saenredam engraving [Copy 10]); Von Frimmel, 1898, p. 111 (by Lucas), and 1920–1921, p. 150; Vienna, Liechtenstein Collection, 1925, p. 206 (by Lucas, although the attribution is not secure; earlier attributed to Israel van Mecheln); Wolter, 1926, p. 229; Hoogewerff, 1936–1947, 3:318 (copy of the painting in Madrid [Copy 2]).

A painting by Hendrick Terbrugghen of the same subject (North Carolina

Museum of Art, Raleigh, 1972 *Masterpieces* catalogue, no. 24) seems to have been inspired by Lucas's engraving (B.26) as well as by the lost painting. See Judson, 1961, p. 347.

7. Washington, National Gallery, 1983, p. 214.

Cat. C5. *Fall of Man*

1. Kloek, 1978, pp. 450–51, no. 20. This drawing is dated ca. 1520 by Vos, 1978a, p. 194, no. 225, which is surely too late.

Cat. C6. *Judgment of Solomon*

1. This may be the drawing of the *Judgment of Solomon* attributed to Lucas in the 1662 sale of the collection of Johan Chrisostomus de Backer, The Hague (Obreen, 1976, p. 314, no. 293, sold for twenty-seven guilders).

2. J. G. Van Gelder, 1957, p. 96.

3. Van Mander, 1604, fol. 238r; Van Regteren Altena, 1939, p. 227, no. 8, and Lugt, 1968, p. 33.

4. A date of 1526 is found on a painting of the same subject with a similar compositional structure (sale G. J. Gould and others, London [Sotheby], June 22, 1960, no. 43, as School of Lucas, panel, 110 x 95). Numerous differences, including a more elaborate architectural setting, suggest this painting was not a direct copy, but it might well have been influenced by Lucas's painting or one of the later copies.

Another variation is a glass painting in the Cleveland Museum of Art, inv. no. 68.188 (69.2 x 46.4), where it is attributed to the circle of Lucas. See Gibson, 1970a, and color plate following p. 89. He dates the glass painting ca. 1530. This work is similar only in its composition. The poses, costumes, and background architecture of the figures have been altered.

5. Lugt, 1968, p. 33, noticed the left-handed gestures of the main figures.

Cat. 7. *Moses after Striking the Rock*

1. This was probably the painting mentioned by Scannelli da Forli, 1657, p. 142: "di Luca una grande historia in quadro assai capace, e molto ben conservata, nella quale con tutto che le figure non siano più longhe d'un braccio espresse con la solita maniera, si palesa pero cosi bella, ed abbondante l'inventione, e le figure particolari tanto capricciose, e ben osservate, che un quadro simile di quelto Autore al sicuro non si vede in altro luogo dell' Italia" (by Lucas a large history in a very large and very well preserved painting, in which although the figures are no longer than a *braccio* they are expressed in the usual manner; but still it proves to be so beautiful and filled with invention, and the particular figures so

whimsical and well observed, that a similar painting by that artist certainly can't be found in any other place in Italy). The description of the painting as large and well preserved, with figures no larger than a *braccio* (roughly two feet), could have easily applied to *Moses*. The praise of the invention and observation of the bizarre figures is also appropriate, although Scannelli did not describe the subject of the painting.

By 1693 the painting was listed in an inventory of the Borghese collection as "a large painting on canvas of Moses with a number of figures, N.235, with a gilded frame, by Lucas of Holland"; see Della Pergola, 1964, p. 224, no. 86. Despite Lucas's monogram it was later listed in the Borghese Collection as "Rest of a caravan, painting of the Ferrara School"; see Piancastelli, 1898. There is unfortunately no proof for Vos's speculation (1978c, p. 500, n. 97) that the painting might have been sold to Cardinal Scipione Borghese by the Countess of Santa Fiore.

2. Piancastelli, 1898, noted that the painting became the property of the Principessa Piombino as a result of the shuffling of art objects in the Borghese villa and palazzo. This followed the death of D. Marcantonio Borghese in 1888.

3. The influence of Lucas's painting on Cornelis Engebrechtsz. is noted by Gibson, 1977, p. 149, who compares the children, the headdresses, and the rounded faces of the women. No specific poses were borrowed by Cornelis, but the genre atmosphere of his *Feeding of the Five Thousand* is heavily dependent on Lucas's *Moses* and his later *Dance around the Golden Calf.* Bangs, 1975, p. 149, observed the similarities between *Moses* and the left wing of a triptych in Kassel attributed to Aertgen van Leyden (the central panel represents the *Crucifixion*). The later artist borrowed the pose of the woman and child in the left foreground, the clustering of the main figures, and details of the background landscape.

4. Von der Osten's description of the self-portrait as "a bit dwarfish in size but with an eloquent profile" matches none of the profile figures in the painting. The three men facing the spectator all have dark hair, but their facial hair and, more important, their close-set eyes are quite different from the two most likely portraits of the artist, Lucas's Braunschweig *Portrait of a Man* (Fig. 14) and Dürer's silverpoint drawing in Lille (Fig. 70). See the Appendix for further information on the many "portraits" of Lucas.

5. Dülberg, 1900b, p. 160; Beets, 1913, p. 105; and Silver, 1973, p. 401.

6. The sacrifice of animals by Aaron is described in Leviticus (16:9–11). Although Silver (1973, p. 401, n. 5) recognized the bells worn by this figure, he did not consider it likely that a priest would be shown with a sword. Beets, 1913, p. 105, described this figure as the military leader. Bangs, 1975, p. 148, was the first to identify the figure with the sword as Aaron, and he mentioned the turban with embroidered sash, the ephod with two shoulder pieces, and the checkered tunic as a part of Aaron's costume described in Exod. 28:7 and 39.

7. The drawing by Vellert is signed and dated and is one of a series by the artist

representing scenes from the life of Moses (see Beets, 1912b, p. 144, no. 4, and Glück, 1901, pp. 18-20). The D.I.A.L. illustration (71 E 14.2) is incorrectly dated 1531.

Cat. 8. *Rebecca and Eliezer at the Well*

1. Dirck van Sonneveldt and Johan Adriaensz. Knotter are mentioned several times in *Het Schilder-Boeck* as collectors of art in Leiden. Van Sonneveldt owned a painting by Cornelis Cornelisz. Kunst, for example, and Knotter's collection included works by Lucas Cornelisz. de Kock and Aertgen van Leyden, among others. See Vos, 1978c, p. 500, nn. 95-96, and Greve, 1903, pp. 297-98.

2. Van Mander, 1604, fol. 213v.

3. Dülberg, 1900b, p. 163, and 1909, p. 15; also Hoogewerff, 1936-1947, 3:306. Cf. Filedt Kok, 1978, pp. 6, 169, n. 133, and Silver, 1973, p. 407.

Cat. C9. *Susanna in Her Bath*

1. Ovid, *Metamorphoses,* 3.138-253; see also Hall, 1974, pp. 101-2.

Cat. C10. *Meeting of David and Abigail*

1. The measurements were provided by the museum and differ from those cited by J. G. Van Gelder, 1957, p. 94 (25.2 x 38.9).

2. A reworking of this composition is found in a drawing in the Städelsches Kunstinstitut, Frankfurt (inv. no. 13477; pen and brush in ink, with gray wash). It is attributed by J. G. Van Gelder, 1957, p. 98 and fig. 6, to a student or follower of Lucas; see also Gibson, 1970a, p. 86 and fig. 11. The format is now vertical rather than horizontal, and only the pose of David, wearing a heavily plumed helmet and leaning from his horse toward the kneeling Abigail, is directly quoted. Other details are drawn from Lucas's engravings. The man running alongside David's horse is comparable to a figure in the *Triumph of Mordecai* of 1515 (B.32), and the man at the extreme left is found in two prints from the 1512 series of the *History of Joseph* (B.21, 23). There is no relationship to Lucas's earlier engraving of *David and Abigail* (B.24), which represents the moment prior to the actual meeting.

Cat. 11. *Dance around the Golden Calf*

1. Van Mander, 1604, fol. 213v. See Amsterdam, Rijksmuseum, 1986, 2:151, for the speculation that this triptych belonged to a member of the Van Swieten family, who also commissioned Lucas's *Last Judgment*. Aegje van Swieten died in 1627 in the Calverstraat.

2. In notes written in 1671 in the margin of a copy of Van Mander's *Het Schilder-Boeck* (now in the Rijksprentenkabinet, Amsterdam), the Medemblik lawyer

Hendrick Houmes mentioned that this triptych was in the possession of Mr. Woiutiers (see Moes, 1889, pp. 150–51). Woiutiers lived at that time on the Herengracht and had acquired the painting by inheritance from Jasper Losschert.

3. This was mentioned by Joachim von Sandrart in his *Teutsche Academie* of 1675, who says Lossert was a bookkeeper (see Peltzer, 1925, p. 87). From 1671 to 1709 the triptych apparently remained with a single family, judging by the repetitions and variations of the names Losschert (Lossert, Loskart) and Woiutiers (Wuytiers).

4. Bredius, 1913, and Amsterdam, Rijksmuseum, 1956, pp. 117–18.

5. Hoet, 1752–1770, 1:135, no. 25, and Bille, 1961, p. 144.

6. An identical description of the triptych is in Orlers, 1641, p. 362.

7. See Chapter 2 for this work and two other early sixteenth-century paintings of the *Feeding of the Five Thousand* from the Leiden school (Figs. 68–69). Lucas's painting also served as inspiration for later works of the *Dance around the Golden Calf*. The inverted composition, with the dance represented in the background and the foreground filled with scenes of the feast, is found again in paintings by Frans Francken II in Dresden (Gemäldegalerie, 1962, no. 13), by Carel van Mander in Haarlem (see Vos, 1978c, p. 499, n. 92), and by Jan Steen in Raleigh (Kirschenbaum, 1977, fig. 85).

8. Beets, 1952a, p. 191 (this date was accepted by Parshall, 1974, p. 135); Van Schendel, 1953, p. 7 (also *Verslagen,* 1952, p. 14); Wurfbain, 1971; Filedt Kok, 1978, p. 101; Vos, 1978a, p. 124.

9. Kloek, 1978, nos. 26–27. A silverpoint drawing of an old man in the British Museum (Kloek's no. 23) was considered by Beets, 1952a, p. 190, n. 12, to be a preparatory study for the head at the left of the right wing. There are too many discrepancies among pose, facial type, and costume to warrant the conclusion, and the drawing should be dated closer to the other silverpoint works of 1520–1521.

Cat. 12. *Virgin and Child with Angels*

1. According to Von Frimmel, 1898, p. 65, the painting was in the Galerie Angoisse, Vienna, in 1821, and later at Felsenberg, but this is unverifiable.

2. The two fruits are symbolically interchangeable (see Friedmann, 1947, p. 70, and Bergström, 1955, p. 304). The "beloved" in the Song of Solomon (2:3), a typological precursor to Christ, is praised "as the apple tree among the trees of the wood." Lucas originally painted two cherries in this spot, as shown in an X-radiograph (Filedt Kok, 1978, p. 45, fig. 45). Ferguson, 1976, p. 29, explains that the cherry or "Fruit of Paradise" symbolizes the sweet character of the Saved, who perform good works. Cherries were often included in paintings of the *Virgin and Child,* and Lucas probably substituted the larger fruit to balance the cluster of grapes just above it. In Joos van Cleve's *Holy Family* in New York, an apple, a pear,

a bunch of grapes, and several cherries appear on a platter in the foreground (Friedländer, 1967–1976, 9a:no. 65).

3. Levi d'Ancona, 1977, p. 80. A carnation or other flower symbolizing Christ's divine love frequently appears in representations of the *Virgin and Child:* in Dirk Bouts's London painting, St. Paul hands a carnation to Jesus, and in Gossaert's Palermo altarpiece an angel, similar in appearance to the one in Lucas's panel, offers another (Friedländer, 1967–1976, 3:no. 21, and 8:no. 2). In Lucas's engraving of 1523 (B.84), the Virgin dangles a carnation before Christ.

4. Bode, 1895, p. 118; see also Riegel, 1900, p. 110, for the idea of a self-portrait. The round face, upturned nose, fleshy lips, and small chin resemble the portrait in Braunschweig, but the color of the hair is different. See the Appendix for a discussion of the numerous so-called portraits of the artist.

5. There is also a resemblance to the face of the Magdalene in the 1519 engraving B.77; Friedländer, 1963a, p. 60. See Filedt Kok, 1978, pp. 42–43, 45, and 55, for a discussion of the underdrawing style in the Berlin and Munich paintings.

6. The painting of the leaves in the Berlin *Virgin and Child* is extremely close to the detailed description of the foliage in the background of the Munich panel, as are the tight clusters of grapes in both works. For parallels with *Emperor Maximilian,* see Friedländer, 1963a, p. 60.

7. Baldass dated the painting as early as 1515 (1923, pp. 22, 31), while Hoogewerff suggested 1522–1525 (1936–1947, 3:279–81). The three most recent citations agree on a date of ca. 1520 (Berlin, Staatliche Museen, 1978, p. 230; Filedt Kok, 1978, p. 42; and Vos, 1978a, p. 141).

8. Buchelius, 1928, p. 49, and Amsterdam, Rijksmuseum, 1958, p. 100. Jacob Cornelisz.'s painting is also now in Berlin (Staatliche Museen, 1978, pp. 116–17, no. 607).

Cat. C13. *Virgin and Child with Joseph, Anne, and Two Male Saints*

1. Lugt, 1968, p. 32, suggests that the figure at the left in the drawing, tentatively identified as Zacharias, could also be one of Anne's two earlier husbands, Cleophas or Salome.

2. Lugt (ibid.) notes that the drawing in the Louvre (Copy 1) was earlier thought to be German. Lucas's drawing of Maximilian in pen and brush is a preparatory study for his engraving of 1520 (B.172); see Kloek, 1978, pp. 452–53, no. 23.

Cats. 14 and 15. *Virgin and Child with Mary Magdalene and a Donor* and *Annunciation*

1. The inscription on the Magdalene's box of ointment was added at a later date: "Unguentu[m] Nardi Spicati ptios [=pretiosum]" (from Mark 14:3, refer-

ring to the costly nard oil she used). This was almost certainly painted sometime between 1604 and 1627, at the same time that the two wings were joined, the strip at the top was added, and the changes were made in the figure of the donor. See Filedt Kok et al., 1975, p. 242. This article by Filedt Kok, Eikemeier, and Van Asperen de Boer proved an invaluable and virtually complete source, providing most of the information given here.

2. In 1604, Van Mander, fol. 213v, described the painting in detail: "There was another most excellent little painting or diptych owned by the nobleman Frans Hooghstraet, in a manor outside Leyden; it showed a very well painted Madonna at half length, the rest of her below the knees hidden as if behind a rock. The Child was also very lovely holding in its hands a bunch of grapes with a tendril that reaches the ground, probably in order to show that Christ is the true vine; the fabrics were painted excellently. The other panel shows a woman in adoration, with the Magdalene behind her, pointing out to her the Christ Child on Mary's lap. The background of fields and trees was quite exceptional and worthy of admiration. On the outside was an Annunciation to Mary with full-length figures, very strong in proportion, poses and the depiction of fabrics, with handsome folds in the draperies. This little painting now belongs to Emperor Rudolph, the greatest art lover of our day; this precious piece was dated '22, and had the 'L', which was Lucas van Leyden's normal signature."

See Filedt Kok et al., 1975, pp. 245 and 256, n. 28, for the suggestion that the donor might have been Franchoys van Hoogstraten, who probably lived in the Castle Teijlingen, Voorhout (near Leiden). He was mayor of Haarlem from 1521 to 1524 and died in 1559. His son, Gerrit, who died a debtor in 1612, might have sold the inherited painting to Count Simon zur Lippe, Rudolf's agent in the Netherlands around 1600. See also Bangs, 1980, p. 93.

3. The diptych was not included in the inventory of 1621 taken nine years after Rudolf's death (see Zimerman, 1905), so presumably by that time it had been purchased by Duke Maximilian (Filedt Kok et al., 1975, p. 246). The two wings of the diptych had already been joined ca. 1627–1628, as described in the inventory of paintings in the Kammergalerie, no. 33: "A panel, 2 feet 5½ inches high and 2 feet 5 inches broad [ca. 74.9 x 73.7], on which is Our Beloved Lady, with the little Child, St. Mary Magdalene and St. Philip, and behind them a building, along with a beautiful landscape, all painted in a very flowing manner by Lucas van Leyden in the year 1522, with the No. 33." Von Reber, 1892, p. 42, and Filedt Kok et al., 1975, p. 246. The measurements given here include a horizontal strip about 20–25 cm in height that must have been added after 1604. The variations among the measurements given in 1627 (2' 5½" x 2' 5"), in the Schleissheim catalogue of 1775 (2' 1¾" x 2' 1¼"), and in the Munich catalogue of 1839 (2' 1" x 1' 6") are presumably the result of faulty measuring, a change in frames, or measuring with and without the frame at subsequent times. See note 10 for a discussion of the erroneous identification of the male figure as St. Philip.

After Maximilian's death in 1651, the painting apparently remained in the Bavarian Electors' collection, although no trace of it appears between 1627 and 1729.

4. *Beschreibung der Gemaelden in der Churfürstlichen Residenz zu Schleissheim,* 1770, no. 293; see Filedt Kok et al., 1975, p. 251, for the full quote. A description of the panel in 1775 is found in Van Weizenfeld, 1775, p. 92, no. 342.

5. Von Mannlich, 1810, p. 71, no. 1708.

6. Van Mander's report, including its mistakes, was repeated verbatim by Orlers in 1614 (Orlers, 1641, pp. 361–62) and by Von Sandrart in 1675 (Peltzer, 1925, p. 87).

7. Bullart only described the figures in the left half of the diptych: "The Emperor Rudolph had by him [Lucas] a half-length Virgin with the child Jesus, who holds a bunch of grapes: this work is signed with an 'L' and the number, 'XXII', which leads one to believe that Lucas painted it when he was twenty-two."

8. Her lower legs are cut off by the edge of the frame, not "hidden as if by a stone" as noted by Van Mander, fol. 213v. Van Mander criticized the practice of using the frame to crop figures without the intermediary of a rock or similar object (*Den Grondt der edel vry Schilder-const* [Haarlem, 1603], ch. 5, paragraph 24); see Vos, 1978c, p. 498, n. 84, for the complete text of this criticism, and Filedt Kok et al., 1975, p. 252, n. 1.

9. Hoogewerff, 1936–1947, 3:282, suggests that Van Mander's *vrouw priant* (praying woman) was a typographical mistake for *vroom priant* (pious prayer), but Filedt Kok et al., 1975, pp. 241, 255, n. 14, observe that in the early seventeenth century *vroom* would have meant "brave, bold." They also (p. 255, n. 15) corrected Reznicek-Buriks's theory (1965, p. 243) that Lucas represented a woman who was overpainted at a later date. The underdrawing shows that the figure was intended to be a man from the start.

The representation of a female saint interceding on behalf of a male donor was unusual in the Netherlands at this time, which may help to explain Van Mander's confusion; see Friedländer, 1967–1976, 6a:no. 10, and Panofsky, 1971b, pls. 128 and 255. Representations of a male saint with a female donor were more common.

10. Filedt Kok et al., 1975, pp. 242–43, have already shown that these additions and alterations to the figure were probably the result of Joseph's rise in popularity during the later sixteenth and seventeenth centuries; see Mâle, 1932, pp. 313–25, and Knipping, 1974, 1:117–19. X-rays reveal that the collar of the brown undershirt was originally larger, a white shirt once covered the neck, the collar and cuffs of the jacket have changed in color, and the ring on the man's left index finger has been painted out; Filedt Kok et al., 1975, figs. 9, 11, 13.

The erroneous identification of this figure as St. Philip in the inventory of 1627–1628 (see note 3) was perhaps the result of a misreading of the surveyor's rod as Philip's attribute, the cross-topped staff; Ferguson, 1976, pp. 139–40. Several scholars, who believed that the attributes of Joseph were painted by Lucas, suggested that the donor and his wife were being portrayed as their patron saints, Joseph and Mary Magdalene (Beets, 1913, pp. 90–92; Rome, Galleria Borghese, 1928, pp. 7–8; and Baldass, 1937b, p. 206).

11. De Jongh, 1974, p. 184, and Timmers, 1978, p. 146, no. 370. See also Mak, 1948, pp. 124–25.

12. In the *Annunciation* on the exterior of a small triptych in Leiden, from the early sixteenth-century Leiden School, the letters *MARIA* appear prominently in the tiles of the foreground. The composition and placement of the figures are roughly similar to those in the Munich diptych. See Van Brussel, Moerman, and Wurfbain, 1978, p. 4, for a reproduction. They make a tentative attribution of the triptych to Lucas's brother Dirck Hugensz. For information on the significance of the lilies, see Mak, 1948, p. 39.

13. See Filedt Kok et al., 1975, pp. 233–34, for evidence that the *Annunciation* was on the reverse of the *Mary Magdalene with Donor* rather than the *Virgin and Child*. It also was probably semicircular at the top, like the interior panels (pp. 243–45). A painting of the *Rest on the Flight* in the Hessisches Landesmuseum, Darmstadt, inv. 83, was by 1872 believed to be the long-lost exterior of the second panel (Hofmann, 1872, no. 191, and Marggraff, 1872, pp. 156–57, no. 743). It is approximately the same size as the exterior panel in Munich (42 x 30, rounded above), and its subject would have been appropriate. It is signed with Lucas's monogram on a stone in the foreground and was first attributed to Lucas by Seeger, 1843, p. 29, no. 150. This attribution was soon rejected (e.g., by Woltmann and Woermann, 1882, p. 533). The work shows no similarity to Lucas's painting style and certainly has no connection with the Munich diptych. Filedt Kok et al., 1975, p. 245, suggested that the exterior of the left wing (the wing that was permanently against the wall) was probably painted with a dark priming layer.

14. See notes 2 and 3 for the full texts of 1604 and 1627. Van Mander used the word *kasken* to refer to both diptychs and triptychs. He also described the Rijksmuseum *Dance around the Golden Calf* (Fig. 32) as a "kasken" (fol. 213v).

15. This artist was adept at simulating the style of the early sixteenth century and made a number of changes to other German and Netherlandish paintings of this period. It has been suggested that he was Georg Vischer (Von Reber, 1892, p. 25, n. 1, and Filedt Kok et al., 1975, pp. 247–50, for a complete review).

16. Filedt Kok et al., 1975, p. 252; also pp. 235–39 for the alterations and restorations. The *Annunciation* was seriously damaged as a result of the procedure in 1874; a large part of the central composition, including the lower drapery of Gabriel and Mary, was lost. See Filedt Kok et al., 1975, fig. 8, for the X ray showing the paint loss.

17. Filedt Kok, 1978, pp. 48–55.

Cat. C16. *Christ as Man of Sorrows and Virgin of Sorrows*

1. These may also be the panels that were in the sale Frank Lust Abbot, New York (Sotheby), June 7, 1978, no. 9 (school of Lucas).

2. One of the pendant paintings listed here (Copies 1–9) may be the item in the inventory of Antoinette Wiael, July 5–7, 1627: "Two portraits of Our Saviour and Our Beloved Lady in double frame, after Lucas van Leyden" (cited in Denuce, 1932, p. 42). "A Christ and a Beloved Lady, by Lucas van Leyden" was sold in 1662 with the collection of Johan Chrisostomus de Backer, The Hague; see Obreen, 1976, p. 301, nos. 154–55.

3. This has been suggested by Benesch, 1970, p. 151, and Amsterdam, Rijksprentenkabinet, 1978, p. 106, n. 176. The wings may have been joined before the two engraved copies were made showing the figures in one frame (Copies 20–21). These printmakers may also have simply united the two panels on the plate in order to facilitate the production of the print. The *Virgin and Child with Mary Magdalene and a Donor* diptych in Munich (Fig. 12, Cat. 14) was joined in the early sixteenth century, and the Leningrad triptych of *Christ Healing the Blind Man* (Fig. 35, Cat. 25) was united in the eighteenth century.

4. Ringbom, 1965, p. 127, discusses the interest in this theme among late fifteenth-century Netherlandish artists. Examples by Dirk and Albert Bouts are numerous (e.g., Friedländer, 1967–1976, 3:pls. 74–79, 92–93; see also 6a:pls. 91–92, and 7:pl. 12, for the workshops of Hans Memling and Quinten Massys).

Cat. C17. *Virgin and Child in the Clouds*

1. Because De Bisschop made drawn copies of a number of paintings in this collection, Van Gelder, 1957, p. 98, makes a connection between the drawing in Vienna (Copy 1) and a description in the inventory of 1662, no. 20: "een lieven vrouwen hemelvaart" (an Assumption of the Beloved Lady). See also Obreen, 1976, p. 296, which mentions that the painting was sold for 125 guilders to Pr. Disponteijn.

2. This drawing is dated ca. 1522 by Filedt Kok, 1978, p. 55, and Vos, 1978a, p. 196, no. 236, while Kloek, 1978, p. 454, no. 24, places it ca. 1527–1528. The earlier date seems more plausible, especially since the decoration is found in engravings from Lucas's middle period (e.g., B.114, 171, and 172).

Cat. C18. *Adoration of the Magi*

1. The panel was cleaned in 1962, uncovering the signature and date; Karlsruhe, Kunsthalle, 1966, p. 172.

2. This work was first mentioned in the manuscript inventory of 1823, no. 305; ibid., p. 172.

3. In this copy the servants are shown in full length and a strip is added to the panel at the top (information from the Kunsthalle, Karlsruhe, 1978).

4. Versions in which the figures of the Virgin and Child are isolated and placed in the context of the *Rest on the Flight* include: (1) Coll. A. Goekoop, San Antonio Abad Iliza (Baleares), 1969, as Joos van Cleve and Joachim Patinir; (2) formerly Coll. Agnes Seitz, Ebenhausen; copper, 39.5 x 45.5; (3) formerly with Malmedé, Cologne, 1932, as G. von Coninxloo; 75 x 106.5; (4) Private Coll., Bordighera, as Flemish, in the manner of Jan de Cock; (5) Fürstlich Fürstenbergische Sammlungen, Donaueschingen, as David Vinckeboons; 51 x 66 (Woltmann, 1870, p. 51, no. 114); (6) Private Coll., Stuttgart; 52 x 34. A partial copy was also cited by Steinbart, 1929, p. 236, in the Coll. Fugger-Babenhausen, Augsburg.

Paintings of the *Adoration* attributed to Lucas frequently appear in early inventories and sales but cannot be definitively associated with this composition because of incorrect measurements or insufficient evidence. See Rathgeber, 1844, cols. 216-18, nos. 759-71; Kramm, 1860, 4:974; Parthey, 1864, pp. 30-31, nos. 5-11; Hymans, 1884, pp. 151-52; and Moes, 1889, p. 151. At least three other compositions of the *Adoration* have been associated with Lucas in the past: (1) The Art Institute, Chicago, inv. no. 33.1045 (Cat. A6); (2) Barnes Foundation Museum of Art, Merion, Pa., inv. no. 443 (Cat. A7); (3) Provinzial Museum, Bonn, inv. no. 116, 57 x 86 (1914, pp. 59-60, after Lucas), also known in a partial copy engraved by Jacob Matham and signed "L" (B.173, 170; Hollstein, 11:218, no. 40). None of these compositions appears to be by Lucas.

5. The Virgin in the Mainz copy has a halo, unlike the same figure in Karlsruhe; the black servant at the extreme left in Karlsruhe is more closely cropped than the one in Mainz and wears a billowing scarf on his peaked hat.

6. Similar spectators are found in Lucas's engraving of the *Adoration*, dated 1513 (B.37).

7. Hoogewerff, 1936-1947, 3:393, draws specific parallels between this composition and a *Crucifixion* in Verona, attributed by him to Aertgen. The rather flaccid style and poses of the Verona painting are very different from the more detailed and controlled *Adoration*. Also compare the *Holy Family* triptych in Antwerp, attributed to Aertgen; Bruyn, 1960, fig. 36.

8. Friedländer, 1967-1976, 6a:no. 1 (and a variant in Bruges, no. 2) and 8:no. 12. In Gossaert's painting, as in Lucas's, the figure of Joseph is half-hidden in a doorway in the middle distance and acts as the terminus of the diagonal line leading from the kneeling Magus up through the Virgin. It is unlikely, however, that Lucas could have seen this painting during his journey (see Brussels, Palais des Beaux Arts, 1977, p. 23, for the early provenance). The fact that Gossaert's work is clearly within the tradition of Flemish representations helps to confirm the source of Lucas's inspiration. A similar figure in the middle ground, although not a figure of Joseph, appears in an *Adoration* in Nuremberg by the Master of the Female Half-Lengths (Friedländer, 1967-1976, 12:no. 56).

9. See Berlin, Staatliche Museen, 1978, p. 184. Copies by the Master of Frankfurt are in Vienna and Antwerp, and motifs were also taken over by Geertgen tot sint Jans.

10. See Dirk Vellert's triptych in Rotterdam and a panel in Cologne by an unknown master, ca. 1515 (Friedländer, 1967-1976, 12:no. 139, and Hiller and Vey, 1969, fig. 4). The same is true for Jacob Cornelisz.'s *Adoration* of 1520 in an American private collection (Friedländer, 1967-1976, 12:no. 239; cf. 5:no. 48, and 10:no. 49, for several other examples of northern Netherlandish centralized representations).

11. The swaying, mincing poses and the frequent use of a figure seen from the back in the foreground corner of many Antwerp Mannerist paintings could have influenced Lucas's later style; see the *Adoration* in Antwerp by an unknown master (Friedländer, 1967-1976, 11:no. 46) or such works by the so-called Pseudo Bles as the *Adoration* in Cambridge (11:no. 6) and the *Beheading of John the Baptist* in Berlin (11:no. 4).

12. Beets, 1913, p. 103. Also close to the poses of the two Magi are the female figures in two pen drawings by Lucas from the early 1520s: *Jael Killing Sisera* in Rotterdam and *Judith with the Head of Holofernes* (Kloek, 1978, pp. 444-45, nos. 10-11).

Cat. C19. *John the Baptist Preaching in the Wilderness*

1. The *computat digitas* was used several times by Lucas: in *The History of Joseph* engravings from 1512 (B.19, 22, 23) and in *Susanna before the Judge,* formerly in Bremen (Fig. 6, Cat. 3).

Cat. 20. *Last Judgment*

1. In the most detailed document concerning this commission, dated July 12, 1577, five descendants of Claes Dircsz. claim rights to a painting by Lucas then in St. Catherine's Hospital and agree on its removal to the burgomaster's chamber: "The heirs of Claes Dirczn., deceased timber merchant, being Dirc Jacopsz. van Montfoort, Jan Gerritsz. Buytewech, Mr. Reyer Jacobsz., Mr. Symon Jansz. and Gysbert Dirczn. Gool lay claim to the altar or memorial picture that was located in St. Peter's church next to the font and has been stored in St. Jacob's hospital. The aforementioned heirs, who had it fetched and brought to St. Catherine's hospital, have shown a receipt of the expenditure for this painting, commissioned on the sixth of August 1526 to Master Lucas Huychz., for the amount of thirty-five Flemish pounds paid by their aforementioned ancestors; adding that they had certain rights from the church-wardens at the time. From this it appears that the church had received three Flemish pounds for the installation, but at the wish of

the burgomasters the heirs agreed that the painting shall be brought to the burgomaster's room and hung there" (Hermesdorf et al., 1978, p. 411, doc. 1).

Although no reference is made in this document to the subject of the painting, it was mentioned as a Last Judgment in a record of August 10, 1571, recently discovered by Bangs (1980, p. 95). This is a payment for repairs made to the triptych by Ysaack Claesz. van Swanenburgh. The painting can also be related to an entry in the treasury accounts for September 11, 1577, recording payment for the transferal of a Last Judgment painting, artist unnamed, from St. Catherine's hospital to the burgomasters' room.

No mention is made of the donors in these documents, but they were almost certainly family members. Claes died in 1525 or early 1526, leaving three or four children still living (see Bangs, 1974a, for the question of his death date, and Hermesdorf et al., 1978, pp. 318–20, for a discussion of possible donors). The most detailed information on the provenance and early history of this triptych may be found in Dülberg, 1899a, pp. 31–37; Vos, 1978a, pp. 115–19; and Hermesdorf et al., 1978, pp. 318–22, 325–30.

2. The painting is described in the document of July 12, 1577 (see note 1), as originally hanging "next to the font" (*nae aent vont*). It is not known exactly when the triptych was completed and hung in the church. Hoogewerff, 1936–1947, 3:291, gave the date as 1527, but there is no proof of this (see Hermesdorf et al., 1978, p. 400, n. 54).

3. For documents concerning the iconoclastic riots in Leiden, see Kist and Moll, 1862, pp. 426–41, and Bangs, 1974b, p. 226, n. 29. On August 28, 1566, two days after the plundering of the churches, a council resolution was passed urging that all objects that had been saved be taken to St. Jacob's Hospital. An unreliable "eyewitness" account—supposedly written by a sixteenth-century Leiden priest but known only in an eighteenth-century copy—reports that the triptych was bought by one of the burgomasters for safekeeping from the "rabble" (Kist and Moll, 1862, p. 441, and Hermesdorf et al., 1978, p. 326, and esp. nn. 59–60).

4. Hermesdorf et al., 1978, pp. 326 and 411.

5. In 1614, Orlers gave more information about this foreign potentate, indicating that Emperor Rudolf II offered to buy the triptych in 1602 for the number of ducats it would take to cover the painting surface (1641, p. 361). The note in the margin beside the June 1583 entry in Buchelius's diary was probably written later, repeating the story told by Orlers (see Buchelius, 1928, p. 21, and Hermesdorf et al., 1978, p. 402, n. 65).

A number of letters survive documenting the efforts of Count Simon zur Lippe (Rudolf's envoy in Holland), Jan Muller (an engraver in Amsterdam), and Hans von Aachen (a painter in Prague, who acted on the emperor's behalf). Letters by Prince Maurits and the States General urged the Leiden Council to facilitate the sale. The request was refused, however, and according to Muller in a letter of

November 6 to the count, then in The Hague, this was due in part to the actions of Carel van Mander and Hendrick Goltzius. A year later the emperor tried again unsuccessfully to buy a painting by Lucas, this time his *Christ Healing the Blind Man* (see Cat. 25). Finally in 1604 he purchased Lucas's *Virgin and Child* diptych (Cats. 14–15). See Hermesdorf et al., 1978, pp. 402, n. 65, 411–13; Dodt van Flensburg, 1844, p. 106; and Van der Burch, 1887. For a general discussion of the events in 1602, see especially Elsevier, 1862; Dülberg, 1899a, pp. 34–35 (who suggests the city government resisted Rudolf's offer because the triptych was owned by the heirs of Claes Dircsz., rather than because of some upsurge of local patriotism); and Vos, 1978c, p. 497, n. 81.

6. This could not refer to the restoration of 1737, since the documents describe only a general cleaning and repair at that time. For a detailed discussion of the nineteenth-century restorations, see Hermesdorf et al., 1978, pp. 333–37.

7. On the significance of the Trinity in sixteenth-century northern Last Judgment scenes, see Harbison, 1976, pp. 159–66. The image of God the Father in Lucas's painting was overpainted, probably in the late sixteenth or seventeenth century, with the tetragrammaton in red surrounded by a golden aureole. For Calvinist attitudes toward images of God and the use of the tetragrammaton in the sixteenth and seventeenth centuries, see Krücke, 1959, pp. 71, 76–77, and 82, and Knipping, 1974, 2:244. For the history of the cleanings and overpaintings of Lucas's image of the Father, up to its final reappearance in 1935, see De Stuers, 1914; Coert, 1935–1936; and Hermesdorf et al., 1978, pp. 332, 334–35, 338–39. A watercolor copy of Lucas's figure of God was done before the repainting described by De Stuers (Copy 1).

8. For the Copenhagen panel, see Hoogewerff, 1936–1947, 3:123–24; Harbison, 1976, p. 166; and Boon, 1966.

9. For the different traditions of representing God the Father, see Réau, 1956, 1:8.

10. For the Alkmaar panel, see Hoogewerff, 1936–1947, 2:530–38, and figs. 264–67, and for the triptych by Mostaert or Geertgen, see Boon, 1966, p. 66, fig. 3. In both of these works the *psychostasis* is prominently in the foreground. See Salinger, 1941, for Joos van Cleve's painting.

11. Examples include several *Last Judgment* scenes by Jan Provost (Friedländer, 1967–1976, 9b:pls. 169, 172). Prints of the scene omit the Archangel, perhaps because of their small format, as in Jacob Cornelisz.'s woodcut of ca. 1520 (Hollstein, 1949–1974, 5:6, no. 66). As noted by Harbison, 1976, pp. 133–35, the decline in importance of the weighing of souls in the sixteenth century was paralleled by the decline in importance of the doctrine of good works. In this period a corresponding emphasis was given to salvation through faith alone. This was true especially in Protestant thought, but also to an extent in reform Catholicism. See also Hoogewerff, 1936–1947, 3:298–300. Bangs, 1985, p. 13, suggests that the absence of Michael weighing individual souls may be due to the unusually high mortality rate in Leiden in 1525–1526 because of a plague.

12. Wurfbain (in Hermesdorf et al., 1978, pp. 323–24) suggests the books on the rock at Paul's right are an allusion to the charters of Leiden, which were kept in the church tower until its collapse in 1512. Buried in the debris for six months, these books were finally recovered and stored in the town hall. Wurfbain uses as confirmation the quatrain, now lost, that was painted in 1595 under the triptych in the burgomasters' room. The calligraphy, done by Pieter Bailly, reads: "Everyone who is prohibited by his office, / from sailing on seas and lakes / what happens in the world / from chart[er]s must learn" (Wurfbain's translation). According to this theory, the "Chaerten" would refer not only to mariners' charts but also to the municipal charters. Several speculations have been made about this theory. Wurfbain assumed the lines were copied from an earlier verse written on the magistrate's bench in St. Peter's, but it is unknown whether the calligraphy by Bailly referred to the *Last Judgment* at all. Elsevier, 1875, transcribed the poem but doubted any connection between it and the triptych. Wurfbain also based his theory on the possibility that Claes Dircsz. had been a churchwarden prior to 1515 and in that capacity was closely involved in the events of 1512–1515, but there is no evidence of this. Until further documentation for this interesting hypothesis comes to light, it is best to conclude that the books lying between Peter and Paul were intended only as Paul's attribute. Although Paul is customarily shown with only one book (e.g., in Lucas's engravings B.88, 105, 106), the large number of his epistles might have prompted Lucas, in search of a further compositional link between the two panels, to add more volumes.

13. The theory that the triptych was originally placed at the high altar of St. Peter's was first suggested in Van Mieris, 1770, 2:370 (directly contradicting the information in his 1:29, which describes the triptych as hanging in the baptismal chapel). A number of nineteenth-century writers followed this theory, beginning with Kramm, 1860, 4:972–73, and Elsevier, 1875, p. 86.

14. Bangs, 1972; see also Pelinck, 1948, p. 175, and Hermesdorf et al., 1978, pp. 320–22, 325, for a discussion of the possible location and its relation to the size and content of the picture. According to Bangs (correspondence, June 15, 1981), the attached column on the west wall of the church near the baptistery shows evidence that the triptych may have hung there. During the recent restoration of the church, a coating was removed from the column, revealing an inserted block of new stone filling a hole probably made for an iron hook. The height would have been appropriate for hanging the *Last Judgment,* although Bangs adds that there is no proof the hook was used for this particular painting. There is no hole in the column attached along the north end of the west wall. Bangs also mentioned that Claes Dircsz. owned the three central crypts at the west end of the church, which would help to explain this placement of the memorial triptych (the documentation is from the First Gravebook of St. Peter's, 1581; see Bangs, 1985).

15. Bangs, 1974a; Hermesdorf et al., 1978, pp. 318–19. On contemporary Leiden government, see Blok, 1884a, pp. 130–63.

16. For the use of Last Judgment representations in town halls in northern Europe, see Harbison, 1976, pp. 51–64, 177–81, and Troescher, 1939. Hermesdorf et al., 1978, pp. 326–27, mention that the subject of the Leiden triptych as well as its large size explain the move of the painting to the town hall in 1577 rather than to the private home of one of the heirs of Claes Dircsz.

17. Dülberg, 1899a, p. 33, identified the elderly man on the left wing as a portrait of Claes Dircsz. and the man being led by the angel at the left of the central panel as a portrait of Claes's son, accompanied by his wife. Dülberg cites as evidence their strongly individualized features and family resemblance (cf. Lafenestre and Richtenberger, 1894–1907, pp. 171–72, who followed the traditional identification of the elderly man as Lucas's father and the seated man in the central foreground as a self-portrait). Dülberg further identified as portraits two of the seated men in the foreground of the central panel. This rather loose interweaving of portraits with generalized figures would have been contrary to the traditional grouping of kneeling donors in Last Judgment representations. In addition, the nudity of the figures would have been sharply contrasted to the sober, formal dress of other fifteenth- and early sixteenth-century northern donor portraits. Overvoorde and Martin, 1902, p. 20, agree with Dülberg. Those in disagreement include Beets, 1912a, p. 214, and J. G. Van Gelder, 1938, pp. 45–46. Van Gelder suggested a now-lost predella with portraits (cf. Hoogewerff, 1936–1947, 3:300). An example of a triptych with a predella for the donor portraits is Cornelis Engebrechtsz.'s *Crucifixion* in Leiden (Friedländer, 1967–1976, 10:pl. 60).

18. An infrared reflectography study of the underdrawing of the Leiden painting revealed that the sword was originally drawn pointing inward and reversed during the painting process (Filedt Kok, 1978, p. 82 and fig. 93). The points are generally turned inward, probably to symbolize the Word of Judgment issuing directly from Christ's mouth. The less common reversal is perhaps a representation of the sword as the instrument of Christ's condemnation. As such it is usually coupled with a symbol of his grace on his right, as in Rogier van der Weyden's *Last Judgment* in Beaune, perhaps the first example of the sword and lily both pointed away from Christ.

Several *Last Judgment* panels by Jan Provost in which the sword is positioned with the point toward the damned (e.g., Hamburg, Kunsthalle) are roughly contemporary with Lucas's triptych. In a painting by Provost in Bruges (ca. 1524–1525; Friedländer, 1967–1976, 9b:pls. 169, 172), Christ brandishes the weapon in his left hand, so that it is clearly intended as the active instrument of damnation (see Künstle, 1928, p. 550, who considers this a complete misunderstanding by Provost of Rev. 1:16 and 19:15). In Van Orley's Antwerp triptych, Christ is flanked by two angels, the one on his right carrying the lily and the one on his left wielding the sword. The sword facing outward, coupled with the lily, acts as a more legible and dynamic symbol of Christ's judgment than the traditional placement originally planned by Lucas.

19. Gibson, 1977, p. 149.

20. Valentiner, 1919.

21. Friedländer, 1967-1976, 12:pl. 59, and Harbison, 1976, figs. 54-55. Rather problematic in its relationship to Lucas's work is a *Last Judgment* in Valenciennes, now recognized as a painting by Aertgen van Leyden (Bangs, 1979a, fig. 96). On p. 137, n. 1, Bangs suggests the possible influence of Lucas as well as the more obvious stimulus of Maarten van Heemskerck. It appears that Aertgen's figures, particularly those in the left foreground, derive from the group in the same position in the Leiden School *Last Judgment* in New York (and thus only secondarily from Lucas's triptych).

Cat. C21. *Rest on the Flight into Egypt*

1. See Friedländer, 1967-1976, 10:83, and 1963a, p. 72, for the information on the Berlin and Zurich private collections. There is no way of knowing whether the "Vlucht in Egypte van Mr. Lucas tot Leyden," which was among the paintings at Mariënpoel, is related to this composition; see Elsevier, 1869, pp. 21-22; Dülberg, 1899c, p. 72; and Bangs, 1979a, p. 21.

2. Hiller and Vey, 1969, p. 64.

3. Information concerning Copies 3 and 4 was found in the Rijksbureau voor Kunsthistorische Documentatie, The Hague, along with photographs. The files there suggested they are fragments of a painting that originally measured 65 x 80.

4. Leiden, Stedelijk Museum, 1983, p. 206, identifies this as the collection of Hermann Schrieder, Heidelberg.

5. Kloek, 1978, pp. 454-55, no. 25 and fig. 1. See also Filedt Kok, 1978, pp. 166-67, n. 117.

Cat. C22. *Virgin and Child*

1. Perhaps this painting is the *Virgin and Child* by Lucas in the Escorial, cited by Michiels, 1847, p. 130, no. 33, or the *Virgin and Child* in Madrid mentioned by Blanc, 1861, p. 12. The museum file revealed only that the painting came from Spain.

2. German List of Stolen Art-Works, no. 116; Recovery 1947, Collecting Point, Munich, no. 8438.

3. The panel was never cut down; there is still a narrow, unpainted border about 2 mm wide along all four sides (Filedt Kok, 1978, p. 171, n. 151).

4. In certificates dated 1952, both Valentiner and Friedländer agreed that the

Norfolk painting was the better of what they considered to be two original versions (Provincetown, Chrysler Art Museum, 1958, p. 38).

5. Some rudimentary underdrawing is visible beneath the flesh areas of both the Norfolk and the Amsterdam paintings, which does not rule out the possibility that both works were copies; see Filedt Kok, 1978, p. 132, fig. 140, for the reproduction of infrared reflectogram details of the Amsterdam panel.

6. A number of scholars have suggested a date of ca. 1520, apparently by comparison with the Berlin *Virgin and Child with Angels* (Fig. 11, Cat. 12). See Beets, 1914, p. 59; Wescher, 1929, p. 169; Neugass, 1957; and Marette, 1961, p. 193. The poses of the Virgin and Christ Child are indeed similar, but the Virgin's facial features and the heavy build of her body are more typical of Lucas's late style.

Cat. 23. *Virgin and Child*

1. Compare the prefiguration of Christ as an apple tree in the Song of Solomon (2:3). Discussions of the apple as symbol in Netherlandish Virgin and Child representations are found in Ferguson, 1976, pp. 27-28, Panofsky, 1971b, 1:144, and Bergström, 1955, p. 304. For the concept of Mary as the new Eve in Catholic liturgy, see Timmers, 1978, p. 130; see also an early sermon, "In Natali Domini" (Migne, 1844-1864, 39:col. 1991, and 65:col. 899).

2. Ringbom, 1965, pp. 13, 59-60, 93-94, and Siebert, 1906, p. 27. Lasareff, 1938, pp. 27-36, analyzes the iconography of the *Virgo lactans*. See Künstle, 1928, p. 550, for this motif in the late fifteenth-century Dutch block book the *Speculum humanae salvationis,* ch. 39.

3. "Facta est Maria fenestra coeli, quia per ipsam Deus verum fudit saeculis lumen," from a sermon ("In Natali Domini") attributed to both St. Augustine and St. Fulgentius; Migne, 1844-1864, 39:col. 1991, and 65:col. 899, and quoted in Ringbom, 1965, p. 43.

4. Timmers, 1978, p. 216. The plant in the right foreground of the Oslo panel appears to be the *Primula officinalis Jacquin,* which was associated in the Middle Ages with the *flos campi* of Song of Solomon 2:1. As a symbol of the Virgin it appeared in Konrad von Megenburg's *Buch der Natur,* written ca. 1350; see Behling, 1957, pp. 25 and 120, and pls. 25, 65; also Levi d'Ancona, 1977, p. 323. Reznicek-Buriks, 1965, p. 245, suggests it is a strawberry plant in bloom.

5. Bartsch, 1803-1821, 7:436, and Hollstein, 1949-1974, 7:34, no. 193. There is no symbolic difference between the apple in the Oslo painting and the pear in the etching, both held by the Christ Child; see Friedmann, 1947, p. 70. Simon Frisius also made prints after the Strasbourg *Betrothal* (Fig. 26, Cat. 44) and after a lost composition by Lucas of *Christ as Man of Sorrows and Virgin of Sorrows* (Fig. 47, Cat. C16).

6. Compare Filedt Kok, 1978, figs. 108, 120-21, 130; see also ibid., p. 41,

Kloek, 1978, pp. 454–55, no. 25, and Parshall, 1978–1979, p. 52. The black-chalk drawing (21 x 17.1) is only slightly smaller than the painting itself.

7. Van Mander, 1604, fol. 214r. The Berlin *Virgin* measures 74 x 44 and is much larger than the Oslo painting. See Vos, 1978c, p. 501, n. 103, for a discussion of Ferreris as an art collector. Further references to Virgin and Child paintings by Lucas are found in: (1) the 1612 sale of the estate of Claes Rauwart, Amsterdam (Bredius, 1915–1922, 5:1744); (2) the 1653 inventory of Jeremias Wildens, Antwerp (Denuce, 1932, p. 161, no. 291); (3) the 1662 sale of Johan Chrisostomus de Backer, The Hague (Obreen, 1976, p. 296, no. 18); (4) the 1663 inventory of Catharina Dey, Antwerp (Denuce, 1932, p. 240); (5) the 1685 inventory of Alexander Voet, Antwerp (Denuce, 1932, p. 315); (6) the 1687 inventory of the estate of Catharina Deyl, Amsterdam (Bredius, 1915–1922, 2:545, no. 131); (7) the 1732 taxation of the paintings of Catharina Grypestar, The Hague (Bredius, 1915–1922, 4:1240).

Cat. C24. *Christ Healing the Lepers*

1. This drawing in the Louvre (pen, brush, and wash, 25 x 19.5) is not accepted by Kloek, 1978, p. 457, but is included in Lucas's oeuvre by Vos, 1978a, no. 242 (ca. 1530) and Filedt Kok, 1978, pp. 97–98 (ca. 1530). Cf. Kloek and Filedt Kok, 1983, p. 12, where the drawing is described as a copy. The rejection of it is not convincing. The lively hatching of the flesh areas and the description of the tree trunk are similar to Lucas's drawing of the *Fall of Man* in Hamburg, ca. 1528–1530 (Kloek, 1978, p. 455, no. 26). The awkward poses of John the Baptist and Christ and the "untidy" figures in the background, noted by Kloek, are reminiscent of Lucas's late style in the painting of *Christ Healing the Blind Man* in Leningrad (Fig. 35, Cat. 25).

Cats. 25 and 26. *Christ Healing the Blind Man* and *Shield-Bearers*

1. The coats of arms on the exterior were first identified by Beets, 1910.

2. Van Mander, 1604, fol. 212v. The *Shield-Bearers* seem to have influenced Goltzius's drawing of the same subject in Oxford, dated 1586 (Reznicek, 1961, 1:317, no. 199). They also inspired Aertgen van Leyden in his representation of *Shield-Bearers* on the exterior of a *Last Judgment* triptych in Valenciennes. Like Lucas's painting, this work was commissioned by members of the Van Montfoort family (see Bangs, 1979a, pp. 128, 137, n. 1, and fig. 92, and Amsterdam, Rijksmuseum, 1986, 2:329–30, no. 208).

3. *Catalogues de ventes,* 1909, p. 87, no. 338.

4. According to De Somof, 1899, p. 260, the wings passed through a number of hands before ending up in the Kauffmann collection. He recorded that Kauffmann bought the wings from an art dealer for 100 rubles (Wrangell, 1913, p. 64,

says 30) and sold them back to The Hermitage for 8,000 rubles. See also Nikulin, 1978, p. 309, n. 3.

5. Tilmann was entrusted by the count to buy paintings for the collection of Emperor Rudolf II. In this letter he reported that the painting by Lucas was badly damaged, with the paint peeling from the panel in five or six places, and that it was overpriced at 2,000 imperial guilders. Hirschmann, 1916, pp. 36, 40, suggests Tilmann was trying to excuse his failure to purchase the painting by overemphasizing its damage. At roughly the same time, Van Mander remarked on its good condition. Perhaps after Rudolf failed to acquire the *Last Judgment,* now in Leiden (see Cat. 20), his agents turned their attention to this painting. Peltzer, 1911–1912, p. 106, says Hans von Aachen was the primary agent in the unsuccessful attempts to acquire the *Last Judgment* and *Christ Healing the Blind Man* and the successful purchase in 1604 of the *Virgin and Child* diptych now in Munich (Cats. 14–15).

6. Van Mander, 1604, fol. 213r. For information on the coats of arms, see Beets, 1910, pp. 157–58, and Kekule von Stradonitz, 1910, pp. 186–90, and 1911, pp. 44–45. The four smaller coats of arms above the heads of the two *Shield-Bearers* might be those of the donors' grandparents. Neither scholar could identify the arms above the woman, and Kekule von Stradonitz questioned the identification of the coat of arms at the far left. It is possible they were overpainted, along with much of the background of this panel (see Kekule von Stradonitz, 1910, p. 190, and 1911, p. 45; also Nikulin, 1978, p. 308).

7. The drawing by Gabriel de Saint Aubin (Copy 3) reveals that the *Shield-Bearers* had been separated from the front and cut down by 1771–1772. The lost segments would have fit into a rectangle measuring approximately 27 x 33.5. Most likely, they were painted with a continuation of the architectural decoration (Nikulin, 1978, p. 304). The date could have been painted as if chiseled into the stone, a variant of the method used in the 1527 *Moses after Striking the Rock* in Boston (Fig. 24, Cat. 7) (cf. Beets, 1913, p. 114). It could also have been displayed on a cartouche or small globe, as in some of Lucas's late ornamental prints (B.160–62).

8. Amsterdam, Rijksmuseum, 1986, 2:152.

9. Nikulin, 1978, p. 309, n. 6. The 1740 catalogue of the Crozat collection describes the painting as a triptych, with the wings painted on both sides. The 1755 catalogue refers to the painting as *formerly* a triptych, and the measurements confirm that the interior had been united. No mention is made of the *Shield-Bearers,* which might still have been in their original location on the exterior (Nikulin, 1978, p. 309, n. 4). The drawing by Saint Aubin (Copy 3) shows the wings sawn apart and attached separately. The original shape of the triptych is impossible to determine. Several suggestions have been made, including a rounded as well as a more decorative format (see, e.g., Beets, 1913, p. 114; Hoogewerff, 1936–1947, 3:311–12; Nikulin, 1965, p. 15, and 1978, pp. 305–6 and fig. 4;

and Vos, 1978a, p. 92). The most significant change to the figures of the interior occurs in the area overpainted along the join of the central panel and right wing. The head of a man, originally tonsured (as in the Aachen copy), was transformed into a peculiar type of feathered female headdress. See Nikulin, 1965, p. 17, and 1978, pp. 307–8, for a discussion of the overpainting on the exterior wings.

10. Nikulin, 1972, p. 116; also 1964, pp. 17–18, for the identification of the self-portrait. See the Appendix for a detailed discussion of the various "portraits" of Lucas.

11. See Utrecht, Centraal Museum, 1955, figs. 6, 31, 93, for similar landscape, mountains, and architecture.

Cat. 27. *History of St. Hubert*

1. Van Mander, 1604, fol. 211v.

2. Vos, 1978c, p. 483, n. 22; this was suggested earlier by Beets, 1913, p. 81, who identified Dürer's engraving as *St. Hubert*. See Bernen, 1973, p. 136, for the legend of the saint's conversion from the *Acta Sanctorum*.

3. Information on the Lochorst family is in Gavelle, 1929, pp. 252–58, and Vos, 1978c, p. 483, n. 23. For a less felicitous connection between Lucas's family and Gerrit van Lochorst, involving the sheriff's punishment of Lucas's brother for escaping from prison, see Dülberg, 1899c, pp. 70–71.

Bangs, 1979a, pp. 93–95, suggested the commission came from Adriaen van Poelgeest, who at that time was living in the Lochorst house in Leiden. Van Poelgeest had been instrumental in fixing the price for an altarpiece by Lucas's father, Huygh Jacobsz.

4. See Cats. 2, 7, 8 for further information on the practice of painting in tempera or watercolor on canvas; also Vos, 1978c, p. 483, n. 21. Typical measurements for Netherlandish paintings in this medium are 90 x 74.2 (Dirk Bouts; see Friedländer, 1967–1976, 3:no. 3), 108 x 158 (Joos van Gent; see 3:no. 101), and 97 x 110 cm (Quinten Massys; see 7:no. 28). Van Mander, 1604, fols. 203r–v, said of a painting in tempera on canvas by Rogier van der Weyden, "At this period it was fashionable to paint large canvases with tall figures in them. They were used to decorate rooms when tapestries were not used."

Cat. 28. *St. Andrew*

1. The Flemish practice of adding dramatic peaks and cliffs to the background had by this time become prevalent in the northern Netherlands as well (e.g., Amsterdam, Rijksmuseum, 1958, figs. 6, 19, 30, 36, and 49). That it was frequently used by Leiden artists of the early sixteenth century could of course have influenced Lucas's representation, but none of the mountains depicted by the

Lamentation Master (named after a painting in Vienna) are close enough to be considered a direct source (Gibson, 1977, figs, 17, 38, and 61).

2. Ferguson, 1976, pp. 165, 171; Ryan and Ripperger, 1948, pp. 12-13; and Braunfels, 1973, 5:138-39. Cf. a shutter of *St. Andrew* by Jan Provost, also with an open book in the hands of the apostle and an X-shaped cross behind him (Friedländer, 1967-1976, 9b:no. 161).

3. See Filedt Kok, 1978, pp. 56-57, and fig. 59 for the X-radiograph. The top could have been similar in shape to the simple rounded arch of Jacob Cornelisz.'s *Adoration of the Magi* (American private collection; Friedländer, 1967-1976, 12:no. 239), or to the ogival arches of Jan Mostaert's *Last Judgment* in Bonn and Lucas's own *Last Judgment* (Figs. 17-19, Cat. 20). The figure of St. Peter on the exterior of Lucas's *Last Judgment* (Fig. 23) is oriented away from the center, but there may have been a specific reason for contradicting the traditional format; see Cat. 20.

4. As in Bernard van Orley's altarpiece in Kassel (Friedländer, 1967-1976, 8:no. 83, who dates it ca. 1518).

5. See, for example, *St. Jacob* from the circle of Geertgen tot Sint Jans (location unknown; now a fragment, 24 x 14; Rotterdam, Museum Boymans–van Beuningen, 1936, fig. 16), and Cornelis Engebrechtsz.'s *Mary Magdalene and John the Baptist* in Aachen (oval, 33 x 24, originally probably full length and rectangular; Friedländer, 1967-1976, 10:no. 105). The *Temptation of St. Anthony* in Brussels is also a fragment, although a much larger one. Once attributed to Lucas, it is now given to Aertgen (66.5 x 71; see Bruyn, 1960, p. 73, fig. 20, for a reconstruction). For Provost's triptych, see Friedländer, 1967-1976, 9b:no. 122 (on loan from the Rijksmuseum; central panel 44 x 31; wings 52 x 15); also no. 125, a slightly smaller triptych of the *Adoration* also attributed to Provost (Kunsthaus, Zurich; central panel 27 x 19; wings 27 x 7.5).

6. For an early date see Hoogewerff, 1936-1947, 3:247, Lauts, 1957, pp. 34, 44, and Friedländer, 1967-1976, 10:83, among others. Vos, 1978a, p. 187, and Filedt Kok, 1978, p. 57, both date the painting ca. 1518. Filedt Kok also notes that even the use of infrared reflectography shows no underdrawing.

7. See Chapter 2 for further discussion of the technique of this panel in relation to Lucas's other polyptychs. Also Filedt Kok, 1978, pp. 31, 34-35, 57, for his discussion of the paint technique in the Rotterdam, Wilton House, and Karlsruhe panels.

Cat. C29. *St. George*

1. Ryan and Ripperger, 1948, pp. 233-35, and Ferguson, 1976, pp. 121-22.
2. Ferguson, 1976, p. 122. E.g., Panofsky, 1971b, 2:fig. 248; also Friedländer, 1967-1976, 6a:no. 63, and 9a:nos. 16-17.

Cat. C30. *St. James the Greater Raising a King and Queen of Spain*

1. Hall, 1974, p. 165.

Cat. 31. *Portrait of a Man Aged 38*

1. A receipt, now in the Gemeente Archief, Leiden (dated March 23, 1686), records payment to Carel de Moor, father and son, for the restoration of a damaged painting by Lucas belonging to the late Mr. Doeswerffe—apparently Cornelis van Doeswerff, grandfather of Alexandre le Breton van Doeswerff, who sold the painting in 1775. This information was kindly provided by M. L. Wurfbain (correspondence, March 26, 1981), who also noted that a Vincent van Doeswerff was married to the granddaughter of the burgomaster Claes Adriaensz. van Leeuwen. See Van Mander, 1604, fol. 214r: "a painting of a nearly life-size head, belonging to a burgomaster of Leyden whose name is Claes Ariaensz., it shows its character very well and precisely." See Vos, 1978c, pp. 474–75, 500, nn. 100–101. Gavelle, 1929, p. 43, considered this a reference to the portrait in Braunschweig (Fig. 14, Cat. 32), although that painting is closer to half life-size.

2. The entry in the sale catalogue reads: "The portrait of the master himself, half-length, holding a roll of paper marked 38, painted in a very detailed and beautiful manner on panel, height 18, breadth 16 inches." The portrait sold for eight guilders, fifteen stuivers.

3. Van Hall, 1963, p. 186, no. 3 (see also no. 5); the measurements are the same as above, and the figure is described as half-length, with a roll of paper in his hand.

4. Gleadowe, 1922, p. 179.

5. London, Royal Academy of Arts, 1902, no. 157, and Friedländer, 1902, p. 146.

6. Kloek, 1978, pp. 428–29, 446–49, nos. 13–18.

7. Bruyn, 1969, p. 46.

8. Friedländer, 1967–1976, 12:supp. 415. Gossaert's Carondelet diptych in the Louvre features an inscription around the frame of the left wing giving Jan Carondelet's age (8:no. 4). His *Portrait of a Benedictine Monk* in the Louvre has the monk's age and the date inscribed on the background above the sitter's head (8:no. 72). The numbers 42 and 40 are written on the windowsill in the background of two pendant portraits of a man and woman, sometimes attributed to Cornelis Engebrechtsz. (Musées Royaux des Beaux-Arts, Brussels; 10:no. 109). Cf. the number 25 in the background of a *Portrait of a Man* once given to Lucas (Cat. A14). The inclusion of the age of the sitter in German portraits is common in works by Dürer, Holbein, Hans Suess von Kulmbach, and Bartholomäus Bruyn the Elder. A number of examples are found in Berlin, Staatliche Museen, 1978, nos. 557D and E (Dürer), 586B–D (Holbein), 1834 (Kulmbach), and 556A (Bruyn).

9. Early sixteenth-century examples of blank scrolls in Netherlandish portraits include Jacob Cornelisz.'s *Portrait of Jacob Pijnssen* (Rijksmuseum Twenthe, Enschede; Friedländer, 1967–1976, 12:no. 291) and Gossaert's *Portrait of a Man* (Pushkin Museum, Moscow; 8:add. 165). The man in Bernard van Orley's portrait in the

Gemäldegalerie, Dresden (8:no. 148), holds a piece of paper on which the date 1527 is written. The man in Massys's portrait holds a piece of paper with the inscription "ETAS MEA 51 DUM SCRIBERETUR 1.5.0.9. FUI IN TERRA SANCTA" (7:no. 38). The *Portrait of a Man* in the Louvre (inv. R.F.120) is probably by a minor northern artist working in the first half of the sixteenth century and influenced by Italian portraiture (see Edouard Michel, 1953, pp. 254-55 and fig. 150, for the attribution to Van Scorel). The man holds in his left hand a paper dated 1501 or 1521 and inscribed "anno etatis mee. 32." In a portrait of a woman (location unknown) that was incorrectly considered a work by the Master of Alkmaar, a small piece of paper with the number 45 appears on the foreground balustrade (Friedländer, 1967-1976, 10:no. 59III).

10. The inscription on Dürer's portrait reads "Dem pernh . . . zw . . ." (Anzelewsky, 1971, p. 260, and Brussels, Palais des Beaux-Arts, 1977, p. 48), and on Gossaert's "(pm?)rpses / Joannes,m / malbodius / pingeba . . . dnz / oty" (Friedländer, 1967-1976, 8:no. 63; cf. a slightly different reading in Rotterdam, Museum Boymans–van Beuningen, 1965, p. 65). For Van Cleve's *Portrait of a Man* in Vaduz, see Friedländer, 1967-1976, 9a:no. 80.

Cat. 32. *Portrait of a Man*

1. Incorrect measurements are given in the catalogues for the exhibitions in Rotterdam, Museum Boymans–van Beuningen, 1936; Amsterdam, Rijksmuseum, 1958; and Delft, Prinsenhof, 1964-1965.

2. The ducal museum later became the Herzog Anton Ulrich-Museum. The panel was first mentioned in the museum inventory of 1789-1803; in the section listing those paintings acquired from 1772 to 1779, p. 346, no. 4, it is called a self-portrait by Hans Holbein: "His portrait with a hat, on panel, height 1 foot, width 9 inches."

3. The seal of the Musée Napoleon was put on the reverse of the panel.

4. Van Mander, 1604, fol. 214r. See Cat. 31, note 1.

5. The drawing has highlighting in white and yellow body-color and underdrawing in black chalk; London, Victoria and Albert Museum, 1972, p. 106, no. 81.

6. Rubens placed the image of Lucas in an oval stone frame surmounted by a curved pediment. The frame is decorated with the head of Minerva and several laurel branches. The banderole below curves around a lighted oil lamp and the attributes of a painter and sculptor. For other drawings by Rubens copied after works by Lucas see Held, 1959, pp. 151-52, and London, Victoria and Albert Museum, 1972, p. 108.

7. No. 1016, which directly follows the entry for Rubens's portrait of Tobias Stimmer, reads as follows: "Another portrait of Lucas van Leyden, painter and engraver, drawn in the same style [as the portrait of Stimmer], with the attributes

of the arts that he practiced, and a laurel branch crowning the border"; Lugt, 1943, p. 100.

8. The literature cited here is in addition to that under the main heading above.

9. Van Mander, 1604, fol. 211v; see Copy 6 for the full text of the inscription.

10. Conway, 1921, pp. 464–66; Goldscheider, 1936, p. 23; Filedt Kok, 1978, pp. 58–60; Vos, 1978a, p. 21; and Parshall, 1978–1979, p. 52.

11. In 1930, Friedländer accepted Stock's date of 1509, adding that nothing concerning Lucas seemed unbelievable (p. 498). He later reiterated his belief in the importance of Stock as a source of information but dated the painting, on the basis of style, closer to 1511 (1963a, p. 10). Stock's reliability is also weakened by his identification of the painting as a self-portrait. He made a number of portrait engravings (see Von Wurzbach, 1910, 2:664), predominantly of seventeenth-century artists or political leaders such as Erasmus and William the Silent whose likenesses were presumably readily available to him. In the case of his engraving of Holbein's "self-portrait," however, there have been doubts similar to the ones expressed recently about Lucas's; see R. N. Wornum, *Holbein* (London, 1867), pp. 80–84, and H. A. Schmid, *Holbein* (Basel, 1945), p. 21, for information on Holbein's self-portraits.

Bock, 1910, p. 405, identified youthful features of the portrait that would have dated it at least a decade earlier than Dürer's portrait drawing of 1521 (Fig. 70). Riegel, 1882, 2:147, considered the sitter to be at least thirty years old.

12. Vermeulen, 1915, p. 100; De Jonge, 1916, p. 251; and Dülberg, 1899c, p. 79.

13. The two black-chalk drawings are in the Stedelijk Museum "De Lakenhal," Leiden, and in the Louvre; Kloek, 1978, pp. 446–47, nos. 13, 16. See Der Kinderen-Besier, 1933, p. 82, and fig. 28A–C for a description of this style of hat.

14. Filedt Kok, 1978, pp. 58–59, 165–66, n. 109, and Müller-Hofstede, 1959, pp. 224–25, 228, and fig. 2.

15. This information was kindly provided by the chief restorer at Braunschweig, Knut Nicolaus (correspondence of June 25, 1981). He noted that even a new, twentieth-century tempera layer applied to an old oil or tempera painting would prove impossible to remove after a short time without damaging the earlier paint.

16. Netherlandish portraits of the late fifteenth and early sixteenth centuries were usually composed either in bust length, with hands, or in half- or three-quarter length; see the portraits of Hans Memling (Friedländer, 1967–1976, 6a:pls. 110–23); Quinten Massys (7:pls. 40–49; but cf. pl. 50, compositionally similar to the Braunschweig portrait); Joos van Cleve (9a:pls. 89–128); Jan Gossaert (8:pls. 44–63); and Jan Mostaert (10:pls. 18–27).

An analysis of the portrait types in the Netherlands and in Italy is given by Ring, 1912–1913, pp. 64–73. Bust-length portraits without hands were more common earlier in the fifteenth century (e.g., in paintings by Jan van Eyck, Rogier van der Weyden, and Petrus Christus; Panofsky, 1971b, 2:figs. 262–63, 364, 377, 405, 413).

The most likely source of inspiration is Dürer—either his drawings or prints such as *Frederick the Wise,* dated 1524 (B.104). For examples of Dürer's drawings, see Brussels, Palais des Beaux-Arts, 1977, pp. 58–61, 63, and illustrations on pp. 17 and 37. The woodcut portraits of Lucas Cranach may also have influenced Lucas's composition (e.g., Jahn, 1972, p. 408).

17. Filedt Kok, 1978, p. 59, was the first to mention the similarity in the use of highlighting between the Braunschweig panel and the *Last Judgment.*

Cat. 34. *Chess Players*

1. Von Frimmel, 1898, pp. 64–65, 206, relates this panel to an entry in the inventories of the Imperial Schatzkammer, Vienna, 1747–1748, no. 46, "A piece, in which some players are represented, by Lucas van Leyden," and 1750, no. 46, "A medium-sized piece with some players by Luca Cornelio von Leyden." These citations are from Zimerman, 1889, pp. 244, 307. The writer of the 1750 entry almost certainly meant Lucas Huyghensz. rather than Lucas Cornelisz., Cornelis Engebrechtsz.'s son.

A number of gaming compositions by Lucas are known, and there is no way of determining which was in the Schatzkammer. Pigler's claim (1936, p. 182) that it was the panel in Budapest (Fig. 53) seems plausible, given the location of a royal castle at Pressburg in Hungary (see Cat. C39, note 2). A much larger painting of chess players attributed to Lucas was owned by Charles I of England: "Above the chimney a picture in water colours, where they are sitting playing at chess, containing some fifteen figures being half so big as the life; in a wooden frame" (3'4" long x 5'9"); cited in Vertue, 1757, pp. 136–37, no. 33. This was incorrectly identified with the panel in Berlin by Cust, 1910, p. 149; see also Kramm, 1860, 4:974.

2. Sterling, 1930, p. 111, n. 1, mentions that the panel was given in 1875 to the Musées des Beaux Arts, Lyon, and was later returned to the Bernard family. The museum has no record of owning the painting, however, and Sterling cites apparently nonexistent museum catalogues of 1877 (no. 153) and 1881 (no. 174, as Lucas Cranach) (correspondence with the museum conservator, May 5 and December 22, 1980).

3. This panel is mentioned in the museum file in Berlin as a late eighteenth-century copy.

4. The game of courier, played on a board measuring twelve by eight squares, is described by Crow, 1944, p. 34, and Murray, 1962, p. 483. The Berlin panel was associated with this game by J. A., 1951, pp. 92–94.

5. Kloek, 1978, pp. 438–39, nos. 1 and 2a.

Cat. 35. *The Fortuneteller*

1. The strokes of the H seen by Wurfbain at the lower left of the composition appear to be only an accidental grouping. In fact, this presumed letter is only partially visible, since what would have been its right vertical is obscured by a dark shadow. The panel was examined out of its frame on June 30, 1980, in company with Jacques Foucart, who agreed with this assessment.

2. Oddly enough, Friedländer, 1963a, p. 48, considered the painting in Nantes to be the better of the two, although he concluded that both were probably copies of a lost original. Most recently Filedt Kok, 1978, p. 26, has accepted the Louvre panel, while Parshall, 1974, p. 100, doubts its authenticity. Wurfbain, 1978, pp. 204-5, tentatively attributes it to Huygh Jacobsz. (see note 1).

3. Filedt Kok, 1978, p. 26.

Cat. C36. *The Betrothal*

1. The information cited here, as well as the photograph, was obtained at the Rijksbureau voor Kunsthistorische Documentatie, The Hague. No other reference to it has been found.

2. In his right hand, the fool holds the end of his jester's wand. This type of nonfigured *marotte* is also seen in Lucas's engraving B.147, ca. 1507.

Cat. 37. *Card Players*

1. The "FM" on the center of the woman's bodice border could have been a later addition. The dull gold paint seems slightly different from the gold of her cuffs or the button at her neck. Several unlikely theories have been proposed to explain these initials. Wurfbain, 1978, p. 202, n. 7, attributes the painting to Frans Minnebroer, who has been identified as Frans Crabbe van Espleghem. Van Mander described the works of this Mechelin artist, active in the first half of the sixteenth century, as similar to those by Lucas (see Van de Wall, 1969, p. 121 and n. 1). Unfortunately, no paintings are securely attributable to him. At any rate, the *Card Players* is in my mind undoubtedly an original work by Lucas, somewhat damaged.

Rosenbaum, in the catalogue of the exhibition in Washington, National Gallery, 1979-1980, pp. 114-15, identifies the young man at the left as Charles V, the older man as Cardinal Wolsey, and the woman as Margaret of Austria. In this case FM would stand for Filia Maximiliani (daughter of Emperor Maximilian). These three met in Bruges in 1521, and Rosenbaum suggests Lucas saw them during his trip south in that year. There are several problems with that theory, however. First, the stylistic evidence shows that this panel could not possibly have been painted as late as 1521. The figure types are much closer to Lucas's early period than to the Berlin *Virgin and Child with Angels,* ca. 1521 (Fig. 11, Cat. 12). Also, the woman's features do not resemble those of Margaret as portrayed by Bernard van Orley (various copies are illustrated in Friedländer, 1967-1976, 8:pl. 126). The young man does have the long, hooked nose of Charles, but then so do a number of other figures in Lucas's prints and paintings (e.g., B.33, B.37, and the Louvre *Fortuneteller* [Fig. 2, Cat. 35]). Also, the prominent, disfiguring Habsburg jaw and lower lip are missing here (see Friedländer, 1967-1976, 8:pl. 120, for portraits of Charles). Finally, the only connection between the man at the right and Wolsey seems to be their corpulence and age, and once again this figure type of the heavy, older man appears repeatedly in Lucas's works (e.g., in the *Chess Players* in Berlin [Fig. 1, Cat. 34] and *Potiphar's Wife Accusing Joseph* in Rotterdam [Fig. 4, Cat. 1]).

2. Stewart, 1977, p. 174, lists no. 88 as a copy, but it is in all probability identical to the Lugano panel (no. 87). The location and measurements cited for no. 88 (private collection, London, 515 x 425 mm) are those used by Friedländer, 1963a, p. 52, with reference to the painting then in the Coll. Lady Dunsany. Stewart was obviously confused by the fact that Friedländer mistakenly used the dimensions (in reverse) of the Eindhoven copy in referring to the panel now in Lugano.

3. This is a very close copy, of poor quality.

4. Filedt Kok, 1978, pp. 36, 162, n. 82, describes the painting as heavily restored, with a number of retouchings and abrasions. Rubbed areas are particularly noticeable in the hands of the three figures and the robe of the man at the right. A thin overpainted wash dulls the surface on the woman's left cheek and headdress and the faces of both men. Part of the background landscape has also been retouched. Smudges of brown overshadow Lucas's characteristic crisp detailing in the foliage of the tallest tree at the left.

5. The thin brush lines seem more delicate than the bold hatching in *Potiphar's Wife Accusing Joseph,* Rotterdam (Fig. 4, Cat. 1); see Filedt Kok, 1978, figs. 17-21. The *pentimento* at the tip of the woman's nose in the Lugano *Card Players* is comparable to a similar change in the face of the man in the middle background of *Potiphar's Wife* (see Filedt Kok's fig. 20).

Cat. 38. *Card Players*

1. An inscription formerly on the tablecloth at the center bottom read "LUCAS VAN LYDEN P." It was certainly added at a later date, however, which was noted as early as Waagen, 1854, p. 152. The inscription was later removed during cleaning.

2. The gaming scene by Lucas mentioned in the inventory of Charles I is described as a chess game and is much larger than the Wilton House *Card Players;* Vertue, 1757, pp. 136-37, no. 33.

3. This painting is an exact copy of the panel in Wilton House, even down to

the number and placement of the coins on the table. It is more crudely painted and seems to date from the later sixteenth century.

4. Friedländer, 1967–1976, 10:no. 141, dates it ca. 1513–1514, while Beets, 1913, pp. 112–13, places it ca. 1530.

Cat. C39. *Card Players*

1. A horizontal strip measuring 1.5 cm has been added to the top border; Pigler, 1968, p. 378.

2. Pigler, 1936, p. 182, identifies the painting now in Budapest with an entry in the inventories of the Schatzkammer, 1747–1748 and 1750, no. 46, in which a painting with some "players" by Lucas is mentioned (see Cat. 34, note 1, for the full text of these entries). Pigler further notes that in 1770 Empress Maria Theresa ordered a group of paintings, including this one, sent to the royal castle at Pozsony (Pressburg). Von Frimmel, 1898, pp. 64–65, 206, relates this same entry to the *Chess Players* in Berlin (Fig. 1, Cat. 34).

3. A number of changes have been made in the more crudely painted copy by Macalester (Copy 2). The two advisers have been omitted, apparently in order to make room for the coats of arms in the upper corners. The background oculus has been transformed into a large rectangular window, through which we see a landscape. The cards being played have also been altered (see Chapter 3).

4. Parshall, 1974, p. 99, and Pigler, 1936.

5. Hoogewerff, 1936–1947, 3:229, n. 2, suggested a link between the *Allegory* and the painting in Budapest. Parshall's theory (1974, p. 100, n. 4) that the *Card Players* is by the artist of *The Betrothal* in the Morris Collection (Fig. 28) seems unlikely. The copyist of *The Betrothal* is more accomplished in his depiction of drapery folds and facial modeling.

Cat. C40. *A Family Surprised by Death*

1. The laurel can in this case be read as a symbol either of eternity or of victory (Ferguson, 1976, p. 33). Symbols of resurrection often appear in later sixteenth- and seventeenth-century *Vanitas* still lifes (e.g., Leiden, Stedelijk Museum, 1970, cats. 7, 12, 20, 27, 32). In the *Emblemata* by Sambucus (3d ed., Antwerp, 1569, p. 110), a winged image of a globe, laurel-wreathed skull, hourglass, open book, and trumpet appears with the motto "In morte vita" (in death is life). As a symbol of victory, the laurel wreath can refer to the victory *of* death over worldly existence and the victory *over* death through Christ. Compare the *Temptation of a Young Man* (Cat. C42, note 1).

Cat. C41. *Allegory of Transience*

1. The composition of the drawing is more restricted and the figures are arranged more compactly than in the painting. Also, the tilt of the head and glance of the eyes in the drawing are at times slightly different; the fool's *marotte* is missing; there are fewer objects on the table; the figure of Death looks around the tree in a different direction; and five or six small figures have been added in the left background. The painting is possibly by the copyist of the *Temptation of a Young Man* (Fig. 52, Cat. C42) and the *Card Players* in Budapest (Fig. 53, Cat. C39); see Cat. C39 for discussion.

2. Bock and Rosenberg, 1930, p. 39, and Filedt Kok, in Amsterdam, Rijksprentenkabinet, 1978, p. 96.

3. See Amsterdam, Rijksprentenkabinet, 1978, p. 40, for a brief discussion of the iconography of the *Young Man with a Skull*. General overviews of the *Vanitas* theme are in Bergström, 1956, pp. 154–90; Haak, 1967–1968; and Leiden, Stedelijk Museum, 1970.

Cat. C42. *Temptation of a Young Man*

1. Tervarent, 1958, col. 232, and Whittlesey, 1972, p. 214. Laurel is a Christian symbol of eternal life and is probably used here in contrast to the symbols of transience (the hourglass and skull); Ferguson, 1976, p. 33.

Cat. C43. *Card Players*

1. Judson, 1961, p. 347.

2. Filedt Kok, 1978, pp. 129–30, has studied the underdrawing and paint technique of this panel and found it uncharacteristic of Lucas.

3. For Van Cleve, see Friedländer, 1967–1976, 9a:nos. 64–65, and for Massys, 7:no. 53. Eisler, 1977, p. 85, suggests the still life in the Washington panel has a *vanitas* significance, but there is nothing to support this; see Bergström, 1956, pp. 154–90. Reznicek-Buriks, 1965, p. 245, considers the still life characteristic of Lucas and compares it to the pot of flowers in the Oslo *Virgin and Child* (Fig. 29, Cat. 23). For the idea that the copy was painted in Spain, see Roger Mandel, 1968, cited in Eisler, 1977, p. 85. Filedt Kok, 1978, p. 132, notes that the clothing and facial types point toward a German artist and that the poplar wood on which the work was painted was rarely used in the sixteenth century in the Netherlands.

4. This date was most recently suggested by Parshall, 1974, pp. 99–100, n. 3, who follows Friedländer, 1963a, pp. 62–63. An early dating was proposed by Fell, 1935, p. 171; Hoogewerff, 1936–1947, 3:258–59; and Friedländer, 1967–1976, 10:54, 84.

Cat. 44. *The Betrothal*

1. A *Betrothal* owned by G. Wildenstein in 1938 was attributed to Lucas, but it is not known whether it was one of the panels listed here (J. G. Van Gelder, 1957, p. 96, n. 5; Paris, Petit Palais, 1965–1966, p. 143).

2. J. G. Van Gelder, 1957, p. 94, observes that the drawing in the Coll. Hagedoorn, 1869, may have been the one now in Brussels (Copy 3).

3. Lucas's composition seems to have influenced another early seventeenth-century artist. Jan Muller's drawing of a couple in Constanz represents two figures in similar poses. While the man offers the ring, however, the young woman reaches for his purse. See Reznicek, 1956, pp. 100 (fig. 22) and 114 (no. 20), and Chapter 3 above.

4. The panel in Antwerp (Copy 1) is essentially the same in size and composition but less well painted. The clumsy modeling flattens the figures, and the harsh outlines and hard drapery folds also indicate that it is the work of a copyist. Like Copies 2–4 it shows more of the man's sleeve at the bottom and less of the scene at the sides. The colors are so similar to those in Strasbourg (e.g., the salmon-red bodice and gold inner sleeve of the woman) that the copyist must have known either the original or another painted version. The women's necklaces are different: a thin, black, beaded chain tucked into the bodice in the Strasbourg version and a thicker, more ropelike necklace in the Antwerp panel (cf. the combination of two necklaces, one a cross pendant and the other a heavier, beaded strand, in *The Betrothal* in the Morris Collection, London [Cat. C45; Fig. 28]).

5. There is a difference of opinion about whether the Strasbourg panel was originally larger (see the listing of Exhibitions). Filedt Kok's recent examination revealed that it was cut along the top and bottom (1978, p. 63).

6. Paris, Petit Palais, 1965–1966, p. 143. For Lucas's use of the flattened arch, see *Jacob Buying Esau's Birthright* in the Louvre and *Emperor Maximilian* in the Fondation Custodia, Paris (Kloek, 1978, pp. 442–43 [no. 7], 452–53 [no. 23]). This arch is not used elsewhere by Frisius, and none of his other prints after Lucas (Figs. 31, 47) has a frame like the one shown here. Copies 2–4 are narrower than the painting, with the composition cropped slightly at the left but more substantially at the right.

7. Wegner, 1959, p. 8; see also Leiden, Stedelijk Museum, 1978, no. 3, and Brown, 1978, p. 782, for an early dating.

8. See Chapter 3 for the painting's relationship to such prints as *The Promenade* (B.144), *Young Couple* (B.148), *Fool Kissing a Woman* (B.150), and the woodcut *Tavern Scene* (B.20). Filedt Kok, 1978, p. 63, Vos, 1978a, pp. 111–12, and Parshall, 1978–1979, p. 52, have all recently dated the painting to the late 1520s.

9. Filedt Kok, 1978, p. 63.

10. Filedt Kok, 1979, p. 511, no. 3, mentions that the painting was poorly received by a number of scholars at the 1978 exhibition in Leiden. He attributes

this to the dirty varnish, to certain restorations in the faces, and to the fact that the work was exhibited behind glass. Filedt Kok, 1978, p. 167, n. 119, describes the paint as generally well preserved, with only minor retouching. See Brown, 1978, p. 782, for the suggestion of overpainting alterations.

Cat. C45. *The Betrothal*

1. Both the signature and date are apparently a later addition; see Paris, Petit Palais, 1965–1966, p. 143, and Vos, 1978a, p. 111.

2. The banderole was revealed during a cleaning of the panel sometime before 1943. Several faulty translations of the inscription have appeared, beginning with Hobhouse, 1959, no. 5. Although he correctly associated it with the closest English proverb—marry in haste, repent at leisure—his German translation has a slightly different meaning: "besser als hastig getraut das lange reut" (lengthy regret is better than hasty marriage). In the exhibition in Nottingham, Midland Counties Art Museum, 1945, p. 5, the translation has a meaning opposite to that intended: "It is better to be married now than to be sorry for a long time." See Paris, Petit Palais, 1965–1966, p. 143, for a similar misreading.

3. Parshall, 1974, p. 100, mentions a copy in the Musée des Beaux-Arts, Dijon, but the museum staff has no knowledge of any such painting (correspondence, January 26, 1981).

4. It has been suggested that the background of the panel in Strasbourg (Fig. 26) is overpainted and that a cleaning would reveal a similar inscription; Brown, 1978, p. 782, and Wurfbain, 1978, p. 207. This is not the case, however, according to a recent X-radiograph; see Filedt Kok, 1978, p. 65, fig. 67, and 1979, p. 511, no. 3.

Cat. C46. *Fluteplayer*

1. For the significance of the flute, see De Mirimonde, 1967, p. 328; Winternitz, 1967, pp. 37–38, 48, 52–53; Brussels, Palais des Beaux-Arts, 1971, p. 175; Kettering, 1977, pp. 33–34; and Braunschweig, Herzog Anton Ulrich-Museum, 1978, pp. 49–50. Discussion of the lute as an erotic symbol is found in Brussels, Palais des Beaux-Arts, 1971, p. 178, and Amsterdam, Rijksmuseum, 1976b, pp. 59–61.

2. See Friedländer, 1967–1976, 10:no. 109, for the Brussels portraits.

Cats. A1 and A2. *Lot and His Daughters*

1. Nicolle, 1901, p. 192, and Edouard Michel, 1953, pp. 155–56. There is no way to know whether any of these paintings was the panel sold for forty-five francs in the sale of the Coll. Pieter Six, Amsterdam, 1703 (*Dictionnaire des Ventes d'Art Mireur* [Paris, 1911], 2:342); see also Hoet, 1752–1770, 1:74, no. 59, who

described the sale as taking place in 1704, with Lucas's painting of *Lot and His Daughters* bought for twenty-one guilders).

2. A link with the school of Patinir was noted by Held, 1966, p. 447, although he suggested the figures might have been added by Lucas. Examples of Patinir's compositional preferences include Friedländer, 1967–1976, 9b:nos. 237, 240, and 245. The variant of *Lot and His Daughters* in Maastricht has a landscape even more characteristic of Patinir. See Friedländer, 1967–1976, 9b:nos. 240–41, 243a, and 251, for the characteristic Patinir School bridge; nos. 237 and 246 for the road; nos. 241, 245, 246 for the tree stump; and no. 246 for the salamanders (and Beets, 1934, p. 55). In Patinir's Escorial painting the main figure is also probably derived from Dürer's engraving of *St. Christopher* (B.51); Friedländer, 1967–1976, 9b:105.

3. Beets, 1934, pp. 53–54, and Hoogewerff, 1936–1947, 3:237.

4. A painting of the same subject in the Detroit Institute of Arts (with a figure grouping roughly comparable to that in the Rotterdam and Paris panels) is generally associated with the Leiden school of Cornelis Engebrechtsz. It is attributed to Lucas Cornelisz. by Beets, 1935a, p. 63 and fig. 54, and Detroit, Institute of Arts, 1944, no. 13. Gibson, 1977, fig. 61, assigns it to the Master of the Vienna Lamentation.

Cat. A3. *Lot and His Daughters*

1. Beets, 1934, pp. 57–59, and Friedländer, 1963a, p. 52.

2. Davies, 1968, p. 81. This was suggested by A. E. Popham, in a letter of May 30, 1924, in the museum files, which also contain a detailed analysis of the costume (September 1954) and a conclusion that the painting should be dated between 1517 and 1522 (Davies, 1968, p. 81). For the speculation about Huygh Jacobsz., see Beets, 1934, p. 58.

Cat. A4. *Job and His Three Friends*

1. The sixteenth-century theologian Molanus described the pictorial tradition of showing Job's friends as musicians (see Bernen, 1973, p. 150).

Cat. A5. *Angel*

1. This suggestion was earlier made by Valentiner, in a letter of November 20, 1929, to Wildenstein & Co., New York (now in the museum file). Valentiner attributed the panel to Gossaert in his early period.

Cat. A6. *Adoration of the Magi*

1. I studied the underdrawing on November 21, 1979, with the help of the museum staff. We used an Infrared Vidicon Television System, with an 87C Red

Filter and two quartz lamps. For underdrawing in the Berlin and Rotterdam panels, see Filedt Kok, 1978, figs. 6–10, 17–23.

2. Friedländer, 1963a, p. 50, and Held, 1966, p. 447, also attribute it to this artist.

3. In 1928, Friedländer believed the panel was painted by Lucas but that the composition derived from a lost painting by Gerard David. In 1930, he suggested that the intermediary was a manuscript illumination from Bruges. No specific source is known.

4. Friedländer, 1967–1976, 6b:no. 182, and 11:no. 127; see also 6b:no. 181A, for a similar arrangement of the main figures in a miniature from the Breviary of Isabella of Spain. The placement of the four figures, from Joseph to the eldest Magus, is similar to that in Dürer's woodcut *Adoration* (B.87), although reversed. See Hoogewerff, 1936–1947, 3:233.

5. Friedländer, 1967–1976, 10:51, noted a general relationship between the two works; see his pl. 55, for a reproduction.

6. Van Mander, 1604, fols. 217r–v. See Gibson, 1977, pp. 203–4, for a discussion of the paintings mentioned by Van Mander. Whether the Chicago *Adoration* is by Gibson's "Hand A" is difficult to judge from photographs. Bulbous-nosed figures in the right foreground of the Chicago panel compare with those in the *Disrobing of Christ* in New York, the *Crucifixion* in Amsterdam, and the *Descent from the Cross* formerly in the Petri Collection (Gibson's figs. 41–43). But Gibson describes the application of paint by "Hand A" as looser, citing details of the hair.

Cat. A7. *Adoration of the Magi*

1. There is no evidence that the painting was formerly in a private collection in Paris, as Friedländer says (1930, p. 498).

2. Held, 1966, p. 447. See also Filedt Kok, 1978, p. 161, n. 71; Vos, 1978a, pp. 32–33; and Renger, 1979, p. 58.

3. This was suggested by Friedländer, 1963a, pp. 54–55, although he attributed the *Adoration* and *Last Supper* to Lucas and associated *Feeding of the Five Thousand* with Lucas's workshop, ca. 1512. Filedt Kok, 1978, p. 161, n. 71, also saw similarities between this *Adoration* and the *Last Supper*. This triptych in the Suermondt Museum, Aachen, inv. no. 273, represents the *Last Supper* (central panel 57 x 44), with *Christ between Peter and John* on the left wing and *Christ Washing the Feet of Peter* on the right (57 x 18 each). It has been associated with Lucas's workshop in several publications (e.g., Friedländer, 1963a, p. 55, and Grimme, 1963, pp. 208–9). See also Friedländer, 1967–1976, 10:81, no. 112; Held, 1966, p. 447; and Filedt Kok, 1978, p. 161, n. 71. Bangs points to a passage in Buchelius's diary from 1638 referring to a painting of the *Last Supper* then in Wittevrouwen and attributed to Lucas (Van Campen, 1940, pp. 71–72). The work in Aachen may have been the painting seen by Buchelius, although his description is unfortunately too general.

The triptych of the *Feeding of the Five Thousand* is in the Mittelrhein-Museum, Koblenz, inv. no. 1968/67 (center panel 76 x 44.5, wings 76 x 18.5). Its provenance is complex: found in Koblenz, 1933; Schloss Museum, Koblenz; stolen during World War II (correspondence with Dr. Kurt Eitelbach, Mittelrhein-Museum, December 22, 1980); with H. M. Schoenemann, New York, 1949-1950; Bob Jones University Collection of Sacred Art, Greenville, S.C. (as Lucas; see the catalogues of 1954, pp. 94-97, and 1962, 3:236-39, no. 131); sale Duke of Northumberland and others, London (Sotheby), March 27, 1968, no. 40 (as Lucas), withdrawn from sale and purchased by the Koblenz museum (see *Het Vaderland,* May 1, 1968, p. 11). It was exhibited in Rotterdam, Museum Boymans–van Beuningen, 1936, no. 89, as by Lucas or from his circle. See also Hoogewerff, 1936-1947, 3:377-79; Friedländer, 1963a, p. 55; Held, 1966, p. 447; and Friedländer, 1967-1976, 10:87, supp. 167.

4. A later date for the triptych in Koblenz is supported by comparison with Lucas's paintings from the 1520s. The framing of the scene with seated figures in the foreground corners is found in *Moses after Striking the Rock,* Boston (Fig. 24, Cat. 7), the *Dance around the Golden Calf,* Amsterdam (Fig. 32, Cat. 11), and *Christ Healing the Blind Man* in Leningrad (Fig. 35, Cat. 25). It is unlikely that the similarities between the seated woman with her child in the central panel in Koblenz and those in a comparable location in Lucas's paintings in Boston and Leningrad are merely coincidental. The group was almost certainly inspired by Lucas's model.

5. Noted by Van Regteren Altena, 1955, p. 111. See also Vos, 1978a, p. 32, figs. 38-39.

6. Dirck was born ca. 1475 and was a painter by 1507. For more information about him, see Bangs, 1979a, pp. 6, 49, 88, 94, and 108. A triptych in Leiden of the *Virgin in Glory* has been attributed to Dirck by Van Brussel, Moerman, and Wurfbain, 1978, p. 4. The paintings in Merion, Aachen, and Koblenz are stylistically unrelated to the *Virgin in Glory;* until more is known concerning Lucas's brother, attribution of these works to him is speculative.

Cat. A8. *Salome Receiving the Head of St. John the Baptist*

1. The wings (36 x 14.3) were added later and are painted with Latin inscriptions referring to the beheading of the saint; see Friedländer, 1967-1976, 10:83.

2. Hoogewerff, 1936-1947, 3:232; Reznicek-Buriks, 1965, p. 245, who also related the woman in profile to one in Lucas's engraving the *Temptation of St. Anthony* (B.117); and Tschudi, 1893, p. 109.

3. For the crossed arms and stance of the executioner see Rogier van der Weyden's *St. John Altarpiece* in Berlin (Panofsky, 1971b, 2:pl. 205) and the exterior of Hans Memling's *Virgin Enthroned* in Bruges (Friedländer, 1967-1976, 6a:no. 11). Beets, 1913, pp. 82-83, and Conway, 1921, p. 474, mention the Flemish influence, with emphasis on that of Antwerp.

This work has similarities with an Antwerp School drawing of the same subject in the Berlin Kupferstichkabinett (see Bock and Rosenberg, 1930, 1:60, no. 4350). The executioner is a mirror image of the man in Philadelphia, down to the placement of his sword. Salome stands at the right, also in profile. The body of John the Baptist is at the left behind the executioner, with crossed arms and legs that are bent beneath him (although in the drawing the saint is kneeling more than in the painting). Hoogewerff, 1936–1947, 3:232, connects the panel with a composition by the Cologne Master of St. Severin, but the only similarity is in the upper torso of the saint (Brockmann, 1924, pl. 4).

Cat. A9. *Salome with the Head of St. John the Baptist*

1. As noted by Dülberg, 1933, p. 8, this painting may have influenced the half-length representation by Jacob Cornelisz., dated 1524 and now in the Rijksmuseum (on loan from the Mauritshuis; Friedländer, 1967–1976, 12:no. 284).
2. Beets, 1940, pp. 43–44.
3. Beets, 1935b, pp. 197–98.

Cat. A10. *St. Jerome Penitent*

1. Filedt Kok, 1978, pp. 127–28. His study of the underdrawing, visible in the drapery with infrared-reflectography, shows the hatching to be longer and flatter than that characteristic of Lucas. A dendrochronological study showed that the tree from which the panel was made was cut ca. 1512, plus or minus five years (information from the museum). See Filedt Kok, 1978, p. 137, who mentions that the panels for Lucas's *Last Judgment* of 1526 (Figs. 17–19, Cat. 20) were taken from trees felled between 1500 and 1510.

Cat. A11. *St. Paul*

1. There is no similarity to the woodcut mentioned by Winkler; see Geisberg, 1974, 1:no. 93.
2. See Rotterdam, Museum Boymans–van Beuningen, 1936, p. 44 (and figs. 17, 98, and 143, for comparable half- or three-quarter-length representations of Paul from the northern Netherlands).
3. This information is from the museum report by M. Kroning, December 28, 1976, in which James Burke, former curator of prints and drawings at the museum, suggested the panel was a fragment of a larger work. This point was made by Friedländer, 1967–1976, 10:87, and Indianapolis, John Herron Art Institute, 1950, no. 46. See Cats. 27–28 for discussion of other representations of standing saints that appear to have been cut down at a later date.
4. Parshall, 1978–1979, p. 53.

5. Compare the similar, although much finer, drawing style around the eyes and in the hands of Lucas's *St. Jerome* in the Ashmolean Museum, Oxford (pen and brush in brown and gray, white highlighting, black chalk, and a blue background; Kloek, 1978, p. 449, no. 19). Paul's furrowed brow, slitted eyes, and sidelong glance are also seen in one of the apostles to the right of Christ in the Leiden triptych, the fourth from the left.

Hoogewerff, 1936–1947, 3:285, also noted similarities between this painting and the figures on the exterior of *Last Judgment*. See also the sword in Lucas's engraving of *Peter and Paul* (B.106), dated 1527.

Cat. A12. *Portrait of Claes van Isendoren*

1. This information was found on a piece of paper attached to the back of the panel. Amsterdam, Goudstikker, 1928, no. 22, dates the paper to the period of the French Revolution.

2. The full name is universally accepted as Claes van Isendoren or Isendoorn, even though part of the last embroidered word is covered by the collar of the cloak. I did not see this painting in person, and my stylistic analysis is based on a photograph.

3. For the *Portrait of a Man*, black chalk, Stedelijk Museum "De Lakenhal," Leiden, see Kloek, 1978, p. 446, no. 13. Filedt Kok has shown that even with the use of infrared reflectography there is no underdrawing visible in Lucas's Braunschweig *Portrait* (Fig. 14, Cat. 32) and only a very summary use of chalk lines in the London panel (Fig. 10, Cat. 31). He mentions the paucity of underdrawing in northern Netherlandish portraits of this period. Exceptions include the rather sparse lines in some portraits by Jan van Scorel, as well as the much more detailed brush lines in the face of the donor in Lucas's Munich diptych (Fig. 12, Cat. 14). See Filedt Kok, 1978, p. 58, and n. 106. Lucas's long, carefully drawn and spaced hatching has no similarity to the more delicate and irregular lines in the *Portrait of Claes van Isendoren*.

4. Baldass's second comparison with the portraits on the right of the Rijksmuseum *Sermon* (a work formerly attributed to Lucas, then to Aertgen van Leyden, and now generally assigned to an anonymous master) is even less valid. These rapidly painted, loosely brushed heads are far removed in style and technique from this portrait.

Cat. A13. *Portrait of a Man*

1. Lubbers was founder of the Ubbena hospital (actually a home for the aged) in the early sixteenth century. There is no proof for this traditional identification. According to the museum curator, Lies Boiten, the frame is original and has an inscription that is now barely legible: ". . . Van Eye e . . ."

2. Friedländer, 1963a, p. 53, also described the Groningen portrait as close in conception and technique to the portrait in Lugano, which he accepted as an original Lucas.

Cat. A14. *Portrait of a Man Aged 25*

1. According to *Connoisseur,* 1954, the frame is original. See also Stuttgart, Staatsgalerie, 1958–1959, p. 47, where the date is read as "151(?)9(?)."
2. The measurements of 42 x 30.5 given at the sale probably include the frame. In *Connaissance des Arts,* 1957, no. 66, the panel is listed as selling for 1,440,000 francs at the Charpentier auction. The names *Rheims* and *Lebel* included in this entry may refer to buyers.
3. Friedländer certified the painting in Amsterdam on August 20, 1953, and Valentiner in Los Angeles on April 11, 1954 (*Connoisseur,* 1954).

Cat. A15. *Portrait of a Man*

1. This painting was not studied in person.
2. *Burlington Magazine* 95 (1953): 33–34.

Cats. A16 and A17. *Portrait of a Man in a Red Hat* and *Portrait of a Man in a Three-Cornered Hat*

1. Panel, in a diamond shape, 23 x 23; see Hoogewerff, 1936–1947, 3:382 and fig. 206, and Gibson, 1977, n. 102 (who considers the Beets panel the only possible portrait by Lucas Cornelisz.). The misshapen face of this portrait (resulting from a misunderstanding of facial structure and of spatial relationships) is quite different from the finely painted panels in the Six collection.

Cat. A18. *Portrait of a Woman*

1. This drawing (36.4 x 33) is in black and red chalk, with the background in brown wash; Kloek, 1978, p. 447, no. 15. Baldass, 1937b, pp. 206–7, observed a similarity to one of the women in Lucas's Berlin *Chess Players* (Fig. 1, Cat. 34), but the facial characteristics have only the most superficial resemblance and even the headdresses are different.
2. Several *pentimenti* are easily visible along the contour of the woman's chin, both to the right and the left.

Cat. A19. *Fortuna*

1. Beets, 1935b, p. 197.

Appendix

1. Rupprich, 1956, 1:174, and Van Mander, 1604, fol. 212v.

2. "Jch hab maister Lucas von Leÿden mit dem stefft conterfet" (I made a portrait of Master Lucas in silverpoint); Rupprich, 1956, 1:174. The drawing in Lille, measuring 24.4 x 17.1, is signed with Dürer's monogram in the upper center and is now in the Musée des Beaux-Arts, Lille; see Winkler, 1936, p. 38, no. 816; Strauss, 1974, 4:2046, no. 1521/26; and Brussels, Palais des Beaux-Arts, 1977, p. 76, no. 82. Evrard, 1884, pp. 9–10, 795–97, presents a confused discussion of the various portraits of Lucas, in which he says that Dürer's drawing is a portrait of Jacopo de Barbari, not Lucas.

3. For Dürer's notations of name or occupation, see, e.g., Brussels, Palais des Beaux-Arts, 1977, pp. 69–73, nos. 62, 65, 66, 72, 73. In Lampsonius's *Pictorum Aliquot Celebrium Germaniae Inferioris Effigies* (Antwerp, 1572), no. 10 is entitled *Lucae Leidano Pictori*. The engraving is in reverse, and wider, showing more of the sleeves. There is also more detail in the lower section; the sitter's right hand is introduced, holding what appears to be a glove (Dülberg, 1899c, p. 79). A smaller copy of the Lille drawing, also in silverpoint, is in the Musée des Beaux-Arts, Rennes; Ephrussi, 1882, p. 309, n. 1, considers it a preparatory sketch by the late sixteenth-century engraver. This print was mentioned by Bullart, 1682, p. 398, as a self-portrait. The first modern scholar to publish the Lille drawing as Dürer's portrait of Lucas was Hymans, 1877, pp. 177–80. See Dülberg, 1899c, p. 79, for this inscription.

4. See Vos, 1978a, p. 19, and 1978b, p. 2; also Van Someren, 1888–1891, 2:412, no. 3352. Riegel, 1882, 2:148–49, describes it as similar in facial structure to the Braunschweig portrait. Only Dülberg, 1899c, p. 80, connects this engraving with the earlier print of 1572, although he accepts the sitter's age as thirty-seven. Kloek, 1978, p. 429, suggests it is a copy after a lost portrait drawing by Lucas, comparable to the group from 1521.

5. Colvin, 1882, p. 134. See Cat. 32, Copy 6, for the complete Latin inscription and for a later dating of ca. 1525–1527.

6. Müller-Hofstede, 1959, p. 231. Cf. Beets, 1940, p. 8, who comments on the striking similarity between the two portraits; also Dülberg, 1899c, p. 79, and Winkler, 1936, p. 38, no. 816. Bock, 1910, dates the panel to shortly after 1510, stating that it must be separated from the Lille drawing by at least a decade. Gleadowe, 1922, p. 180, also notes the remarkable change in appearance from the youth of 1509 to the young man of 1521. See also Goris and Marlier, 1937, p. xxxi.

7. Conway, 1921, p. 465, measured the proportions of the facial features. He showed that the Braunschweig painting and the Lille drawing, as well as a black-chalk drawing in the British Museum that has also been called a portrait of Lucas by Dürer (see below), are all of different men.

8. See Cat. 32 for a discussion of Stock's unreliability as a source and for the dating ca. 1525–1527. The brush drawing by Rubens in the Fondation Custodia (Cat. 32, Copy 2) is probably a modified copy of Stock's engraving rather than a

direct copy of the painting. The most obvious reason for this conclusion is the use of an oval frame by both seventeenth-century artists (Müller-Hofstede, 1959, pp. 236–37, discusses the drawing in detail). The sketch by Rubens is evidence of Lucas's renown a century after his death, as Müller-Hofstede noted, but it can in no way be considered proof that the representation was a portrait of Lucas.

9. Those who use the direct glance to identify this as a self-portrait include Colvin, 1882, p. 134; Dülberg, 1899c, p. 77; and Friedländer, 1967–1976, 10:47. For Dürer's self-portraits of this type, see Panofsky, 1971a, figs. 25–26, 30, and 109–10. Joos van Cleve's painting in the Coll. Thyssen-Bornemisza has been verified as a self-portrait by comparison with figures in the background of two paintings of the *Adoration of the Magi*, both in Dresden (compare Friedländer, 1967–1976, 9a:no. 70 with nos. 27 and 28). Jacob Cornelisz.'s *Self-Portrait* in the Rijksmuseum (12:no. 289), dated 1533, has been described as dependent on Lucas's portrait (Müller-Hofstede, 1959, p. 234). The similarities are striking, and one wonders whether Jacob would have based his painting so closely on a work that he knew was not a self-portrait (see Amsterdam, Rijksmuseum, 1958, p. 101, no. 111). His panel is a fragment of a larger composition, in which he is seated before his easel. See a copy in Toledo, dated 1530 (Friedländer, 1967–1976, 12:no. 289, and p. 119).

10. This drawing is attributed to Dürer by Winkler, 1936, p. 35, no. 809 (who doubts that these traces are original), and Strauss, 1974, 4:2052, no. 1521/30.

11. For an illustration of this etched copy, see Vos, 1978a, fig. 4, and Lavalleye, 1967, no. 157. The work was accepted as an original by Bartsch, 1803–1821, 7:433, no. 173; Riegel, 1882, 2:146 (who identified the inscription as a seventeenth-century addition); and Colvin, 1882, pp. 134–35. By the early twentieth century, the etching was no longer thought to be by Lucas, nor the drawing a portrait of him; e.g., Conway, 1921, p. 465. Vos, 1978a, p. 12, notes that the only known impressions of the etching are on seventeenth-century paper. A stained-glass window in the Rijksmuseum has a full-length portrait of Lucas—holding a palette and brush—made by W. F. Dixon in 1884, using this print as a model for the head (Vos, 1978a, p. 20 and fig. 21).

12. Vos, 1978a, pp. 17, 19. Galle's work was entitled *Illustrium Quos Belgium Habuit Pictorum Effigies;* see no. 10 for the portrait of Lucas.

13. For Coecke van Aelst's work, see Friedländer, 1967–1976, 12:no. 84. See also the *Portrait of a Man* (Brukenthal Museum, Sibiu) by the Master of the Legend of St. Augustine (6b:add. 290), where the sitter points to the skull half-hidden under his cloak much in the manner of Lucas's figure, and Dirck Jacobsz.'s *Portrait of Pompejus Occo*, ca. 1531, in the Rijksmuseum (13:no. 414). The observation about Hondius's publication, entitled *Pictorum Aliquot Celebrum Praecipue Germaniae Inferioris Effigies* (Some portraits of famous, distinguished painters from the Netherlands), was made by Vos, 1978c, p. 493, n. 65.

14. Van Mander's reference is on fol. 212v. See also Bullart, 1682, p. 398. A

painted variant of Lucas's engraving was exhibited in Amsterdam, Rijksmuseum, 1952, p. 42, no. 86, as a *Portrait of a Man* (on loan from the Coll. H. A. Wetzlar, Amsterdam). Van Hall, 1963, p. 186, no. 4, describes a painted oval self-portrait by Lucas from 1523, apparently not the same as above, in which the artist's hand rests on a skull (cited in the sale J. A. Brentano, Amsterdam, May 13, 1822, no. 191). See also Evrard, 1884, p. 797, who mentioned a painting of a young man with a skull in the Coll. Denon.

15. Bruyn, 1960, gave it to Aertgen; Bangs, 1979a, ch. 13, removed it from Aertgen's oeuvre; and Amsterdam, Rijksmuseum, 1986, 2:44–45, no. 44, assigned it the Master of the Sermon, ca. 1530–1535. Friedländer, 1963a, p. 8, among others, identified the man as a self-portrait, and Hoogewerff, 1936–1947, 3:261, went one step further and identified the men in the group as Lucas, Cornelis Engebrechtsz., and Cornelis's three sons. The entry in Amsterdam, Rijksmuseum, 1986, 2:no. 44, describes these six men as donors. Those who attribute it to Aertgen identify the self-portrait as the man with a mustache (also looking out at the viewer) seated at the rear of the foreground group. See Müller-Hofstede, 1959, pp. 232–34, Bruyn, 1960, pp. 61–63, and Friedländer, 1963a, p. 8. On the other hand, Hudig, 1934, p. 66, and Van Gils, 1946, p. 70, have attributed the painting to Lucas and see the seated man with a mustache as a self-portrait.

16. For the Berlin *Virgin and Child,* see Riegel, 1900, p. 110. As Dülberg, 1899c, p. 82, observed, the extreme youth of the figure in this painting can scarcely be reconciled with Lucas's age at the time the work was painted. For the *Last Judgment,* see Lafenestre and Richtenberger, 1894–1907, pp. 171–72, and Dülberg, 1899c, p. 82, and for *Moses,* Von der Osten and Vey, 1969, p. 178 (it is not clear which figure he means). For *Christ Healing the Blind Man,* see Nikulin, 1964.

17. There are a few "portraits" of Lucas that I do not treat here. Bock, 1910, p. 406, singles out a man in the background of *Christ Crowned with Thorns* (B.69) because of his frontal stance, his glance outward, and what Bock sees as a general resemblance to Dürer's silverpoint drawing (cf. Pelinck, 1949, p. 194). Müller-Hofstede, 1959, p. 232, has drawn attention to three figures in Lucas's engravings with the same facial characteristics as the Braunschweig portrait: the man second from the left in *Four Soldiers,* ca. 1507 (B.141), the kneeling man in *Susanna and the Elders,* ca. 1508 (B.33), and the seated man with a jug at the extreme right of the *Dance of the Magdalene,* 1519 (B.122). He is careful to add that these figures cannot be considered true self-portraits. Finally, another figure in roughly the same pose appears in two early engravings from 1507–1508 (B.27, 147). Since one wears a purse around his waist decorated with the monogram *L,* both have been called self-portraits. See Beets, 1913, p. 27, and Pelinck, 1949, pp. 194–95. Vos, 1978a, p. 22, fig. 27, reproduces a lithograph from ca. 1850 by David van der Kellen, *The Last Days of Lucas van Leyden,* in which the likeness of Lucas is modeled after the torchbearer in B.147.

The drawings of the *Standing Boy with a Sword* in the Rijksmuseum Prentenkabinet and the *Standing Young Man* in the collection of Rugby School have also been identified as portraits of the artist by Dülberg, 1899c, p. 78 (Ring, 1912–1913, p. 113, refutes this); Baldass, 1937b; Beets, 1940, p. 6; Müller-Hofstede, 1959, p. 232; and Friedländer, 1963a, p. 74. See Kloek, 1978, pp. 439–40, nos. 3 (black chalk, 25.2 x 18.5) and 4 (black chalk, 30 x 18). Dülberg, 1899c, p. 78, also sees a self-portrait in the British Museum drawing of *Two Allegorical Figures Seated upon a Sphere* (Kloek, 1978, no. 20; silverpoint, 27.6 x 20.3).

See also: (1) *Portrait of a Man* in the Uffizi, once attributed to Lucas as a self-portrait (e.g., Michiels, 1847, p. 135, no. 88, and Riegel, 1882, 2:149) but exhibited since 1908 as a portrait by Bernardino dei Conti (Van Hall, 1963, p. 186, no. 9); (2) *Portrait of a Man at a Table* (sold by Sotheby, May 6, 1970, no. 8), called a self-portrait in *L'Art et les Artistes,* 1921 (see also Van Hall, 1963, p. 186, no. 7). This is certainly a later copy after a drawing by Lucas in the Louvre (Kloek, 1978, p. 448, no. 18, and Paris, Petit Palais, 1965–1966, p. 36, no. 71). See Kramm, 4:975, and Dülberg, 1899c, pp. 82–83, for others.

The most complete discussions of this subject are in Dülberg, 1899c, pp. 77–83; Bock, 1910; Van Hall, 1963, pp. 186–87, 385; and Vos, 1978a, pp. 16–23 (also 1978b and 1978c, pp. 492–93, nn. 63 and 65).

BIBLIOGRAPHY

Note: Museum and exhibition catalogues are listed alphabetically by author or by city and museum. Unless indicated otherwise, the place of publication of catalogues can be assumed to be the same as the location of the exhibition.

A., D. P. 1955. "Ein Lucas van Leyden für Codex Aureus." *Die Weltkunst* 25 (February 15): 11.
A., J. 1951. "L'Exposition au Petit-Palais, des Tableaux des Musées de Berlin." *Aesculape* 32 (April): 89–95.
Aachen, Suermondt Museum. 1902. *Führer durch das Suermondt Museum der Stadt Aachen.*
———. 1932. *Gemälde-Katalog.*
Adriani, Gert. 1976. *Braunschweig, Herzog Anton Ulrich-Museum, Verzeichnis der Gemälde.* Braunschweig.
Amsterdam, Goudstikker. 1928. *XXV Catalogue of the Goudstikker Collection.* Exhibition catalogue.
———. 1930. *Catalogue des Nouvelles Acquisitions de la Collection Goudstikker.* Exhibition catalogue.
———. 1936–1937. *Catalogue of the Goudstikker Collection.* Exhibition catalogue.
Amsterdam, P. De Boer. 1936. *Catalogus van Oude Schilderijen, Nieuwe Aanwinsten.* Exhibition catalogue.
———. 1937. *Catalogue de Tableaux Anciens.* Exhibition catalogue.
———. 1948. *Tentoonstelling van Oude Schilderijen.* Exhibition catalogue.
Amsterdam, Rijksmuseum. 1900. *Catalogus der Verzameling Schilderijen en Familie-*

Portretten van de Heeren Jhr. P. H. Six van Vromade, Jhr. Dr. J. Six en Jhr. W. Six. Exhibition catalogue.

———. 1905. *Catalogue of the Pictures.*

———. 1929. *Catalogus van de Tentoonstelling van Oude Kunst.* Exhibition catalogue.

———. 1939. *Bijbelse Kunst.* Exhibition catalogue.

———. 1948. *Meesterwerken uit de Oude Pinacotheek te München.* Exhibition catalogue.

———. 1950. *120 Beroemde Schilderijen uit het Kaiser-Friedrich-Museum te Berlijn.* Exhibition catalogue.

———. 1951. *Catalogus van de Tentoongestelde Schilderijen Pastels en Aquarellen.*

———. 1952. *Drie eeuwen portret in Nederland, 1500–1800.* Exhibition catalogue.

———. 1956. *Catalogus van de Tentoongestelde Schilderijen Pastels en Aquarellen.*

———. 1958. *Middeleeuwse Kunst der Noordelijke Nederlanden.* Exhibition catalogue.

———. 1976a. *All the Paintings of the Rijksmuseum in Amsterdam.*

———. 1976b. *Tot Lering en Vermaak: Betekenissen van Hollandse genre-voorstellingen uit de zeventiende eeuw.* Exhibition catalogue.

———. 1986. *Kunst voor de Beeldenstorm.* 2 vols. Exhibition catalogue.

Amsterdam, Rijksprentenkabinet. 1978. *Lucas van Leyden-grafiek.* Exhibition catalogue by J. P. Filedt Kok.

———. 1985. *Livelier than Life: The Master of the Amsterdam Cabinet or the Housebook Master.* Compiled by J. P. Filedt Kok. Exhibition catalogue.

Antonucci, Giovanni. 1929. "La Leggenda di Susanna nella Tradizione Giuridica e nella Iconografia. I. Il Proceso di Susanna." *Emporium* 70 (July): 2–10.

Antwerp, Koninklijk Kunstverbond. 1927. *Teekeningen en Prenten van Antwerpsche Meesters der XVIIe eeuw.* Exhibition catalogue.

Antwerp, Musée d'Anvers. 1849. *Catalogue.*

Antwerp, Musée Royal des Beaux-Arts. 1905. *Catalogue descriptif, I: Maîtres anciens.*

———. 1958. *Catalogue descriptif: Maîtres anciens.*

Anzelewsky, Fedja. 1971. *Albrecht Dürer: Das Malerische Werk.* Berlin.

Armstrong, Christine M. 1990. *The Moralizing Prints of Cornelis Anthonisz.* Princeton.

Artaud, Antonin. 1960. "La Mise en Scène et la Métaphysique." *L'Arc* 3 (Spring): 85–88.

L'Art et les Artistes. 1921. "Une intéressante découverte artistique: un portrait présumé de Lucas de Leyde." 3:291–92.

Art News. 1935. "Tomas Harris Galleries Show Flemish Art." 33 (July): 3, 13.

———. 1955. "Entering the Public's Domain." 54 (December): 46.

Art Quarterly. 1955. "'Moses Striking Water from the Rock' by Lucas van Leyden in the Museum of Fine Arts, Boston." 18:314–16.

Augustine. 1950. *The City of God.* Translated by Marcus Dodds. New York.
Baldass, Ludwig. 1923. *Die Gemälde des Lucas van Leyden.* Vienna.
———. 1923–1925. "Sittenbild und Stilleben im Rahmen des niederländischen Romanismus." *Jahrbuch der Kunsthistorischen Sammlungen in Wien* 36: 15–46.
———. 1936. "Die frühholländische Ausstellung in Rotterdam." *Pantheon* 18:252–57.
———. 1937a. "Die Niederländischen Maler des Spätgotischen Stiles." *Jahrbuch der Kunsthistorischen Sammlungen in Wien* 11:117–38.
———. 1937b. "Die Bildnisse des Lukas van Leyden." *Pantheon* 20:205–9.
Bange, E. F. 1949. *Die Deutschen Bronzestatuetten des 16. Jahrhunderts.* Berlin.
Bangs, Jeremy D. 1972. "The Furnishings of the Pieterskerk, Leiden, from before the Reformation." Master's thesis, Rijksuniversiteit, Leiden.
———. 1974a. "Letter to the Editor." *Art Bulletin* 56:309.
———. 1974b. "The Sixteenth-Century Organ of the Pieterskerk, Leiden." *Oud-Holland* 88:220–31.
———. 1975. "Letter to the Editor." *Art Bulletin* 57:148–49.
———. 1976. "Documentary Studies in Leiden Art and Crafts, 1475–1575." Ph.D. dissertation, Rijksuniversiteit, Leiden.
———. 1977. "Further Adventures of Jan Zevertsz., Bookprinter and Parchment-maker of Leiden." *Quaerendo* 7:116–27.
———. 1979a. *Cornelis Engebrechtsz.'s Leiden.* Assen.
———. 1979b. "Reconsidering Lutheran Book Trade: The So-called 'Winkelkasboek' of Pieter Claesz. van Balen." *Quaerendo* 9:227–60.
———. 1980. Review of Vos, 1978a; Amsterdam, Rijksprentenkabinet, 1978; and *Lucas van Leyden Studies, Nederlands Kunsthistorisch Jaarboek* 29 (1978). *Sixteenth Century Journal* 11:91–97.
———. 1985. "The Leiden Pieterskerk West End, 1512–1637: Aspects of Rebuilding and Change." *Bulletin KNOB* 84 (February): 1–15.
Barnes, Albert C. 1937. *The Art in Painting.* 3d ed. New York.
Bartlett, Vernon. 1969. *The Past of Pastimes.* London.
Bartsch, Adam. 1803–1821. *Le Peintre Graveur.* 21 vols. Vienna.
Basel, Kunstmuseum. 1945. *Meisterwerke Holländischer Malerei des 16. bis 18. Jahrhunderts.* Exhibition catalogue.
———. 1974. *Lukas Cranach.* Exhibition catalogue.
Baumgart, Fritz. 1939. "Der Falschspieler Caravaggios." *Das Werk des Künstlers* 1:482–524.
Beets, N. 1908. "De aan Jan van Scorel toegeschreven Warmenhuizer Gewelfschilderingen." *Bulletin van den Nederlandschen Oudheidkundigen Bond,* series 2, 1:62–70.

———. 1910. "De bestellers van Lucas van Leyden's 'Genezing van den blinde van Jericho.'" *Oud-Holland* 28:155-60.

———. 1911. "Ontleeningen IV: Cornelis Engebrechtsz. en Albrecht Dürer." *Bulletin van den Nederlandschen Oudheidkundigen Bond,* series 2, 4:8-12.

———. 1912a. "Lucas van Leyden's Laatste Oordeel in de Laekenhal te Leiden." *Elsevier's Geillustreerd Maandschrift* 22:213-16.

———. 1912b. "Dirck Jacobsz. Vellert. Peintre Anversois. IV. Dessins Posterieurs à 1520." *L'Art Flamand & Hollandais* 18:129-48.

———. 1913. *Lucas de Leyde.* Paris and Brussels.

———. 1914. "De Tentoonstelling van Noord-Nederlandsche Schilder- en Beeldhouw-kunst voor 1575." *Onze Kunst* 13:41-62.

———. 1934. "Zestiende-eeuwsche Kunstenaars. III. Lucas van Leyde." *Oud-Holland* 51:49-59, 151-62, 190-209.

———. 1935a. "Zestiende-eeuwsche Kunstenaars. IV. Lucas Corneliszoon de Kock." *Oud-Holland* 52:49-76, 159-73, 217-28.

———. 1935b. "Een Geschilderde Naaktfiguur van Lucas van Leyden." *Maandblad voor Beeldende Kunsten* 12:194-202.

———. 1936. "Alberto Dürer, Luca di Leida e Marcantonio Raimondi; un triumvirato nel regno dell'incisione." *Maso Finiguerra* 1:149-59.

———. 1940. *Lucas van Leyden.* Amsterdam.

———. 1952a. "De Dans om het gouden kalf, een hervonden triptiek van Lucas van Leyden." *Oud-Holland* 67:183-99.

———. 1952b. "Rijksmuseum verwerft een Lucas van Leyden." *Algemeen Handelsblad* 125 (September 23): 5.

———. 1954. "De Noordnederlandse Schilderkunst in de zestiende eeuw." In *Kunstgeschiedenis der Nederlanden,* vol. 1, edited by H. E. Van Gelder and J. Duverger. 3d ed. Utrecht.

Bégule, Lucien, and Émile Bertaux. 1906. "Un vitrail profane du XVe Siècle." *Gazette des Beaux-Arts* 36:407-16.

Behling, Lottlisa. 1957. *Die Pflanze in der Mittelalterlichen Tafelmalerei.* Weimar.

Benesch, Otto. 1928. *Beschreibender Katalog der Handzeichnungen in der graphischen Sammlung Albertina: Die Zeichnungen der niederländischen Schule des XV. und XVI. Jahrhunderts.* Vienna.

———. 1945. *The Art of the Renaissance in Northern Europe.* Cambridge, Mass.

———. 1970. "Rembrandt and the Gothic Tradition." *Collected Writings, I: Rembrandt.* New York.

Benoist, Luc. 1953. *Catalogue et Guide: Nantes, Musée des Beaux-Arts.* Nantes.

Bercovici, Konrad. 1928. *The Story of the Gypsies.* New York.

Bergström, Ingvar. 1955. "Disguised Symbolism in 'Madonna' Pictures and Still Life." *Burlington Magazine* 97:303-8, 343-49.

———. 1956. *Dutch Still-Life Painting in the Seventeenth Century.* London.
———. 1958. *Dem symboliska nejlikan i senmedeltidens och renässansens konst.* Mälmo.
Berlin, Kaiser Friedrich-Museum. 1906. *Beschreibendes Verzeichnis der Gemälde.* 6th ed.
———. 1911. *Die Gemäldegalerie des Kaiser-Friedrich-Museums.* Vol. 2.
———. 1925. *Ein Beitrag zur Geschichte des Okkultismus.* Exhibition catalogue.
Berlin, Königliche Museen. 1880. *Führer.*
———. 1883. *Beschreibendes Verzeichniss der Gemälde.* 2d ed.
———. 1891. *Beschreibendes Verzeichnis der Gemälde.* 3d ed.
Berlin, Staatliche Museen. 1931. *Beschreibendes Verzeichnis der Gemälde.* 9th ed.
———. 1978. *Catalogue of Paintings.* 2d ed.
Bernen, Satia and Robert. 1973. *A Guide to Myth and Religion in European Painting, 1270–1700.* New York.
Bersier, J. E. 1951. *L'influence de l'Italie dans la peinture hollandaise.* Paris.
Berve, Maurus. 1969. *Die Armenbibel.* Beuron.
Bialostocki, Jan. 1959. "'Opus quinque dierum': Dürer's 'Christ among the Doctors' and Its Sources." *Journal of the Warburg and Courtauld Institutes* 22:17–34.
Bianchi, Lidia. 1968. "La Fortuna di Raffaello nell' Incisione." In *Raffaello.* Novara.
Bielefeld, Deutsches Spielkarten Museum. 1972. *Wahrsagekarten.* Exhibition catalogue.
Bier, Justus. 1957. "Riemenschneider's Use of Graphic Sources." *Gazette des Beaux-Arts* 50 (October): 203–22.
Bijl, A. 1948. "Vermaarde schilders en hun nageslacht." *Nederlandsch Archief voor Genealogie en Heraldiek* 6:26–31, 54–56, 74–77, 105–9, 125–26, 152–57.
Bille, Clara. 1961. *De Tempel der Kunst of het Kabinet van den Heer Braamcamp.* Amsterdam.
Blanc, Charles. 1861. *Histoire des Peintres de Toutes les Écoles: École Hollandaise.* Paris.
Blasius, J. H. 1868. *Verzeichniss der Gemäldesammlung des Herzoglichen Museums in Braunschweig.* Braunschweig.
Bliss, Douglas Percy. 1928. "Love-Gardens in the Early German Engravings and Woodcuts." *Print Collector's Quarterly* 15:90–109.
Blok, P. J. 1884a. *Eene hollandsche Stad onder de bourgondisch-oostenrijksche Heerschappij.* The Hague.
———. 1884b. *Leidsche Rechtsbronnen uit de Middeleeuwen.* The Hague.
Bock, Elfried. 1910. "Die Bildnisse des Lucas van Leyden." *Monatshefte für Kunstwissenschaft* 3:405–7.
Bock, Elfried, and Jakob Rosenberg. 1930. *Staatliche Museen zu Berlin. Die Zeichnungen Alter Meister im Kupferstichkabinett: Die Niederländischen Meister.* Vol. 1. Berlin.

Bode, Wilhelm. 1895. "Die Fürstlich Liechtenstein'sche Galerie in Wien: Die altniederländische und die altdeutsche Schule." *Die graphischen Künste* 18:114–29.

Bol, Laurens J. 1969. *Holländische Maler des 17. Jahrhunderts nahe den Grossen Meistern: Landschaften und Stilleben.* Braunschweig.

Bonn, Provinzial Museum. 1914. *Gemäldegalerie: Katalog.*

Boon, K. G. n.d. *Zelf-portret: Het zelfportret in de Nederlandsche en Vlaamsche Schilderkunst.* Amsterdam.

———. 1953. "Meester van de Khanenkoaanbidding of de Meester van de Kruisingen te Turijn." *Oud-Holland* 58:209–16.

———. 1964. "Lucas van Leyden." *Encyclopedia of World Art.* 9:349–53. London.

———. 1966. "Gertgen tot sint Jans of Mostaert." *Oud-Holland* 81:61–72.

———. 1968. "Werk van een vroege Goudse of Leidse schilder in het Rijksmuseum." *Bulletin van het Rijksmuseum* 16:3–12.

———. 1973. "De vroegste glaskartons uit de Sint Janskerk te Gouda." *Bulletin van het Rijksmuseum* 21:151–75.

———. 1978. *Netherlandish Drawings of the Fifteenth and Sixteenth Centuries in the Rijksmuseum.* The Hague.

———. 1983a. "Sixteenth-century Cartoons for Church Windows." *Apollo* 117:437–42.

———. 1983b. "The Life and Work of Hugh Jacobsz. before 1500." *Essays in Northern European Art Presented to Egbert Haverkamp-Begemann on His Sixtieth Birthday.* Doornspijk, The Netherlands.

Borenius, Tancred. 1923. *The Picture Gallery of Andrea Vendramin.* London.

Bornkamm, Heinrich. 1969. *Luther and the Old Testament.* Translated by E. and R. Gritsch. Philadelphia.

Borromeo, Federico. 1625. *Museum.* Milan.

Bosshard, Emil D. 1982. "Tüchleinmalerei—ein billige Ersatztechnik?" *Zeitschrift für Kunstgeschichte* 45:31–42.

Boston, Museum of Fine Arts. 1969. *Museum of Fine Arts, Boston.* Great Museums of the World series. New York.

Brant, Sebastian. 1944. *The Ship of Fools.* Translated by Edwin H. Zeydel. New York.

———. 1964. *Das Narrenschiff.* Stuttgart.

Braunfels, Wolfgang. 1973. *Lexikon der Christlichen Ikonographie.* Freiburg.

Braunschweig, Herzog Anton Ulrich-Museum. 1978. *Die Sprache der Bilder.* Exhibition catalogue.

———. 1980. *Selbstbildnisse und Künstlerporträts von Lucas van Leyden bis Anton Raphael Mengs.* Exhibition catalogue.

Braunschweiger Presse. 1963. "Ehrenplatz für Lucas van Leyden." 136 (June 14).

Bredius, A. 1901. "Schilderijen van Lucas van Leyden." *De Nederlandsche Spectator* (February 23): 64.

———. 1913. "Schilderijen in oude Inventarissen." *Oud-Holland* 31:205–6.
———. 1915–1922. *Künstler-Inventare: Urkunden zur Geschichte der holländischen Kunst des XVIten, XVIIten, und XVIIIten Jahrhunderts.* 8 vols. The Hague.
Bremen, Kunsthalle. 1948. *Museum-Heute: Ein Querschnitt.*
Bremmer, H. P., ed. 1929. *Beeldende Kunst* 17:2 (December): 9, 12–17.
———. 1932. *Beeldende Kunst* 18 (April): 89–90.
———. 1936. *Beeldende Kunst* 23 (May): 1–2.
Breustedt, Renate. 1966. "Die Entstehung und Entwicklung des Nachtbildes in der Abendländischen Malerei und seine Ausbreitung in den Niederlanden (bis ca. 1510/30)." 2 vols. Ph.D. dissertation, Georg-August-Universität, Göttingen.
Bréviare Grimani. 1903. *Le Bréviare Grimani à la Bibliothèque Marciana de Venise.* Venice.
Briere-Misme, Clotilde. 1924. *École Hollandaise.* Vol. 2 of *La Peinture au Musée du Louvre,* by J. Guiffrey. Paris.
Bristol, Red Lodge. 1946. *Catalogue of the Exhibition of Dutch Old Masters.* Exhibition catalogue.
Brockmann, H. 1924. *Die Spätzeit der Kölner Maler-schule.* Bonn.
Brown, Christopher. 1978. "Leiden: The Lucas van Leyden Exhibition." *Burlington Magazine* 120:782–83.
Bruges, Stedelijk Museum. 1902. *Exposition des Primitifs flamands et d'Art anciens.* Exhibition catalogue.
———. 1907. *Exposition de la Toison d'Or.* Exhibition catalogue.
———. 1953. *Het Portret in de Oude Nederlanden.* Exhibition catalogue.
Brussels, Palais des Beaux-Arts. 1971. *Rembrandt et son temps.* Exhibition catalogue.
———. 1977. *Albrecht Dürer in de Nederlanden.* Exhibition catalogue.
Bruyn, Joos. 1954. "Enige Werken van Jan van Scorel uit zijn Haarlemse tijd (1527–1529)." *Bulletin van Het Rijksmuseum* 2:51–58.
———. 1960. "Twee Antonius-panelen en andere werken van Aertgen van Leyden." *Nederlands Kunsthistorisch Jaarboek* 11:36–119.
———. 1961. "Een drieluik van Aertgen van Leyden." *Jaarboek, Koninklijk Museum voor Schone Kunsten, Antwerpen,* 113–29.
———. 1962. "Lucas van Leyden and the Leyden Painters of His Time." *Cours d'ete, 1962: Comptes rendues des conferences.* Mimeographed.
———. 1965. "The Jan Gossaert Exhibition in Rotterdam and Bruges." *Burlington Magazine* 107:462–67.
———. 1969. "Lucas van Leyden en zijn Leidse tijdgenoten in hun relatie tot Zuid-Nederland." In *Miscellanea I. Q. van Regteren Altena,* 44–47. Amsterdam.
———. 1983. "Over de betekenis van het werk van Jan van Scorel omstreeks 1530 voor oudere en jongere tijdgenoten (2)." *Oud-Holland* 97:217–23.
Buchelius, Arnoldus. 1928. *Diarium, Res Pictoriae, Notae Quotidianae en Descriptio*

Urbis Ultrajectinae (1583–1639). Edited by G. J. Hoogewerff and J. Q. van Regteren Altena. The Hague.

Buchner, Ernst. 1953. *Das deutsche Bildnis der Spätgotik and der frühen Dürerzeit.* Berlin.

Bullart, Isaac. 1682. *Académie des Sciences et des Arts.* Vol. 2. Amsterdam.

Burchard, L. 1913. "Bartholomeus Dolendo." In *Allgemeines Lexikon der Bildenden Künstler von der Antike bis zur Gegenwart,* edited by Ulrich Thieme and Felix Becker, 9:390. Leipzig.

Burckhardt, Jacob. 1879. *Der Cicerone.* 4th ed. Vol. 2. Edited by Wilhelm Bode. Leipzig.

———. 1893. *Das Spiel im deutschen Mittelalter.* Basel.

Burger, Willy. 1925. *Die Malerei in der Niederlanden, 1400–1550.* Munich.

Busch, Werner. 1982. "Lucas van Leydens 'Grosse Hagar' und die augustinische Typologie-auffassung der Vorreformation." *Zeitschrift für Kunstgeschichte* 45:97–129.

Byvanck, A. W. 1937. *La Miniature dans les Pays-Bas Septentrionaux.* Paris.

Castiglione, Baldassare. 1974 (1561). *The Book of the Courtier.* Translated by Sir Thomas Hoby. London.

Catalogues de ventes. 1909. *Les Catalogues de ventes et livrets de Salons illustrés par Gabriel de Saint Aubin, I, Catalogue de la Collection Crozat.* Paris.

The Catholic Encyclopedia. 1910. 15 vols. New York.

Caviness, M. H., et al. 1989. *Stained Glass before 1700 in American Collections: Midwestern and Western States.* Washington.

Châtelet, Albert. 1981. *Early Dutch Painting.* Translated by Christopher Brown and Anthony Turner. New York.

Chicago, Art Institute. 1933. *Art Masterpieces in a Century of Progress Fine Arts Exhibition.* Exhibition catalogue.

———. 1934. *Catalogue of a Century of Progress Exhibition of Paintings and Sculptures.* Exhibition catalogue.

———. 1938. *Masterpieces of the Month.* Exhibition catalogue.

———. 1938–1939. *The Christmas Story in Art.* Exhibition catalogue.

———. 1954. *Masterpieces of Religious Art.* Exhibition catalogue.

———. 1961. *Paintings in the Art Institute of Chicago: A Catalogue of the Picture Collection.*

Chomentovskaja, O. 1938. "Le Comput Digital: Histoire d'un Geste dans l'Art de la Renaissance Italienne." *Gazette des Beaux-Arts* 20 (July–August): 158–72.

Cicerone. 1918. "Die Versteigerung der Sammlung von Kaufmann." *Der Cicerone* 10:24–31.

Clark, Kenneth. 1968. *Rembrandt and the Italian Renaissance.* New York.
———. 1979. *Landscape into Art.* New York.
Cleary, James W., ed. 1974. *Chirologia: or, The Natural Language of the Hand,* by John Bulwer. Carbondale.
Clébert, Jean-Paul. 1963. *The Gypsies.* Translated by Charles Duff. New York.
Clemen, Paul. 1930. *Die Gotischen Monumental-Malereien der Rheinland.* 2 vols. Düsseldorf.
Clive, H. P. 1961. "The Calvinists and the Question of Dancing." *Bibliothèque d'Humanisme et Renaissance* 23:296–323.
Coert, Al. 1935–1936. "Het weder te voorschijn brengen van de beeltenis van God den Vader op het 'Jongste Oordeel' van Lucas van Leyden in de Lakenhall." *Jaarboekje voor Geschiedenis en Oudheidkunde van Leiden en Rijnland* 28:76–83.
Cohen, Walter. 1914. "Die Ausstellung Frühholländischer Malerei und Plastik in Utrecht." *Zeitschrift für Bildende Kunst* 25:25–36.
———. 1928. "Alte Malerei aus Rheinisch-Westfälischem Privatbesitz zu Ausstellung in Düsseldorf." *Der Cicerone* 20:49–60.
Cologne, Kunstgewerbemuseum. 1963. *Die Sammlung Clemens.* Exhibition catalogue.
Cologne, Kunstverein. 1922. *Alte Malerei aus Kölnischem Privatbesitz.* Exhibition catalogue.
Colvin, Sidney. 1882. "Lucas de Leyden." *L'Art* 4 (November): 131–38.
———. 1893. "Eine Sammlung von Handzeichnungen des Lukas van Leyden." *Jahrbuch der Preussischen Kunstsammlungen* 14:165–76, 231–32.
Connaissance des Arts. 1957. "Cours des tableaux anciens." (August): 16.
Connoisseur. 1954. "The Connoisseur's Diary." 134 (December): lxxi, 287.
Conway, Martin. 1921. *The Van Eycks and Their Followers.* New York.
Corwin, Nancy A. 1976. "The Fire Landscape." Ph.D. dissertation, University of Washington, Seattle.
Crofton, Henry Thoman. 1909. "The Former Costumes of the Gypsies." *Journal of the Gypsy Lore Society* 2:193–231.
Crow, W. B. 1944. *The Symbolism of Chess and Cards.* London.
Cust, Lionel. 1910. "Notes on Pictures in the Royal Collections—XIX. Paintings Attributed to Lucas van Leyden." *Burlington Magazine* 18 (December): 149–50.
Cuttler, Charles D. 1984. "Exotics in 15th-Century Netherlandish Art: Comments on Oriental and Gypsy Costumes." In *Liber Amicorum Herman Liebaers,* edited by Frans Vanwijngaerden et al., 419–34. Brussels.
Cuzin, Jean-Pierre. 1977. *La Diseuse de bonne aventure de Caravage.* Paris.

D'Argenville, Desallier. 1745. *Abrégé de la vie des plus fameux peintres.* Vol. 2. Paris.

Davidson, Bernice. 1954. "Marcantonio Raimondi, the Engravings of His Roman Period." Ph.D. dissertation, Harvard University, Cambridge.

Davies, Martin. 1968. *Early Netherlandish School: The National Gallery, London.* 3d ed. London.

Davis, Natalie Z. 1975. "Women on Top." In *Society and Culture in Modern France,* 124–51. Stanford.

De Bosque, A. 1975. *Quentin Metsys.* Brussels.

De Jonge, C. H. 1916. "Costuum-varia I: De datering van het zelfportret van Lucas van Leyden te Brunswijk." *Bulletin van de Nederlandschen Oudheidkundigen Bond* 9:248–51.

De Jongh, E. 1967. *Zinne- en minnebeelden in de schilderkunst van de zeventiende eeuw.* N.p.

———. 1968–1969. "Erotica in Vogelperspectief." *Simiolus* 3:22–74.

———. 1974. "Grape Symbolism in Paintings of the 16th and 17th Centuries." *Simiolus* 7:166–91.

De Jongh, Jacobus. 1764. *Het Leven der Doorluchtige Nederlandsche en eenige Hoogduitsche Schilders, voormaals Byeenvergaderd en beschreeven door Karel van Mander Kunst-Schilder.* Vol. 1. Amsterdam.

De la Marche, Olivier. 1898. *Le Chevalier Délibéré.* London.

De la Roche. 1783. *Voyage d'un amateur des Arts.* Vol. 1. Amsterdam.

Delft, Prinsenhof. 1949. *Oude Kunst.* Exhibition catalogue.

———. 1952. *Prisma der Bijbelse Kunst.* Exhibition catalogue.

———. 1964–1965. *De Schilder in Zijn Wereld.* Exhibition catalogue.

Della Pergola, Paola. 1964. "L'Inventario Borghese del 1693." *Arte Antica en Moderna* 25:219–30.

De Madrazo, Pedro. 1903. *Catalogo de los Cuadros del Museo Nacional de Pintura y Escultura. Museo del Prado.* 9th ed. Madrid.

De Marolles, M. 1666. *Catalogue de livres d'estampes et de figures en taille douces.* Paris.

De Mirimonde, A. P. 1967. "La Musique dans les allegories de l'Amour. II. Eros." *Gazette des Beaux-Arts* 69 (May–June): 319–46.

Demonts, Louis. 1922. *Catalogue des Peintures Exposés dans les Galeries: Musée du Louvre, Paris.* Vol. 3. Paris.

———. 1923. "A Lost Lucas van Leyden." *Burlington Magazine* 43:124–29.

Denuce, Jean. 1932. "Inventare von Kunstsammlungen zu Antwerpen im 16. und 17. Jahrhundert." In *Quellen zur Geschichte der flämischen Kunst.* Antwerp.

Der Kinderen-Besier, J. H. 1933. *Mode-Metamorphosen: De Kleedij onzer Voorouders in de zestiende eeuw.* Amsterdam.

Descamps, J. B. 1753. *La Vie des Peintres Flamands, Allemands et Hollandois.* Vol. 1. Paris.
Descargues, P. n.d. *Art Treasures of the Hermitage.* New York.
De Somof, A. 1899. "Correspondence de Russie: Les Nouveaux Rembrandt et Adam Elsheimer à l'Ermitage Impérial." *Gazette des Beaux-Arts* 21:258-64.
———. 1901. *Leningrad, Ermitage: Catalogue de la Galerie des Tableaux.* Vol. 2. Leningrad.
De Stuers, Victor. 1914. "De schennis van Lucas van Leiden's Laatste Oordeel." *Jaarboekje voor Geschiedenis en Oudheidkunde van Leiden en Rijnland* 11:29-30.
De Tolnay, Charles. 1943-1960. *Michelangelo.* 5 vols. Princeton.
Detroit, Institute of Arts. 1944. *Loan Exhibition of Early Dutch Paintings, 1460-1540.* Exhibition catalogue.
D.I.A.L. 1968. *Decimal Index of the Art of the Low Countries.* The Hague.
Di Lentaglio, Giuseppe. 1929. "Susannah 'La Casta' nell' Arte." *Emporium* 70 (July): 11-19.
Dodt van Flensburg, J. J. 1844. *Archief voor Kerkelijke en Wereldsche Gechiedenissen, inzonderheid van Utrecht.* Vol. 4. Utrecht.
Dominici, Cardinal G. *Regola del governo di cura familiare.* Edited by D. Salvi. Florence.
Dordrecht. 1893. *Kunstgewerbliche Ausstellung.* Exhibition catalogue.
Douglass, Jane Dempsey. 1974. "Women and the Continental Reformation." In *Religion and Sexism,* edited by Rosemary Radford Ruether, 292-318. New York.
Dresden, Gemäldegalerie. 1962. *Alte Meister.* 7th ed. Dresden.
Dresen-Coenders, Lene. 1977. "De strijd om de broek: De verhouding man/vrouw in de begin van het moderne tijd (1450-1630)." *De Revisor* 4:29-37, 77.
Dülberg, Franz. 1899a. "Das jüngste Gericht des Lucas van Leyden." *Repertorium für Kunstwissenschaft* 22:30-61.
———. 1899b. "Die Nachkommen des Lucas van Leyden." *Oud-Holland* 17:156-62.
———. 1899c. "Die Persönlichkeit des Lucas van Leyden." *Oud-Holland* 17:65-83.
———. 1900a. "Das Alkmaarer Jüngste Gericht." *Repertorium für Kunstwissenschaft* 23:203-10.
———. 1900b. "Der Neue Lucas van Leyden im Germanischen Museum." In *Mitteilungen aus dem Germanischen Nationalmuseum,* 157-64.
———. 1903-1908a. *Frühholländer I. Die Altarwerke des Cornelis Engebrechtszoon und des Lukas van Leyden im Leidener Städtischen Museum.* Haarlem.

———. 1903–1908b. *Frühholländer III. Frühholländer in Italien.* Haarlem.
———. 1903–1908c. *Frühholländer IV. Frühholländer in Paris.* Haarlem.
———. 1909. "Lucas van Leyden." *Onze Kunst* 15:1–17.
———. 1923. "The Feeding of the Five Thousand, by Cornelis Engebrechtszoon." *Burlington Magazine* 43 (October): 173–79.
———. 1929. *Niederländische Malerei der Spätgotik und Renaissance.* Wildpark-Potsdam.
———. 1930. "Lot en Avontuur van Beroemde Schilderijen." *Elsevier's Geillustreerd Maandschrift* 40:303–10.
———. 1933. "Lucas van Leyden bij de vierhonderdjarige herdenking van zijn sterfday." *Elsevier's Geillustreerd Maandschrift* 43 (July–December): 1–14.
Duplessis, Georges. 1882. *Oeuvre de Lucas de Leyde.* Paris.
Düsseldorf, Kunstverein. 1928. *Ausstellung Alter Malerei aus rheinisch-westfälischem Privatbesitz.* Exhibition catalogue.
Duverger, Erik. 1957–1958. "Lucas van Leyden en de tapijtkunst." *Artes Textiles* 4:26–38.
Edinburgh, Royal Scottish Academy. 1883. *Catalogue of Loan Exhibition.* Exhibition catalogue.
Ehrenstein, Theodor. 1923. *Das Alte Testament im Bilde.* Vienna.
Eisler, Colin. 1967. "Letter to the Editor." *Master Drawings* 5:66.
———. 1977. *Paintings from the Samuel H. Kress Collection: European Schools Excluding Italian.* Oxford.
———. 1989. *The Thyssen-Bornemisza Collection: Early Netherlandish Painting.* London.
Elsevier, W. J. C. Rammelman. 1858. "Ouders van den Schilder Lucas van Leyden." *De Navorscher* 8:245–46.
———. 1862. "Het laatste oordeel door Lucas van Leyden geschilderd." *De Navorscher* 12:313–14.
———. 1869. "Lucas van Leiden, de schilder." *De Navorscher* 19:20–22.
———. 1875. "Het laatste oordeel: Lucas van Leyden." *De Nederlandsche Spectator* 11 (March 13): 86–87.
Engelman, Jan. 1949. "Oude Kunst in Delft. Het Kostbare en het zeldzame." *De Tijd* (July 9): 3.
Ephrussi, Charles. 1882. *Albert Dürer et ses Dessins.* Paris.
Erasmus, Desiderius. 1971. *Praise of Folly and Letter to Martin Dorp, 1515.* Translated by Betty Radice. Harmondsworth.
Evrard, M. W. 1884. *Lucas de Leyde et Albert Dürer.* Brussels.
Fell, H. Granville. 1935. "From Gallery and Mart." *Connoisseur* 96 (September): 170–72.
Ferguson, George. 1976. *Signs and Symbols in Christian Art.* New York.
Filedt Kok, J. P. 1978. "Underdrawing and Other Technical Aspects in the Paintings of Lucas van Leyden." *Nederlands Kunsthistorisch Jaarboek* 29:1–184.

———. 1979. "Lucas van Leyden: Exhibitions and Recent Publications." *Nederlands Kunsthistorisch Jaarboek* 29:509–20.
Filedt Kok, J. P., et al. 1975. "Das Diptychon des Lucas van Leiden von 1522: Versuch einer Rekonstruktion." *Nederlands Kunsthistorisch Jaarboek* 26:229–58.
Floerke, Hanns. 1906. *Das Leben der niederländischen und deutschen Maler des Carel van Mander.* Vol. 1. Munich.
Florence, Istituto universitario olandese di storia dell' arte. 1971. *Tekeningen van Jan de Bisschop.* Exhibition catalogue.
Forssman, Erik. 1976. "Rembrandts Radierung 'Der Triumph des Mardochai.'" *Zeitschrift für Kunstgeschichte* 39:297–311.
Förster, Ernst, ed. 1867. *Denkmale Deutscher Kunst von Einführung des Christenthums bis auf die Neueste Zeit.* Vol. 11. Leipzig.
Fraenger, Wilhelm. 1923. *Der Bauern-Bruegel und das deutsche Sprichwort.* Munich.
Freedberg, David. 1976. "The Problem of Images in Northern Europe and Its Repercussions in the Netherlands." In *Hafnia: Copenhagen Papers in the History of Art,* 25–45.
Friedländer, Max J. 1899. "Franz Dülberg: Die Leydener Malerschule." *Repertorium für Kunstwissenschaft* 22:328–33.
———. 1900–1901. "Lucas van Leyden." *Bulletin uitgegeven door den Nederlandschen Oudheidkundigen Bond* 2:44.
———. 1901. "Lucas van Leijden." *Das Museum* 6:1–4.
———. 1902. "London: Die Leihausstellung der Royal Academy von 1902." *Repertorium für Kunstwissenschaft* 25:142–47.
———. 1903. "Die Brügger Leihausstellung von 1902." *Repertorium für Kunstwissenschaft* 26:147–75.
———. 1906. "De verzameling von Kauffmann te Berlijn." *Onze Kunst* 5:29–40.
———. 1917. *Die Sammlung Richard von Kaufmann, Berlin.* Vol. 2. Berlin.
———. 1922. "Om Gammel-Nederlandske Billeder i den Langaardske Samling og Flamske Fra det 17. Aarhundrede." *Kunst og Kultur* 10:118–38.
———. 1924. *Lucas van Leyden.* Meister der Graphik, vol. 13. Leipzig.
———. 1928. "A Painting by Lucas van Leyden." *Art News* (April 14), unpaginated.
———. 1930. "Uber die Anfänge des Malers Lucas van Leyden." *Der Cicerone* 22:493–99.
———. 1947. "Quentin Massys as a Painter of Genre Pictures." *Burlington Magazine* 89:114–19.
———. 1949. "Bilder und Zeichnungen in der Sammlung van Beuningen." *Phoenix* 4 (June): 141–66.
———. 1963a. *Lucas van Leyden.* Berlin.
———. 1963b. *Landscape, Portrait, Still-Life.* Translated by R. F. C. Hull. New York.

———. 1967–1976. *Early Netherlandish Painting*. 14 vols. New York.
———. 1969. *From Van Eyck to Bruegel*. Translated by M. Kay. Edited by F. Grossmann. London.
Friedländer, Walter. 1974. *Caravaggio Studies*. Princeton.
Friedmann, Herbert. 1946. *The Symbolic Goldfinch*. Washington.
———. 1947. "The Symbolism of Crivelli's 'Madonna and Child Enthroned with Donor' in the National Gallery." *Gazette des Beaux-Arts* 32: 65–72.
Fritsch-Estrangin, H. 1933. "À l'occasion d'un centenaire oublié un tableau peu connu de Lucas de Leyde." *Chronique des Arts et de la Curiosité. Beaux-Arts* 72 (December 8): 6.
Fuchs, Eduard, and Alfred Kind. 1913. *Die Weiberherrschaft in der Geschichte der Menschheit*. 2 vols. Munich.
Galbiati, Giovanni. 1951. *Itinerario per il visitatore della Biblioteca Ambrosiana*. Milan.
Galpin, Stanley L. 1920. "Les Eschez Amoureux: A Complete Synopsis, with Unpublished Extracts." *Romanic Review* 11:283–307.
Gavelle, Émile. 1929. *L'École de Peinture de Leyde et le Romantisme Hollandais au Debut de la Renaissance: Cornelis Engebrechtsz*. Lille.
Geisberg, Max. n.d. *Anfänge: Die Anfänge des Deutschen Kupferstiches und der Meister E. S.* Leipzig.
———. 1974. *The German Single-Leaf Woodcut, 1500–1550*. 4 vols. New York.
Gerson, Horst. 1936. "Jerome Bosch and the North-Netherlandish Primitives." *Burlington Magazine* 69 (September): 136–37.
———. 1962. *Zes Eeuwen Nederlandse Schilderkunst*. Vol. 1. *Van Geertgen tot Frans Hals*. Amsterdam.
———. 1968. *Rembrandt Paintings*. Amsterdam.
Gibson, Walter S. 1970a. "Two Painted Glass Panels from Circle of Lucas van Leyden." *Bulletin of the Cleveland Museum of Art* 56:81–92.
———. 1970b. "Lucas van Leyden and His Two Teachers." *Simiolus* 4:90–99.
———. 1972. *Hieronymus Bosch*. New York.
———. 1974. "Jan Gossaert de Mabuse: Madonna and Child in a Landscape." *Bulletin of the Cleveland Museum of Art* 61:287–99.
———. 1975. "Bruegel, Dulle Griet, and Sexist Politics in the Sixteenth Century." In *Pieter Bruegel und seine Welt,* edited by Otto von Simson and Matthias Winner, 9–15. Berlin.
———. 1977. *The Paintings of Cornelis Engebrechtsz*. New York.
———. 1978. "Some Flemish Popular Prints from Hieronymus Cock and His Contemporaries." *Art Bulletin* 60:673–81.
———. 1980. Review of *Lucas van Leyden Studies: Nederlands Kunsthistorisch Jaarboek* 29 (1978). *Simiolus* 11:107–12.

———. 1983. "Lucas van Leyden and the Old Testament." *Print Collector's Newsletter* 14:127–30.

———. 1986. "Lucas van Leyden's Late Paintings: The Italian Connection." *Nederlands Kunsthistorisch Jaarboek* 37:41–52.

Gilbert, Creighton. 1952. "On Subject and Non-Subject in Italian Renaissance Pictures." *Art Bulletin* 34:202–16.

Gleadowe, R. 1922. "A Lucas van Leyden for the National Gallery." *Burlington Magazine* 40 (April): 179–80.

Glück, Gustav. 1901. "Beiträge zur Geschichte der Antwerpner Malerei im XVI. Jahrhundert." *Jahrbuch der Kunsthistorischen Sammlungen des Allerhöchsten Kaiserhauses* 22:1–34.

———. 1942. "The Feeding of the Five Thousand in the Painting of the Netherlands." *Art Quarterly* 5:45–57.

———. 1945. "Mabuse and the Development of the Flemish Renaissance." *Art Quarterly* 8:116–38.

Göbel, Heinrich. 1923–1934. *Wandteppiche*. 3 vols. Leipzig.

Goldscheider, Ludwig. 1936. *Fünfhundert Selbstporträts von der Antike bis zur Gegenwart*. Vienna.

Goris, Gerhard. 1712. *Les délices de Leide, une des célèbres villes de l'Europe*. Leiden.

Goris, J. A., and Georges Marlier, eds. and trans. 1937. *Albert Dürer: Journal de Voyage dans les Pays Bas*. Brussels.

Grand Rapids, Art Gallery. 1940. *Masterpieces of Dutch Art*. Exhibition catalogue.

Gray, John M. 1883. *Notes on the Edinburgh Loan Exhibition of 1883*. Edinburgh.

Greenville, S.C., Bob Jones University Collection of Sacred Art. 1954. *Catalogue*.

———. 1962. *Introduction to the Art Collection*.

Greve, H. E. 1903. *De bronnen van Carel van Mander voor 'Het leven der doorluchtighe Nederlandtsche en Hoogduitsche schilders'*. The Hague.

Grimme, Ernst Günther. 1963. "Das Suermondt Museum: Eine Auswahl." *Aachener Kunstblätter* 28.

Grohn, H. W. 1967. "Leyden, Lucas van." In *Kindlers Malerei Lexicon*, 4:132–35. Zurich.

Groningen, Groninger Museum. 1910. *Verslag van den Toestand van het Museum van Oudheden voor de Provincie en Stad Groningen*.

Grosjean, Ardis. 1974. "Towards an Interpretation of Pieter Aertsen's Profane Iconography." *Konsthistorisk Tidskrift* 42–43 (December): 121–43.

Die Grossen Galerien. Kalender 1973. Oslo. Dresden.

Grossmann, F. 1973. *Pieter Bruegel*. London.

Grupp, Claus D. 1973. *Spielkarten und ihre Geschichte*. Leinfelden.

Gysin, F. 1947. *Tapisseries suisses de l'époque gothique*. 2d ed. Basel.

Haak, B. 1967–1968. "De Vergankelijkheidsymboliek in 16e eeuwse portretten en 17e eeuwse stillevens in Holland." *Antiek* 1:23–30, 2:399–411.

Haarlem, Frans Hals Museum. 1969. *Catalogus*. Haarlem.
The Hague, Mauritshuis. 1945. *Nederlandsche Kunst van de XVde en XVIde Eeuw.* Exhibition catalogue.
Hall, James. 1974. *Dictionary of Subjects and Symbols in Art.* New York.
Hamaker, H. G. 1873. *De Middeneeuwsche Keurboeken van de Stad Leiden.* Leiden.
Hamill, Alfred E. 1949. "A Fifteenth-Century Tapestry." *Journal of the Gypsy Lore Society* 28 (July–October): 81–82.
Hanckel, H. 1952. "Narrendarstellungen im Spätmittelalter." Ph.D. dissertation, Albert-Ludwigs-Universität, Freiburg.
Hannema, D. 1937. "De Meester van het Johannes Altaar." *Bulletin Museum Boymans Rotterdam* 1:3–4.
———. 1949. *Catalogue of the D. G. van Beuningen Collection.* Rotterdam.
Harbison, Craig. 1976. *The Last Judgment in Sixteenth Century Northern Europe.* New York.
———. 1979. "Some Artistic Anticipations of Theological Thought." *Art Quarterly* 2:67–89.
———. 1984. "Lucas van Leyden, the Magdalen and the Problem of Secularization in Early Sixteenth Century Northern Art." *Oud-Holland* 98:117–29.
Hargrave, C. P. 1930. *A History of Playing Cards and a Bibliography of Cards and Gaming.* London.
Hasselt, Provincial Begijnhof. 1955. *Kunst uit de 16e–17e eeuw.* Exhibition catalogue. Hasselt.
Haussherr, Reiner. 1973. *Bible Moralisée.* Graz.
Havelaar, Just. 1918. "Lucas van Leyden." *Elsevier's Geillustreerd Maandschrift* 28:1–17, 92–103.
Heidrich, Ernst. 1910. *Altniederländische Malerei.* Jena.
Held, Julius. 1931. *Dürer's Wirkung auf die niederländische Kunst seiner Zeit.* The Hague.
———. 1959. *Rubens: Selected Drawings.* Vol. 1. London.
———. 1966. Review of Friedländer, 1963a. *Art Bulletin* 48:446–47.
Hermesdorf, P. F., et al. 1978. "The Examination and Restoration of 'The Last Judgment' by Lucas van Leyden." *Nederlands Kunsthistorisch Jaarboek* 29:311–424.
Hiller, Irmgard, and Horst Vey. 1969. *Cologne, Wallraf-Richartz-Museum: Katalog der Deutschen und Niederländischen Gemälde.* Cologne.
Hind, Arthur M. 1926. *Catalogue of Drawings by Dutch and Flemish Artists Preserved in the Department of Prints and Drawings in the British Museum.* Vol. 3. London.
———. 1963a. *A History of Engraving and Etching.* New York.
———. 1963b. *An Introduction to a History of Woodcut.* 2 vols. New York.
Hindman, Sandra. 1977. *Text and Image in Fifteenth-Century Illustrated Dutch Bibles.* Leiden.

Hinz, Berthold. 1969. "Das Ehepaarbildnis." Ph.D. dissertation, Westfälischen Wilhelms-Universität, Münster.
———. 1974. "Studien zur Geschichte des Ehepaarbildnisses." *Marburger Jahrbuch für Kunstwissenschaft* 19:139–218.
Hirsch, Rudolf. 1948. "De Münchener Pinakothek in het Rijksmuseum te Amsterdam." *Phoenix* 3:123–44.
Hirschmann, O. 1916. *Hendrick Goltzius als Maler, 1600–1617*. The Hague.
———. 1919. *Hendrick Goltzius*. Leipzig.
Hobhouse, J. R. 1959. *The Morris Loan Collection*. London.
Hoet, Gerard. 1752–1770. *Catalogus of Naamlyst van Schilderyen*. 3 vols. The Hague.
Hoetink, H. R. 1966. "Het laatste oordeel." *Openbaar Kunstbezit* 10:62a–b.
"Hoey." 1924. In *Allgemeines Lexikon der Bildenden Künstler,* edited by Ulrich Thieme and Felix Becker, vol. 17. Leipzig.
Hofmann, Rudolf. 1872. *Die Gemälde-Sammlung des Grossherzoglichen Museums zu Darmstadt*. Darmstadt.
Holl, Karl. 1959. *The Cultural Significance of the Reformation*. Translated by K. and B. Herz and J. Lichtblau. Cleveland.
Hollstein, F. W. H. 1949–1974. *Dutch and Flemish Etchings, Engravings and Woodcuts ca. 1450–1700*. 19 vols. Amsterdam.
Hoogewerff, G. J. 1928. "Vroege Nederlandsche Schilderwerken in Italie." *Mededeelingen van het Nederlandsche Historisch Instituut te Rome* 8:111–22.
———. 1936–1947. *De Noord-Nederlandsche Schilderkunst*. 5 vols. The Hague.
———. 1954. *Het Landschap van Bosch tot Rubens*. Antwerp.
Houbraken, Arnold. 1753. *De Groote Schouburgh der Nederlantsche Konstschilders en Schilderissen*. 2d ed. 3 vols. The Hague.
Hudig, F. W. 1934. "De Preek van Lucas van Leyden." *Oud-Holland* 51:65–69.
Hurm, W. 1892. *Beschreibendes Verzeichniss der Gemälde und Bildhauerwerke des Kunstvereins zu Bremen*. Bremen.
Hutchison, Jane C. 1972. *The Master of the Housebook*. New York.
Hymans, H. 1877. "Albert Dürer et Lucas de Leyde: Leur rencontre à Anvers." *Bulletin des Commissions Royales d'Art et d'Archéologie* 16:172–81.
———. 1884. *Le Livre des Peintres de Carel van Mander*. Vol. 1. Paris.
Immerzeel, J. 1842. *De Levens en Werken der Hollandsche en Vlaamsche Kunstschilders, Beeldhouwers, Graveurs en Bouwmeesters*. Amsterdam.
Indianapolis, John Herron Art Institute. 1950. *Holbein and His Contemporaries*. Exhibition catalogue.
The Interpreters's Dictionary of the Bible. 1962. Vol. 4. New York.
Inventaire. 1913. *Inventaire des Dessins et Aquarelles donnés à l'État Belge par Madame la douairiere de Grez*. Brussels.
Isarlov, G. 1934. "Les maniéristes néerlandais." *L'Art et les Artistes* 27:289–97.

Jaeger, Wolfgang. 1960. *Die Heilung des Blinden in der Kunst.* Konstanz.

Jaffe, Michael. 1965. "Rubens as a Collector of Drawings, Part 2." *Master Drawings* 3:21–35.

Jahn, Johannes. 1972. *1472–1553. Lucas Cranach d.A. Das gesamte graphische Werk.* Munich.

Janson, Horst W. 1952. *Apes and Ape Lore in the Middle Ages and the Renaissance.* London.

Janssen, Han. 1965. *Speelkarten.* Bussum.

Janssens de Bisthoven, A. 1959. *Les Primitifs Flamands, Musée Communal des Beaux-Arts, Bruges.* Antwerp.

Jourdain, C. H. 1699. *Voyages historiques de l'Europe.* Vol. 5. Paris.

Judson, J. Richard. 1959. *Gerrit van Honthorst.* The Hague.

———. 1961. Review of Nicolson, 1958. *Art Bulletin* 43:341–48.

K., J. 1865. "De Pieterskerk te Leiden." *Aurora: Jaarboekjen.* 206–12.

Kahn, Rosy. 1918. *Die Graphik des Lucas van Leyden.* Strasbourg.

Karlsruhe, Kunsthalle. 1929. *Verzeichnis der Gemälde.*

———. 1966. *Katalog Alte Meister.*

Kekule von Stradonitz, Stephan. 1910. "Die Wappen auf den Flügeln des Triptichons: Die Heilung des Blinden von Lucas van Leyden." *Zeitschrift für Museumskunde* 6:185–91.

———. 1911. "Die Wappen auf den Flügeln des Triptichons: Die Heilung des Blinden von Lucas van Leyden." *Zeitschrift für Museumskunde* 7:44–46.

Kettering, Alison McNeil. 1977. "Rembrandt's Fluteplayer: A Unique Treatment of Pastoral." *Simiolus* 9:19–44.

Kiefer, A. 1958. *Das Schachspiel in Literatur und Kunst.* Munich.

Kiewning, D. 1903. "Maler Johann Tilmann." *Mitteilungen aus der lippischen Geschichte und Landeskunde* 1:139–45.

Kirschenbaum, Baruch D. 1977. *The Religious and Historical Paintings of Jan Steen.* New York.

Kist, N. C., and W. Moll. 1862. *Kerkhistorisch Archief.* Vol. 3. Amsterdam.

Kloek, Wouter. 1978. "The Drawings of Lucas van Leyden." *Nederlands Kunsthistorisch Jaarboek* 29:425–58.

Kloek, W. Th., and J. P. Filedt Kok. 1983. "'De Opstanding van Christus', getekend door Lucas van Leyden." *Bulletin van het Rijksmuseum* 31:4–20.

Knappert, L. 1908. *De Opkomst van het Protestantisme in eene Noord-Nederlandsche Stad.* Leiden.

Knipping, John B. 1974. *Iconography of the Counter Reformation in the Netherlands.* 2d ed. 2 vols. Nieuwkoop.

Knuttel, G. 1938. *De Nederlandsche Schilderkunst van van Eyck tot van Gogh.* Amsterdam.

Koch, Robert A. 1965. "La Sainte-Baume in Flemish Landscape Painting of the Sixteenth Century." *Gazette des Beaux-Arts* 56:272-82.

Koechlin, R. 1924a. *Les Ivoires gothiques français.* Paris.

———. 1924b. "La Partie d'Échecs de Huon de Bordeaux et les Ivoires Français du XIVe Siècle." In *Mélanges Bertaux,* 180-84. Paris.

Kohlhaussen, Heinrich. 1928. *Minnekästchen im Mittelalter.* Berlin.

Koning, D. 1959. "Het geboortejaar, de moeder, en de woning van Lucas van Leyden." *Jaarboekje voor Gechiedenis en Oudheidkunde van Leiden en Omstreken* 51:82-90.

Korevaar-Hesseling, E. H. 1948. *Het Landschap in de Nederlandse en Vlaamse Schilderkunst.* Amsterdam.

Koslow, Susan. 1975. "Frans Hals's Fisherboys: Exemplars of Idleness." *Art Bulletin* 57:418-32.

Krahn, Cornelius. 1968. *Dutch Anabaptism.* The Hague.

Kramm, Christiaan. 1860. *De levens en werken der Hollandsche en Vlaamsche Kunstschilders, Beeldhouwers, Graveurs en Bouwmeesters.* 4 vols. Amsterdam.

Kraus, Dorothy and Henry. 1975. *The Hidden World of Misericords.* New York.

Kristeller, Paul. 1907. "Marcantons Beziehung zu Raffael." *Jahrbuch der Königlich Preuszischen Kunstsammlungen* 28:199-229.

Kronenberg, M. E. 1924. "Lotgevallen van Jan Seversz., Boekdrukker te Leiden (c. 1502-1524) en te Antwerpen (c. 1527-c. 1530)." *Het Boek* 13:1-38.

Krönig, Wolfgang. 1936. *Der italienische Einfluss in der Flämischen Malerei im ersten drittel des 16. Jahrhunderts.* Wurzburg.

Krücke, Adolf. 1959. "Der Protestantismus und die Bildliche Darstellung Gottes." *Zeitschrift für Kunstwissenschaft* 13:59-90.

Kugler, Franz. 1867. *Handbuch der Geschichte der Malerei.* 3d ed. Vol. 2. Leipzig.

Künstle, K. 1928. *Ikonographie der Christlichen Kunst.* Vol. 1. Freiburg.

Kunz, George F. 1917. *Rings for the Finger.* Philadelphia.

Kurth, Betty. 1926. *Die Deutschen Bildteppiche des Mittelalters.* 2 vols. Vienna.

Kurth, Willi. 1963. *The Complete Woodcuts of Albrecht Dürer.* New York.

Kuznetsov, Y. 1975. *Peinture d'Europe Occidentale.* Leningrad.

Laclotte, Michel. 1967. "Vingt Ans d'Acquisitions au Musée du Louvre. 1947-1967." *Revue du Louvre et des Musées du France* 17:295-344.

———. 1970. *Musée du Louvre.* Paris.

Lacroix, Paul. 1871. *Moeurs, usages et costumes au Moyen-Age et à l'époque de la Renaissance.* Paris.

Lafenestre, Georges, and Eugene Richtenberger. 1894-1907. *La Peinture en Europe. V. La Hollande.* Paris.

Lampsonius, Domenicus. 1572. *Pictorum Aliquot Celebrium Germaniae Inferioris Effigies.* Antwerp.

Lankheit, Klaus. 1959. *Das Triptychon als Pathosformel.* Heidelberg.

Lasareff, V. 1938. "Studies in the Iconography of the Virgin." *Art Bulletin* 20:26–65.

Lauts, Jan. 1957. *Meisterwerke der Staatlichen Kunsthalle Karlsruhe.* Karlsruhe.

Lavalleye, Jacques. 1967. *Pieter Bruegel the Elder and Lucas van Leyden: The Complete Engravings, Etchings and Woodcuts.* London.

Le Blanc, Charles. 1854. *Manuel de l'amateur d'estampes.* Vol. 1. Paris.

Le Blant, E. 1878. *Études sur les sarcophages chretiens antiques de la ville d'Arles.* Paris.

Le Comte, Florent. 1702. *Cabinet des Singularitez d'Architecture, Peinture, Sculpture et Graveure.* 2d ed. Vol. 3. Brussels.

Leendertz, P., ed. 1845. *Dirc Potter: Der Minnen Loep.* 2 vols. Leiden.

Lehrs, Max. 1969. *Late Gothic Engravings of Germany and the Netherlands.* New York.

Leiden, Stedelijk Museum. 1886. *Catalogus.*

———. 1949. *Beschrijvende Catalogus van de Schilderijen en Tekeningen.*

———. 1970. *IJdelheid der IJdelheden.* Exhibition catalogue.

———. 1978. *Lucas van Leyden: Rondom het Laatste Oordeel.* Exhibition catalogue.

———. 1983. *Catalogus van de schilderijen en tekeningen.*

Leningrad, Hermitage. 1870. *Catalogue de la Galerie des Tableaux.* 2d ed. Vol. 2.

———. 1955. *Iskusstvo Niderlandov Flandrii i Golandii.*

———. 1958. *Katalog Zhivopisi.* Vol. 2.

Lennep, J., et al. 1870. *Nederlands geschiedenis en Volksleven in schetsen.* Vol. 2. Leiden.

Levi d'Ancona, Mirella. 1977. *The Garden of the Renaissance: Botanical Symbolism in Italian Painting.* Florence.

Lewinson-Lessing, W. F. 1965. *Meisterwerke aus der Eremitage: Malerei des 14. bis 16. Jahrhunderts.* Leningrad.

Leymarie, Jean. 1956. *Dutch Painting.* Paris.

Lindsay, Thomas M. 1925. *A History of the Reformation.* Vol. 2. New York.

Liverpool, Walker Art Gallery. 1963. *Foreign Schools Catalogue.*

London, Arcade Gallery. 1961. *Exhibition of Paintings.* Exhibition catalogue.

London, British Institution for Promoting the Fine Arts. 1849. *Catalogue of Pictures by Italian, Spanish, Flemish, Dutch, French and English Masters.* Exhibition catalogue.

London, Burlington Fine Arts Club. 1892. *Exhibition of Pictures by Masters of the Netherlandish and Allied Schools of XV. and Early XVI. Centuries.* Exhibition catalogue.

———. 1920. *Catalogue of a Collection of Pictures and English Furniture of the Chippendale Period.* Exhibition catalogue.
London, Eugene Slatter. 1949. *Masterpieces Dutch and Flemish Painting.* Exhibition catalogue.
London, National Gallery. 1929. *Catalogue.*
———. 1939. *Catalogue.*
———. 1973. *Illustrated General Catalogue.*
London, Royal Academy of Arts. 1902. *Exhibition of Works by the Old Masters.* Exhibition catalogue.
———. 1929. *Exhibition of Dutch Art, 1450–1900.* Exhibition catalogue.
———. 1952–1953. *Dutch Pictures, 1450–1750.* Exhibition catalogue.
London, Tomas Harris. 1935. *Catalogue of the Exhibition of Early Flemish Paintings.* Exhibition catalogue.
London, Victoria and Albert Museum. 1972. *Flemish Drawings of the Seventeenth Century from the Collection of Frits Lugt. Institut Neerlandais.* Exhibition catalogue.
Lucas, Henry S. 1934. *The Renaissance and the Reformation.* New York.
Lugano-Castagnola, Villa Favorita, Collection Thyssen-Bornemisza. 1977. *Ausgestellte Kunstwerke.*
Lugt, F. 1943. "Rubens and Stimmer." *Art Quarterly* 6:99–114.
———. 1968. *Musée du Louvre. Inventaire General des Dessins des Écoles du Nord: Maîtres des Anciens Pays-Bas, né avant 1550.* Paris.
Lutz, Heinrich. 1961. "Albrecht Dürer und die Reformation, Offene Fragen." In *Miscellanea Bibliothecae Hertziana zu Ehren von Leo Bruhns, Frans Graf Wolff Metternich, Ludwig Schudt,* 175–83. Munich.
Maastricht, Bonnefantenmuseum. 1958. *Catalogue van Schilderijen en Beeldhouwwerken.*
Macfie, Scott. 1943. "Gypsy Persecutions: A Survey of a Black Chapter in European History." *Journal of the Gypsy Lore Society* 22:65–78.
Magasin Pittoresque. 1842. "Musées et Collections Particulières des Departements: Musée de Nantes." 10:324–25.
Mainz, Mittelrheinisches Landesmuseum. 1911. *Katalog.*
———. 1925. *Katalog.*
Mak, J. J. 1948. *Middeleeuwsche Kerstvoorstellingen.* Utrecht and Brussels.
Mâle, Emile. 1925a. *L'Art Religieux de la Fin du Moyen Age en France.* 3d ed. Paris.
———. 1925b. *L'Art Religieux du XIIIe Siècle en France.* 6th ed. Paris.
———. 1932. *L'Art Religieux après le concile de Trente.* Paris.
Manchester. 1857. *Exhibition of Art Treasures.* Exhibition catalogue.
Marette, J. 1961. *Connaissance des Primitifs par l'étude du bois.* Paris.
Marggraff, Rudolf. 1872. *Katalog der älteren königlichen Pinakothek zu München.* 3d ed. Munich.

Markx-Veldman, I. 1973. "Het 'Vulcanus-triptiek' van Maarten van Heemskerck." *Oud-Holland* 87:95–123.

Marlier, Georges. 1954. *Erasme et la Peinture Flamande de Son Temps.* Damme.

Maurer, Friedrich. 1963. "Der Topos von den 'Minnesklaven.'" *Dichtung und Sprache des Mittelalters.* Bern.

Mercier, Fernand. 1937. "La Valeur Symbolique de l'Oeillet dans la Peinture du Moyen-Age." *Revue de l'Art* 71:233–36.

Meyer, E. R. 1954. "Jan van Scorels 'Nieuwe Manier.'" *Oud-Holland* 69:189–93.

———. 1964. *The Rijksmuseum, Amsterdam.* New York.

Meyer, Maurits de. 1970. *Populäre Druckgraphik Europas: Niederlande, Vom 15. Bis zum 20. Jahrhundert.* Munich.

Michel, Edouard. 1926. "Nieuwe Aanwinsten in het Louvre-Museum." *Onze Kunst* 23:90–93.

———. 1953. *Musée National du Louvre: Catalogue Raisonné des Peintures du Moyen-Age, de la Renaissance et des Temps Modernes, Peintures Flamands du XVe et du XVIe Siècle.* Paris.

Michel, Emile. 1893. *Rembrandt.* Paris.

Michiels, Alfred. 1847. *Histoire de la peinture Flamande et Hollandaise.* Vol. 3. Paris.

———. 1868. *Histoire de la peinture Flamande et Hollandaise.* 2d ed. Vol. 5. Paris.

Moedema, Hessel, and Meijer, Bert. 1973. "De introduktie van gekleurde schildergrond en de invloed daarvan op de stilistische ontwikkeling van de schilderkunst." *Proef* (July): 123–50.

Migne, Jacques Paul. 1844–1864. *Patrologiae cursus completus. Series Latina.* Vol. 4. Paris.

Moes, E. W. 1889. "Aanteekeningen van Mr. Hendrik Houmes op van Mander's Schilder-Boeck." *Oud-Holland* 7:149–54.

Morehead, Albert. 1957. *The Fireside Book of Cards.* New York.

Moschini, Vittorio. 1943. *Disegni di Jacopo Bellini.* Bergamo.

Moscow, Pushkin Museum of Fine Arts. 1965. *Exhibition of Paintings of West-European Artists from the Louvre, the Municipal Museum of Bordeaux, and Other Museums in France.* Exhibition catalogue.

Moxey, Keith P. 1977. *Pieter Aertsen, Joachim Beuckelaer, and the Rise of Secular Painting in the Context of the Reformation.* New York.

———. 1989. *Peasants, Warriors, and Wives: Popular Imagery in the Reformation.* Chicago and London.

Müller, Ernst. 1820. *Verzeichniss der Gemälde-Sammlung von Dr. Friedrich Gotthelf Baumgärtner.* Leipzig.

Muller, F. 1853. *Beschrijvende Catalogus van 7000 Portretten van Nederlanders.* Amsterdam.

Müller-Hofstede, Cornelius. 1951. "Zuschreibungs- und Restaurierungs-fragen bei Bildern des Herzog-Anton-Ulrich-Museums in Braunschweig." *Kunstchronik* 4 (October): 242–43.

———. 1959. "Das selbst-bildnis des Lucas van Leyden im Herzog-Anton-Ulrich Museum zu Braunschweig." In *Festschrift Friedrich Winkler,* 221–37. Berlin.

Munich, Alte Pinakothek. 1859. *Verzeichniss der Gemälde.*

———. 1884. *Katalog der Gemälde-Sammlung.*

———. 1936. *Amtlicher Katalog.*

———. 1963. *Katalog, II. Altdeutsche Malerei.*

Münz, Ludwig. 1952. *A Critical Catalogue of Rembrandt's Etchings.* 2 vols. London.

Murray, J. H. R. 1962. *A History of Chess.* Oxford.

Nagler, G. K. 1845. *Neues allgemeines kunstler-lexicon.* 22 vols. Munich.

Nantes, Musée des Beaux-Arts. 1846. *Catalogue des Tableaux et Statues.* 5th ed.

———. 1876. *Catalogue des Objets.* 8th ed.

Nares, Robert. 1859. *A Glossary.* Edited by J. O. Halliwell and T. Wright. Vol. 2. London.

Neugass, Fritz. 1957. "Die Sammlung von Walter P. Chrysler, Jr., New York." *Die Welt-kunst* 27:9.

New York, E. and A. Silberman Galleries. 1955. *An Exhibition of Paintings.* Exhibition catalogue.

New York, Metropolitan Museum of Art. 1970. *100 Paintings from the Boston Museum.* Exhibition catalogue.

New York, World's Fair. 1939. *Masterpieces of Art.* Exhibition catalogue.

Nicolle, Marcel. 1901. "Les recentes acquisitions du Musée du Louvre, Département de la Peinture, 1897–1901." *Revue de l'Art ancien et moderne* 10:189–200.

———. 1913. *Nantes, Musée des Beaux-Arts: Catalogue.* Nantes.

Nicolson, Benedict. 1958. *Hendrick Terbrugghen.* London.

Niemeijer, J. W. 1961. *Schaken als Thema in de Beeldende Kunst.* Wassenaar.

Nikulin, N. 1962. *Detali Kartin Ermitazha: Zapadno-europeiskaya Zhivopis, XV–XVI Vekov* (Details of Paintings in the Hermitage: Western European Painting, 15th and 16th Centuries). Leningrad.

———. 1964. "Ob odnom awtoportrete Luky Lej-denskogo" (On a Self-portrait of Lucas van Leyden). *Soobscenija Gosudarst-wennogo Ermitara* 25:17–19.

———. 1965. "K Istorii Triptikha Luki Leidenskogo 'Istselenie Ierikhonskogo Sleptsa'" (Regarding the History of Lucas van Leyden's *Healing of the Blind man of Jericho*). *Soobscenija Gosudarstwennogo Ermitara* 26:14–18.

———. 1972. *Niderlandskaya Zhivopis XV–XVI Vekov v Ermitazhe* (Netherlandish Painting of the 15th–16th Centuries in the Hermitage). Leningrad.

———. 1978. "Some Data Concerning the History of the Triptych 'The

Healing of the Blind Man' by Lucas van Leyden.'" *Nederlands Kunsthistorisch Jaarboek* 29:299–310.

Nottingham, Midland Counties Art Museum. 1881. *Exhibition*. Exhibition catalogue.

———. 1945. *Exhibition*. Exhibition catalogue.

Nuremberg, Germanischen Nationalmuseums. 1909. *Katalog der Gemälde-Sammlung*. 4th ed.

Oberheide, Albert. 1933. "Der Einfluss Marcantonio Raimondis auf die nordische Kunst des 16. Jahrhunderts." Ph.D. dissertation, Universität, Hamburg.

Obreen, D. O. 1976. *Archief voor Nederlandsche Kunstgeschiedenis*. Soest.

Opmerus, Petrus. 1611. *Opus cronographicum orbis universi*. Antwerp.

Orlers, I. I. 1641 (1614). *Beschrijvinghe der Stadt Leyden*. 2d ed. Leiden.

Oslo, Nasjonalgaleriet. 1973. *Katalog over Utenlandsk Malerkunst*.

Overvoorde, J. C. 1907. "De St. Pieterskerk te Leiden." *Het Huis Oud & Nieuw* 5:133–49.

———. 1915. *Archieven van de Kerken: Gemeente-Archief, Leiden*. 2 vols. Leiden.

Overvoorde, J. C., and W. Martin. 1902. *Stedelijk Museum te Leiden*. Leiden.

Ozment, Steven. 1983. *When Fathers Ruled: Family Life in Reformation Europe*. Cambridge, Mass.

Pächt, O., and J. J. G. Alexander. 1966. *Illuminated Manuscripts in the Bodleian Library, Oxford*. Vol. 1. Oxford.

Panofsky, Erwin. 1969. "Erasmus and the Visual Arts." *Journal of the Warburg and Courtauld Institutes* 32:200–227.

———. 1971a. *The Life and Art of Albrecht Dürer*. Princeton.

———. 1971b. *Early Netherlandish Painting*. 2 vols. New York.

Pape, L. 1836. *Verzeichniss der Gemälde-Sammlung des Herzoglichen Museums in Braunschweig*. Braunschweig.

———. 1849. *Verzeichniss der Gemälde-Sammlung des Herzoglichen Museums zu Braunschweig*. 3d ed. Braunschweig.

Paris, Exposition Universelle. 1900. *Catalogue des Oeuvres d'Art Figurant dans le Pavillon de la Belgique à l'Exposition Universelle de Paris et appartenant a M. L. de Somzée*. Exhibition catalogue.

Paris, Institut Néerlandais. 1959. *Exposition Lucas de Leyde. Gravures*. Exhibition catalogue.

Paris, Musée Cernuschi. 1958–1959. *Orient-Occidents*. Exhibition catalogue.

Paris, Musée des Arts Decoratifs. 1936. *Exposition Retrospective de la vigne et le vin dans l'art*. Exhibition catalogue.

Paris, Orangerie des Tuileries. 1946. *Les Chefs-d'Oeuvres des Collections Privées Françaises retrouvés en Allemagne par la Commission de Récupération Artistique et les Services Alliés*. Exhibition catalogue.

———. 1967–1968. *Vingt ans d' acquisitions au musée du Louvre, 1947–1967.* Exhibition catalogue.
Paris, Petit Palais. 1952. *Chefs-d'Oeuvre de la Collection D. G. van Beuningen.* Exhibition catalogue.
———. 1965–1966. *Le Seizième Siècle European: Peintures et Dessins dans la Collections Publiques Française.* Exhibition catalogue.
Parival, Jean de. 1669. *Les Délices de la Hollande.* Paris.
Parshall, Peter W. 1974. "Lucas van Leyden and the Rise of Pictorial Narrative." Ph.D. dissertation, University of Chicago.
———. 1978. "Lucas van Leyden's Narrative Style." *Nederlands Kunsthistorich Jaarboek* 29:185–237.
———. 1978–1979. Review of Amsterdam, Rijksprentenkabinet, 1978, and Vos, 1978a. *Simiolus* 10:51–54.
———. 1987. "Kunst en reformatie in de noordelijke Nederlanden." *Bulletin van het Rijksmuseum* 35:164–75.
Parthey, G. 1864. *Deutscher Bildersaal.* Vol. 2. Berlin.
Passavant, Johann David. 1833. *Kunstreise durch England und Belgien.* Frankfurt.
———. 1860. *Le Peintre-Graveur.* Leipzig.
Pauli, Gustav. 1907. *Katalog der Gemälde und Bildhauerwerke in der Kunsthalle zu Bremen.* Bremen.
Pelinck, E. 1948. "Petrus en Paulus van Lucas van Leyden." *Apollo: Maandschrift voor Literatur en Beeldende Kunsten* 3:172–77.
———. 1949. "Het Geboortejaar van het 'Wonderkind' Lucas van Leyden." *Oud-Holland* 64:193–96.
Peltzer, R. A. 1911–1912. "Der Hofmaler Hans von Aachen, seine Schule und seine Zeit." *Jahrbuch der Kunsthistorischen Sammlungen des Allerhöchsten Kaiserhauses* 30:59–182.
———. 1925. *Joachim von Sandrart: Teutsche Academie der Bau- Bild- und Mahlerey-Künste, Nuremberg 1675.* Munich.
Philadelphia, John G. Johnson Collection. 1972. *Catalogue of Flemish and Dutch Paintings.*
Phillips, J. A. 1984. *Eve: The History of an Idea.* San Francisco.
Piancastelli, Giovanni. 1898. "Un quadro attribuito a Luca da Leyda enz." *L'Arte* 1:219.
Pigler, Andreas. 1936. "Ein Frühwerk des Lucas van Leyden." *Oud-Holland* 53:182–86.
———. 1954. *Budapest, Orszagos Szepmuveszeti Muzeum: A Regi Keptar Katalogusa.* Budapest.
———. 1968. *Katalog der Galerie Alter Meister.* Budapest.

Piper, Reinhard. 1916. *Das Liebespaar in der Kunst.* Munich.

Pit, A. 1894. *Les Origines de l'Art Hollandaise.* Paris.

Pittsburgh, Carnegie Institute. 1954. *Pictures of Everyday Life: Genre Painting in Europe, 1500–1900.* Exhibition catalogue.

Poch-Kalous, M. 1965. Review of Friedländer, 1963a. *Mitteilungen der Gesellschaft für Vergleichende Kunstforschung in Wien* 18:5–8.

Popelka, Liselotte. 1963–1965. "Susanna Hebraea." *Mitteilungen der Gesellschaft für Vergleichende Kunstforschung in Wien* 16–17:45–50.

Popham, A. E. 1932. *Catalogue of Drawings by Dutch and Flemish Artists Preserved in the Department of Prints and Drawings in the British Museum.* Vol. 5. London.

Portland, Oregon, Art Museum. 1956. *Paintings from the Collection of Walter P. Chrysler, Jr.* Exhibition catalogue.

Princeton, Art Museum. 1969. *Symbols in Transformation: Iconographic Themes at the Time of the Reformation.* Exhibition catalogue.

Provincetown, Mass., Chrysler Art Museum. 1958. *Inaugural Exhibition.* Exhibition catalogue.

R. 1915. "Hoe een 18de eeuwsch 'kunstliefhebber' over Leiden oordeelde." *Jaarboekje voor Geschiedenis en Oudheidkunde van Leiden en Rijnland* 12:181–82.

Randall, L. M. C. 1966. *Images in the Margins of Gothic Manuscripts.* Berkeley.

Rathbone, Perry T. 1970. "Director's Choice." *Apollo* 91:56–67.

Rathgeber, Georg. 1844. *Annalen der Niederländischen Malerei, Formschneide- und Kupferstecherkunst.* Gouda.

Réau, Louis. 1912. "La Galerie de Tableaux de l'Ermitage et la Collection Semenov." *Gazette des Beaux-Arts* 54:471–88.

———. 1956. *Iconographie de l'art chrétien.* 6 vols. Paris.

Renger, Konrad. 1970. *Lockere Gesellschaft: Zur Ikonographie des Verlorenen Sohnes und von Wirtschausszenen in der niederländischen Malerei.* Berlin.

———. 1979. Review of Leiden, Stedelijk Museum, 1978, and Amsterdam, Rijksprentenkabinet, 1978. *Kunstchronik* 32:57–63.

Reznicek, E. K. J. 1956. "Jan Harmensz. Muller als tekenaar." *Nederlands Kunsthistorisch Jaarboek* 7:65–120.

———. 1961. *Die Zeichnungen von Hendrick Goltzius.* 2 vols. Utrecht.

———. 1968. "Enkele Gegevens uit de Vijftiende Eeuw over de Vlaamse Schilderkunst in Florence." In *Miscellanea J. Duverger,* 83–91. Ghent.

Reznicek-Buriks, E. I. 1965. Review of Friedländer, 1963a. *Oud-Holland* 80:241–47.

Rich, D. C. 1933. "The Paintings of Martin A. Ryerson." *Art Institute of Chicago Bulletin* 27:59–60.

Riegel, Herman. 1882. *Die niederländischen Schulen im herzoglichen Museum zu Braunschweig.* 2 vols. Berlin.

———. 1885. *Die Vorzüglichsten Gemälde des Herzoglichen Museums zu Braunschweig*. Berlin.

———. 1900. *Beschreibendes und kritisches Verzeichniss der Gemälde-Sammlung*. Braunschweig.

Ring, Grete. 1912–1913. *Beiträge zur Geschichte Niederländischer Bildnismalerei im 15. und 16. Jahrhundert*. Leipzig.

Ringbom, Sixten. 1965. *Icon to Narrative: The Rise of the Dramatic Close-up in Fifteenth-Century Devotional Painting*. Abo.

———. 1966. "Nuptial Symbolism in Some Fifteenth-Century Reflections of Roman Sepulchral Portraiture." *Temenos* 2:68–97.

Ritchie, Andrew C. 1962. "Recent Gifts and Purchases." *Yale Art Gallery Bulletin* 28 (December): 6–7, 49.

Ritz, G. M. 1972. *Hinterglasmalerei*. Munich.

Rombouts, P., and T. Van Lerius. n.d. *De Liggeren en andere historische Archieven der Antwerpsche Sint Lucasgilde*. Vol. 1. The Hague.

Rome, Galleria Borghese. 1928. *Mostra di Capolavori della Pittura Olandese*. Exhibition catalogue.

Rooses, M. 1886–1892. *L'oeuvre de P. P. Rubens*. Vol. 5. Antwerp.

———. 1903. "Die Vlämischen und Niederländischen Meister in der Ermitage zu St. Petersburg: Lucas van Leiden." *Zeitschrift für Bildenden Kunst* 14:13–16.

Rosenberg, Adolf. 1877. "Lucas von Leyden." In *Kunst und Künstler des Mittelalters und der Neuzeit*, edited by Robert Dohme, vol. 1. Leipzig.

Rosenberg, Jakob. 1943. "Early Flemish Painting." *Bulletin of the Fogg Museum of Art* 10 (November): 47–49.

Rostworowski, Marek. 1973. "Le Vent dans le Paysage Hollandais du XVIIe Siècle." *Bulletin du Musée National de Varsovie* 14:13–30.

Rotterdam, Museum Boymans–van Beuningen. 1930–1931. *Catalogus van de Kersttentoonstelling*. Exhibition catalogue.

———. 1936. *Jeroen Bosch: Noord-Nederlandsche Primitieven*. Exhibition catalogue.

———. 1938. *Meesterwerken uit Vier Eeuwen, 1400–1800: Tentoonstelling van Schilderijen en Teekeningen uit Particuliere Verzamelingen in Nederland*. Exhibition catalogue.

———. 1949. *Meesterwerken uit de Verzameling D. G. van Beuningen*. Exhibition catalogue.

———. 1955. *Kunstschatten uit Nederlandse Verzamelingen*. Exhibition catalogue.

———. 1962. *Catalogus schilderijen tot 1800*.

———. 1965. *Jan Gossaert genaamd Mabuse*. Exhibition catalogue.

Rupprich, Hans, ed. 1956. *Dürer: Schriftlicher Nachlass*. 3 vols. Berlin.

Ryan, G., and H. Ripperger, trans. 1948. *The Golden Legend of Jacobus de Voragine*. New York.

St. Gallen, Kunstmuseum. 1947. *Hauptwerke der Staatlichen Kunsthalle Karlsruhe.* Exhibition catalogue.
Salinger, Margarete. 1941. "Two New Flemish Paintings." *Bulletin of the Metropolitan Museum of Art* 36 (May): 109–11.
Sarna, Nahum. 1966. *Understanding Genesis.* New York.
Scannelli da Forli, Francesco. 1657. *Il Microcosmo della Pittura.* Cesena.
Schaffhausen. 1951. *Meisterwerke Europäischer Malerei.* Exhibition catalogue.
Scheibler, L. 1883. Review of *Beiträge zur niederländischen kunstgeschichte* by Herman Riegel. *Repertorium für Kunstwissenschaft* 6:189–99.
Schlegel, Friedrich. 1823. *Sämmtliche Werke.* Vol. 6. Vienna.
Schleissheim, Königlichen Gallerie. 1885. *Verzeichniss.*
Schleissheim, Königlichen Gemäldegalerie. 1914. *Katalog.*
Schlosser, Hanspeter. 1966. "Die Daniel-Susanna-Erzählung in Bild und Literatur der christlichen Frühzeit." In *Tortulae: Studien zu Altchristlichen und Byzantinischen Monumenten,* edited by W. N. Schumacher, 243–49. Freiburg.
Schnaase, Karl. 1834. *Niederländische Briefe.* Stuttgart.
Schneider, Jenny. 1960. "Die Weiberlisten." *Zeitschrift für Schweizerische Archäologie und Kunstgeschichte* 20:147–57.
Scholten, H. J. 1904. *Musée Teyler à Haarlem: Catalogue Raisonné des Dessins des Écoles Française et Hollandaise.* Haarlem.
Schöne, Wolfgang. 1938. *Dieric Bouts und seine Schule.* Berlin.
Schreiber, W. L. 1937. *Die ältesten Spielkarten.* Strasbourg.
Schröder, Edward. 1882. "Das Goldene Spiel von Meister Ingold." In *Elsässischer Litteraturdenkmäler aus dem XIV–XVII Jahrhundert,* edited by E. Martin and E. Schmidt, vol. 3. Strasbourg.
Schubert, Dietrich. 1973. "Quentin Massys porträtiert von Jan van Scorel?" *Musées Royaux des Beaux-Arts de Belgique, Bruxelles, Bulletin* 22:7–32.
Schultz, Alwin. 1892. *Deutsches Leben im XIV. und XV. Jahrhundert.* 2 vols. Vienna.
Schuyer, E. H. 1968. *Het Schaakspel in de Kunst en Cultuurhistorie.* Bussum.
Seeger, Carl. 1843. *Das Grossherzogliche Museum zu Darmstadt.* Darmstadt.
Seguin, Jean-Pierre. 1968. *Le Jeu de Carte.* Paris.
Seligman, Dorothy C. 1923. "A Roundel of Painted Glass Attributed to Lucas van Leyden." *Connoisseur* 66 (May): 13–15.
Semenov, P. 1885–1886. *Etiudy po istorii niderlandskoi jivopisi* (Studies in the History of Dutch Painting). Leningrad.
Semrau, Franz. 1910. *Würfel und Würfelspiel in Alten Frankreich.* Halle.
Shestack, A. 1967. *Master E. S.* Philadelphia.
Sidney, 16th Earl of Pembroke. 1968. *A Catalogue of the Paintings and Drawings in the Collection at Wilton House, Salisbury.* London.
Siebert, Margarete. 1906. *Die Madonnendarstellung in der Altniederländischen kunst von Jan van Eyck bis zu den Manieristen.* Strasbourg.

Sieper, Ernst. 1898. "Les Échecs Amoureux." *Litterarhistorische Forschungen* 9:1–251.
———. 1903. *Lydgate's Reson and Sensuallyte.* 2 vols. London.
Silver, L. A. 1973. "The 'Sin of Moses': Comments on the Early Reformation in a Late Painting by Lucas van Leyden." *Art Bulletin* 55:401–9.
———. 1974a. "The Ill-Matched Pair by Quinten Massys." *Studies in the History of Art, The National Gallery, Washington* 6:104–23.
———. 1974b. "Quinten Massys." Ph.D. dissertation, Harvard University, Cambridge.
———. 1974c. "Reply." *Art Bulletin* 56:310–11.
———. 1975. "Reply." *Art Bulletin* 57:149.
———. 1976. "Of Beggars—Lucas van Leyden and Sebastian Brant." *Journal of the Warburg and Courtauld Institutes* 39:253–57.
———. 1983. "Fools and Women: Profane Subjects by Lucas van Leyden." *Print Collector's Newsletter* 14:130–34.
———. 1986. "*Figure nude, historie e poesie:* Jan Gossaert and the Renaissance Nude in the Netherlands." *Nederlands Kunsthistorisch Jaarboek* 37:1–40.
Silver, L. A., and S. Smith. 1978. "Carnal Knowledge: The Late Engravings of Lucas van Leyden." *Nederlands Kunsthistorisch Jaarboek* 29:239–98.
Simon, Edith. 1966. *The Reformation.* New York.
Sjöblom, Axel. 1928. *Die Koloristische Entwicklung in der Niederländischen Malerei des XV. und XVI. Jahrhunderts.* Berlin.
Smith, Elise Lawton. 1992. "Women and the Moral Argument of Lucas van Leyden's *Dance around the Golden Calf.*" *Art History* 15 (September).
Smith, John. 1842. *Supplement to the Catalogue Raisonné of the Works of the most eminent Dutch, Flemish, and French Painters.* Vol. 9. London.
Smith, Susan. 1978. "To women's wiles I fell: The Power of Women 'Topos' and the Development of Medieval Secular Art." Ph.D. dissertation, University of Pennsylvania, Philadelphia.
Snyder, J. E. 1971. "The Early Haarlem School of Painting. Part III. The Problem of Geertgen tot Sint Jans and Jan Mostaert." *Art Bulletin* 53:444–58.
Spelman, Leslie P. 1951. "Luther and the Arts." *Journal of Aesthetics and Art Criticism* 10 (December): 166–75.
Spiers, Historisches Museum. 1957. *Ein Grosses Jahrhundert der Malerei.* Exhibition catalogue.
Sporham-Krempel, L. 1958. *Eine Handvoll Glück: Plaudereien um Spielkarten und Kartenspieler.* Munich.
Starkie, Walter. 1957. "Jerome Bosch's 'The Hay-wain.'" *Journal of the Gypsy Lore Society* 36:83–87.
Stechow, Wolfgang. 1966. *Northern Renaissance Art, 1400–1600: Sources and Documents.* Englewood Cliffs.

Steele, Martha L. 1978. "The Development of the Netherlandish Marriage Portrait, 1425–1550." Bachelor's thesis, Reed College, Portland.

Steinbart, Kurt. 1929. "Nachlese im Werke des Jacob Cornelisz." *Marburger Jahrbuch für Kunstwissenschaft* 5:213–60.

Sterling, Charles. 1930. "Réplique d'une composition perdue de Lucas de Leyde." *Bulletin des Musées de France*, 109–12.

Stewart, Alison G. 1977. *Unequal Lovers: A Study of Unequal Couples in Northern Art*. New York.

Stiassny, Robert. 1888. "Altdeutsche und Altniederländer in oberitalienischen Sammlungen." *Repertorium für Kunstwissenschaft* 11:369–95.

Stockholm, Rapps Art Dealer. 1948. *Gamla Nederländska Mästare*. Exhibition catalogue.

Strasbourg, Musée des Beaux-Arts. 1899. *Verzeichnis der Städtischen Gemäldesammlung*.

―――. 1938. *Catalogue des Peintures Anciennes*.

Straus-Ernst, Luise. 1921. "Die Sammlung Clemens." *Zeitschrift für bildende Kunst* 58:14–18.

Strauss, Walter L. 1974. *The Complete Drawings of Albrecht Dürer*. 6 vols. New York.

Stuffmann, Margret. 1968. "Les Tableaux de la collection de Pierre Crozat." *Gazette des Beaux-Arts* 72:11–143.

Stuttgart, Staatsgalerie. 1958–1959. *Meisterwerke aus badenwürttembergischem Privatbesitz*. Exhibition catalogue.

Suida, William E., and Fern Rusk Shapley. 1956. *Paintings and Sculptures from the Kress Collection Acquired by the Samuel H. Kress Foundation, 1951–1956*. Washington.

Sulzberger, Suzanne. 1965. "Considerations sur la chef-d'oeuvre de Quentin Metsys: Le prêteur et sa femme." *Bulletin Musée Royaux des Beaux-Arts* 19:27–34.

Swain, Barbara. 1969. *Fools and Folly during the Middle Ages and the Renaissance*. New York.

Swan, Charles, trans. 1872. *Gesta Romanorum*. 2 vols. New York.

Swillens, P. T. A. 1957. "Carel van Manders kritiek op de schilderijen van Jan van Scorel en diens tijdgenoten." In *Miscellanea Prof. Dr. D. Roggen*, 267–77. Antwerp.

Tabarrini, Marco, ed. 1890. *Trattato della pittura di Leonardo da Vinci*. Rome.

Talbot, Charles W. 1981. "Baldung and the Female Nude." In *Hans Baldung Grien: Prints and Drawings*, 19–37. Exhibition catalogue. Washington, D.C.

Taurel, C. E. 1881. *De Christelijke Kunst in Holland en Vlaanderen*. Vol. 2. Amsterdam.

Taylor, E. S. 1973. *The History of Playing Cards*. Rutland, Vt.

Taylor, G. S., ed. 1930. *The Book of the Knight of La Tour-Landry*. London.

Tea, Eva. 1932. *La Pinacoteca Ambrosiana di Milano*. Milan.
Tervarent, Guy de. 1958. *Attributs et Symbols dans l'Art Profane 1450–1600*. Geneva.
Tietze, Hans. 1935. *Meisterwerke europäischer Malerei in Amerika*. Vienna.
Tietze-Conrat, E. 1957. *Dwarfs and Jesters in Art*. London.
Timmers, J. J. M. 1978. *Christelijke Symboliek en Iconografie*. 3d ed. Haarlem.
Tirion, I. 1742. *Hedendaagsche Historie of Tegen-woordige Staat van alle Volkeren*. Vol. 14. Amsterdam.
Toledo, Museum of Art. 1935. *Catalogue: French and Flemish Primitive Exhibition*. Exhibition catalogue.
Toth, Karl. 1943. *Die Alten Niederländer von Eyck bis Brueghel*. Bielefeld.
Troescher, Georg. 1939. "Weltgerichtsbilder in Rathäusern und Gerichtsstätten." *Wallraf-Richartz-Jahrbuch* 11:139–214.
Trumpf, Peter. 1958. *Spielkarten und Kartenspiele*. Heidelberg.
Tschudi, Hugo von. 1893. "London: Die Austellung altniederländischer Gemälde im Burlington Fine Arts Club." *Repertorium für Kunstwissenschaft* 16:100–116.
Tümpel, Christian. 1969. "Studien zur Ikonographie der Historien Rembrandts." *Nederlands Kunsthistorisch Jaarboek* 20:107–98.
Utrecht, Aartsbisschoppelijk Museum. 1962. *Het Wonder: Miracula Christi*. Exhibition catalogue.
Utrecht, Centraal Museum. 1933. *Catalogus der Schilderijen*.
———. 1955. *Jan van Scorel*. Exhibition catalogue.
Utrecht, Gebouw voor Kunsten en Wetenschappen. 1913. *Tentoonstelling van Noord-Nederlandsche Schilder- en Beeldhouw-kunst voor 1575*. Exhibition catalogue.
Utrecht, Gemeentelijke Archiefdienst. 1976. *Recht en Slecht*. Exhibition catalogue.
Valentiner, W. R. 1913. *Catalogue of a Collection of Paintings and Some Art Objects: John G. Johnson*. 3 vols. Philadelphia.
———. 1919. "Gemälde des Lucas van Leyden in Amerika." *Der Kunstwanderer* 1 (September): 117–19.
Valentiner, W. R., and P. Wescher. 1950. *A Catalogue of Paintings in the Collection of Louis and Mildred Kaplan*. New York.
Van Asperen de Boer, J. R. J., and Wheelock, Arthur K. 1973. "Underdrawings in Some Paintings by Cornelis Engebrechtsz." *Oud-Holland* 87:61–94.
Van Balen, C. L. 1930. *De Blijde Inkomst der Renaissance in de Nederlanden*. Leiden.
Van Brussel, Ton, Ingrid Moerman, and Maarten Wurfbain. 1978. *Het Laatste Oordeel*. Leiden.
Van Campen, J. W. C. 1940. *Notae Quotidianae van Aernout van Buchell*. Utrecht.
Van der Burch, A. H. H. 1887. "Rapiamus." *Oud-Holland* 5:72.
Van der Linde, A. 1874. *Geschichte und Literatur des Schachspiels*. 2 vols. Berlin.
———. 1875. *Schaakspel in Nederland*. Utrecht.

Van de Waal, H. 1952. *Drie Eeuwen Vaderlandsche Geschied-Uitbeelding. 1500–1800. Een Iconologische Studie.* The Hague.

Van de Wall, Constant. 1969. *Carel van Mander. Dutch and Flemish Painters.* New York.

Van de Wetering, Cornelis. 1938. *Die Entwicklung der niederländischen Landschaftsmalerei vom Anfang des 16. Jahrhunderts bis zur Jahrhunderermitte.* Berlin.

Van Gelder, H. A. Enno. 1959. *Erasmus, Schilders en Rederijkers: De religieuze crisis der 16e. eeuw weerspiegeld in toneel- en schilderkunst.* Groningen.

Van Gelder, H. E. 1976. *De Nederlandse Munten.* 6th ed. Utrecht.

Van Gelder, J. G. 1938. "Het Altaarstuk van Lucas van Leyden in het Stedelijk Museum 'De Lakenhal' te Leiden." *Beeldende Kunst Maandblad* 25 (October): 41–48.

———. 1946. " 'De Kerkprediking' van Lucas van Leyden." *Oud-Holland* 61:101–6.

———. 1957. "Verloren werken van Lucas van Leyden." In *Miscellanea Prof. Dr. D. Roggen,* 91–100. Antwerp.

———. 1971. "Jan de Bisschop 1628–1671." *Oud-Holland* 86:201–59.

Van Ghert, Florent, ed. 1840. "Lucas van Leyde." *Kunstkronijk* 1:13–14.

Van Gils, J. B. F. 1946. "Lucas van Leyden met knevel." *Oud-Holland* 61:70–72.

Van Hall, H. 1963. *Portretten van Nederlandse Beeldende Kunstenaars.* Amsterdam.

Van Kappen, O. 1962. "Three Dutch Safe-Conducts for 'Heidens' Granted by Charles Duke of Egmont." *Journal of the Gypsy Lore Society* 41:89–100.

Van Mander, Carel. 1604. *Het Schilder-Boeck.* Haarlem.

Van Marle, Raimond. 1971. *Iconographie de l'Art Profane au Moyen-Age et à la Renaissance.* 2 vols. New York.

Van Mieris, Frans. 1762. *Beschryving der Stad Leyden.* 2 vols. Leiden.

Van Moorsel, P. P. V. 1966. "Rotswonder of Door-tocht door de Rode Zee." *Mededelingen van het Nederlands Historisch Instituut te Rome* 33:1–129.

Van Regteren Altena, J. Q. 1939. "Aertgen van Leyden." *Oud-Holland* 56:74–87, 226–30.

———. 1955. "Hugo Jacobsz." *Nederlands Kunsthistorisch Jaarboek* 6:101–17.

Van Rijckevorsel, J. L. 1932. *Rembrandt en de Traditie.* Rotterdam.

Van Rijnberk, Gerard. 1947. *Le Tarot.* Lyon.

Van Schendel, A. 1953. "Lucas van Leyden's 'Dans om het Gouden Kalf' terug in Amsterdam." *Bulletin van het Rijksmuseum* 1:2–7.

Van Someren, Jan Frederik. 1888–1891. *Beschrijvende catalogus van gegraveerde portretten van Nederlanders.* 3 vols. Amsterdam.

Van Thiel, P. J. J. 1965. "Cornelis Cornelisz. van Haarlem as a Draughtsman." *Master Drawings* 3:123–54.

Vasari, Giorgio. 1906. *Le Vite de' Piu Eccellenti Pittori Scultori ed Architettori scritti da Giorgio Vasari.* Edited by Gaetano Milanesi. 9 vols. Florence.

———. 1970. *The Lives of the Painters, Sculptors, and Architects.* Translated by A. B. Hinds. Vol. 2. London.

Vaughan, Malcolm. 1939. "Old Masters at the Fair." *Parnassus* 11 (May): 4–13.

Vaux de Foletier, François de. 1961. *Les Tsiganes dans l'Ancienne France.* Paris.

———. 1966. "Iconographie des 'Egyptiens.'" *Gazette des Beaux-Arts* 67:165–72.

Vergote, J. 1959. *Joseph en Egypte.* Louvain.

Vermeulen, Frans. 1915. "Eenige Opmerkingen bij het zelfportret van Lucas van Leyden te Brunswijk." *Onze Kunst* 27:98–104.

Verslagen. 1952. "Rijksmuseum van Schilderijen. Aanwinsten." *Verslagen's Rijks Verzamelingen van Geschiedenis en Kunst* 74:10–16.

Vertue. 1757. *A Catalogue and Description of King Charles the First's Capital Collection.* London.

Veth, Cornelis. 1936. "Rotterdam. De tentoonstelling in Boymans: Jeroen Bosch, Van Geertgen tot Scorel, Noord-Nederlandsche Primitieven." *Maandblad voor Beeldende Kunsten* 13:286–90.

Veth, Jan. 1906. "Rembrandt's Zoogenaamde Jodenbruid uit de Kollektie van der Hoop." *Oud-Holland* 24:41–44.

Veth, J., and S. Muller. 1918. *Albrecht Dürers Niederländische Reise.* 2 vols. Berlin.

Vetter, Ewald M. 1966. "Necessarium Adae Peccatum." *Ruperto-Carola* 18:144–81.

Vienna, Liechtenstein Collection. 1780. *Description des Tableaux, et des Pièces de Sculpture, que Renferme la Gallerie de son Altesse François Joseph, Chef et Prince Regnant de la Maison Liechtenstein.*

———. 1885. *Katalog der Fürstlich Liechtensteinischen Bilder-Galerie.*

———. 1925. *Führer durch die Fürstlich Liechtensteinsche Gemäldegalerie.*

Voet, Leon. 1973. *Antwerp, the Golden Age: The Rise and Glory of the Metropolis in the Sixteenth Century.* Antwerp.

Vogelsang, W. 1927. "Een onbekend Schilderij van Lucas van Leyden." *Maandblad voor beeldende Kunsten* 4:3–5.

Volbehr, Theodor. 1888. *Lucas van Leyden. Verzeichniss seiner Kupferstiche Radirungen und Holzschnitte.* Hamburg.

Volkmann, J. J. 1783. *Neueste Reisen durch die Vereinigten Niederlande.* Leipzig.

Von der Osten, Gert. 1961. "Studien zu Jan Gossaert." In *De Artibus Opuscula XL: Essays in Honor of Erwin Panofsky,* edited by M. Meiss, 454–75. New York.

Von der Osten, Gert, and Horst Vey. 1969. *Painting and Sculpture in Germany and the Netherlands, 1500–1600.* Baltimore.

Von Dillis, J. G. 1839. *Catalogue des Tableaux dans la Pinacothèque Royale à Munic.* Munich.

Von Frimmel, Theodor. 1898. *Galeriestudien: Geschichte der Wiener Gemäldesammlung.* Vol. 1. Leipzig.

———. 1907. "Ein Neu Aufgefundener Lukas van Leyden." *Blätter für Gemäldekunde* 4 (December): 34–40.

———. 1920–1921. "Zu den Davidbildern des Lukas van Leyden: Ein neu aufgefundenes Gemälde." *Studien und Skizzen zur Gemäldekunde* 5:149–53.

Von Heinecken, C. H. 1769. *Nachrichten von Künstlern und Kunst-Sachen.* Vol. 2. Leipzig.

Von Lehner, F. A. 1883. *Fürstlich Hohenzollern'sches Museum zu Sigmaringen: Verzeichnis der Gemälde.* Sigmaringen.

Von Löhneysen, H. W. 1956. *Die Ältere Niederländische Malerei. Künstler und Kritiker.* Eisenach.

Von Mannlich, C. 1810. *Beschreibung der Churpfalzbaierischen Gemäldesammlungen zu München und Schleissheim.* Vol. 3. Munich.

Von Reber, F. 1892. *Kurfürst Maximilian I von Bayern als Gemäldesammler.* Munich.

Von Simson, Otto. 1977. "Gerard Davids Gerechtigkeitsbild und der spätmittelalterliche Humanismus." In *Festschrift Wolfgang Braunfels,* edited by F. Piel and J. Traeger, 349–56. Tübingen.

Von Uffenbach, Z. C. 1754. *Merkwürdige Reisen durch Niedersachsen, Holland und Engelland.* Vol. 3. Ulm.

Von Weizenfeld, J. N. E. 1775. *Beschreibung der Churfürstlichen Bildergallerie in Schleissheim.* Munich.

Von Wurzbach, Alfred. 1885. *Geschichte der holländischen Malerei.* Leipzig.

———. 1910. *Niederländisches Künstler-Lexikon.* 2 vols. Vienna.

Vos, Rik. 1978a. *Lucas van Leyden.* Bentveld.

———. 1978b. *Rijksmuseum Kunst-Krant* 5 (September): 1–4.

———. 1978c. "The Life of Lucas van Leyden by Karel van Mander." *Nederlands Kunsthistorisch Jaarboek* 29:459–507.

Waagen, G. F. 1854. *Treasures of Art in Great Britain.* Vol. 3. London.

———. 1860. *Handbook of Paintings.* Vol. 1. London.

———. 1862. *Handbuch der deutschen und niederländischen Malerschulen.* Stuttgart.

———. 1864. *Die Gemäldesammlung in der Kaiserlichen Ermitage zu St. Petersburg.* Munich.

Waetzoldt, Wilhelm. 1908. *Die Kunst des Porträts.* Leipzig.

Waldburg-Wolfegg, Johannes. 1957. *Das mittelalterliche Hausbuch.* Munich.

Walker, John. 1975. *National Gallery of Art, Washington.* New York.

Walvis, J. 1714. *Beschryving der Stad Gouda.* Vol. 2. Gouda.

Warburg, Aby. 1932. "Austauch Künstlerischer Kultur Zwischen Norden und süden im 15. Jahrhundert." In *Gesammelte Schriften,* 1:179–84. Leipzig.
Warsaw, National Museum. 1969. *Catalogue of Paintings: Foreign Schools, I.*
Washington, National Gallery. 1948. *Paintings from the Berlin Museums.* Exhibition catalogue.
———. 1965. *Summary Catalogue of European Paintings and Sculpture.*
———. 1967–1968. *Fifteenth Century Engravings of Northern Europe.* Exhibition catalogue.
———. 1975. *European Paintings: An Illustrated Summary Catalogue.*
———. 1979–1980. *Old Master Paintings from the Collection of Baron Thyssen-Bornemisza.* Exhibition catalogue.
———. 1983. *The Prints of Lucas van Leyden and His Contemporaries.* Exhibition catalogue by Ellen S. Jacobowitz and Stephanie Loeb Stepanek.
Watson, Elkanah. 1790. *A Tour in Holland in MDCCLXXXIV by an American.* Worcester, Mass.
Watson, J. S., trans. 1902. *Quintilian's Institutes of Oratory.* 2 vols. London.
Wegner, Wolfgang. 1959. "Mittelalterliche Kunst der Nördlichen Niederlande: Die Jubiläumausstellung des Rijksmuseums in Amsterdam." *Kunstchronik* 12:5–12.
Wehle, Harry B. 1947. "The Chess Players by Francesco di Giorgio." *Bulletin, The Metropolitan Museum of Art* 5:153–56.
Weigand, W. 1959. *Das königliche Spiel.* Berlin.
Weisz, E. 1913. *Jan Gossaert, gen. Mabuse.* Parchim.
Weller, Allen. 1940. "A Reconstruction of Francesco di Giorgio's 'Chess Game.'" *Art Quarterly* 3:162–72.
Welsford, E. 1935. *The Fool.* London.
Wescher, Paul. 1929. "Leyden, Lucas Hugensz. van." In *Allgemeines Lexikon der Bildenden Künstler,* edited by Ulrich Thieme and Felix Becker, 23:168–70. Leipzig.
Westhoff-Krummacher, Hildegard. 1965. *Barthel Bruyn der Altere als Bildnismaler.* Munich.
White, John. 1972. *The Raphael Cartoons.* London.
Whittlesey, E. S. 1972. *Symbols and Legends in Western Art.* New York.
Wichmann, Hans and Siegfried. 1960. *Schach.* Munich.
Wilde, Johannes. 1974. *Venetian Art from Bellini to Titian.* Oxford.
Wilkinson, N. R. 1907. *Wilton House Pictures.* Vol. 1. London.
Willshire, W. H. 1876. *A Descriptive Catalogue of Playing and Other Cards in the British Museum.* London.
Winkler, Friedrich. 1924. *Die Altniederländische Malerei.* Berlin.
———. 1936. *Die Zeichnungen Albrecht Dürers.* Vol. 4. Berlin.

Winternitz, Emanuel. 1967. *Musical Instruments and Their Symbolism in Western Art.* London.

Winzinger, F. 1963. *Albrecht Altdorfer Graphik.* Munich.

Wolfthal, Diane. 1989. *The Beginnings of Netherlandish Canvas Painting, 1400–1530.* Cambridge.

Wolter, Franz. 1926. "Ein wiedergefundenes Originalbild des Lucas von Leyden." *Oud-Holland* 43:228–34.

Wolters, W. P. 1874. *Het Laatste Oordeel van Lucas van Leiden.* Leiden.

Woltmann, Alfred. 1870. *Fürstlich Fürstenbergische Sammlungen zu Donauschingen: Verzeichniss der Gemälde.* Donauschingen.

Woltmann, Alfred, and Karl Woermann. 1882. *Geschichte der Malerei.* Vol. 2. Leipzig.

Worringer, Wilhelm. 1919. *Die Altdeutsche Buchillustration.* 2d ed. Munich.

Wrangell, B. N. 1909. *Les Chefs-d'Oeuvre de la Galerie des Tableaux de L'Ermitage Impérial à St. Petersbourg.* Munich.

———. 1913. "Iskusstvo i Gosudari Nikolai Pavlovich" (The Arts and the Tzar Nikolai Pavlovich). *Starye Gody* 7:64, 87.

Wurfbain, M. L. 1971. "Lucas van Leyden, 'De Dans om het Gouden Kalf.'" *Openbaar Kunstbezit* 15:17a–b.

———. 1978. "De genreschilderijen van Lucas van Leyden." *Antiek* 13 (October): 199–210.

Wyntjes, Sherrin. 1977. "Women in the Reformation Era." In *Becoming Visible: Women in European History,* ed. Renate Bridenthal and Claudia Koonz. Boston.

York, City Art Gallery. 1955. *The Lycett Green Collection.* Exhibition catalogue.

———. 1961. *Catalogue of Paintings.* Vol. 1.

Zarncke, Friedrich, ed. 1964. *Sebastian Brant, Narrenschiff.* Darmstadt.

Zimerman, Heinrich. 1889. "Inventare, Acten und Regesten aus der Schatzkammer des Allerhöchsten Kaiserhauses." *Jahrbuch des Kunsthistorischen Sammlungen des Allerhöchsten Kaiserhauses* 10:cci–cccxxiv.

———. 1905. "Das Inventar der Prager Schatz- und Kunstkammer, vom 6. Dezember 1621." *Jahrbuch der Kunsthistorischen Sammlungen des Allerhöchsten Kaiserhauses* 25:xiii–lxxv.

INDEX

Page numbers in italics refer to illustrations

Aachen, Suermondt Museum: artist unknown (copy after Lucas van Leyden), *Christ Healing the Blind Man,* 141, 143, *235;* Leiden School, *Last Supper,* 12, 189, 190
Aertgen van Leyden, x, 72, 73, 82, 84, 99, 100, 120, 122, 124, 127, 131, 132, 141, 303*n*3, 304*n*1, 311*n*7, 317*n*21, 319*n*2, 322*n*5, 337*n*4
Aertsen, Pieter, 83
Aldegrever, H., 53
Amsterdam, Rijksmuseum: artist unknown, *Allegory of Transience,* 278*n*23; artist unknown (copy after Lucas van Leyden), *Christ as Man of Sorrows and Virgin of Sorrows,* 117; artist unknown (copy after Lucas van Leyden), *Virgin and Child,* 36, 133, 134–36; artist unknown, *Works of Charity,* 278*n*23; Leiden School Master of the Sermon (Aertgen van Leyden?), *Sermon,* x, 198–99, 272, 337*n*4; Master of the St. John Panels (?), *St. Anne with the Virgin and Child, Saints and Donors,* 279*n*27. *See also* Van Leyden, Lucas, Paintings: *Dance around the Golden Calf*
Amsterdam, Rijksprentenkabinet: workshop of Huygh Jacobsz.(?), cartoon series, 11. *See also* Van Leyden, Lucas, Drawings: *Standing Boy with a Sword*
Amsterdam, Six Collection: artist unknown, *Portrait of a Man in a Red Hat* and *Portrait of a Man in a Three-Cornered Hat,* 199–200
Anthonisz., Cornelis (also known as Cornelis Anthonisz. Theunissen), 53–54, 65

Antwerp, Koninklijk Museum voor Schone Kunsten: artist unknown (copy after Lucas van Leyden), *Betrothal,* 176–77

Baldass, Ludwig, x
Bangs, Jeremy D., 7, 9, 13, 69, 72, 76
Basel, Historisches Museum: artist unknown, tapestries with gaming scenes, 47, 52, *266*
Beatrys (stepmother of Lucas van Leyden), 6
Beets, N., x
Bellegambe, Jean, 131
Bellini: Gentile, 25; Giovanni, 100; Jacopo, 41
Bening, Simon, 187–88
Benson, Ambrosius, 187–88
Berlin-Dahlem, Kupferstichkabinett, Staatliche Museen Preussischer Kulturbesitz: artist unknown (copy after Lucas van Leyden), *Allegory of Transience* (drawing), 173, *250. See also* Van Leyden, Lucas, Drawings: *Head of a Young Man Looking Upward; Virgin Annunciate*
Berlin-Dahlem, Staatliche Museen Preussischer Kulturbesitz: artist unknown (copy after Lucas van Leyden), *Adoration of the Magi,* 121; artist unknown (copy after Lucas van Leyden), *St. Jerome Penitent,* 193–94. *See also* Van Leyden, Lucas, Paintings: *Chess Players; Virgin and Child with Angels*
Bloemaert, Abraham, 84
Bode, Wilhelm, x

Bonn, Provinzial Museum: artist unknown, *Adoration of the Magi,* 311n4
Boon, K. G., 11
Bosch, Hieronymus, 18, 53, 57, 67, 82, 126, 182, 284n35, 296n93
Boschuysen, Elysabeth van (wife of Lucas van Leyden), 3, 7, 276n14
Boston, Museum of Fine Arts. *See* Van Leyden, Lucas, Paintings: *Moses after Striking the Rock*
Bouts, Dirk, 28, 36, 282n22, 306n3, 310n4, 321n4
Brant, Sebastian (author of *Das Narrenschiff*), 53, 55, 62, 64, 66, 268, 291n43, 292n48
Braunschweig, Herzog Anton Ulrich-Museum. *See* Van Leyden, Lucas, Paintings: *Portrait of a Man*
Brunswick Monogrammist, 54, 83, 183
Brussels, Musées Royaux des Beaux-Arts: Jan de Bisschop (copy after Lucas van Leyden), *Betrothal,* 177–78; Jan de Bisschop (copy after Lucas van Leyden), *Procession of the Holy Sacrament,* 160–61, 256
Bruyn, Joos, x
Buchelius, Arnoldus, 9–10, 83, 334n3
Budapest, Museum of Fine Arts: artist unknown (copy after Lucas van Leyden), *Card Players,* xii, 54–56, 171–72, 173, 175, 179, 250; Circle of the Master of Delft(?), *Entombment,* 279n27
Burgkmair, Hans, 53

Calvin, John, 64, 70
Cambridge, Mass., Busch-Reisinger Museum: artist unknown (Netherlandish), *Angel,* 186
Caravaggio, 84, 290n34
Cards, 45–46, 50–56
Chess, 45–50, 51
Chevalier délibéré, 10–12 *passim*
Chicago, Art Institute: Cornelis Cornelisz. Kunst(?), *Adoration of the Magi,* 187–89, 311n4
Christus, Petrus, 17, 326n16
Classical sources, 32, 33
Cologne, Kunstgewerbemuseum: artist unknown (copy after Lucas van Leyden), *Rest on the Flight into Egypt,* 132–33
Copies after lost originals, xi–xii
Cornelisz., Cornelis (also known as Cornelis Cornelisz. Kunst), 187–89, 285n48, 304n1
Cornelisz., Jacob, 81, 110, 112, 129, 131, 191, 270, 274n2, 283n23, 283n24, 284n41, 312n10, 314n11, 322n3, 323n9, 336n1
Cornelisz., Lucas (son of Cornelis Engebrechtsz., also known as Lucas Cornelisz. de Kock), 9, 200, 304n1, 333n4, 338n1
Cornelisz., Pieter (also known as Pieter Cornelisz. Kunst), 11, 280n28, 296n96

Darmstadt, Hessisches Landesmuseum: artist unknown, *Rest on the Flight,* 309n13
David, Gerard, 94, 187–88, 281n12, 282n22
De Bisschop, Jan, xii, 16, 22–23, 25, 43–44, 77, 83, 98, 99, 100, 105–6, 119–20, 138–39, 148–49, 155, 160, 177–78, 226, 242, 244, 254–56
De Bruyn, Nicolas, 83, 100, 123–24, 149, 246, 252, 254
Dijon, Musée des Beaux-Arts: artist unknown (copy after Lucas van Leyden), *Christ as Man of Sorrows and Virgin of Sorrows,* 117
Dolendo, Bartholomaus, 83, 179–80, 257
Doncaster, South Yorkshire, Doncaster Museum Art Gallery: artist unknown, *Portrait of Claes van Isendoren,* 196–97
Dülberg, Franz, x, 10
Dürer, Albrecht, xi, 3–8 *passim,* 17, 23–25 *passim,* 27–29 *passim,* 32, 34, 37, 38–39, 41, 69, 71, 77, 80, 83, 94, 101, 110, 112, 114, 120, 125, 126, 134, 136, 140, 143, 145, 147, 151, 153, 154, 156, 158, 172, 182, 184, 187, 195, 201, 202, 262, 269, 270, 271, 272, 277n19, 278n25, 281n3, 284n38, 285n50, 288n16, 295n79, 323n8, 326n16, 333n2, 334n4

Engebrechtsz., Cornelis, xi, 3, 6, 9, 13, 16, 26, 40–41, 42, 79, 82, 101, 102, 107, 126, 131, 162, 164, 180, 185, 187, 188, 189, 262, 273n1, 275n8, 284n35, 316n17, 322n5, 323n8, 333n4
Erasmus, Desiderius, 53, 59, 70, 291n48, 296n91, 325n11

Feeding of the Five Thousand, 40–41, 82, 262–62
Filedt Kok, Jan Piet, xi, 12, 13, 22, 76
Fouquet, Jean, 26, 27
Frankfurt, Stadelsches Kunstinstitut: Master of the Turin Crucifixion, *Crucifixion*, 10
Friedlander, Max J., x, 9, 16, 79
Frisius, Simon, 28, 83, 118, 136–37, 177–78, 229, 245, 318n5

Gibson, Walter, x–xi, 10, 13, 14, 26, 42, 64
Giorgio, Francesco di, 48
Glass paintings, ix, 4, 20, 98
Goltzius, Hendrick, 83–84, 95, 98, 121, 125, 140, 314n5, 319n2
Gossaert, Jan, xi, 3, 5–6, 25, 29, 30, 32, 35–39 *passim*, 42–44 *passim*, 80, 122, 126, 134, 135, 136, 153, 197, 282n21, 306n3, 323n8, 323n9, 325n16, 333n1
Graf, Urs, 55
Groningen, Groninger Museum: artist unknown, *Portrait of a Man*, 197–98
Gypsy imagery, 65, 66–68

Haarlem, Museum Teyler: Jan de Bisschop (copy after Lucas van Leyden), *Betrothal* (drawing), 177–78
Hamburg, Kunsthalle. *See* Van Leyden, Lucas, Drawings: *Adam and Eve*
Heynricxdr., Marie (mother of Lucas van Leyden), 6
Hoey, Dammes Claesz de (son-in-law of Lucas van Leyden), 92, 276n12, 276n14
Hoey, Jan de (grandson of Lucas van Leyden), 92, 93, 276n12
Hoey, Lucas Dammesz. de (grandson of Lucas van Leyden), 4, 276n12

Holbein the Younger, Hans, 151–53 *passim*, 197, 270, 281n2, 323n8, 325n11
Hondius, Hendrick, 269–71 *passim*
Hoogewerff, G. J., x, 10
Hooghstraet, Frans (collector), 81, 114
Hoogstraten, Franchoys van (donor?), 81
Huyghensz., Dirck (stepbrother of Lucas van Leyden), 9, 171, 190, 191, 309n12

Ingold, Johannes (author of *Das Guldin Spil*), 48, 52, 62, 64
Isenbrandt, Adriaen, 25, 188

Jacobsz., Huygh (here identified as the Master of the St. John Panels), 3–4, 6, 9–13, 16, 17, 79, 90, 185, 189, 259–60, 275n8, 276n16, 321n3, 327n2

Karlsruhe, Staatliche Kunsthalle: artist unknown (copy after Lucas van Leyden), *Adoration of the Magi*, 120, 123. *See also* Van Leyden, Lucas, Paintings: *St. Andrew*
Koblenz, Mittelrhein-Museum: Leiden School, *Feeding of the Five Thousand*, 12, 40–41, 190

Leiden, Stedelijk Museum: attributed to Hans Liefrinck (copy after Lucas van Leyden), *Rest on the Flight into Egypt*, 132, 134, 253; Jan de Bisschop (copy after Lucas van Leyden), *Christ Healing the Lepers*, 138–39, 256. *See also* Van Leyden, Lucas, Paintings: *Last Judgment*; Van Leyden, Lucas, Drawings: *Portrait of a Man*
Leipzig, Kupferstichkabinet, Museum der bildenden Künste: Jan de Bisschop (copy after Lucas van Leyden), *Meeting of David and Abigail*, 105–6, 255
Leningrad, The Hermitage: artist unknown (copy after Lucas van Leyden), *Procession of the Holy Sacrament*, 160–61. *See also* Van Leyden, Lucas, Paintings: *Christ Healing the Blind Man*
Lille, Musée des Beaux-Arts: Albrecht Dürer, *Portrait of Lucas van Leyden*, 8,

143, 153, 154, 156, *262*, 269–72 *passim, 303n4, 325n11*
Liverpool, Walker Art Gallery: artist unknown (copy after Lucas van Leyden), *Christ as Man of Sorrows and Virgin of Sorrows*, 116
Lochorst, Lord of (patron), 81, 145
London, British Museum: Jan de Bisschop (copy after Lucas van Leyden), *St. George* (drawing), 22–23, 147–48, *242;* Albrecht Dürer(?), *Portrait of Lucas van Leyden(?)* (drawing), 271. See also Van Leyden, Lucas, Drawings: *Head of a Young Man with a Fur Hat; Judith with the Head of Holofernes; Two Nude Men on a Sphere; Virgin and Child*
London, Courtauld Institute Galleries: artist unknown, *Job and His Three Friends*, 185–86
London, National Gallery: artist unknown (in the style of Lucas van Leyden), *Lot and His Daughters*, 184–85. See also Van Leyden, Lucas, Paintings: *Portrait of a Man Aged 38*
Love Triangle, theme, 54–55
Lugano, Thyssen-Bornemisza Collection: sixteenth-century Leiden School, *Portrait of a Man*, x. See also Van Leyden, Lucas, Paintings: *Card Players*
Luther, Martin, 64, 68–72

Maastricht, Bonnefantenmuseum: artist unknown (circle of Patinir?), *Lot and His Daughters*, 183
Madrid, Prado: artist unknown (copy after Lucas van Leyden), *The Entry of David into Jerusalem*, 95–97
Mainz, Mittelrheinisches Landesmuseum: artist unknown (copy after Lucas van Leyden), *Adoration of the Magi*, 120, 123, *250*
Marconi, Rocco, 94
Marijtgen (daughter of Lucas van Leyden), 7, *276n14*
Massys, Quentin, 18, 23–25 *passim*, 26, 28, 56, 61, 80, 81, 82, 84, 153, 169, 170, 176, *275n6, 286n1, 289n20, 310n4, 321n4, 325n16*
Master bg, 50, 55
Master BR, 46

Master E. S., 47, 49, *295n79*
Master IB, 77
Master of Frankfurt, 25, 122
Master of the Berlin Passion, 47
Master of the Housebook, 52, 54, *268;* circle of, 60
Master of the Love Gardens, 52
Master of the Morrison Triptych, 25
Master of the St. John Panels. See Jacobsz., Huygh
Master of the Turin Crucifixion, 10
Memling, Hans, 26–28 *passim*, 31, 122, *282n22, 310n4, 325n16, 335n3*
Merion, Pa., Barnes Foundation Museum of Art: Leiden School, *Adoration of the Magi*, 12, 189–90, 311*n4*
Michelangelo, 34
Michiels, Alfred, x
Milan, Galleria della Biblioteca Ambrosiana: artist unknown (copy after Lucas van Leyden), *Triumphal Entry of David into Jerusalem*, 95, 97–98, *240*
Mostaert, Jan, 81, 128–31 *passim, 278n25, 284n38, 294n79, 322n3, 325n16*
Muller, Jan, 60–61, 83, *313n5, 331n3*
Munich, Alte Pinakothek. See Van Leyden, Lucas, Paintings: *Virgin and Child with Mary Magdalene and a Donor* and *Annunciation* diptych

Nantes, Musée des Beaux-Arts: artist unknown (copy after Lucas van Leyden), *The Fortuneteller*, 164–66, *205*
New Haven, Yale University Art Gallery: artist unknown (circle of Lucas van Leyden), *St. Paul*, 195–96
Norfolk, Chrysler Museum: artist unknown (copy after Lucas van Leyden), *Virgin and Child*, 36, 133–36, *253*

Oslo, Nasjonalgalleriet. See Van Leyden, Lucas, Paintings: *Virgin and Child*
Oxford, Ashmolean Museum. See Van Leyden, Lucas, Drawings: *St. Jerome*

Paris, Fondation Custodia, Institut Neerlandais: Pieter Paul Rubens (copy after Lucas van Leyden), *Portrait of a Man* (drawing), 155, *216, 339n8*. See

also Van Leyden, Lucas, Drawings: *Portrait of Maximilian*
Paris, Musée du Louvre: artist unknown (circle of Patinir?), *Lot and His Daughters*, 181–82, 185; artist unknown (copy after Lucas van Leyden), *Virgin and Child with Joseph, Anne, and Two Male Saints* (drawing), 112–13, *243*; attributed to Aertgen van Leyden (copy after Lucas van Leyden), *Judgment of Solomon* (drawing), 99–101; attributed to Simon Bening, *Adoration of the Magi*, 187–88. *See also* Van Leyden, Lucas, Paintings: *The Fortuneteller;* Van Leyden, Lucas, Drawings: *Baptism of Christ*
Parshall, Peter, xi, 49, 60, 64, 71, 76, 77
Patinir, Joachim, 23, 31, 80, 121, 182–84, 186, 311n4
Philadelphia, John G. Johnson Collection: artist unknown (Flemish), *Salome Receiving the Head of John the Baptist*, 191–92, 193, 202; Master of the St. John Panels, *John the Baptist Preaching, with Christ and His Disciples*, 10, 11, 12, 190, *260*
Potter, Dirc (author of *Der Minnen Loep*), 62, 63
Power of Women theme, 45, 49–50, 57, 61–62, 64, 81
Provost, Jan, 22, 27, 147, 314n11, 316n18, 322n2

Raimondi, Marcantonio, xi, 29, 30, 32–34, 37, 38, 41, 44, 80, 125, 126, 181, *263–66*
Raphael, 29, 33, 34, 42, 281n2, 285n50
Rathgeber, Georg, ix
Rembrandt, 298n17
Renger, Konrad, 54
Rotterdam, Museum Boymans–van Beuningen: artist unknown (circle of Patinir), *Lot and His Daughters*, 182–84; artist unknown (early sixteenth-century Dutch), *Portrait of a Woman*, 197, 200–201; Master of the St. John Panels, *Birth of John the Baptist*, 10; Master of the St. John Panels, *Flight of Elizabeth*, 10, 11, *259*. *See also* Van Leyden, Lucas, Paintings: *Potiphar's Wife Accusing Joseph;* Van Leyden, Lucas, Drawings: *Jael Killing Sisera*
Rubens, Pieter Paul, 96, 155, 160, *216*, 339n8
Rudolf II of Prague (Emperor), 83–84, 96, 114, 116, 124–26 *passim*, 140, 313n5
Rugby, Warwickshire, Rugby School: artist unknown (copy after Lucas van Leyden), *Triumphal Entry of David into Jerusalem*, 96–97. *See also* Van Leyden, Lucas, Drawings: *Standing Young Man*

Saenredam, Jan, 83, 95, 96–97, *241*
San Francisco, California Palace of the Legion of Honor: artist unknown (copy after Lucas van Leyden), *Christ Healing the Lepers*, 138–39
Schäufelein, Hans Leonhard, 51
Silver, Larry, 65, 71, 72, 76, 77
Steen, Jan, 73, 84, 85, 107, 293n61, 305n7
Stock, Andries Jacobsz., 153–56, 270, *217*
Strasbourg, Musée des Beaux-Arts: artist unknown, *Fortuna*, 192, 193, 201–2. *See also* Van Leyden, Lucas, Paintings: *Betrothal*
Swart, Jan, van Groningen, 73, 199

Tempera on canvas paintings, ix, 4, 18, 74, 92, 101, 104–5, 138, 145–46
Terbrugghen, Hendrick, 84–85, 301n6
Turin, Galleria Sabauda: Master of the Turin Crucifixion, *Crucifixion* triptych, 10, *258*

Utrecht, Rijksmuseum Het Catharijneconvent: artist unknown (copy after Lucas van Leyden), *Christ as Man of Sorrows*, 118

Van Cleve, Joos, 23, 24, 27, 30, 36, 58, 80, 122, 129, 137, 151, 153, 176, 270, 275n6, 284n38, 305n2, 311n4, 325n16
Van der Weyden, Rogier, 27, 30, 282n21, 294n79, 316n18, 321n4, 325n16, 335n3
Van Haarlem, Cornelis, 84

Van Heemskerck, Maarten, 153, 270, 299n3, 317n21
Van Hemessen, Jan, 81, 83, 84
Van Honthorst, Gerrit, 84
Van Leyden, Lucas
—Paintings: *Betrothal* (Strasbourg, Musée des Beaux-Arts), 37, 58–60, 135, 152, 176–80, *225–26; Card Players* (Lugano, Thyssen-Bornemisza Collection), 19–20, 21, 22, 54–56, 62, 167–68, *208; Card Players* (Wilton House, Collection of the Earl of Pembroke), 20–22, 37, 54–56, 111, 147, 148, 152, 158, 164, 168, 169–71, 194, *210*, 274n3; *Chess Players* (Berlin-Dahlem, Staatliche Museen Preussischer Kulturbesitz), 4, 11, 16–19, 21, 48–51, 62, 90, 91, 94, 158, 162–69 *passim,* 178, 188, 191, 201, *203*, 328n1, 329n2, 338n1; *Christ Healing the Blind Man* (Leningrad, The Hermitage), 4, 12, 15, 37, 42–43, 44, 68, 76, 77, 81–82, 84, 100, 103, 106, 108, 109, 138, 139–44, 154, 160–61, 178, 180, 202, *234, 236–38*, 272, 274n3, 298n17, 314n5, 319n1, 335n4; *Dance around the Golden Calf* (Amsterdam, Rijksmuseum), xi, 3–4, 6, 22, 37, 39–42, 43, 64–66, 67–68, 72, 74, 75–76, 80, 82, 84, 102, 105, 106–9, 133, 137, 141, 142, 161, *230–32*, 309n14, 335n4; *The Fortuneteller* (Paris, Musée du Louvre), 4, 16–17, 22, 56–58, 91, 162, 164–66, 167, *204*, 328n1; *History of Joseph* (location unknown, presumably lost), 4, 74, 91–92, 104; *History of St. Hubert* (location unknown, presumably lost), 4, 5, 16, 18, 74, 81, 145–46; *Last Judgment* (Leiden, Stedelijk Museum), 3, 6, 8, 15, 22, 30–35, 38, 42, 69, 70–72, 76, 81, 83, 103, 105, 122, 123, 124–31, 133, 136, 149, 154, 158–59, 177, 178, 196, 202, *218–22*, 272, 274n3, 276n16, 298n17, 322n3, 336n1; *Moses after Striking the Rock* (Boston, Museum of Fine Arts), 6, 15, 38–39, 42, 43, 67–68, 72–75, 76, 100, 101–3, 104, 108, 109, 122, 123, 133, 137, 139, 145, 149, 158–59, 161, 176, 178, *223–24*, 272, 335n4; *Portrait of a Man* (Braunschweig, Herzog Anton Ulrich-Museum), 110, 111, 153–59, 180, 199, 200, *215–17*, 270, 271, 272, 303n4, 337n3; *Portrait of a Man Aged 38* (London, National Gallery), 4, 24, 151–53, 158, 180, 197–201 *passim, 211,* 272; *Potiphar's Wife Accusing Joseph* (Rotterdam, Museum Boymans–van Beuningen), 10, 17–19, 20, 21, 22, 62–63, 80, 89–94 *passim,* 147, 158, 164, 166, 168, 188, 198, *206,* 328n1, 328n5; *Rebecca and Eliezer at the Well* (location unknown, presumably lost), 4, 74–75, 101, 103–4; *St. Andrew* (Karlsruhe, Staatliche Kunsthalle), 21–23, 146–47, 148, 194, *209,* 284n35; *Susanna before the Judge* (formerly Bremen, Kunsthalle), 18–20, 21, 63–64, 89, 90, 91, 92–95, 105, 147, 168, 170, 192, 198, *207,* 312n1; *Virgin and Child* (Oslo, Nasjonalgalleriet), 4, 36–37, 123, 133, 135, 136–38, 152, 176, 178, *228,* 330n3; *Virgin and Child with Angels* (Berlin-Dahlem, Staatliche Museen Preussischer Kulturbesitz), 25–27, 28, 99, 110–12, 113, 119–20, 133, 134, 138, 152, 154, 194, *212,* 272, 318n6; *Virgin and Child with Mary Magdalene and a Donor* and *Annunciation* diptych (Munich, Alte Pinakothek), 3, 15, 22, 26–27, 28, 31, 37, 81, 84, 103, 111–16 *passim,* 119, 120, 123, 152, 170, 171–72, 194, 196, *213–14,* 274n3, 314n5, 337n3
—Copies after lost originals: *Adoration of the Magi,* 120–23, 124, *251; Allegory of Transience,* 28–29, 171–74, 175, *249–50; Betrothal* (London, Collection M. Q. Morris), xii, 58–60, 179, *227,* 329n5, 331n4; *Betrothal* (location unknown), 60, 166–67, *239; Card Players* (Washington, National Gallery of Art), xii, 28–29, 54–56, 171–72, 173, 175, 179, *250,*

291n46; *Card Players* (Mainz, Mittelrheinisches Landesmuseum), 37, 38, 54–56, 171, 175–76, *251; Christ as Man of Sorrows and Virgin of Sorrows,* 28, 116–19, 149, *245; Christ Healing the Lepers,* 43–44, 76, 138–39, *256; Fall of Man,* xii, 23, 62, 98–99, *242; A Family Surprised by Death,* 28–29, 172, *247; Fluteplayer,* 179–80, *257; John the Baptist Preaching in the Wilderness,* 68, 123–24, *252; Judgment of Solomon,* 44, 99–101, 149, *254; Meeting of David and Abigail,* 43–44, 105–6, 139, *255; Procession of the Holy Sacrament,* 44, 77, 160–61, *256; Rest on the Flight into Egypt,* 8, 36, 132–34, *253; St. George,* 22–23, 147–48, *242; Susanna in Her Bath,* 44, 104–5, 149, *254; Temptation of a Young Man,* 28–29, 171–72, 174–75, *250; Triumphal Entry of David into Jerusalem,* 4, 20, 84, 95–98, *240–41; Virgin and Child,* 4, 36, 133, 134–36, *253; Virgin and Child in the Clouds,* xii, 25, 28, 99, 119–20, *244; Virgin and Child with Joseph, Anne, and Two Male Saints,* 26, 112–13, *243*

—Drawings: *Adam and Eve* (Hamburg, Kunsthalle), 41, 62, 108, 319n1; *Baptism of Christ* (Paris, Louvre), 139; *Head of a Young Man Looking Upward* (Berlin, Staatliche Museen Preussischer Kulturbesitz, Kupferstichkabinett), 164; *Head of a Young Man with a Fur Hat* (London, British Museum), 164; *Jael Killing Sisera* (Rotterdam, Museum Boymans–van Beuningen), 312n12; *Judith with the Head of Holofernes* (London, British Museum), 312n12; *Portrait of a Man* (Leiden, Stedelijk Museum), 24, 152, 197; *Portrait of a Young Woman* (Weimar, Schlossmuseum), 201; *Portrait of Maximilian* (Paris, Fondation Custodia), 113; *St. Jerome* (Oxford, Ashmolean Museum), 24, 337n5; *Standing Boy with a Sword* (Amsterdam, Rijksprentenkabinet), 341n17; *Standing Young Man* (Rugby, Warwickshire, Rugby School), 342n17;

Two Nude Men on a Sphere (London, British Museum), 99, 342n17; *Virgin and Child* (London, British Museum), 108, 133, 136–38, *229; Virgin Annunciate* (Berlin-Dahlem, Staatliche Museen Preussischer Kulturbesitz, Kupferstichkabinett), 120

—Prints: *Abraham Renouncing Hagar* (B.17), 164, 184, 294n71; *Adoration of the Magi* (B.37), 84, 188, 311n6; *Baptism of Christ* (B.40), 40, 43, 294n71; *Beggars* (B.143), 55; *Beheading of John the Baptist* (B.111), 191; *Burial of Christ* (B.54), 119; *Calvary* (B.74), 43, 97, 106, 170; *Christ Appearing to Mary Magdalene* (B.77), 99, 111, 112, 178; *Christ before Annas* (B.59), 95; *Christ Crowned with Thorns* (B.69), 10, 341n17; *Conversion of Paul* (B.107), 43, 44, 157; *Creation of Eve* (B.1), 39; *Dance of Mary Magdalene* (B.122), 7, 27, 43, 65, 99, 106, 123, 170, 173, 341n17; *David and Abigail* (B.24), 11, 44, 304n2; *David Playing the Harp before Saul* (B.27), 11, 17, 163, 341n17; *The Dentist* (B.157), 29; *Descent from the Cross* (B.53), 68; *Ecce Homo* (B.71), 5, 40, 44, 91, 94, 123, 149; *Emperor Maximilian* (B.172), 111, 112, 331n6; *Esther before Ahasuerus* (B.31), 113, 170, 200; *Expulsion* (B.4), 32; *Fall of Man* (engravings: B.3, 7–10; woodcuts: B.1–2), 59, 62, 99, 202; *Fides* (B.127), 43, 77; *Four Soldiers* (B.141), 341n17; *Hagar and Ishmael* (B.17–18), 75; *The History of Joseph* series (B.19–23), 19, 63, 89, 91, 92, 95, 98, 167, 304n2, 312n1; *Holy Family* (B.39, 85), 11, 185; *Jael Killing Sisera* (B.7), 176; *Lamech and Cain* (B.14), 108; *Lamentation over the Body of Abel* (B.6), 41; *Lot and His Daughters* (B.16), 66, 293n62; *Lucretia* (B.134), 30, 33, *263; Mars, Venus, and Cupid* (B.137), 63, 293n62; *Mary Magdalene* (B.123), 30; *The Milkmaid* (B.158), 20, 38, 65, 184; *Mohammed and the Monk Sergius* (B.126), 4, 16–17, 163; *Murder of Abel* (B.5, 13), 39–40, 108;

The Musicians (B.155), 29, 59–60; *Pallas Athena* (B.139), 41; *Power of Women* series (B.1–2, 5–13, 16), 50, 80; *The Promenade* (B.144), 176, 331n8; *Pyramus and Thisbe* (B.135), 98, 184; *Raising of Lazarus* (B.42), 11; *Rest on the Flight* (B.38), 185; *Return of the Prodigal Son* (B.78), 43, 98, 149; *Round Passion* series (B.57–65), 13, 94, 273n1; *St. Jerome* (B.113), 193, 194; *St. Jerome* (B.114), 24, 39, 149; *Sts. Peter and Paul Conversing* (B.106), 72, 103, 149, 337n5; *Sts. Peter and Paul with Veronica's Veil* (B.105), 196, 295n79; *Seven Theological and Cardinal Virtues* (B.127–33), 77, 100, 105, 133, 137, 139, 178; *Small Passion* series (B.43–56), 24, 28, 113, 119; *Susanna and the Elders* (B.33), 29, 44, 64, 65, 80, 105, 341n17; *Tavern Scene* (B.20), xii, 58, 61, 157, 173, 331n8; *Temptation of St. Anthony* (B.117), 184, 192, 293n62, 335n2; *Triumph of David* (B.26), 98; *Triumph of Mordecai* (B.32), 170, 282n18, 304n2; *Two Couples in a Wood* (B.146), 20; *Venus and Cupid* (B.138), 105, 137; *Virgil Suspended in a Basket* (B.136), 29, 39, 108, 150, 157, 176; *Virgin and Child* (B.84), 111, 113, 123, 306n3; *Virgin and Child on a Crescent Moon* (B.82), 24; *Virgin and Child with Angels* (B.84), 24, 27, 28, 29; *Virgin and Child with St. Anne* (B.79), 113; *Young Couple Followed by a Fool* (B.147), 58, 341n17; *Young Couple Seated in a Landscape* (B.148), 176, 178, 331n8; *Young Man with a Skull* (B.174), 3, 173, 269, 271

Van Mander, Carel, ix, xi, 3–8 *passim*, 13, 16, 59–60, 66, 74, 79, 81, 82, 83, 84, 91–92, 95, 96, 98, 100–102 *passim*, 104, 115, 116, 124, 136, 138, 140, 142, 145, 146, 154, 156, 189, 269, 271, 277n16, 284n35, 286n53, 304n2, 305n7, 308n8, 314n5, 321n4, 327n1

Van Meckenem, Israhel, 41, 50, 52, 59, 278n25

Van Montfoort, Jacob Florisz. (donor), 81–82, 140, 142, 143, 319n2

Van Orley, Bernard, 30, 80, 125, 128, 129, 276n16, 316n18, 322n4, 323n9, 328n1

Van Regteren Altena, J. Q., 11

Van Reymerswaele, Marinus, 84

Van Scorel, Jan, 29, 30, 43, 80, 81, 82, 126, 140, 141, 144, 152, 153, 274n2, 281n2, 284n35, 337n3

Van Swieten family (patrons), 77, 81, 82, 124, 130, 131, 304n1

Vasari, Giorgio, 8, 16, 83

Vellert, Dirk, 102

Vienna, Albertina: Jan de Bisschop (copy after Lucas van Leyden), *Fall of Man* (drawing), xii, 23, 62, 98–99, *242*; Jan de Bisschop (copy after Lucas van Leyden), *Portrait of a Man* (drawing), 155; Jan de Bisschop (copy after Lucas van Leyden), *Virgin and Child in the Clouds* (drawing), xii, 25, 28, 99, 119–20, *244*; Nicolas de Bruyn or Jan de Bisschop (copy after Lucas van Leyden), *Judgment of Solomon* (drawing), 100, *254*

Vos, Rik, xi

Waagen, G. F., x

Washington, National Gallery: artist unknown (copy after Lucas van Leyden), *Card Players*, 37, 38, 54–56, 171, 175–76, *250*

Weimar, Schlossmuseum. *See* Van Leyden, Lucas, Drawings: *Portrait of a Young Woman*

Wilton House, collection of the Earl of Pembroke. *See* Van Leyden, Lucas, Paintings: *Card Players*

Wurfbain, Maarten, 75–76

York, City of York Art Gallery: artist unknown (copy after Lucas van Leyden), *Judgment of Solomon*, 99, 101

Zasinger, Martin, 52, 55, 267

Zevertsz., Jan, 68–69, 295n80